THE SPECTACLE

Media and the Making of the O. J. Simpson Story

PAUL THALER

PRAEGER

Westport, Connecticut
London

Library of Congress Cataloging-in-Publication Data

Thaler, Paul.
    The spectacle : media and the making of the O. J. Simpson story /
by Paul Thaler.
      p. cm.
    Includes bibliographical references and index.
    ISBN 0–275–95319–X (alk. paper).—ISBN 0–275–95320–3 (pbk.)
    1. Simpson, O. J., 1947—Trials, litigation, etc. 2. Trials
(Murder)—California—Los Angeles. 3. Free press and fair trial.
4. Mass media and criminal justice. I. Title.
KF224.S485T48 1997
345.73′02523′0979494—dc21   97–5593

British Library Cataloguing in Publication Data is available.

Library of Congress Catalog Card Number: 97–5593
ISBN: 0–275–95319–X
      0–275–95320–3 (pbk.)

First published in 1997

Praeger Publishers, 88 Post Road West, Westport, CT 06881
An imprint of Greenwood Publishing Group, Inc.

Printed in the United States of America

The paper used in this book complies with the
Permanent Paper Standard issued by the National
Information Standards Organization (Z39.48–1984).

10 9 8 7 6 5 4 3 2

Copyright Acknowledgments

The author and publisher gratefully acknowledge permission to use excerpts from the following:

Kathy Butler, "The Accidental Feminist," December 10, 1995, and David
Shaw, "Obsession: Did the Media Overfeed a Starving Public?" October
9, 1995, Copyright 1995, *Los Angeles Times*. Reprinted by permission.

Gerald Uelmen, *Lessons from the Trial*, Kansas City: Andrews and
McMeel, 1996. Courtesy of Universal Press Syndicate.

THE SPECTACLE

To Rosie

For taking such loving care of us all

CONTENTS

ACKNOWLEDGMENTS

This book is built on a premise and an impossibility. The premise will unfold shortly in my introduction. The impossibility stems from the sheer scope of the O. J. Simpson case and the sweeping role that the media played in this epic saga. Thousands of journalists, editors and technicians carried the image and the word of the event across the globe, leaving behind an incredible trove of videotape and articles of the single most covered trial in American history.

For a media critic to make sense of the voluminous Simpson record required choices. Fortunately, I had the benefit of many of those who shared an inside seat on the Simpson trial, along with colleagues and family who supported this project and helped to keep me on track. A few brief words then about them and this book.

No single cultural event in our recent history has generated a library—some 60 books to date—as exhaustive as the Simpson case. Most of the literature has focused on the personal subplots and the legal and political machinations surrounding a double murder and the subsequent trial of one of the most celebrated athletes of our time. I have taken on a different task in this book. The Simpson case, and the well-known controversies surrounding it, form the backdrop to another story, this one about the American media.

Throughout, I have tried to keep my eye focused on the media without diverting too far afield into the tired narratives that have been told and recycled elsewhere. I have relied heavily on the insights of the journalists who daily covered the Simpson event. The book examines the national media machine, but it is equally a story of these individual men and women who brought their talent, judgment and ethic to the Simpson story and impelled it forward.

Here again I have made choices, selecting some 30 reporters, writers, editors, columnists, TV executives, anchors, and talk-show personalities to speak for a media contingent that could be counted in the thousands. They have risked being criticized by speaking candidly about themselves and their role in the trial but particularly about the controversial media issues that confronted them. They are individually cited in the appendix, and I am grateful to them for their honest appraisals. A number of news organizations also graciously provided access and research materials for the book, most notably NBC, ABC, the *Los Angeles Times*, the *Philadelphia Inquirer*, and Court TV. The media-relations people at the National Judicial College also supplied me with tapes of their annual conference that focused on media and the courts.

For the past 15 years, I have looked to Mercy College as a second home where such research can take on a life. My ability to work on this book was greatly enhanced by a faculty development grant, which helped to underwrite my initial research. I could also count on the college's library staff, among them the always diligent Shriveli Rao, who managed to make the intricacies of computer research more user friendly.

My students continue to be a source of inspiration; a special recognition to Frank McAlonan who helped with some of the early research. Sean Dugan and Betty Krasne in the Literature, Language, and Communication Department have been there to lean on for their feedback and friendship. Despite having to endure more than three years of Simpson-talk, they remain valued colleagues.

More than a decade ago, Neil Postman introduced me to some ideas that made extraordinary sense. Since then, those ideas continue to be a driving intellectual force and have taken shape in this book and in my other work. My good colleagues from New York University have also provided sustenance for the mind and spirit. A sincere thanks to Thom Gencarelli, Casey Lum, William Petkanas, Jay Rosen, and Lance Strate for managing to straighten out my thinking over the years.

I have also been fortunate to work with a dedicated group of people at Greenwood Publishers. Peter Covenny helped me to get the project moving until he passed the ball to Nina Perlstein. I have also benefited from the administrative support of Jim Sabin, who saw this book as an important addition to the Greenwood line, and Scott Wich, who so ably helped to market my first book and has been an enthusiastic supporter of this one. I can't imagine having a more diligent production editor than Catherine Lyons, who has not only attended to the fine detail that lends to the overall look of this book, but has managed to calm the concerns of a persistent author in search of a perfect manuscript. I am grateful for her equanimity as much as the special care she has given this book. Her cohort, Jason Azze, also came to the rescue during critical times in the production process.

The Spectacle was born from an extended family. Leslie Jean Thornton has taught her old teacher about the grace and power of language. Her hand is on every page here—she is as much a collaborator as editor—and I am indebted to her singular commitment to this book, and, of course, her friendship over these many years.

I would like to extend my thanks to Moshe Botwinick for closely reading through a weighty manuscript and offering, as always, an incisive critique. Through good fortune, I also have come to know Robert Silverstein, a great agent, who believed in this book and worked tirelessly on my behalf.

Mel Wolfson, my "coach" and friend, has again taken his editor's pen in hand to polish my prose and dust off the remnants of more than a few misbegotten phrases. I have yet to win a bet in our ongoing contest over editorial style points and have the strange feeling I never will.

His daughter and my wife, Amy Wolfson, has also pored over each of these pages and her ideas and insights have shaped my own. She is a partner in this book as in my life. It is no small matter to acknowledge her unfailing patience that has allowed this book to flourish in a household that includes a three-year-old whirlwind named Matthew Benjamin, a constant source of energy and light.

Finally, this book is in memory of Rose Cohen Thaler, my mother. A day does not pass in which I don't feel Rosie's wondrous spirit, her nurturing love, her incandescence. This was her gift that helps carry me through.

INTRODUCTION:
THE STORYMAKERS

In the Year of Simpson we kept our eyes fastened on the big story. Few could argue that the story was not of epic dimensions. Indeed, no other single news event in our history could match the sheer scope and intensity of coverage given to the murder case in Los Angeles.

From June 1994 through October 1995, the Simpson story overtook our culture, sweeping away all other news—in fact, virtually all other public discussion—in its path. This was an event, one critic so aptly noted, that had "hijacked" American culture. To not know SimpsonSpeak circa 1994-95 spoke to a person's cultural illiteracy, as well as to where America regrettably had arrived in the fading moments of the twentieth century.

Simpson was a story of obsession. Even in the aftermath of the criminal trial, it became a weary recitation by the trial's winners and losers. Typically, the replays argued over the legal machinations and the personal subplots that infested the case. But for all the chatter, the bitter perception remained that something had gone horribly awry in Judge Lance Ito's courtroom—that justice had failed miserably. The blame was placed on virtually every major trial participant: from the judge who lost control, to the "inept" prosecution, to the defense team that unabashedly played its race card at every turn, to the jury that blinked at the massive evidence before coming to its near-instant decision.

Strangely, for all the post-trial finger pointing, lost in the sound and fury was a broad critique about the pivotal role the media had played in the so-called Trial of the Century. As the sentinels of a democratic society, the media were perceived as a natural part of the Simpson legal scene, belonging to the trial environment as much as the evidence, the testimony, the lawyers, the judge, the defendant, even the very courtroom furniture. Whatever critical commentary existed typically pointed to their overzealous pursuit of Simpson news, a lapse forgiven as a consequence of serving the interests of an engaged national audience.

But the media were not just highly involved observers acting on our behalf. Their presence, inside and outside of the courtroom, changed the very course of justice in the Simpson case. No other force—not even the force of truth and reason—had as influential a role in the day-to-day workings of the courtroom. In the end, the media themselves may have been the *single most decisive factor* contributing to the legal strategies and decisions coming from the presiding judge and trial attorneys. As well, the media not only shaped the American consciousness regarding the case, but also helped to trigger a political and racial juggernaut that pounded past the gallery of spectators and reporters, the defense and prosecutors' tables, Ito's bench, the witness stand, and the jury box. No one was left untouched.

The media were more than mere storytellers: They were storymakers. They first told—and made—the Simpson story as a tale of celebrity and the fall of a "great man." Then they continued to reinvent the story as a tale of domestic violence, wealth, status, and, finally, race. Whether such stories actually were tied to the real social fabric of American life was largely irrelevant. The media insisted that the Simpson story contained a lasting narrative about the human condition and, through the sheer pervasive nature of their stories, we mostly bought into it.

In reality, though, the media's search for "deeper truths" was a convenient rationale to justify their excessive and frantic coverage. Having instigated the public frenzy, they collectively shrugged at the chaos, while arguing that they were giving their viewers and readers the story they now demanded. With righteous fervor, the media pronounced to their audiences: "Speaketh and we shall follow." In a plainer vernacular, the media followed their readers, ratings, market share, and money to the point of no return. One critic said the media's rabid attention to the Simpson story reminded him of Eskimos capturing the great whale, destroying it, and then stripping away every last part of the carcass until nothing remained except the furtive idea that something once existed here. Indeed, the Simpson story was carved up by the great media machine leaving nothing except, finally, the national psychic wreckage in its wake.

In the final analysis, the media did not just report the Simpson case but were instrumental in creating it. They transformed a murder trial into a cultural event the likes of which we had never seen before—a spectacle of such stupendous proportions that it reached across the globe as a leading export of American culture. Simpson was a cultural happening, a Woodstock of the courtroom, with its own pulsating beat and adulating audience calling for more. And the media played on—a story so intoxicating that the hordes of reporters, editors, directors, and pundits could not find a way to extricate themselves even if they had chosen to. The few news outlets that resisted entering the communal gathering were seen as sentimental entities, out of touch with modern culture, not to mention new market realities about newsmaking. To be crazed in the Year of Simpson meant ignoring the great story.

But if this book was simply about the media clamor surrounding the Simpson case, it would just be half of the story. The media's role and influence were far more powerful and insidious. The storymakers not only shaped public perceptions of the case but the very trial itself. And it couldn't have happened without the camera in the court. In my previous book, *The Watchful Eye*, I argue that the trend in televised justice has been a dangerous Faustian bargain, where the judicial "soul" of the American courtroom has been traded for what we perceive as progress and enhanced freedom. In the Simpson trial, we paid the devil his due.

Whatever hope there was to contain the Simpson trial within the normal boundaries of the courtroom was shattered by the camera. The medium was a two-way street. It instantaneously brought court-room images, wrapped in the never-ending commentary of TV pundits, to American living rooms and business places. Almost as quickly, media coverage sifted into the courtroom itself, where it percolated before the bench and often became the central focus of the day's proceedings. Media and legal issues tangled, making it often impossible to distinguish the actual murder trial from the larger media spectacle. In such a milieu, the absurdity of watching reporters testify as witnesses, or court sessions devoted to gag orders, cameras in the court, a scandalous book, and the vast array of problems involving the media and the trial participants seemed perfectly normal.

Television's presence, of course, did more than merely confuse and elongate the legal process. It changed the very workings of the court and, very likely, the outcome of the trial. With a national audience and a legion of media "experts" hovering over their shoulders each day, participants shifted between Lance Ito's courtroom and the court of public opinion.

This television trial was a global stage and no participant was free from acting out before the world watching. To ignore the camera meant to ignore the media commentary and the public clamor, and no principal player was willing to turn his back on what was being said about the trial, and about him. Even jurors, seated "offstage" from the camera eye, clearly understood that they were a central part of the great Simpson conversation, and that their role had transcended the mere matter of deciding Simpson's culpability in the double murder. They were arbiters of a much higher political order. And they were reminded of that status by Johnnie Cochran in his closing argument, when he asked them to reach beyond the courtroom and send a message to the Los Angeles Police Department, as well as to America. Only in a trial that had become a touchstone for American race politics would such an appeal, however cynically manipulated, have relevance.

That the trial evolved into "racial theater" should not have come as a surprise. Once the media moved the hot-buttoned issue of race into the realm of popular culture, it exploded everywhere—especially inside Ito's courtroom. Even Simpson's lawyers could not have imagined how fast and furious their theory—an unproven story about a racist cop aided by a police conspiracy out to frame Simpson— would travel into the tinderbox of American race relations, before catapulting back into Department 103. With television pundits and a huge audience watching and commenting from early morning to late night, the collision between the courts and the medium was inevitable. By the time the case was nearing its end, the Simpson trial no longer was a question about who killed Nicole Simpson and Ron Goldman, but a perverse contest about civil rights. The Simpson story had evolved into a national referendum about race.

Judge Lance Ito had hoped to illuminate the court system by allowing the Simpson case to be televised. In place of a civics lesson, Americans were largely entertained. The story with its ties to murder, sex, domestic violence, and race conflict was absorbed into a vast entertainment industry, intent on turning the trial into a product to be sold to millions of viewers, who in turn were sold to advertisers.

The media critic Neil Postman had warned a decade ago that Americans were "amusing [themselves] to death," by allowing television to take over the public discussion of politics, business, and religion. Commercial television was not interested in serious discourse, he said, but in "trivializing" those things that matter most to a culture. Since his writings, the courts have become the next great show under the big tent. Simpson was just the latest, albeit the best known, among the pantheon of celebrated defendants from William Kennedy Smith to the Menendez brothers to recently parade across the television screen and our collective consciousness—the newest stars in an age of image idolatry.

For more than a year, we were held captive to the great murder story, and it was spectacular drama unmatched in the annals of criminal law. But in the making of the Simpson story, the media were not only telling us what had become of justice in this country, but what had become of them. This is that story.

PART ONE

MURDER IN LOS ANGELES

PROLOGUE

BUNDY AND ROCKINGHAM

JUNE 12-16, 1994

The corpses of Nicole Brown Simpson and Ronald Goldman lay outside Nicole's condominium at 875 South Bundy Drive in the Brentwood section of Los Angeles. The bodies were nearly bled dry from the multiple slashes and stab wounds inflicted by the killer. A white Akita belonging to Nicole howled into the soft summer breeze for his lost mistress, a sound that woke neighbors.

Steven Schwab, a neighbor walking his own dog in an area behind Nicole's home, came upon the desperate, barking animal. He bent down and noticed the dog's expensive collar, but there was no identification. Then he noticed the dog's paws—they were covered in blood.

Unable to identify the animal Schwab turned to leave, only to find the Akita following him back to his apartment complex. The dog waited there on a second-floor landing. Other neighbors finally took the dog in for the night, but the agitated animal scratched at their door, urging them outside. The man and woman thought a walk might calm the dog down, but once they were out on the street the Akita desperately pulled them to the house on Bundy.

Shortly after midnight the couple found the bodies, sprawled along a darkened walkway awash in blood. Nicole, her throat cut through to the spine, was lying at the bottom of four steps that led to the front door, engulfed in a pool of blood. Ron was slumped against a metal fence, his shirt pulled over his head, his torso savagely ripped open.

The Akita had been the only witness said to have seen the face of the killer.

*   *   *

O. J. Simpson has a corner house at Rockingham and Ashford, and we gathered at where the two streets cross. Reporters were lined up like dominoes. There were at least 30 tripods with reporters connected to each tripod, and cables from live trucks were laid everywhere. It was like the set-up that you'd see for the Super Bowl with TV crews laying cable a week in advance of the big event. But they laid all this cable in a matter of hours to cover O. J. Simpson's comings and goings.

Twenty police officers kept a constant vigil at each entrance of Simpson's home, the gates, back walls, making sure none of the reporters jumped the fence and did anything crazy because there were a lot of reporters out there.

There were at least another 30 still photographers. There was the paparazzi. The *Enquirer*, the *Star*, all of them were there. This was a bonanza for freelance photographers as well. They were up on ladders, they had lenses three-feet long, lenses that you'd think could go through walls.

Then there were the looky-loos, people would just walk by simply because we were there. All kinds of people were walking by our live shots. Eventually police roped off an area where we could do live reports, and they put up blockades so cars couldn't drive past the home because it was just—I hate to call it this but it really was—a media circus, full of chimpanzees, gorillas, apes, elephants, everything. Every kind of animal you wanted to see was represented there in the media circus.[1]

Marc Watts, CNN reporter

1

THE CHASE

"It is the chase we will remember the most."
Forrest Sawyer, ABC-TV

JUNE 17, 1994

Like falling ducks at a shooting gallery, the networks, one by one, dropped all scheduled programming to follow O. J. Simpson and the Ford Bronco on its flight north along the San Diego Freeway.

Sacrificed in the rush to coverage, ABC's *20/20* pushed aside its featured newsmagazine piece on flesh-eating bacteria; CNN broke from *Larry King Live*; NBC pulled the plug on the fifth game of the National Basketball Association championship series between the New York Knicks and the Houston Rockets; and CBS interrupted its featured prime-time program that night called *Diagnosis Murder*.

The commerce of television—the medium's ultimate sacrifice—ground to a halt because of a runaway van on a Los Angeles freeway. The networks lost an estimated $7 million in advertising to air nearly uninterrupted coverage of the chase and Simpson's subsequent arrest. But it turned out to be a small price to pay: The Simpson story would soon yield tremendous dividends.

It was a startling moment for many Americans who could not reconcile Simpson's image of likability, imprinted by thousands of media moments, with his flight from justice and reports that he was holding a blue-steel handgun to his head. Adding to the surreal nature of the story was a subliminal message about our umbilical relationship to television. Television's routine is comforting, a techno-biological clock that ticks from daytime to prime time. When the medium is pulled from its commercial moorings, we suffer the empty, anxious feeling that something has gone terribly wrong. At those times, Americans have come to expect the very worst news: a country at war, an assassination, an earthquake, a plane crash. It is the medium's equivalent to the bad-news telegram, and when the news finally comes, we react together, a nation of viewers huddled around our TV sets.

That the Simpson story itself may have had little relationship to how Americans view and conduct their daily lives was hardly the point. We rarely look for relevance; we look for pictures, and this is, of course, what television vividly brings to us. In the world of television, the image rules, an indelible imprint on the culture's collective memory. On June 17, 1994, pictures of "the chase" became a part of television's history, and of our own.

So impressed by the historic significance of the chase, Jim Moret, the CNN anchor, posed that inevitable rhetorical query: the "Where were you . . ." question, as in, "Where were you when Simpson took flight from justice along the California freeways?" He said: "I could ask you where you were when Kennedy was shot. I could likewise ask where you were when an American landed on the moon. One is a national tragedy, the other a national triumph, that we shared in collectively as a nation. Now look at the event we are sharing in now. It's so bizarre. This is an American tragedy, a personal tragedy."[1]

Simpson's ascendancy to the zenith of American history may have been apropos to CNN celebrity culture, but it was also a telling commentary on where we had arrived in the late twentieth century. Indeed, in the beginning, it was the very personal nature of the story that made us watch. Later, the case would be seen in larger terms dealing with race, spousal abuse, and police corruption. But on that first day, TV pictures of the Simpson chase were tied to something more primal: life and survival. Absent were the devastating pictures we had come to expect from television's breaking story. Instead, ordinary images filled the screen—inexplicably jarring for their plainness, and riveting to about 95 million American viewers, more than the number who watched the first man walk on the moon some 25 years before. This was the car chase of the century—soon to be followed by a trial bearing a similar marquee.

From the vantage point of helicopter cameras, the scene unfolded in slow motion as a white van cruised along the maze of palm-tree-lined freeways followed by a phalanx of police cruisers. Faced with arrest on the charges he stabbed to death his former wife, Nicole Brown Simpson, and her friend, Ron Goldman, Simpson had bolted from a friend's home in Orange County after agreeing to turn himself in to police. Described by newscasters as a "chase," the 30-mile-per-hour pursuit leading to Simpson's estate in Brentwood viscerally reminded viewers more of a funeral procession than the furtive flight of a fugitive. Network anchors were more somber than breathless in their commentary, wondering how Simpson, with his shining media persona—and, in a larger sense, the country itself, with its escalating level of violence—could have come to this.

But beyond any social or psychological pondering, the chase, by virtually any journalistic standard, was a tremendous story. The media's mantra, however, that the story warranted so much attention because of Simpson's fame, missed the point. Other American celebrities, most recently Mike Tyson, the former heavyweight boxing champion convicted of raping a beauty queen, had also been embroiled in felonious trouble. But two things were different now. Simpson was perceived as a friendly personality, a familiar face on the media landscape for a quarter century: He was, for many, the last person capable of committing so heinous a crime. But, more significantly, never had anyone as famous as Simpson found himself hanging so precariously in the glare of live national television.

Five days had passed since the bodies of Ron Goldman and Nicole Simpson had been discovered, and throughout the week the local and national media covered the story with varying degrees of restraint. Pictures flashed across American television screens: raw images of the bloody murder scene; a dazed-looking unshaven Simpson being led somewhere in slow motion; Simpson, in handcuffs, being questioned by police prior to his arrest. But it was the chase that stamped the starting point for what soon would become a seminal media event. The chase marked the moment when television itself became a major player in the Simpson story and a force to be reckoned with. This convergence would ominously foreshadow the events to unfold in the coming year.

The freeway pursuit began very much as a Los Angeles happening. The city is connected by arterial roadways that do not bring together its disparate communities as much as act as a buffer between the rich of Santa Monica and the poor of central L.A. Simpson himself had made the personal journey from a bowlegged slum kid with rickets to a gridiron star. As newscasters filled us in on his bio and evoked the Greeks to speak of the fall of a great man, the irony was unmistakable. At no time in his celebrated life had Simpson achieved such breadth of national and international recognition.

That the setting for the chase was Los Angeles also played in the context of television's awed reaction to Simpson's flight. Los Angeles resonates in the nation's subconscious as the "promised land" and the "matrix of countless American myths."[2] Here on the freeways, television caught Simpson in a wild ride more identifiable with the celluloid world of the dream factory called Hollywood, his van passing an airport named for one of its own mythic heroes: John Wayne.

For some observers, it was this strange connection to film and television that tapped into the American consciousness: The Simpson chase was instantly recognizable because we had seen this scene enacted so many times before in celluloid form. Some observers were astounded by how much the chase reminded them of a cinematic experience—the charismatic outlaw on the run from authorities, in search of escape, but ultimately brought to some form of justice. The more cynical critics posited the notion that Simpson himself may have *intentionally* chosen this public display knowing it would boost him into the role of a lifetime. "It is the best role he ever played," said media critic Neal Gabler. "Here was a guy who was a very minor actor who has gotten more fame, more notoriety for being a murder suspect than in all his years in football or as a minor character actor. Life is a movie and his life movie is better than anything he's ever done."[3]

Ironically, the televised flight of O. J. Simpson was so unlike normal TV for viewers weaned on police and crime dramas crafted for their dramatic confrontation and embellished by premonitory musical underscores. The chase was a far different television experience. Taken as a whole, the hours of live coverage of the slow-speed pursuit amounted to little more than newscasters recounting lane changes along the interstate, accompanied by a chorus of pleas from friends and family to the reportedly despondent and suicidal Simpson. "Real television" as viewers know it hardly existed. Instead of fast-moving images, emotional close-ups and five-second cuts, the hovering helicopters' cameras captured grainy pictures of the Bronco moving at a snail's pace in their long-distance lens. It was crude footage more like that of a home movie that had the effect of heightening the viewers' emotional connection to the screen.

[The chase was ubiquitous, and with the disappearance of all regular network programming, viewers were left with the dreamlike reality that nothing else existed anywhere but this slow-motion car chase.] Nothing on the screen moved very fast and no one did anything daring as the cameras—and millions of viewers—stayed glued to the inaction.

Curiously, it was the very emptiness of information that moved the story forward and kept the networks and their viewers watching. The chase, in effect, was a fascinating event for its sheer vacuousness. Through television, Americans could pour into the image of the moving Bronco whatever feelings, intuition, and apprehension they had about Simpson's state of mind. These unyielding images had captured the public imagination, and the medium refused to relinquish it until the mystery was resolved.

The power of TV images did not lie in the information that the medium conveyed, but rather in each viewer's interpretation. (The chase was, simply, inscrutable, a puzzle to contemplate) Underlying any possible dark secret inside this mysterious van were more basic questions about *our* role in a media-created celebrity world. Could this be the "real" O. J. Simpson, that celebrated member of our popular culture we had known and admired for so long? Had we been deceived so completely? Television's pictures of the Bronco chase presented a mass cognitive dissonance—a disbelief that what we were seeing was actually occurring. We had to keep watching to confirm somehow that this scene, as it unfolded on TV, was, in fact, real.

NBC: A "Problem" in L.A.

Even television insiders found it difficult to comprehend the full scope of the story. In the course of the week following the killings, Simpson's public persona was suddenly transformed from bereaved husband to murder suspect. NBC executive David Bohrman said Simpson's flight was "one of those small handfuls of unforgettable days."[4]

Inside NBC, network execs scrambled to cover the chase, at first with brief news updates and then with full live coverage as anchor Tom Brokaw solemnly informed viewers that Simpson, charged with two counts of murder and now a fugitive at large, was being pursued along a California freeway. Brokaw was only the visible part of an organizational decision to push aside regular broadcasting to cover the chase. Behind the scenes, network president Andrew Lack, Bill Wheatley (vice president of NBC news), Dick Ebersol (president of sports), and Bohrman (executive producer of NBC news specials) grappled with the problem of whether or not to break from the NBA championship—a network sports jewel.

Bohrman had come to NBC two years earlier and was placed in charge of "special events." His job, essentially, was to get the network on the air with live coverage when major stories broke. Without question, the Bronco chase was a major story. "We couldn't ignore it," he said. "There could be an endless debate about how much attention we should have paid to it. I don't know where the middle ground is—but I know there was no way we should have ignored it. It was a moment that people who saw it will never forget. It was the beginning of this drama."

The previous day, Bohrman had returned to New York with stacks of videotape from interviews with Hillary Rodham Clinton on health-care reform. But now the First Lady was on hold: A "problem" had been reported from Los Angeles. First came the police statement that Orenthal James Simpson had been arrested and charged with the murder of two people. And then the staggering postscript: After agreeing to voluntarily turn himself over to police, Simpson fled.

The LAPD announcement that Simpson was now a fugitive rippled through the stunned control room. One NBC news staffer remarked in jest that it being a Los Angeles story, he expected at the very least to see a car chase. And then the police announcement— Simpson had fled in a white Bronco van driven by a close friend, Al (A. C.) Cowlings. "We were thunderstruck," Bohrman said. "I couldn't believe this was happening. All of a sudden Simpson is a fugitive, and he's being sought, and then he's in this car, police are chasing him, reports that he has a gun, and then there is this letter—for all intents and purposes a suicide letter—that gets read. I could see Brokaw react visibly to that moment. It's usually unexpected, surprising news that puts us on the air. It's not very often when we're on the air and then hear really unexpected news."

The network's decision to break from the basketball game began with a phone call from Lack to Ebersol. Minutes into the second half of the basketball contest, NBC pulled out. "I said, we've got to go now," recounted Bohrman. "We told Al Michaels to give it to Brokaw."

"We knew it was going to be a difficult night and it was," said Bohrman. "No one had thought through this scenario before. This was not a geopolitical crisis, this was just an incredible story which was happening while we were there. The most famous person ever charged with murder in this country, a beloved athlete, someone everyone knew. It had taken this turn and for all these reasons we were all drawn to it as people who wanted to put a news story on the air."

A grim Tom Brokaw, now on the air, brought viewers up to date. Simpson had been on the run for eight hours before police—monitoring his cellular telephone—finally caught up with him on Interstate 5. Simpson had told a dispatcher that he had a gun to his head and that he would hurt himself. He wanted to go see his mother.

The network anchor could not push aside his own feelings of bewilderment. Simpson had been a charismatic sports personality at NBC. Now, the network that had so long promoted Simpson's popularity was the messenger by which his public image would collapse. Brokaw said, wistfully: "For people who have known the public O. J. Simpson or even the private, it is inconceivable that it could come to this—that he would be the only suspect in two brutal murders, that he would leave after giving his word for a peaceful surrender, and that it would then play out on television. A man who has spent most of his adult life in the public eye, almost always in adulation. Now the dark side of his role in public life."[5]

Brokaw's on-air presence confirmed another subliminal message about this story: Among all stories, this one was of supreme national consequence. The chase had become a collective network experience with Dan Rather, Connie Chung, Peter Jennings, Barbara Walters, and Brokaw grappling to find a definitive explanation of what this story actually meant. Stunned by the scene unfolding on their monitors, their confusion drifted into American homes, a disconcerting effect for viewers used to taking their cues from television news' leading players. "When the nation's guides to everything are all at sea," said critic Walter Goodman, "the audience, too, must feel adrift."[6]

NBC's choice to cut from the NBA championship to the Simpson chase (before returning to the game's remaining few minutes) added to the kaleidoscopic coverage. For the greater part of the 1960s and 1970s, Simpson performed as a college and professional football star before millions of television viewers. Now, on national television, his image was trapped between the celebrated world of the sports arena—where he was once revered—and the real world of violent passions.

In a larger sense, the chase was the nexus for television news. Not since the 1991 Persian Gulf War had coverage of a breaking story been so all-encompassing. But even the war coverage could not compare with the media frenzy surrounding the chase, a story that would not just push the envelope of modern-day journalism, but ultimately rip it to shreds. Journalism was no longer yellow in the 1990s; the color had changed to purple: hyperbolic, breathless stories filled with gossip and personality. Especially in local TV coverage, celebrity journalism had become the staple of "news." Accompanying this trend was a shifting tide of language more suited for the boardroom than the traditional TV newsroom: Market share had become the critical factor in determining, in fact, the news of the day.

The Simpson story appeared to be the next great show in the plethora of made-for-television spectacles to come out of Los Angeles in the previous five years. The medium had barely rebounded from the Michael Jackson story with its child abuse accusations; the patricide and matricide trials of Lyle and Erik Menendez; the brutal beating of Rodney King at the hands of Los Angeles police officers, and the subsequent riots that shook the city.

As the chase unfolded over two hours, television had staked out not just a story but a moral stance. Enlisting the support of Simpson's friends and family, the networks exhorted Simpson to turn himself in to the police. Former pro football player Vince Evans implored Simpson on TV and radio simulcasts to give himself up, sobbing that "lots of people love you, man."

Those who did not abide by television's professed moral high ground were sharply rebuked or censored. When one Los Angeles television station located Simpson's first wife, Marguerite, and then asked what she would tell her former husband, her response was, "Run." A stunned anchor asked: "Did you say 'run'?" "Go O. J., RUN!" she exclaimed. "They pulled the plug so fast on her," one reporter later said, "you could almost hear the pop."

Simpson's ex-wife was not the only one rooting for the former football hero to make a break from the law. Television brought out his fans. Hundreds of local residents pulled lawn chairs to the side of the road, and waited for the cortege to pass; others lined the overpasses, waving, cheering, holding up signs they had taken the time to write—"GO Juice GO," as if number 32 were trying to elude a pack of motorized tacklers. The freeways of Los Angeles, so long a metaphor for the uprootedness of California culture, had become yet another symbol—a final playing field, and last refuge, for the onetime sports star turned fugitive. The city—and television—had never seen anything quite like this before. The medium had tapped a carnival nerve, frayed with edges of rebelliousness.

Commentators quickly branded onlookers as aberrant offshoots of a celebrity-worshiping culture. Condemning freeway spectators for rooting for Simpson, television found little time to examine its own culpability. For the better part of a half-century the medium had fostered what the social critic Christopher Lasch called a "cult of celebrity": America had evolved into a nation of fans. But the prevailing thought that Simpson's celebrity provoked the crowds around the freeways missed the essential point. Simpson's name was only partly responsible—it was the television experience itself that had mobilized the masses. The freeway "fans" wanted simply to be a part of the great chase.

The Simpson pursuit was actually the second major chase to galvanize Los Angeles residents within the month. A few weeks earlier, helicopter TV cameras captured another truck on the Los Angeles freeways being pursued by police at speeds of 15 to 30 miles per hour. The story was routine: A man had reportedly taken or borrowed a truck from his boss and fled down the freeway. In the course of the chase, the truck lost a tire, and sparks flew from the wheel rim. The pursuit lasted an hour and a half, and television news stations covered it live in its entirety.

In recounting the incident, Leo Wolinsky, the L.A. *Times* metro editor, said: "It all ended very peacefully, but at the end of the chase, the crowd gathered just as they did in the O. J. Simpson thing. They were all around there, people brought their kids out. And it was because the television media followed this thing minute by minute; local TV stations preempted their news that night. There was no other news that night but the stupid chase."[7]

That earlier televised chase carried another message about the trend in TV news coverage: Important news is sacrificed in the news stations' mad pursuit to acquire action-packed pictures. The "car chase," very much a Hollywood movie cliché, had evolved as a genre of television newsmaking—especially in Los Angeles. Howard Rosenberg, the L.A. *Times* television critic, caustically noted: "You and I can put on clown suits and run down a freeway and pretty soon there will be six choppers doing live coverage for no reason other than it makes good pictures. [The Bronco chase] was the logical outrageous extension of the kind of news coverage this city has been getting for some time."[8]

As the Bronco moved inexorably toward its final destination at the Simpson estate in Brentwood, the media revived the hero myths they had been so instrumental in creating. Not merely a celebrated sports figure, Simpson status was exalted by the same media that now traced his flight from the law. By a strange paradox, saturation coverage of the chase on all network channels only helped to legitimize and heighten Simpson's celebrity. Even as a suspected murderer, Simpson enjoyed the rarefied air given to our culture's "heroes," cheered by his highway fans and mourned as the great man toppled from the heights of fame and public adoration.

Headlines the following day declaring the "tragedy" and the "fallen hero" moved the media to wax philosophical. This was the American Hamlet. Even the venerable *New York Times* in its editorial saw Simpson as the archetypal tragic figure ensnared by the "fates" in a type of medieval morality play: "As one who was given great gifts and has been brought to a grim pass by either fate or frailty, he fits the fearsome pattern that lurks in our ancestral memory."[9]

A few media voices tried to bring Simpson's heroic image down to earth. "[Simpson] is a minor pop star—a onetime running back, a rental-car salesman, a modestly gifted actor—in big trouble," stated *Time* magazine columnist Richard Corliss. "Perhaps in an age long depleted of kings, we can come no closer to Greek tragedy than Oedipus Hertz."[10]

For the previous decade, the former football star was better known as a good-natured, media personality, whether shilling for Hertz Rent-A-Car or playing bit parts in slapstick movies. But in television's universe, such credentials qualified Simpson as a bona fide celebrity, and the 50-mile chase as an irresistible Hollywood spectacular. Simpson had "arrived"—if he had once been considered a minor celebrity, by the end of the televised pursuit and the medium's exaltations, his name was on the tip of every American's tongue.

Images of Simpson's flight moved the television networks into extended coverage, and the live footage gave a sense of chilling immediacy. With the story breaking during prime-time evening hours for most of the country, few viewers could escape, compelled to watch on all major broadcast and cable-news stations. For television—and for the country—"the chase" would become just the beginning of a 16-month-long obsession with the Simpson case. If the chase was prelude, then the soon-to-be Trial of the Century was epiphany. In retrospect, the televised chase had become a zeitgeist: From that moment, the Simpson story would abduct the culture. It suddenly became the common national experience of Simpson that everyone could track that day and in the days to come. Everywhere at once, instantaneously from that point on, the Simpson story was no longer just a celebrity crime story. This was something else.

Inside the *Los Angeles Times*

The chase was the type of made-for-TV breaking story that left the print press scrambling to compete. At the *Los Angeles Times*, the pursuit was an astounding chapter in a murder story that had evolved over the previous week. The newspaper had been at the forefront of coverage from the start.

Word of the brutal murders of Nicole Simpson and Ron Goldman had first come across the City News Service, a local news group that sends computer advisories to media organizations, including the *Times*. The first story, that two bodies were found in the fashionable Brentwood area, was unusual in itself. The second advisory that the bodies had been found in front of Nicole Simpson's condominium at 875 South Bundy, made it more interesting. "At first, we didn't even know that it was her; we thought that maybe two bodies were dumped," said Leo Wolinsky of the *Times*. "We sent one person initially at that point. We still were thinking of it as a curiosity."

Later, the violent nature of the gruesome murders would become central to the media's story. The murder scene, indeed, was horrific. Nicole Simpson's blood stained the pathway outside her home; dozens of paw prints belonging to her pet Akita pockmarked the wash of blood. The 35-year-old woman, curled in a near-fetal position, had her carotid arteries and jugular vein severed, knife wounds cutting so deeply as to nearly decapitate her. She had lost seven-eighths of the blood in her body. Goldman's body lay nearby, one eye opened, his torso oozing blood from the scores of knife wounds. The killer's knife had sliced across his neck and throat. A waiter at a nearby restaurant, Goldman had been on a goodwill mission to deliver a pair of eyeglasses left by Nicole Simpson's mother, a deed that cost him his life.

In no sense were these ordinary homicides. As one investigating detective stated: this was an attack of rage. If so, it was an act of calculated, cold-blooded rage. A trail of bloody, size-12 footprints belonging to the killer first led away from the bodies then back again to the victims. Murderers generally flee a killing scene quickly. But, as law-enforcement officials surmised, in this case, the killer's stride was short, indicating that he was unhurried, seemingly amazed at his own butchery.

A day after the discovery of the bodies, when Simpson himself was questioned by police detectives—and captured on videotape standing in handcuffs—the *Times* still lacked a firm handle on the story. "Police were still insisting he wasn't a suspect and we were talking about where this story would go," recounted Wolinsky. "At one point, a city editor suggested we bury the story inside on page B3 in the metro section. But our sources were telling us something different late that day—Simpson was a suspect, and the only suspect."

The early decision to go with the Simpson-as-suspect story was a particularly tough one for the *Times*. Simpson was not an ordinary citizen or suspect. Other newspapers shied away from the declaration, and the police continued to deny the allegations. Working for the hometown paper put added pressure on staffers. "But we thought because of the reporters we put on it, and the good sources that they had, that the story was safe, it was real," said Wolinsky. "We continued to feel way out on a limb for days because it was still days before police would confirm he was a suspect."

The newspaper would continue to be tenaciously single-minded in its coverage while deploying a unit of reporters, photographers and editors to concentrate on the story. As the story snowballed in the days following the Brentwood murders, a team of five reporters was assigned to work nearly full-time on the case. Other staffers would contribute as well on a part-time basis. Few crime stories could have galvanized the paper's forces to this extent.

The *Times'* lead police reporter was Jim Newton. An aggressive 31-year-old journalist, Newton was on the Simpson story from the start. His exclusive story first publicly targeting Simpson as a murder suspect skirted on dangerous grounds. But Newton trusted his bevy of well-placed sources, and his editors trusted him. Three days later, Newton followed up, reporting that Simpson would soon be arrested and charged with the homicides. In the first month after the murders, he wrote 19 page-one Simpson stories and he, and the paper at large, were credited with setting professional standards for investigative journalism—as well as criticized for fanning a media frenzy.

Much of the city's media fed off Newton's daily stories, and for reporters on the Simpson beat the early-morning edition of the *Los Angeles Times* was required reading. Newton had become a primary "source" for television updates. "Every day we took our cue from what he wrote on the front page," said CNN reporter Marc Watts. "We all had our sources, but no one was as plugged in as Jim was. I would arrive at Simpson's home at 3 a.m. for my daily duties, and we would wait for the early edition of the L.A. *Times* to come up to see what Newton had written."[11]

Newton began the day of June 17, 1994, believing it would be a relatively easy one at the paper. Heading to police headquarters at Parker Center, he became part of a chaotic scene, joining reporters jammed into a press conference for the latest police update. Outside headquarters, 18 television trucks circled the building and four media helicopters hovered overhead. The Simpson story had already grown into an astounding news event; however, no one could possibly have anticipated the latest development

Newton continued to ponder a CNN report aired the previous day, that a possible second murder suspect reported to be Simpson's friend, A. C. Cowlings, was being sought by police. His sources could not confirm the report, and he entered police headquarters somewhat wary. "It was a frustrating morning, trying to confirm or definitively disconfirm [the CNN story]. All I could get were people saying that they had not heard of a second suspect. So I went to Parker Center with little trepidation that there was a single suspect being sought. It never occurred to me that we were going to have no suspect in custody."[12]

For the reporter, the day proved to be anything but typical. A perturbed Deputy Chief David Gascon, the LAPD press relations officer, announced to reporters and a national audience tuned to the televised press conference that O. J. Simpson had failed to turn himself in to police as he had promised. He now was a fugitive at large. Over the conference room microphone a collective gasp was emitted from the more than 100 reporters. Newton later heard his own spontaneous reaction to the announcement caught on his tape recorder: "Oh, my fucking god!"

"Coming back to the paper afterward, people were shell-shocked, not sure what we would really do," he said. Reports started to filter into the newsroom that Simpson was headed to his house to kill himself—rumors buttressed by a press conference at Robert Shapiro's law office that late afternoon. Shapiro, who had recently taken on the case, instructed Robert Kardashian, a friend of Simpson's, to read a letter written by Simpson earlier that day. For reporters, the words sounded all too much like a suicide note. The letter, addressed "To Whom It May Concern," plaintively appealed not to an individual but to the public—Simpson's fans—pleading with them to "think of the real O. J. and not this lost person."

The media scene soon echoed with a series of sound bites from the principal players. There was Shapiro pleading with Simpson to surrender immediately "for the sake of your children."

The LAPD's David Gascon had a more pointed statement to reporters: "Mr. Simpson is out there somewhere and we will find him."

At the time of the police press conference, Wolinsky was attending an academic conference at the University of Southern California analyzing another hard-rock media issue: coverage of the Los Angeles riots. Not one of the "news junkies" at the conference had heard the breaking news that Simpson had disappeared after being officially charged with murder. When Wolinsky announced what had happened, the audience gasped in astonishment. "They couldn't believe that Simpson could be a fugitive," he said.

Speculation spread like brushfire following the police press conference. Heading back to the *Times* office, Wolinsky first thought that Simpson most likely was already dead, possibly at his Brentwood estate, his body waiting to be found by authorities. When reports came in that his Bronco van had been spotted on the Los Angeles freeways, Wolinsky laughed at the thought that the accused celebrity was now in the middle of a Los Angeles police chase. "Oh, what a joke," he said, thinking wryly. "I'm sure that must be him." But 15 minutes later, Wolinsky and the *Times* staff were fully convinced that Simpson, armed with a gun, was in flight. Like a reflex action, the newsroom scrambled reporters and photographers to follow the Bronco route from Orange County to the West Side.

Newton went over to Brentwood, which he described as "rocking and rolling" with police, spectators, and media besieging the exclusive neighborhood that is home to many Hollywood celebrities. The reporter was fast approaching his deadline as the Bronco chase continued to unfold. Newton learned that the police department's 24-man SWAT team, assembled at Brentwood, was prepared to kill

Simpson if he exited the van pointing a gun. "That was everybody's nightmare scenario," he said. "Something would go wrong, and there would be a riot."

The story was pushing the *Times'* deadline very hard. It was almost 5 p.m., and the lead to the next day's Simpson story had yet to be resolved. At the copy desk, Shawn Hubler had written several different tops for the main story: Simpson is captured; Simpson gets away; Simpson is dead. But even at that confused moment, Newton realized that in this city, with its strained history of police brutality, its social and class divisions, "there were not only kinds of endings for the Simpson story, but all kinds of outcomes for the city."

On CNN and the major networks, the Simpson chase percolated between a media event and a public celebration keenly resembling a modern "day of the locusts." Even before Simpson's eventual surrender at his estate, the chase was spinning as legendary in the annals of Hollywood criminal folklore, being compared with the Lana Turner scandal in the 1950s (her daughter, Cheryl Crane, stabbed to death Turner's longtime boyfriend, and underworld hoodlum, Johnny Stompanato) and the infamous case of Roscoe "Fatty" Arbuckle, the silent film comedian who was accused of rape and manslaughter in the death of a model in the 1920s.

While reveling in the sordid history of Hollywood, some reporters were nevertheless chagrined at the celebratory mood along the freeways and around Brentwood. Jane Wells, a local television reporter, described the side streets surrounding Simpson's home as having "a party atmosphere," with music playing and children coming into the neighborhood to join the Simpsonfest. Said one KTTV anchor: "To have a worldwide celebrity named as a murder suspect flee and then turn around and come back to his own home to a party atmosphere is distasteful. It's the most bizarre thing I've ever seen."

At ABC, Barbara Walters, with a different slant, vapored about "the love everyone feels." Alongside, Peter Jennings mused on whether the spectators saw the celebration as a chance for becoming "a participant" in television's instant history-making, a point picked up by media critics. "You can imagine them hurrying home and turning on their sets in anticipation of seeing themselves in a replay," said Walter Goodman, the *New York Times* television critic. "Until they did that, they were outsiders."[13]

Viewers also rushed to the scene, zeroing in with the help of helicopter cameras. From network to network, Americans watched as

Simpson's Bronco turned the corner to his Rockingham estate and pulled up to his home. Howard Rosenberg, the L.A. *Times* TV critic, said that television itself should have stopped there instead of lingering on the scene, waiting for the moment when Simpson would leave the van, armed with a gun and dangerous. It was widely speculated that Simpson would be gunned down by police or blow himself away. Live television has an awful potential—it can show, without warning, something that most people don't want to see. "The problem with live TV, there is no safety net," said Rosenberg. "What happens, happens, then it's gone. There is no way to control it. That's why it's dangerous."

Just after 9 p.m. East Coast time, Simpson finally surrendered to police, and the fears of looming violence dissipated over the airwaves. Sweeping into the television vacuum following Simpson's arrest were the "legal experts," quickly brought on-air for their post-chase analysis. Featured that night on ABC's *Nightline* was Johnnie L. Cochran, Jr., billed as a "distinguished defense attorney," having recently represented Michael Jackson against accusations of child abuse. His defense-minded spin was not lost on Simpson: soon, the lawyer would be shifting to another public stage as the murder case unfolded.

And so the Simpson story began, a wrenching human event. already caught in the throes of a media extravaganza. Live TV coverage of the Bronco chase had more than simply produced a sensational "event of the moment." It was the catalyst that triggered an incredible media frenzy—the likes of which were unprecedented in American culture—that was already whipping across the nation. Indeed, even before the famed football star had been taken to county jail, the media were hooked. For the next 16 months, Simpson's plight would be at the core of their obsession.

FRENZY IN L.A.

JUNE-JULY 1994

Winning Hearts and Minds

The Los Angeles district attorney's office and the Los Angeles Police Department quickly launched their opening blitz in an effort to win public support for their case.

Prosecuting and trying to convict someone as popular as Simpson would be a war waged on two fronts. Later, the D.A.'s office would take its case to the courtroom, but at this early juncture the office tried its case in a different venue, euphemistically referred to as the court of public opinion. In the days leading up to and after the Bronco chase, the D.A.'s office and the LAPD were a sieve of leaks—a quasi public-relations unit—promoting Simpson's guilt. Their intensive investigation had delivered what officials called a "mountain of evidence" against Simpson. Reports that a fake goatee and mustache, $8,750 in cash, a fully loaded Smith & Wesson .357 Magnum handgun, and a passport were taken from the Bronco van in the aftermath of the chase buttressed charges that Simpson was, in fact, guilty of murder.

District Attorney Gil Garcetti's intent to play political hardball was evident. To win his case, the D.A. had to change public perceptions of the popular football legend. At a televised press conference following the chase, Garcetti told reporters he was concerned about portrayals of Simpson as a "fallen American hero." "Let's remember we have two innocent people who have been murdered," he said, and that their families, including the Simpson children—six-year-old Justin and nine-year-old Sydney—"will have to live with this tragedy forever."

Immediately after Simpson's arrest, Garcetti cut a wide swath through TV interview shows, going so far as to predict that Simpson would confess and plead "mitigating circumstances." In a nationally televised interview on *This Week with David Brinkley,* two days after the chase, he asserted: "It's not going to shock me if we see an O. J. Simpson sometime down the road—it could happen very soon, it could happen months from now—say, 'OK, I did do it, but I'm not responsible.'"

Garcetti played up Simpson's stormy history with his wife as a "classic" example of domestic violence, and went so far to roundly criticize the municipal court judge in Simpson's 1989 prosecution for battering Nicole. The district attorney accused the judge of giving Simpson a slap on the wrist by placing him on probation—a charge that did not sit well with the judge, who produced the transcript of the hearing. The judge called Garcetti a liar for misrepresenting the facts: Indeed, he had imposed the precise sentence the prosecutors had requested in the case.

An all-too-availing media welcomed the first wave of off-the-record comments, reports of evidence and spins coming from the D.A. and LAPD. These "orchestrated leaks," as later described by Johnnie Cochran, were a deliberate strategy to persuade the people of Los Angeles—and the pool of potential jurors—that Simpson was solely responsible for the Brentwood murders. The Simpson team had yet to coalesce, and soon the "Dream Team" itself would aggressively use impromptu press conferences, leaks, and contrived courtroom sound bites to manipulate press coverage and win public support. In the opening act, however, it was the city's chief law enforcement authorities who persistently played the media at every turn.

The Simpson case entered into a murky political maelstrom. Although the district attorney's office prosecuted 70,000 felonies a year and claimed a 93 percent conviction rate, public perception still persisted that the office had not been very competent over the previous decade, especially in trying high-profile cases. The D.A.'s office and the LAPD had suffered severe credibility problems after a recent history of devastating setbacks. Televised trials had vividly brought their failures to a national audience.

In 1990, the highly publicized trial of Ray Buckey, a man accused of molesting children at the McMartin preschool in Los Angeles, ended with an acquittal. The *Twilight Zone* case involved John Landis, a Hollywood filmmaker accused of endangering the lives of three actors, two of them children, who were killed during a helicopter stunt. Landis and his co-defendants were acquitted. And then there was the videotaped beating of Rodney King in March 1991 and the ensuing trials of six Los Angeles police officers—a case that only widened the rift between the police department and the heavily black inner-city community. The prosecutor's office had been accused of presenting a less-than-effective case in the first police trial at Simi Valley, which ended in acquittals—a verdict that convulsed into a riot. Subsequently, two of the officers were convicted of violating King's civil rights in a federal trial, but this time critics accused the court of meting out far too lenient sentences.

In several other high-profile cases, Garcetti's office also wound up short. Two men accused of severely beating a truck driver during the riots were convicted on relatively minor charges. In what had also seemed an open-and-shut case, the first trial of Lyle and Erik Menendez, brothers who had admitted to the shotgun killings of their parents at their Beverly Hills estate, ended in two hung juries.

Simmering under the surface was a turbulent history involving the LAPD and the minority communities of Los Angeles. The King incident was yet another detonation point in a long, fractious, and dangerous relationship. The LAPD had been branded as racist since the hard-line regime of Police Chief Daryl Gates. With the riots, the anger finally tumbled into the streets and criminal courtrooms of the city.

Ironically, in the aftermath of the chase, the police faced a different type of criticism: They had gone soft on Simpson, and they had given the famous football legend special treatment despite the long trail of incriminating evidence they said existed.

Critics charged that, in the days after the bodies of Nicole Simpson and Ron Goldman were found sprawled on a walkway outside Nicole's Brentwood condominium, police had permitted Simpson to come and go freely from his estate two miles from the murder scene. Also, a police sergeant working privately with Simpson had helped him avoid reporters and photographers at Nicole's funeral by using a decoy. Photographs of the decoy, accompanied by the police sergeant, were published and aired on television. Simpson's short-lived flight from justice only fueled second-guessing about police performance. Even anonymous police sources took aim at their own department. Free from being identified, one such source charged that "you don't let a suspect who killed two people run the streets."[1]

A defensive Deputy Chief David Gascon responded: "We are not prepared to say we did anything wrong." But Simpson's flight on national television was a public relations debacle. Garcetti, a highly visible D.A. facing re-election in 1996, refused to blame the police for allowing Simpson to slip away. Seeking damage control, the police went to the media offering interviews with the investigating detectives.

The prevailing thought was that Garcetti's office and the LAPD could not escape the political machinations surrounding the case even if they had seriously sought a lower profile. Simpson's celebrity, combined with the widespread antagonism swirling around law enforcement in Los Angeles, automatically turned the case into a political free-for-all. This case was either going to raise up or bring down the major participants, a realization Garcetti recognized from the start. "The D.A.'s office has had a very bad record prosecuting big cases up to now," said Leo Wolinsky, the L.A. *Times* metro editor. "Garcetti's going to be judged by what happens here. So whether he wants to get involved or not, he is—and people are looking at his performance."[2]

Bad News

Following the chase, police leaks began in earnest. The secret disclosure of evidence potentially incriminating to Simpson was embraced by the media. Reporter and source had mutual self-interests that were satisfied in such an arrangement. A determined LAPD sold the idea that it had captured the Simpson-Goldman killer—and he was O. J. Simpson. Police sources played to an accommodating media. Reporters continued to advance the story, refusing to let the Simpson case and the Simpson story just settle. Whether or not such leaks could later influence public sentiment and ultimately prejudice Simpson's trial was beside the point. Reporters are paid to get the story quickly, regardless of whether those stories are detrimental to the court's search for justice. To that end, their appetite was voracious and nondiscriminative.

In their twisted relationship, the media continued to eagerly go along with the district attorney's gambit—yet lambasted the very tactics used to sell Simpson's guilt to the public. It wouldn't be the first or last time that the media engaged in a bout of self-denial.

While willing to feed the public with a steady stream of leaked stories from "unidentified investigators," the media found themselves caught in a trap of their own making. The cycle became predictable, with reporters running fast and furious with "inside" stories from "sources familiar with the case," then turning around to shake a righteous finger at what they characterized as abusive conduct among city law-enforcement officials.

In the week following the chase, the media pressed the LAPD to make public a taped 911 emergency call made by Nicole Simpson after her ex-husband had broken into her home. A furious O. J. Simpson could be heard screaming obscenities as he entered her home. When the tapes were finally released, June 22, the story exploded across the airwaves and in newsprint. The national media not only ran with the story but beat it into the ground. For the next week, television sounded like a tape recorder that had gone awry.

The 911 tape was played over and over, thousands of repetitions that effectively conveyed the prosecution's message that Simpson was a guilty man. Yet, after freely exploiting the police tapes, news organizations turned around to rail against the prosecution's campaign to discredit Simpson. The L.A. *Times* chastised law enforcement authorities for releasing the tapes to gain maximum media exposure. With indignation, the newspaper charged: "The timing of the material's release—just in time for Wednesday's early evening newscasts—reeked of advance planning by the prosecution."[3] The *Times* editors, however, failed to mention that their newspaper had been among those that had aggressively pushed authorities to first hand over the tapes to the media.

Although quick to criticize overzealous prosecutors and police officials, reporters continued to pounce on even the smallest piece of new information. Having unleashed a runaway train, the media were unable, or unwilling, to apply the brakes. And, at times, they crashed.

News sources often proved to be wrong, and reporters swept away by frenzied competitive pressures failed miserably at times to verify information. Coverage was unsettling, creating a journalistic schizophrenia. Important "breakthroughs" in the case were reported one day, and would disappear the next. When the *Los Angeles Daily News* reported that police had found a possible murder weapon near the crime scene—a bloodstained, military-style, entrenching tool—it was a dramatic news exclusive. Soon the story was spiked without comment. Other reports stated that the murdered victims had been decapitated, adding another horrific element to the crime. The story was fact one day, fiction the next. The victims had suffered grievous neck wounds but had not been decapitated.

KCBS was also wrong when it reported the "bombshell" that police had found incriminating evidence in the golf bag that Simpson had taken on his overnight plane trip from Los Angeles to Chicago in the hours following the murder. Other news organizations embellished on the story—still unverified—citing sources who reported that blood had been found on the golf bag. When a local Los Angeles television station reported a bloody ski mask had been found at the murder scene, it came across as a chilling piece of evidence. But it was one that did not exist. The police had actually found a hat—a dark blue watch cap—not a ski mask. The problem extended beyond factual error. As Jim Newton, of the L.A. *Times*, noted: "There is a big difference in the malevolence you attribute to a watch cap than a ski mask."[4] These errors not only undermined the credibility of the media and clouded public perception, but served to demonize Simpson even before he stood before the court as a defendant.

KCBS found itself in the middle of another controversy a month after the murders, when its investigative correspondent Harvey Levin reported that Deputy District Attorney Marcia Clark had been videotaped at Simpson's estate prior to the issuance of a court-ordered search warrant of the property. A time code on the tape was used as evidence against Clark to show that the prosecutor had arrived at Simpson's estate at 10:28 on the day of the search. The warrant for Simpson's home was signed by a judge at 10:45 a.m.

Levin pushed the story, pronouncing that Clark's impropriety could have seriously jeopardized the prosecution's case, as well as her role as the lead prosecutor—a charge disputed by more incisive legal experts. Speaking on a local radio talk show, Levin could barely contain his excitement over the possibility that his "exclusive" might somehow impact the Simpson case. "I have a feeling that this tape is going to be subpoenaed today," he said. "It's going to end up being, perhaps, an important element in the case."

KCBS's heavy promotion of Simpson coverage boasted of Levin's "bombshell," although the station's sister network, the *CBS Evening News*, opted to ignore the report. Levin himself made the rounds of the media talk shows, crediting his shrewd reportorial skills for uncovering Clark's alleged impropriety. As one of the media's "constitutional police officers," he declared that he had protected the public interest against sloppy law-enforcement work.

What Levin had failed to protect against was sloppy journalism: specifically, his own. Levin's report turned out to be untrue, a mistake more embarrassing for the station's incessant self-promotion. The day his report was aired, the district attorney's office issued a blunt denial of Levin's charges, corroborated by other sources, that Clark had not arrived at Simpson's estate until two hours *after* the service of the search warrant. Levin's story was unraveling, but even in the face of Clark's refutation, the station stood by its story, continuing to broadcast the controversial footage in its newscasts. Two days after the erroneous report, the station was still pushing the story: A promotional spot airing during the network's morning news show listed the story among the KCBS "exclusives" in its coverage of the Simpson case.

Levin finally went on the air to apologize to viewers and to the maligned Marcia Clark, an apology picked up by the networks. The videotape's time code reading of 10:28 did not indicate when the footage was shot, but rather when it was fed to the station's studio in Hollywood. The tape was fed from a satellite truck outside of Simpson's home at 10:28 *in the evening*.

Leo Wolinsky characterized the Levin report as endemic of the type of loose reporting by local television news outlets. "Where they fall down is in their chasing the 'hot' story and getting carried away with it, not having it down tight," he said. KCBS's problem was exacerbated by the station's recalcitrant attitude when faced with its own mistake—an arrogant and dangerous attitude exhibited by any station that "stands by its reports" even when those reports are wrong. "[KCBS] made a big deal about their story and then they were forced to retract," said Wolinsky. "The retraction throughout the day got more vague and more vague until they weren't even retracting it anymore. That kind of stuff looks very bad for the television media."

Marc Watts was a product of local television news for 12 years before joining CNN in 1994. He said that local stations suffered from lower professional standards than those at CNN, a reportorial sloppiness that gave rise to the rush of bad stories early in the Simpson case. Unlike local news stations, CNN required reporters to triple check their information before going on the air. (The network, though, was not immune from careless reporting when it erroneously disclosed, prior to the Bronco chase, that police were seeking two suspects in the murders.)

Local television stations made a practice of running too fast with the news, he contended. "An attorney plugged into the case in the prosecution office could [tell a reporter] something he was discussing over the water cooler," he said, and local stations would likely report the "scoop" that night on its evening newscast. "On local TV, one source, they're going on the air—and one source wasn't enough for all the leaks involved in the O. J. Simpson story."[5]

The KCBS foul-up hardly gave the news industry a moment's pause. The media juggernaut continued to surge ahead. "If this episode was unique, you could accept it," said L.A. *Times* critic Howard Rosenberg. "As bad as Channel 2 is, it's merely the goofiest circus clown in the crowded Volkswagen. . . . In fact, the case may have become a seminal moment in the regression of TV journalism, with the electronic cannonballs careening out of control as never before. Amy Fisher was bad. Michael Jackson was worse. But now has become the ultimate horror, the recurring nightmare."[6]

Compounding media mistakes was the problem of "the echo chamber" effect. Here, news organizations picked up erroneous stories from other media outlets and, failing to fact-check, ran with them. The repetition of bad news had the effect of contaminating the entire media, from small local news stations to the national wire services. While it is normal practice for the news media to carry stories coming from different newspapers and TV stations, and accept a certain amount of risk, the Simpson story was equivalent to handling a live grenade. No one knew when one story would blow up, destroying the credibility of one or more news organizations.

Bad reporting also fueled a rising level of acrimony between journalists and public officials. When KNBC wrongfully reported that the police had taken bloody clothes out of Simpson's washing machine, Gil Garcetti publicly criticized the report. Acknowledging its mistake on the air, KNBC still refused to take the entire blame, indicting other news outlets for repeating the story, including the *Los Angeles Times*. But KNBC was wrong, again. The *Times* never reported that bloody clothing had been found by police, only that Simpson's clothing was being examined by the police.

"I was just about to rip the roof off of KNBC," said *Times* reporter Jim Newton. "What we reported was that police seized clothes from the washing machine and were testing them to see if blood was found on them. Those tests did not find blood."

Finally, KNBC corrected itself, a second time, but only after tainting its print brethren at the *Times*.

As reporting became increasingly undependable, some news outlets, including the *Times*, adopted a policy strictly forbidding reporters from crediting information to other media organizations. Although reporters at the *Times* were under severe internal pressure to "get ahead of the story," an editorial decision was reached that only stories based on primary sources would be printed. Wary that the epidemic of "bad" stories was spreading rapidly, the *Times* was intent on staying accurate. Reporters assigned to the Simpson beat were told to be on guard against inaccurate or unverified accounts coming from other media outlets.

Still, Simpson mania was in the air. The feverish competition to ferret out exclusives pushed reporters, who were all too quick to go with highly speculative information from unreliable sources. "When the *Los Angeles Daily News* reported a trenching tool [a possible murder weapon] had been found, and it moved on the wires, there was a lot of pressure put on me here to match that, but we couldn't get it from our sources," said Newton. "We had an option to say, 'According to the *Los Angeles Daily News*, sources say. . . .' We didn't say that. [Our editors] agreed if we couldn't find it through our own people, we just weren't going to repeat it."

Beyond the media's carelessness and fratricidal fighting, a serious question loomed: Did the massive coverage detonate public sentiment against Simpson, making a fair trial more difficult, if not impossible? Simpson had yet to be indicted, much less brought to trial, and critics were already charging that the police were launching a campaign of vilification, provoking a "lynch mob mentality," assisted by the local and national media.

"The presumption of innocence has been assassinated in this case," said F. Lee Bailey, a member of Simpson's defense team. "The conduct of law enforcement has been reckless, and the press has not been far behind. It is reprehensible, the worst case I've seen in 40 years."[7]

For all his public posturing, the famed attorney was well aware that Simpson's presumed innocence was essentially irrelevant in the eyes of the media. As opposed to the courts, the media work under a wholly different set of principles, where matters such as the "presumption of innocence" are usually little more than legal niceties. Few reporters wait for official disclosures, such as those made in the courtroom. The idea—always—is to "get ahead" of the story. Simply, the virtue of patience is anomalous to the profession grounded in the here and now. "[For reporters] news is what they know today, this

minute," said the *Times* media critic David Shaw. "By instinct or
training, they want to report what they know as soon as they know
it."[8]

The credo holds natural dangers for a defendant's fair-trial
rights, and the Simpson case would be the latest to carry the burden
of what euphemistically is called "pretrial publicity." The "evidence"
and "testimony" brought before a newspaper or TV station may later
be modified or found inadmissible in court. Other disclosures may
simply be used to "sell" the news that day regardless of whether such
stories inflame public passions and prejudice a future panel of jurors.
It was highly doubtful whether these concerns even fleetingly passed
through the consciousness of any member of the Simpson press corps.

One such piece of inflammatory evidence was the coroner's report
that was unofficially released to ABC and other news organizations.
Photos accompanying the report depicted the full extent of the fatal
and gruesome wounds to the victims' bodies. Nicole Simpson's throat
had been severely slashed, exposing her spinal cord. Ron Goldman
had 64 stab wounds; his throat had multiple slash wounds, his ear
was nearly severed, there were knife wounds on his upper torso and
back. Said an unidentified ABC source: "They knew they were being
killed."

From the media's perspective, the battle for the Simpson story
was well under way. The intensity of the competition was something
most reporters never envisaged or experienced before. The story
dominated their news pages and broadcasts. It also took a
psychological toll. While working around the clock, reporters were
expected not simply to report the news, but to provide stories no one
else had. Although breaks in the story were quickly vacuumed into
the media mainframe, reporters took mental note of their "exclusives"
like gunslingers counting notches on their guns. Local TV stations
trumpeted their exclusives in promotions for upcoming newscasts,
regardless of whether their "bombshell" was significant at all to the
case. Often, it was the *appearance* of being ahead of the competition
that counted in the stations' drive for ratings.

Although reporters worked independently, the cumulative effect
was that of a massive media machine constantly pushing the story
forward, to the next revelation, the next piece of evidence, the next
episode of the Simpson saga. There was not a moment when the
Simpson story—or reporters—could simply rest. KCBS's Harvey Levin
described the working conditions as nightmarish, with journalists
putting in 18-hour days while working under the most intense

scrutiny. Levin was told by his executive producer that he would be going live on the air during the day with breaking developments in the case, and then be expected to lead every evening newscast. "It was lunacy at the beginning," he said. "I think there was a general lack of quality control. I was getting physically sick. . . putting in insane hours."[9]

Coverage had already breached the walls of reason, and the media, unrestrained and caught in a frenzy of competition, embraced one revelation after the next. Virtually anyone with any connection to Simpson could become the latest media focal point. And sources lined up, anxious to tell their stories, some for momentary fame, some for money. On *A Current Affair,* Simpson's caddie told the TV tabloid show that Simpson had exploded in anger over a perceived insult by a companion during a golf outing hours before the murder. A source for the Associated Press, described as a friend of Nicole's, charged that Simpson had stalked his former wife and threatened to kill her if he saw her with another man. Former pro-football star Jim Brown, on ABC's *Good Morning America*, painted Simpson as a drug user, charging that "it's known that the Juice has dealt with cocaine."

Seeking the spotlight could have unintended consequences. Susan Forward, a clinical social worker, faced professional disciplinary action after a spate of television interviews in which she disclosed her confidential discussions with Nicole Simpson during two therapy sessions. Nicole had spoken privately of being battered and threatened by Simpson following their divorce in 1992. Professing to further the nation's awareness of wife abuse, Forward had violated her patient's privacy rights, as well as the ethical standards of her profession.

In the days preceding the pretrial hearings, the media continued to do the prosecution's bidding, weaving a sinister scenario that pointed to Simpson as being the killer. ABC-TV disclosed that Simpson made several recent visits to a local cutlery store, and then tied the report to a detailed description of the victims' autopsy results. Nicole Simpson and Ron Goldman were attacked from behind with a serrated knife and slashed in the head, neck, chest, and torso, the network reported. KCBS-TV then reported that a knife was missing from Simpson's weapons collection and that he could not account for it. Still other sources told of seeing Simpson at the Los Angeles International Airport the day after the bodies were found, digging through a duffel bag. The clear inference was that Simpson was looking to hide incriminating evidence.

An overlay of speculation and innuendo plagued the early coverage. Once drawn into the Simpson story, no one connected to the case was exempt from the media's minute scrutiny. Even the victims' families were left open to the worst kind of idle gossip. No longer considered private citizens, their lifestyles—indeed the very way in which they comported themselves—were dissected and crassly exploited. Tabloid television shows and cable talk programs were notorious, like the CNBC *Rivera Live* show—a hotbed of chatter and gossip in the early days of the case. Geraldo Rivera himself floated mean-spirited stories with flimsy news value. During one segment, Rivera accused Nicole Simpson's parents of being "co-opted" by O. J. Simpson for financial gain: that, in effect, Simpson had bought their loyalty. According to the talk-show host: "One of the reasons Simpson was treated by Nicole's family more as a bereaved husband than potential perpetrator of a heinous murder, was O. J. had co-opted Nicole's parents, giving them a Hertz franchise." The "source" for his story was a "buddy" who, Rivera said, had "socialized" with the Simpsons.

To corroborate his accusation, Rivera turned to the show's guest, a helicopter pilot-reporter who had covered the Bronco chase. Following Rivera's lead-in, he remarked: "Family members are upset with the father and mother; they turned their back on Nicole—O. J. was a meal ticket, he meant a lot of money." In the next breath, the guest astoundingly extended his argument, blaming Nicole Simpson for her own demise. "She had to share some of the blame because she had a great lifestyle, drove a white Ferrari, was the wife of O. J. Simpson. But there's a lot to say why she didn't leave town—the woman should have split town."

Waves of speculation and rumor enveloped the case before it had even come to court. In a highly unusual public statement, President Bill Clinton implored the nation, after having watched in "excruciating detail" the chase and its aftermath, that "the time has now come for the legal process to take its course." Said Clinton: "I think the less the rest of us say from now on until the legal process takes its course, the better." If Clinton hoped that reason would prevail and that the press would back off, if only a step or two, he had sorely misjudged the prevailing mood. Clearly, the media weren't listening.

THE GREATEST STORY EVER

JUNE-JULY 1994

The chase was merely a prelude, not only to the O. J. Simpson case but to the O. J. Simpson *story*. Network and cable television's power to turn the focus of an entire nation on to one defendant and one courtroom in Los Angeles was astonishing. Newspapers and radio stations across the country also filled in the day-to-day coverage. But the Simpson story was distinctly a television event, and the medium's greatest story ever if measured by the thousands of hours of coverage. No other story in television's 50-year history had so singularly dominated the airwaves.

Television's reach during the pretrial hearings and the subsequent trial was remarkable. Beginning in late June 1994, the swirling images of a sports legend turned murder suspect transformed the American workplace and living room into an electronic courtroom. The Simpson case was, simply, inescapable. The nation was so distracted that by the time the case was resolved more than a year later, American businesses had lost $40 *billion* in productivity costs from workers caught up in Simpson gossip around the water cooler and copy machine.[1]

The Television Trial

The murder case would come to serve as the quintessential television trial, a vast experiment in teledemocracy that has reshaped public perceptions of the justice system. In recent years,

television had presented to the public stage such celebrated defendants as William Kennedy Smith; Lorena and John Bobbitt; Erik
and Lyle Menendez; the Los Angeles police officers responsible for the
beating of Rodney King; Jeffrey Dahmer; Christian Brando; Amy
Fisher; and Tonya Harding. But when Simpson was first brought
before a Los Angeles municipal judge—and, in effect, a public
courtroom filled with millions of television viewers—the fledging
relationship between the camera and the courtroom changed forever.
For better or worse, the Simpson case pushed American justice
system headlong into the new age of the "television trial."[2]

With television attached to its hip, the Simpson trial was an
extraordinary *cultural* event. And, in the beginning at least, those
who dared to criticize this techno-legal relationship were characterized as being out of touch with the modern world. *New York Times*
columnist Anna Quindlen was one of the most ardent champions of
the televised pretrial hearings, marveling at the civics lessons they
gave Americans. Dismissing critics of court television as "tut-tutters"
and stodgy "neo-Luddites," she contended that the medium opened
the courtroom to a vast public gallery. "[And] in the case of *People* v.
Simpson," she said, "the people have shown up in force."[3]

Other supporters contended that the very question of whether
television belonged in the courtroom was moot. "To ask about the
impact of cameras on the judicial system is beginning to be an
irrelevant question," said media critic Jay Rosen. "People see
television as a part of the system. It's almost like asking, 'What's the
impact of the courtroom on the judicial process?' A proper reply would
be, 'What do you mean? The courtroom is the judicial process.' So is
television."[4]

Without pictures from the courtroom, the Simpson case may
have soared no higher than other recent, nontelevised trials featuring
such celebrated defendants as Mike Tyson, Leona Helmsley, and
Manuel Noriega. While all were cases of national interest, a measure
of media normalcy prevailed. In the course of the next 16 months, the
Simpson case would overshadow every other important judicial event,
including the nontelevised federal trial of the terrorists responsible
for bombing New York's World Trade Center.

With video pictures coming from the small courtroom in the Los
Angeles County Criminal Courts Building, the Simpson case vaulted
into the culture's daily consciousness. Pretrial hearings—beginning
with Simpson's arraignment—were unprecedented for the sheer scope
and density of television coverage they earned. The case dominated

early morning, daytime, prime-time, late-night, and overnight programming. Rather than lose interest in the tedious proceedings, viewers hung on as yet another piece of tantalizing evidence—a bloody glove, a mysterious sealed envelope, the autopsy results—was disclosed, discussed, and dissected ad infinitum.

The media feeding frenzy that ensued quickly moved the Simpson case into a larger-than-life telegenic spectacle that played to a global audience. If the Earth did not stand still during the Los Angeles hearings, it at least slowed down in the dizzying cycle of gavel-to-gavel coverage, and the endless spins and analyses. The media's capitulation to the Simpson case, Rosen said, was "just a complete surrender to the lure of the story on everyone's part—audience, journalists, tabloids, producers, conversants at cocktail parties, everyone."

The Grand Jury Falls

From the start, the courts could not cope with the cyclone of pretrial publicity spinning around the case. With the escalating level of media attention, the grand jury proceedings became the first casualty. Superior Court Judge Cecil Mills called a halt to the panel's secret review, already five days old, charging that the media had overwhelmed the court's chance of keeping grand jury members free from the torrent of Simpson coverage.

Mills was no neophyte in his dealings with the media. Following the frenzy surrounding celebrity madam Heidi Fleiss' recent court appearances—and the trampling of innocent passersby by overzealous reporters and photographers—he had issued a set of rules governing press behavior inside the courthouse. But Mills found himself powerless to control the media mayhem outside the criminal court building.

The swell of inflammatory publicity peaked with the release of Nicole Simpson's 1993 emergency police calls. Even before presented in court, the tapes of the 911 calls were given to the media, the public at large, and, ostensibly, community members who could soon become jurors. No other single disclosure to date had so publicly incriminated Simpson. In its campaign to recast Simpson's public image into that of a killer, the prosecution had scored a decisive blow.

Public release of the tapes was seen as a retaliatory move by law-enforcement authorities in a public relations scramble with Simpson's defense attorneys. By the time Marcia Clark acknowledged that a bloody ski mask (mistakenly touted in numerous press reports as having been recovered by police from Simpson's home) did not exist, the prosecution was already losing its edge. Later, it was disclosed that the "ski mask" was, in fact, a blue knit watch cap recovered near the victims.

Efforts to "reconstruct" Simpson's public persona continued, and the police went on the offensive just hours after Clark's admission. The release of Nicole Simpson's frantic telephone calls to police was in time for the 5 p.m. newscasts in Los Angeles. That day, Garcetti's office and the LAPD won the news cycle from the defense. Footage of the tapes surpassed coverage given to the nonexistent bloody ski mask. It was a victory of sorts in the battle to dominate the television airwaves.

The two 911 calls Nicole Simpson made to police from her home on October 25, 1993, eight months before her murder, became the media's next fixation. Transcripts ran in all major newspapers, but this was not a story to be read: The tapes were meant to be heard. Nicole Simpson's frightened voice, and the background sounds of an enraged O. J. Simpson breaking into her townhouse were a powerful indictment. "He's fucking going nuts," she said desperately to an emergency police operator. "He's going to beat the shit out of me." Despite her pleadings that he leave, O. J. Simpson is heard furiously ranting at his ex-wife, "I don't give a shit anymore. I'm not leaving."

On television, the tapes were played in awkward juxtaposition against photos of O. J. and Nicole smiling, arm in arm, at happier times on vacation. Conjuring a mental image of a volatile and menacing O. J. Simpson, the tapes carried a visceral implication. If Simpson was capable of this level of intimidation and abuse, what else could he do? That question hung in the air as the tapes, again and again, filled television and radio airwaves across the country.

If the release of the police tapes was intended to blunt public sympathy for Simpson, Garcetti could not have been happier. Prior to the disclosure, public opinion polls reported that the clear majority of Americans believed Simpson was probably innocent. After the tapes were given to the media, the numbers reversed, with six out of ten Americans now believing Simpson was guilty. But the airing of the tapes also had an unintended side effect: It cast Garcetti as a manipulative and strong-armed official making political hay out of the tragedy. "He looks like a cheap politician on television," stated Harland Braun, a former Los Angeles deputy D.A.[5]

"I think we've seen a district attorney who has basically made a fool of himself by holding press conferences, by leaking information," said Steven Brill, the president and founder of Court TV. "Indeed, he hasn't even leaked it. He's done it in the kind of public way that makes a spectacle of the prosecutor's office."[6]

Whether Garcetti was still smarting over the recent Menendez brothers' stunning mistrials—certainly a distinct possibility—his tactics were evident. He refused to allow another high-profile defense team to sell its story to the public unchallenged. But by taking the offensive, he opened himself to charges of unfairly attacking Simpson before going to trial. Leslie Abramson, Erik Menendez's attorney and now an ABC commentator, suspected that Garcetti was looking to reach the potential jury pool before the Simpson defense team became organized. Deriding the strategy, Abramson charged that the prosecutor's office was "out of control," seeking to "poison the panel [its] way, before the other side poisons the panel" against the prosecution. Asked if the airing of the tape had hurt Simpson's ability to get a fair trial, Garcetti replied with intentional naiveté that he was "confident that we can find 12 jurors who know very little if anything about this tape."

The 911 tapes propelled a tidal wave of police leaks detailing Simpson's turbulent and sometimes violent relationship with his wife. Unidentified police sources released news of a 1985 incident in which Simpson reportedly shattered a car windshield with a baseball bat; the car belonged to his wife Nicole.

This latest strategic move to paint Simpson as a violent personality was followed by a wave of media stories reopening a 1989 battery case. That case involved yet a previous 911 call made by Nicole Simpson on New Year's eve. The distraught woman told police, "He's going to kill me, he's going to kill me." When police arrived at the Brentwood estate, they found Nicole hiding in the bushes outside the couple's home wearing only soiled sweatpants and a bra. She had been beaten around the face and neck. Although she refused to press charges, the city attorney had O. J. Simpson arrested. Pleading "no contest" to beating his wife, Simpson was given a small fine and ordered to perform 100 hours of community service. Subsequently, the Simpsons issued a joint statement: "Our marriage is as strong as the day we were married."

Cumulatively, the leaks created an uphill struggle for Simpson's defense, but a public backlash was beginning to grow against law-enforcement authorities seen as conspiring against Simpson. Police officials began to backtrack. To explain the flurry of anti-Simpson police announcements and leaks, LAPD officials argued they were compelled to release the 911 tapes, and other reports, under the Freedom of Information Act.

Still, the police and prosecutors were seen as going too far. The winds of public opinion were shifting prompting Garcetti to call for a moratorium on police leaks to the press. His office, he said, had no intention of trying the case in the media. Garcetti went further, telling reporters he would refuse to honor media requests for legal or police records involving Simpson. After a widespread publicity campaign designed to pummel Simpson before his trial, the district attorney now imposed a virtual news blackout.

"I'm going to fight as hard as I have to, to make sure that information is not improperly released," he said. Garcetti insisted he was chiefly concerned that Simpson receive an impartial trial, and that the public see that Simpson was being treated fairly. The release of the 911 tapes, he finally conceded, was "not fair to Mr. Simpson [and] not fair to the public."

Garcetti's involvement with the case continued to be linked with political expediency and his attempts to micro-manage public opinion. With each decision now seen as part of a larger political agenda, Garcetti left himself open to criticism at each step in the case. His selection of Marcia Clark as the lead prosecutor, and Christopher Darden, a black associate prosecutor, struck the press and the legal community as an overt attempt to remain politically correct in a trial involving spousal abuse and murder and the prosecution of a black American sports legend. By playing the political card from the start, each move by the district attorney's office now became suspect.

Critics charged that the district attorney's most questionable move was to try the case in downtown Los Angeles with its large population of black residents, rather than in predominantly white Santa Monica in West Los Angeles where the crimes occurred. Garcetti had met with the city's Urban League before making his decision. The chief prosecutor was now accused of trying to insulate himself from potential repercussions that could arise if Simpson were convicted—a factor he denied. He insisted that the Santa Monica courthouse, weakened by earthquake damage, could not have withstood the media crush. And then, in response to charges that his office was engaged in racial gerrymandering, Garcetti said it was not politics but a "general rule" to try lengthy cases at the Los Angeles

County Courthouse, a facility better equipped to handle security matters.

His critics did not buy it. "This is nonsense," said Gregg Jarrett the Court TV co-anchor during the Simpson proceedings. "I can point to ten long-term cases that have been tried, and Menendez is just one of them, outside of Los Angeles." Although some observers said Garcetti's choice of downtown L.A. made sense—it was equipped with metal detectors and also housed the D.A.'s "special-trials" division—in the world of legal gamesmanship, the move was considered a terrible tactical mistake. For all of Garcetti's pretrial "arrogance" in declaring to the nation Simpson's unequivocal guilt, Jarrett predicted that the prosecutor's choice of venue to downtown Los Angeles "will go down in the history of American jurisprudence as one of the biggest mistakes made by an elected district attorney if O. J. Simpson is acquitted."[7]

The very same media that had so closely followed Garcetti's lead were about to turn around and bite him during the secret grand jury hearings. A key eyewitness was found to have lied to prosecutors, not about her connection to the case, but her involvement with the media. Under Marcia Clark's examination, Jill Shively told the grand jury her story: Driving her car on the night of June 12, she narrowly missed colliding with a large white vehicle racing past the intersection of Bundy and San Vicente. Shively said the driver began honking his horn and screaming to "move your damn car." She quickly realized that he was O. J. Simpson. As the only witness to claim to have seen Simpson near the murder scene the night of the murders, Shively was a critical component in the prosecution's case.

But then she lied. Before taking the stand, Shively assured Clark that no one, except her mother and law-enforcement officials, had been told of her experience. In fact, she had told millions of people. That same evening she appeared on the TV tabloid show *Hard Copy,* described as an unidentified grand jury witness, holding her grand jury subpoena before a camera, and embellishing her testimony by describing Simpson as "just screaming and freaking out." Said Shively: Simpson looked like "a madman gone mad, insane" that night. She was paid $5,000 for her story, and another $2,600 from the *Star* to reprint the interview.

Clark was furious when she learned that Shively had lied and threatened "to make an example" of her key witness. Shively wound up leafing through the telephone book yellow pages to find a lawyer to represent her against Clark's possible retribution. The prosecutor responded by taking Shively before the grand jury a second time to have her explain her misleading statements. Then Clark asked the grand jury to "completely disregard" Shively's testimony before she threw her off the prosecution's witness list.

As the grand jury wound its way through the hearings, the press leaks overtook the legal process. Indeed, two unidentified grand jurors now joined the leaking mania, violating the court edict by giving press interviews. Jurors also acknowledged that they had heard the 911 tapes on television. In the end, the grand jury had capitulated to the basic reality of the Simpson case: The normal workings of the courtroom could not prevail in this media-charged environment. Even a change of venue would be of little use—the case dominated the airwaves and newsprint everywhere. Only those living a life of solitude could escape the screaming headlines and endless TV and radio chatter.

Robert Shapiro complained loudly that the district attorney's office, aided by the police, had politicized the case by running its investigation in the media. He accused Garcetti of inciting a propaganda campaign with false and misleading statements about the investigation and even Simpson's possible defense strategy. Garcetti, in fact, had appeared on a half-dozen network programs, claiming the slayings were "a classic case of domestic violence," and that he would not be surprised if Simpson confessed to the killings, perhaps claiming a "diminished capacity" (insanity) defense.

Shapiro then took aim at the litany of media mistakes compounded by the zealous prosecutor's office. Before a single charge had even been brought against him, Simpson had been tried and convicted in a media trial. The public was told of bloodstains on driveways, matching blood types, bloody gloves, a ski mask at the murder scene, and a military-style shovel described as a potential murder weapon—information that was unverified, premature, or outrightly erroneous. (DNA tests had yet to be completed on blood evidence, and a ski mask and murder weapon had not been found by police.)

Ironically, Garcetti's aggressive publicity campaign played right into the hands of the defense, which had searched anxiously for a way to move the case from the grand jury into a more favorable legal venue: a preliminary hearing. The grand jury "investigation" was heavily weighted in favor of the prosecution, severely limiting the defense's options. Indeed, the "fact-finding" mission of the panel is controlled solely by prosecutors, since no judge or defense lawyers are allowed in the grand jury room. By having the prosecution present its case at a preliminary hearing, the defense now had the chance to probe witnesses in advance of a jury trial, challenge evidence for its admissibility, and, if it chooses, to present a case of its own.

Shapiro prevailed upon Judge Mills, "on an emergency basis," to take action against the district attorney's defamation campaign. He charged that the D.A.'s unethical public posturing had promoted a presumption of guilt for his client that was bound to influence jury members.

After nearly a week of grand jury deliberations, Mills had come to an important decision. The unrelenting media coverage could likely infiltrate and influence the jurors' final decision. Then he took the extraordinary step of disbanding the jury. A judge, instead of a secret panel of citizens, would decide if Simpson were to be tried for murder. The Simpson case would now be taken before the world in a televised preliminary hearing.

Obsession

More than 80,000 preliminary hearings were held in California in 1993 with few even nudging the media's consciousness. The Simpson hearing was something else entirely—a legal proceeding turned into a spectacular made-for-TV event—a neat, week-long preview of the upcoming trial.

The purpose of the hearing was to determine whether a crime had been committed and, if so, whether Simpson was the likely assailant. Under routine circumstances, the proceedings would have been fairly perfunctory, but the case had already overstepped the bounds of normalcy. With America watching, the hearing became a national obsession.

During the six-day hearing, the three major networks saw their daytime entertainment ratings soar as high as 40 percent above regular levels. Simpson's preliminary hearing, beginning in late June, was a TV blockbuster, especially in Los Angeles where an estimated three out of four households were glued to the proceedings.

Having built the proverbial bandwagon, the networks now jumped on, making the hearing the centerpiece of programming throughout their 24-hour day. Eight out of ten Americans tuned to at least some coverage, an astounding figure not lost on network executives. Even ABC-TV's respected *Nightline* devoted its entire weekly lineup to cover the proceedings and was rewarded with some eight million viewers for each broadcast—a number equal to its 1980 groundbreaking coverage of the Iranian hostage crisis. CNN's audience also jumped fivefold: Nearly as many watched its Simpson coverage as those who tuned in to the network's 1991 Persian Gulf War coverage.

Abstract notions of "news value" among the networks were soon pushed aside for a more pragmatic consideration: ratings. At the start, the "Big Three" had serious questions about clearing out their entire daytime schedules to cover the preliminary hearings and considered other options. One was a plan to rotate trial coverage among their channels, but even that idea soon gave way to competitive and financial pressures. Still, the major networks refused to allow viewers to just slip away to CNN or Court TV, both featuring gavel-to-gavel coverage. They had learned a hard lesson from CNN's aggressive reporting of the Persian Gulf War, which proved to be a tremendous boost to the prestige and financial coffers of the struggling news organization.

"If the networks walked away from this story, it would help build the news dependence on CNN," said David Poltrack, CBS's executive vice president of research.[8] The prestige of the major networks had been chipped away during the past decade—about 25 percent of their audience had gone elsewhere, namely to cable, for news, information, and entertainment. The lure of the Simpson story was simply too great for the networks to just hand over to their cable adversaries.

Once the decision to carry the hearings was made, the three networks toyed with the notion of carrying the hearing without advertising, a decision that could cost them a combined $4.5 million in ad revenue for each day of coverage. Instead, they chose to air the entire proceedings with sporadic ad breaks that would run during court recesses. That decision paid off in ratings, with each network showing a dramatic hike in viewership during the morning and afternoon time slots.

From that decision to go gavel to gavel, the gravitational pull of the story was nearly inescapable. Networks refused to back off the story even when the day's proceedings were over—the Simpson story was *sui generis*, galvanizing both news and entertainment divisions. The news side took every opportunity to squeeze more programming out of the hearing, showcasing it on all their prime-time newsmagazines. Once the fire was lit, the Simpson story flashed across the entire media landscape. Said Fred Graham, the Court TV anchor: "TV producers are like lemmings. They run to cover the story that is being covered. And they don't know when to quit, and they sure as hell don't want to be the first to quit."[9]

As it pertained to news coverage, the Simpson hearing appeared to be the single most important story of the day, everyday, on all network channels. As the hearing took on a media life of its own, virtually all other news became mere electronic blips. The hearing dominated a week that saw Yasir Arafat arrive in Jericho, marking a historic chapter in the Middle East peace process, and the death of North Korean leader Kim Il Sung during critical negotiations with the United States and South Korea over nuclear arms—stories that came and then quickly disappeared, blotted out by the Simpson story.

For viewers, the Simpson story was TV's equivalent of a calamitous car crash. It forced them to slow down and not to dare look away from the wreckage and bloody victims strewn on the road. Although viewers continued to avidly watch the case, they carried a growing sense of anger that the medium was exploiting the story— and exploiting them. The relationship between networks and viewers was mutually schizophrenic. Viewers, admittedly hooked on the case, complained that networks were giving it "too much coverage," and "important news" was suffering as a result. Others said they would prefer to scrap gavel-to-gavel coverage altogether and return to their regular soap operas.

Reaction to viewer complaints was swift and mixed. Tom Brokaw, the NBC *Nightly News* anchor, said he could not recall another story that created "so much angst" at the network. Brokaw acknowledged that NBC staffers were constantly questioning their own roles in producing and showcasing the story: "How much is too much?" he asked. "Are we all prostituting ourselves to the O. J. thing? Have we been driven by the lowest common denominator?"[10]

CBS anchor Dan Rather admitted that to turn your back on Simpson was to ignore the everyday economic reality of television news. "In a tight ratings fight, O. J. spikes it up there," he said, "and you better keep that in mind." It wasn't just the networks but every news station piggybacking onto the Simpson phenomena. "The average local station news director is a guy with his back to the wall, his shirttail on fire, the bill collector at the door and a guy with a straight razor right at his throat," said Rather. "If his ratings don't get up, he may be out of a job in three months, six months, nine months. So when somebody says, 'Listen, O. J. gets the ratings,'

even if his better sense or his conscience tells him to go with
something else as the lead [story], he's gonna go long and strong with
[Simpson]."[11]

ABC's Ted Koppel offered no excuses. Instead, he targeted those
critics of *Nightline* and other programs with concentrated Simpson
coverage. Television was simply delivering the goods to viewers, who
apparently wanted more and not less of the Simpson story, he
insisted. Indeed, Koppel was miffed that viewers were ungrateful. He
concluded a *Nightline* special about the media coverage of the case
with a televised tongue-lashing. Speaking directly to his audience, he
said: "If all of you profess [that television] is shoving [coverage] down
your throats," then viewers can act accordingly. "All TV sets," he
piously reminded his audience, "are equipped with an on-off button."

Having spent the previous two hours with a group of media
critics, talk-show personalities, and commentators, discussing such
notions as the journalistic "high ground," Koppel had boiled network
decision-making down to its fundamental value: audience share.
Koppel's message was clear: Ratings ruled and high-minded values
of "newsworthiness," a term bandied about by his illustrious panel,
were secondary to the medium's base reality. As a sure-fire seller, the
Simpson story could not be ignored by any major commercial media
organization. Whether it was *Hard Copy* or *Nightline,* the media
followed the money.

This of course was not a startling revelation for media watchers.
But the notion that television "news" was merely a crass commercial
product, with stories chosen for their market appeal and advertising
potential, served only to heighten cynicism directed toward the
media. "Is this [a story] that demands every bit of television time
and talent that can be mustered?" *New York Times* television critic
Walter Goodman asked derisively. "By the standards of show
business, the hour after hour of the Simpson case on all four major
networks plus CNN and Court TV are resoundingly justified; the
ratings prove it."

Goodman's counterpart at the *Los Angeles Times*, Howard
Rosenberg, also lambasted the networks for failing to set a more
serious national news agenda, choosing to whet the public appetite
for more and more of Simpson. "Somebody has to decide what is and
what is not important for the country. Somebody has to say there are
priorities."[12]

But instead of backing off, the news media continued to search
for "larger meanings" to justify its swamping Simpson coverage. The

most far-reaching connection was made in a *New York Times* editorial stating that it was Americans' own "primal curiosity" in the gruesome and the murderous that had been aroused by the murders in Brentwood. The interest in the Simpson story, the *Times* postulated, had been instigated by the dark obsessive forces lurking under the surface of humanity. The story fed the "archetypal appetite" for tales of familial murder. As the *Times* reminded its readers, such narratives had evolved from biblical beginnings: "It is only a few pages, after all, that the reader is confronted with Cain."[13]

Whether the Simpson story stirred the primordial or simply the prurient, Americans *en masse* were compelled to turn on television, buy newspapers and magazines, phone in talk radio, and cyberchat on the Internet about the case. They jolted TV ratings scales, raised circulation rates of newspapers and magazines (for tabloids like the *National Enquirer*, as much as 500,000 more readers per issue), and subscribed to on-line computer services promoting Simpson as the "hot topic" of cyberspace.

However, the public's relationship with the media was complex and belied an underlying and mutual resentment. Like a personal relationship gone sour, each side blamed the other for failing to be rational and mature. The media titillated the public's imagination for the sensational and the celebrated. In turn, Americans continued to complain about the media's hard and persistent sell. But the media could not stop selling, nor could their audiences extricate themselves from the compulsion to watch, read, and talk about Simpson.

This link between television and its viewers was categorically expressed in rating points. ABC's rating instantly plummeted—a drop of 32 percent—when it cut away from the hearing to return to its regularly scheduled soap opera, *One Life to Live*. Viewers switched over to NBC and CBS, and ABC never fully rebounded the rest of the day, even after returning to the hearing. When CNN broke away from its coverage of the proceedings to present breaking news stories, its Atlanta headquarter's phone lines were immediately jammed by outraged viewers.

Having helped to create a Simpson addiction, the networks now turned against the very people they had helped to hook. The result resembled a dysfunctional family fight. Network programs, in fact, often posed as stern parents who scolded their children for behaving badly, having forgotten that they were the very ones who had set the bad example. On ABC's *20/20*, one segment assailed visitors to Los

Angeles who had come to "gawk" at Simpson's Brentwood estate and Nicole Brown's condominium. Such reactions prompted reporter Tom Jarriel, with self-righteous indignation, to condemn this frenzied public reaction.[14]

Said Jarriel: "People have always flocked to Hollywood to star gaze. But fans who are clustering around one fallen star lately have shown bizarre behavior, behavior so strange that fact is becoming stranger than fiction. Just three weeks after the murders, tourists had begun to flock by the hundreds to the Simpson Brentwood estate and the home of Nicole Brown. . . . People are diverting their vacations, coming up in their motor homes, selling [Simpson] paraphernalia; they are ripping bark off the trees to have as part of the mementos of their life."

His outrage barely contained, Jarriel found Ben Stein, a Hollywood writer, to serve as his alter ego. And Stein delivered, offering jaunty sound bites, provocatively designed for the program.

"Blood sells," he said. "Famous innocent beautiful blood really sells. People want to be connected with that innocent, beautiful blonde blood. It's like people want to be washing in the blood of Nicole Simpson and somehow have their lives transformed."

Jarriel summed up: "It's not quite dancing on a grave, but it's close."

For the correspondent, the behavior of the crowd coming to Los Angeles was "a case of morbid curiosity which had run amok." More to the point, he said their actions seemed to be indicative of a breakdown in the culture and the cheapening of human life. "There is virtually no reverence for the dead," he pronounced. "A man whose good reputation once sold rental cars today is being hawked on the street with cheap, almost obscene merchandising. If this is a case of being as American as apple pie, we may need a national psychiatric task force to bail us out."

The Jarriel segment reached its unintended and perversely ironic peak when Hugh Downs, the program's anchor, posed the very idea that television itself—and, specifically, the medium's frantic Simpson coverage—could be partly responsible for the celebrity-crazed culture denounced in Jarriel's commentary. "You know I'd be a hypocrite if I didn't admit at the same time that I say I find it repugnant," said Downs, "that I was riveted to TV [coverage of Simpson] all day."

But Jarriel was in denial, refusing to be sidetracked by the possible notion that television bore responsibility for creating the manic public environment he now decried. Yet, 20/20 itself would produce an astounding 22 segments related to the Simpson case over the coming months—no other story in the history of the program had been as prevalent or so widely promoted. Declaring that "there's nothing wrong with the national curiosity" about the trial coverage, Jarriel then bemoaned, without even blinking at the apparent hypocrisy, that "you hate to see people making money on real-life tragedy."

Big Business

The preliminary hearing was in fact more than just big news or grand entertainment. Simpson was big business, a huge money-maker that infiltrated into virtually every part of the media's vast entertainment and news industry.

In addition to the major networks, cable and syndicated stations vied for a piece of the action. Programs like CNN's *Larry King Live* and CNBC's *Rivera Live* dissolved their usual formats to cover almost exclusively the Simpson story; other shows were created, like the short-lived, syndicated *Premiere Story*, with Simpson the centerpiece of each episode. Talk-show luminaries like Rivera and King were placing bets that the hearing and subsequent murder trial would do for them what the Iranian crisis in 1980 did for Ted Koppel and his nightly news special, then called *America Held Hostage*. "This isn't a one or two-day blowout like the World Trade bombing," said Peter Brennan, the executive producer of *Premiere Story*. "This has all the drama needed to build a franchise."[15]

The span of television coverage was astonishing. No other single event in the medium's history could rival the sheer density of coverage given to the case. From the beginning, television had become Simpsonized, as if the story had swallowed whole the entire TV industry. At ABC alone, by the end of the trial, the network's magazine and news shows—*Nightline*, *PrimeTime Live,* and *20/20*—produced more than 100 Simpson stories.

Court TV, the brainchild of Steven Brill, joined alliances with NBC's *Dateline* with the hope of boosting its number of cable subscribers. Meanwhile, *Dateline*, aggressively sought preeminence over the Simpson story on its thrice-weekly prime-time program. Syndicated TV tabloids like *Hard Copy* and the sister shows, *Inside Edition,* and *American Journal*, prepared their battle plans against the networks, rigging up a special O. J. unit of reporters, producers, and technicians.

CNN also geared up for a ratings war, ripping up its entire day-time schedule to cover the preliminary hearing and, later, the trial—a move that continued to distance the network from its original mission as an all-news medium. Since its Gulf War coverage in 1991, the network's far-reaching international and national news coverage had decidedly slipped into a "softer" news-entertainment format. In its decision to carry the entire Simpson proceedings, CNN would usurp most of its remaining hard-news programming, scale back *World News* to a half-hour nightly, and eliminate altogether *Inside Politics*. With the exception of the occasional news update or coverage of a late-breaking news event, few stories in the world could upset the network's preoccupation with Simpson.

Like the networks, not many major newspapers or magazines could resist the Simpson story. A few prominent dailies, among them the *New York Times*, showed considerable restraint in their coverage, but most newspapers followed television's lead. Even *USA Today*, a publication more akin to television with its color pages and penchant for sound-bite-size news stories, devoted more inches and front-page space—nearly 150 front-page articles over the next 16 months—to the Simpson story than to any other.

The Simpson preliminary hearing was above all else a phenomenal Los Angeles story, and the local media responded as if it belonged to them. Many considered the *Los Angeles Times* the official "paper of record" during the trial, with huge sections of its news hole devoted each day to the case. The *Times* metro editor Leo Wolinsky called the paper the Simpson "bible," and he was close to the truth. No other paper was more devout in its coverage of the story.

A day after the bodies of Nicole Simpson and Ron Goldman were discovered, the Simpson story was page one of the *Los Angeles Times*. The story did not leave the front pages until well over a year later. By the trial's end, the newspaper had run 398 front-page articles about the case—more than 1,500 stories in all—compared with the *Washington Post* and *New York Times*, which ran 70 and 52 front pagers, respectively. In terms of total space on its pages, the *Los Angeles Times* devoted ten times more than its competitors. The saturating coverage was like nothing ever seen before in the paper's history. For the *Times* staff, the preliminary hearing was a perfect dry run to prepare for covering the anticipated murder trial. "We could give tremendous intensive coverage in a very short time without burning ourselves out and also give ourselves a practice run on what the trial was going to be about," said Wolinsky.[16]

Of the news weeklies, *Newsweek* would be the most aggressive, publishing six covers and 100 Simpson stories over the next ten months. *Time* magazine, having been burned by its cover on June 27, 1994, featuring a controversial "darkened" Simpson mug shot, was more gun-shy, producing half that number of stories. Simpson was also a mainstay for pictorial magazines. *People* magazine devoted an entire issue to the case as the trial began, featuring a "Who's Who in Court," an extensive "scorecard" of the players in the trial, and a full-page artist's rendering of the murder victims sprawled along the gated pathway at 875 South Bundy.[17]

Radio talk shows became the central meeting point for discussion of the Simpson case. On most computer services, Simpson "chat boards" overwhelmed almost all other electronic conversation with the exception of sex and dating forums. Publishers caught up shortly afterwards releasing 30 Simpson books even before the trial had ended.

Hollywood's movie industry also took advantage of the Simpson hearing, openly exploitative of the huge audience captivated by the case. The relentless TV coverage of Simpson's flight, arrest, and pretrial hearings gave Hollywood a good reason to alter its movie-selling schemes already planned for the summer. Studios poured advertising dollars into the gavel-to-gavel TV coverage and evening news wrap-ups, a strategy that proved to be a boon for the industry.

On occasion, the studios came up with alternative Simpson-related marketing strategies of questionable merit. An 18-wheeler truck, plastered with prominant ads for Universal's new release, *The Shadow*, was leisurely driven alongside a media-packed courthouse as TV cameras rolled. "It boils down to this," said one MGM marketing source. "What's a studio to do when they've got close to 100 million viewers watching?"[18]

4

METAMORPHOSIS

JUNE-JULY 1994

The Drama

The inherent drama of the preliminary hearing actually had little to do with the legal question at hand since it was widely assumed that O. J. Simpson would be held over for trial. Similar hearings in California are won 95 percent of the time by the prosecution. Even Robert Shapiro, who recognized that there was little chance of winning, declined to present a strong rebuttal but, instead, used the hearing to lay the groundwork for the defense in the upcoming trial.

What *was* astonishing about the hearing was its metamorphosis as a made-for-television event. The medium's challenge by going gavel to gavel was to convert the tedious proceedings into compelling television that would somehow captivate millions of viewers over an extended period of time. TV executives faced an ongoing dilemma: How were they to entice viewers to come back each day? They hardly struggled for an answer. The trial experience had to be transformed into drama, exploited for its entertainment or cinematic possibilities.

Suspense had to be generated beyond the mere matters of law. Networks could not afford to mimic C-SPAN by presenting an uninterrupted view of the proceedings. They were driven to emphasize, hype, and, in fact, *create* the very layers of intrigue needed to push the Simpson story forward. Proceedings had to be presented as conflict, with adversarial tensions magnified. The primary players in the trial had to be "reconstructed" as "characters" easily identifiable to viewers accustomed to fictional scenarios featuring steely prosecutors and savvy, high-priced defense lawyers.

Simply, the role of television was to "narratize" the Simpson case by remaking the often dense hearing—and, later, the criminal trial—into a story imbued with the very qualities of the conventional TV courtroom drama. And television succeeded. Following the verdict more than a year later, viewers remarked that their experience with the televised trial seemed somehow familiar. "It had the budget of a movie, it had the casting of a movie, it had the tension of the movie, and [for me] the happy ending of a movie," said Emory law professor Kathleen Cleaver.[1]

There was little question that the elements of the case—the famous defendant, the gruesome murders of two young, attractive people—had tremendous media resonance. But that in itself would not sustain ongoing interest in the case. The defense theory—that Simpson was framed—would. "You can almost see it as the brilliant twist at the end of a movie script—a flashback to the psycho cop sneaking through the night to drop the bloody glove that will damn an innocent man to Death Row," said Mike Royko, the *Chicago Tribune* columnist.[2]

Neal Gabler, the social critic, went further. He said that the very defense story may have been deliberately formulated during the preliminary hearing to play to the emotions of viewers—and, more specifically, the pool of prospective jurors weaned on television dramas. The defense theory, he argued, seemed like the premise of a Hollywood creation, that Detective Mark Fuhrman had waylaid Simpson by planting evidence at the famed athlete's estate. Simpson was the victim of a racist cop out to get him. The theory would later expand indicting the LAPD in a massive conspiracy to manufacture evidence against Simpson.

According to Gabler, the defense team was counting on a jury that believed in television's make-believe picture of the world. But the picture of a racist cop setting up a famous black celebrity by first smearing blood on a glove before smuggling it to another crime scene is not the stuff of real life, he said. "This is not part of our own experience. What is it? It's the television experience. On *Hunter* or *Columbo,* or any number of unrealistic police dramas, this is the kind of thing that a villain might do. And so in concocting their theory, what they are really doing is concocting a TV theory for a TV age. It's not rational, it's not logical, it's more Rube Goldbergian than Rube Goldberg. But in this TV age what they are playing on is the notion that one of the jurors might say I saw something like that on television, therefore it might have happened in real life."[3]

Gabler's analysis was intriguing but only partly on target. TV dramas in themselves take their cues from "real life," and there was no question that Simpson's lawyers, as the writer Jeffrey Toobin noted, "played to experiences that were anything but fictional—above all, the decades of racism in and by the Los Angeles Police Department." But there was also little doubt among critics like Gabler and Toobin that the defense was intent on creating its own "alternative reality" in a last-ditch effort to win an acquittal in a case where evidence was so overwhelmingly stacked up against Simpson. The Dream Team's public storytelling, with its repeated references to a police conspiracy and rogue cops, was filled with fantastic, evil machinations. It was great fiction that was "bold elegant and dramatic," said Toobin. "It was also, of course, an obscene parody of an authentic civil rights struggle, for this one pitted a guilty 'victim' against innocent 'perpetrators.'"[4]

Sustaining Suspense

Much of the first day of the hearing was taken up by the great "hair battle" in which the lawyers spent hours quarreling about the number of hair strands that Simpson was obliged to hand over to the court. A lab analysis would determine if Simpson's hair matched those found at the crime scene. The lawyers took extreme positions with regard to the samples: Prosecutors had demanded 100 hair strands from Simpson's head, the defense agreed to supply just one. Robert Shapiro also demanded that his team be present during the lab analysis to ensure that the results were not tampered with. ABC commentator Robert Philibosian was being only partially facetious in suggesting that Judge Kathleen Kennedy Powell appoint yet another judge—a "special master"—to preside over the chemists' lab.

TV legal experts joined in the incessant talk about the hair strands, and the sheer weight of such coverage left the impression that a riveting point of law had been argued and that a dramatic decision was to be reached. On ABC, Leslie Abramson perceptively called the great hair debate "a tempest in a teapot," although, with nothing more to say about the ensuing court debate, her discussion with Peter Jennings became a commentary on Jennings' bald spot.

Powell's decision to allow 40 and 100 hairs to be taken from Simpson's head quickly expedited the matter. But television had, for at least that day, suffused the legal wrangling with an overreaching sense of importance. By comparison, in the *New York Times* the following day, the hair debate appeared on page 20, relegated to two short paragraphs at the end of a secondary Simpson article.

Newspapers could reorder events and provide context concerning the most and least important legal issues of the day. On the other side, the ability of television to bring events immediately to its viewers' attention forced commentators to follow the camera's lead. Their microanalysis of each legal point, each piece of evidence, each witness, became the foci of the moment ensuring that the smallest legal matters were given as much attention as the larger ones. Pundits lived in the present tense and left the impression that today's witness, today's legal motion, today's evidence, were all that mattered. Clearly, this process worked against the way in which the court cumulatively made sense of the case—a conflict of interests that would widen in the coming months.

Knowing they were being watched by television, both sides were suspected of elongating the process by contesting legal points regardless of how small or obtuse they may have been. By taking control of the courtroom, lawyers also believed they took control of media perceptions about the case, and thereby those of the jury pool watching. They placed their bets that future jurors, and, as well, the presiding judge, might possibly be influenced by what they saw during the hearing.

A process that ordinarily should have taken two or three days stretched twice as long. The actual murder trial would run more than a year, one of the longest in California's history. With the judges in both the preliminary hearing and the trial reluctant to constrain lawyers—likely fearing that pundits would paint them as being unfair—lawyers took every opportunity to hammer away at the smallest of points and, of course, to "upstage" their opponent. Without the camera, the matter over hair strands could have been dealt with more quickly and with less heat. But, given the leeway by the court, no lawyer could afford to appear conciliatory on television. And certainly the medium was not asking them to. Drama, after all, was key.

Granted, the actual courtroom experience had moments of intense and genuine emotional strains. Even reporters watching the hearing from the courthouse pressroom grew silent when a neighbor of Nicole Simpson described the victim's dog wailing in the night, grieving for his mistress, and wandering the streets with his paws covered in blood, before leading a frightened couple to the murder scene. In his column the next day, Bill Boyarsky pondered the difficulty in capturing in words "the haunting nature of the testimony." Nor could he convey "the terror on neighbor Bettina Rasmussen's face as she told of finding Nicole Simpson's body—or the look on the face of the accused murderer as he listened."[5]

Throughout the hearing, and later the trial, there were such transitory sight bites in which the medium's live coverage conveyed a powerful sense of immediacy and urgency. But even these moments, however chilling or profound, were hyped to larger-than-life proportions in an effort to enhance the drama.

Take the case of the mysterious yellow envelope kept under seal by Judge Powell. It was presented in open court by Judge Cecil Mills and the defense team. Speculation that the package contained the murder weapon was left dangling before the court and millions of viewers. Throughout the hearing, this mystery envelope would tantalize TV gossips and rumormongers—a perfect theatrical device to complement the ongoing spins.

The defense team played up the intrigue to the hilt. Having first uncovered the "evidence" before handing it over to Mills, Shapiro strenuously objected when Powell said she wanted to open the package in court. The evidence belonged to the defense, he claimed, and Simpson's side was under no obligation to open it—a controversial point since all evidence acquired by either side must be handed over to the court. Shapiro, though, was well aware of the envelope's contents: a knife belonging to Simpson clean of forensic evidence. While searching Simpson's home for evidence, police had failed to check a built-in dressing table with large, beveled mirrors. Simpson himself directed his lawyers to the wooden shelf behind the mirror where the knife, still in its original open box, was stored.

The sealed envelope resonated throughout television-land like a fantastic quiz show. Viewers felt free to make their best guess in the Simpson game. Telephone calls from throughout the world flooded police headquarters and the district attorney's office. Marcia Clark's secretary said 180 messages were left on the office answering machine in response to the envelope mystery. From self-described legal experts to the man-on-the-street, theories abounded that the package contained the bloody knife, a clean knife, or another article of blood-soaked clothing. *Newsweek* reported that two well-placed sources confirmed that a knife was indeed inside the envelope. Undeterred by the revelation, the public leaped at the opportunity to solve the mystery. One person, drawn to Simpson's Brentwood neighborhood, said she found a large kitchen knife with a steel blade about eight inches long near Simpson's home.

When Shapiro accused Clark of "grandstanding" in court—a media savvy choice of words—as she opened a different envelope purportedly containing incriminating phone records, the prosecutor, in astonishment, replied: "I can't believe I'm hearing this from Mr. Shapiro." Clark certainly had in mind Shapiro's own envelope ploy that was the featured clip on every network newscast that evening. Photographs of Powell holding aloft the envelope were also carried in all major newspapers.

The Shapiro-Clark exchange played again and again on newscasts. Like a wise politician seizing the day's sound bite, Shapiro had captured the media moment. In producing the mystery envelope, the lawyer had, in essence, distracted the media's attention from the thorny legal issues confronting his case and, instead, substituted a shroud of intrigue. Could this envelope contain the "smoking gun" or, more precisely, the bloody knife? That it would later be shown to be Simpson's knife—but not the murder weapon— only added to the embarrassment of the prosecution and police who had failed to find it in their extensive searches. According to legal pundits, Shapiro had won the day not by sheer force of argument but by producing a prop that was dangled before the national stage. As the media pondered the envelope story, Shapiro was seen as outmaneuvering the prosecution, at least for this day.

In a trend that was to mark the nature of trial coverage, analysts boiled down the legal complexities of the case into everyman language—a hybrid language that joined the sports arena to the battlefield. TV legal pundits created a "who's winning, who's losing" commentary, and a running scorecard as to which lawyer had scored the "decisive blow" and which side had suffered a "knockout." In producing the so-called mystery envelope, Shapiro earned points for keeping the prosecution "off balance." One CBS analyst pronounced that the prosecutors' "momentum" had stopped, and they needed to "regroup" over the weekend.

Dan Rather, anchoring the coverage, replied: "The prosecution wants to punt for the weekend."

At Court TV, Roy Black, the former defense counsel for William Kennedy Smith turned legal expert, had a different spin: "I think [the defense team] is trying to win the hearts and minds of the public."

And Gerry Spence, another celebrity defense lawyer, asserted authoritatively: "The fight is for credibility."

The Actors

To sustain the Simpson case over a long time, the medium had to do more than create a dramatic show. Major players had to be molded into identifiable personalities with distinct roles. They had to be seen, in other words, as "character actors." There was the driven prosecutor in Marcia Clark; the neo-mythical "Dream Team"; the famous but enigmatic defendant, O. J. Simpson. Later, at trial, the brooding, tortured prosecutor Christopher Darden, the slick, smooth Johnnie Cochran, and the sagacious Judge Lance Ito would join the cast. All would be featured players in the Trial of the Century.

In some inexplicable way, it seemed as if the trial participants themselves had been suddenly transformed by being part of this television event. Indeed, they seemed *familiar*, made-for-TV stereotypes. *Time* magazine's Richard Corliss, in a bout of free association, linked the principal players to a cast of supporting actors right out of Central Casting:

> Brian Kaelin, with his sleepy-surfer blondness, is a part-time actor whose films include *Beach Fever*. Robert Shapiro, the Rupert Murdoch look-alike, and Gerald Uelmen, a less telegenic *Matlock,* play bad cop-good cop for the defense. Clark's witnesses have a nice racial mix out of *Hill Street Blues*: Greek-American male nurse, Chinese-American criminalist, middle-American detectives. And just as the hearing is a sneak preview of the murder trial, so these bit players seem to be auditioning for a second career. *The Tonight Show*'s Jay Leno imagined them all thinking, 'Gee, I hope I get to play myself in the TV movie.'"[6]

As media-made "characters" now, trial participants could easily cross over into the TV studio—and did. By day, lawyers and witnesses would perform in the televised proceedings and then, later that evening, take their act to another realm of television programming, as guests on newsmagazines, tabloids, and talk shows. During the trial, Laura Hart McKinny, owner of the infamous Fuhrman audiotapes, testified before millions of ABC viewers even before taking the stand. Johnnie Cochran and F. Lee Bailey had an open door at ABC and CNN, but it was the ubiquitous Alan

Dershowitz who was the primary celebrity TV surfer, appearing almost everywhere across the dial.

Television's instinctive tendency to typecast backfired in at least one significant instance. During the preliminary hearing, Mark Fuhrman's clean-cut looks and even-headed keel played well into television imagery of the prototypical professional cop, despite evidence from his personnel records that he held racist attitudes. So telegenic was Fuhrman's appearance on the witness stand that he received scores of sexually suggestive letters and photographs from women throughout the country. Fuhrman was in transcendence thanks to television—he had arrived as the next media sex symbol. Only much later would audiotapes of Fuhrman spewing hate rhetoric finally compel the medium to retype the detective as the "bad cop."

Role-Playing

Inexperienced with covering the courts, the networks and local stations devised strategies to make the trial more television-friendly. Some stations sought to mimic the trial experience by using their stage sets as quasi-courtrooms. Typically, two legal commentators, taking adversarial viewpoints, would be guided by an anchor playing the role of judge. Viewers were also assigned a role. No longer cast as passive audience members, they were now asked to join a "public jury" and express their opinions on TV and radio phone-in talk shows, or in the seemingly endless polls, media devices only a half-step removed from the "truth meter" used by one local New York station to measure audience call-in responses to witness testimony.

The public was not the only group changed by television. All trial participants—the judge, the lawyers, the witnesses, and the defendant—had to confront the camera in the court and by extension, the media and public reviews of their performances. No single member of the court could escape the inevitable reality that television was watching and judging *them*. This was not a point lost on commentators, who went so far as to question the very motives of each of the participants—even those without speaking roles. Simpson, mostly silent at the hearing, would continue to be examined for his body language. Was he genuinely emotional? Or was he the consummate performer playing to the camera when his facial muscles twitched or when his eyes misted over at the sight of photos of the mutilated victims?

At Simpson's televised arraignment two weeks prior to the hearing, his haggard appearance became a major point of discussion among TV commentators. Some used his telegenic image to connote his suicidal state of mind, and guilt. Others discussed Shapiro's behavior toward his client, drawing sweeping generalizations. When Shapiro placed his arm over Simpson's shoulder as criminal charges were being read in court, he appeared to be offering a gesture of comfort to his visibly tense and despondent client. But the most cynical interpretations described Shapiro's physical maneuver as a deliberate attempt at stagecraft, even naming it the "Abramson Hug" after the defense lawyer Leslie Abramson, who took the same tack with her client Erik Menendez. Later, during a televised pretrial hearing, Simpson's teary-eyed response to a witness's graphic description of the murder scene elicited another response from Shapiro. This time, he offered a cup of water and whispered a few words that appeared to relax Simpson. Whether such professional graces were spontaneous or not, with television watching, Shapiro was suspected of deliberately crafting his image to go beyond that of a defense lawyer, to that of a sensitive parent or caring friend.

Rather than scoff at Shapiro for manipulating his client's public persona, the lawyer scored points in the media's estimation. His public relations coup had distracted public attention away from the double murders and propped up Simpson as a more sympathetic figure. Whether or not Shapiro consciously played to the camera on these occasions, pundits believed he did. They in fact *assumed* that savvy lawyers like Shapiro had learned to play the media game—not to do so would have been a professional naiveté unforgivable in this new television environment.

"What the defense was doing was working on the image of O. J. Simpson as a broken, dejected, depressed man—he appeared almost out of it," stated Laurie Levenson, a law professor and now an ABC legal commentator. "And then his lawyer put his hand on his shoulder and made requests for things for his comfort, and talked about how lonely and dejected he is in prison. All of that, I think, was to focus on O. J. Simpson so the public would not focus on the crime and the victims."[7]

If there were two presumptions made by most pundits, they were these: first, the camera in the court was a benign, unobtrusive mirror of the courtroom, merely reflecting the processes of law as they unfolded; second, most participants played to the camera. The inherent contradiction between these positions would echo throughout the trial. While at once declaring that the medium was merely observing the proceedings, with little or no effect, media observers continued to ascribe underlying motives to participants whom they believed were well aware that the world was watching.

Of course, both presumptions could not be correct. Either the camera was just another quiet "spectator" or it was something else—an active, motivating presence. Later, at trial, the Simpson courtroom would turn into a seminar on the issue of "cameras in the court." But even now, the answer was evident—the Simpson case was the quintessential television trial. With their images broadcast to a worldwide audience, no single participant could escape the scrutiny of the medium. Even if participants consciously chose to block out the camera, they could not step aside from the saturated media analysis and public perceptions of their performance. And that had to affect their behavior.

Barry Scheck, a member of the defense team, acknowledged that television's "surveillance" of the courtroom scene changed each participant in the case. "Everybody's human," he said. "They watch what happens on television, and they try to ignore it—but it affects you. Anybody who says differently, ain't being truthful with you."[8]

For participants to have control in the courtroom also meant they had to take command of the medium. Lawyers, witnesses, and the judge continually addressed two audiences, one in the courtroom and the other in the American living room (or workplace or bar). Television could be purposefully used to reach an enormous audience, and the trial attorneys clearly saw the camera as a weapon in their own strategic arsenal. Grandstanding had less to do with playing to the courtroom than with playing to the camera to win public attention and support.

Both sides in the Simpson case understood that game and sought any edge to influence public opinion. Even the choice of language to describe the crime and the defendant suggested two different realities. For the prosecution, the murders were a "bloody massacre." Shapiro had once advised lawyers, in an article about how to handle the press, never to call a homicide "a tragedy," but rather "a horrible human event." He took his own advice, and when matters arose dealing with Simpson's violent behavior toward Nicole Simpson, he called it "domestic discord." Language in the Simpson case was taken to its most abstruse level.

In bizarre fashion, television's discourse—the legal "spins" alluding to the winners and losers of the day—directly influenced the lawyers. Gerald Uelmen, a defense team member, said that the daily television emphasis on which side was "ahead" and which was "behind," drove the trial attorneys to "win" the day by coming up with a dramatic media moment that was bound to lead TV evening newscasts. "Winning and losing became a daily event," he admitted, "and the lawyers were motivated to capture the momentum for the evening news with a dramatic put-down of the other side. It was a sure sound bite and an easy way to regain momentum on a bad day."[9]

If the American courtroom was ideally meant to be an island of quietude amid the raging public storms that surround high-profile cases, that ideal was crushed at the Simpson hearing and, subsequently, the trial. At no time could participants push aside the unrelenting media attention that radiated from the in-court camera. To ignore television meant to push aside the overwhelming media and public commentary about the case. More significantly, during the preliminary hearing, it also meant ignoring the reality that future jurors were also watching. This was *their* preliminary hearing as well. Just what effect the televised coverage had on their thinking— and on their ultimate verdict—was impossible to fully predict. In any event, the lawyers in the Simpson case were taking no chances.

The Critics

The role of TV legal commentators could not be underestimated. Having been positioned by the networks and stations as "experts," they were left to tell their audiences what they had seen on television, what it meant, and, essentially, what they should believe. They were the filters through which court images had to pass before reaching into American homes. Although most projected an on-air confidence—a vital quality for any successful TV pundit—their intellectual range varied from the very good to the very bad.

For some critics, relying on lawyers to tell the Simpson story was a bad practice filled with ethical pitfalls. "It's a lazy journalistic practice to turn over your analysis to lawyers," said Everette Dennis, executive director of the Freedom Forum Media Studies Center at Columbia University. "You don't know what their vested interest is. The networks wouldn't turn over the floor to a politician."[10]

But television did turn over its stage to the legions of lawyers turned TV commentators—and watching the proceedings meant listening to their incessant microanalysis. The medium created the illusion that viewers were watching unfettered pictures of the courtroom, but, in actuality, they were given the equivalent of captioned pictures. Viewers watched and then were told what is was they had just seen.

Lofty claims that such commentary "educated" viewers to the legal intricacies of the case was highly debatable. At stake was hardly the legal education of the American public. More to the point, commentators provided a type of insidious propaganda that controlled audience perceptions and shaped national expectations about the case. The motives of the legal experts were first to establish *themselves* as authorities—whether or not they held such distinction—and then to hype the Simpson story for their network employer. Simply, they were compelled to heighten the hearing's dramatic aspects and encourage viewers to continue watching. Some parlayed their on-screen, adversarial-like punditry into a future career as a television personality. Following Simpson's criminal trial, Gerry Spence was offered his own show. So were Roger Cossack and Greta Van Susteren, two attorneys who landed their own CNN show following their stint as commentators for the network.

The one critical observation that pundits neglected to share with their viewers during the hearing was that there was virtually no chance that Simpson would go free. To do so would have meant undercutting the very suspense that provoked viewers to come back for more. By stating the obvious—that Simpson would in fact be held over for trial—they would trample television's most sacrosanct rule: Never, but never, give the ending away. "On camera, none of the lawyers on any of the networks mentioned what they all knew," said critic John Gregory Dunne, "that no municipal court judge was going to take the heat for throwing the most spectacular murder case of the century out of court on a constitutional technicality."[11]

Television seemed to enlist any lawyer ever involved in a high-profile case, giving them the imprimatur as "expert" for the great Simpson show. Leslie Abramson, coming off a defense of Erik Menendez, was coveted by Court TV before she joined ABC. Johnnie Cochran, best known for representing Michael Jackson against charges that he had sexually abused a young boy, bounced between CNN, ABC, and NBC as a legal commentator, before joining Simpson's defense team. Roy Black, who defended William Kennedy Smith at his rape trial, moved between Court TV and NBC. CBS featured Gerald Lefcourt, who had represented militant Abbie Hoffman and real estate tycoon Harry Helmsley.

Many attorneys were hired as "legal consultants" by local stations or networks. ABC reportedly paid Abramson as much as $4,000 a day for her legal commentary.[12] Other lawyers, though, worked for nothing, seeking the tremendous publicity and momentary fame attached to their front-stage positions. Such attention was not necessarily a career boost. Los Angeles attorney Barry Tarlow contended that his high profile had only brought his practice "a bunch of crackpots," like the one who asked him to file a civil-rights action, claiming that the FBI planted a "bug" in his head.

Pundits were expected to offer pithy, authoritative statements about the day's proceedings, whether or not they truly were qualified to explain the specific legal intricacy of the day. Their primary obligation was to keep viewers watching, and to do so they had to rely on controversy, conflict and drama. While intelligent discussions of thorny legal issues sometimes took place, many programs relied on the fiery point-counterpoint technique so popular in entertainment programming. Others offered little more than a cacophony of second-guessing that invited comparison to an ugly family fight. There was William Kunstler railing against Robert Shapiro for entering a plea bargain in the 1990 trial of Christian Brando, the son of the famous actor. Kunstler, in turn, was admonished by another legal analyst, who said, "I think it's disgraceful that Kunstler is saying these things."

Meanwhile, Court TV's Roy Black had a moment of conscience regarding the rampant speculation surrounding the preliminary hearing. "All of us love to speculate, [but] we're running far ahead of the evidence. It's an unfortunate thing. We ought to suspend judgment." Some lawyers, like Black, qualified for their on-air stint by having first starred in other celebrated television trials. F. Lee Bailey, a regular at the cable network, changed hats to become a member of the Simpson defense team. Across the dial, a panoply of former celebrity lawyers now came back for a return engagement. Making the rounds were Ira London, who defended child-killer Joel Steinberg; Vincent Bugliosi who prosecuted Charles Manson; and Barry Slotnick, who represented New York subway-shooter Bernhard Goetz.

Critics of these media-enhanced legal eagles complained that lawyers were often expected to provide expertise in legal areas in which they had little experience (some had never even tried a criminal case). Others were simply unprepared. Alan Dershowitz blamed the general "mediocre" commentary for creating serious misconceptions about the case. "It was obvious that several of the frequent commentators—busy lawyers—rarely watched the day's proceedings," he charged. "They were grossly inaccurate in assessing what had occurred. It was often embarrassing to watch [them] speculating wildly about issues they knew little about."[13]

The constant judgmental TV gab, said critics, could poison the public's view of the defendant, or, for that matter, the state's case. Others questioned the attorneys' neutrality, especially those once connected to L.A.'s district attorney's office, like Robert Philibosian, the former county D.A. known for his strong law-and-order views, and a regular commentator for ABC. His counterpart on *Nightline* was Abramson, whose verbal darts were mostly aimed in the direction of the prosecutors.

The "experts" called attention to themselves in other ways. The running feud between Abramson and writer Dominick Dunne was not forgotten as the Simpson case began. Dunne's critical articles in *Vanity Fair* attacked Abramson's attempt to portray the Menendez brothers—admitted killers—as victims themselves of an abusive upbringing that finally exploded into murder. The defense attorney lambasted Dunne for "his little venomous pieces that are completely false," and described his stable of sources as "unscrupulous liars."[14]

Dunne acknowledged he carried an "inner rage" after his own daughter was murdered: Her attacker was tried but handed a light sentence. He had no tolerance for excuse-ridden defense theories that sought to shift the blame from the defendant to the victim. "I have learned more about fiction from Leslie Abramson than anyone," he said. "This [Menendez] defense is a skilled fabrication."[15] Dunne conceded that Abramson's powerful courtroom presence was the determining reason why the first trials of the brothers ended in two hung juries. But, he argued, the nonverdicts had failed to dispense justice.

Ironically, Abramson now found herself part of Dunne's media world as a high-profile TV legal critic.

Footnote: Sheppard's Ladder

In the middle of the preliminary hearing, on July 4, 1994, the court recessed in honor of Independence Day. But the day was another historical marker as well, and one that carried a darker significance for the Simpson case.

On July 4, 1954, a Cleveland woman had been found brutally bludgeoned to death in her home. The victim, Marilyn Sheppard, was the wife of a successful osteopathic surgeon, Dr. Sam Sheppard. Soon he would be charged with her murder, despite his claim that he confronted the actual killer before being knocked unconscious (a scenario that inspired the television series, *The Fugitive*). As in the Simpson case, Sheppard came under attack in a wild media debacle. Newspaper headlines reviled Sheppard, fomenting public passions against him with stories about "bombshell witnesses" who had described Sheppard's "Jekyll-Hyde" personality and fierce temper. Other news reports disclosed that Sheppard had refused to take a lie detector test—a factor that was clearly inadmissible in court, but highly prejudicial to community residents yet to be selected as jury members for the case. Caught in the throes of such media-inspired public pandemonium, Sheppard was swiftly convicted.

Aside from the frantic media environment that surrounded them, Sheppard and Simpson had another common connection: F. Lee Bailey. Ten years after Sheppard was imprisoned, Bailey argued his appeal before the U.S. Supreme Court—and won. The Court overturned the conviction on the grounds that the presiding judge had failed to curb the inflammatory publicity that all but destroyed Sheppard's chance for a fair trial. At his retrial in 1966, Sheppard was acquitted, but he died a broken man a few years later.

The Sheppard decision would hover in the shadows of the Simpson case. In its ruling, the U.S. Supreme Court condemned the rampant media coverage for undermining Sheppard's rights. Then it set down recommendations to protect defendants against future media intrusions. These recommendations included the use of gag orders forbidding participants from speaking to the press and jury sequestration. If judges could not constitutionally restrain the press, the High Court ruled, then it was their duty to protect the legal process by other means.

Later, at the Simpson trial, Judge Lance Ito would try these coping mechanisms but without much success. This trial was taking place in a far different country—and before a vastly different national media—than the one that existed 40 years before. The huge expansion of media outlets and the rise of sophisticated technologies had transformed America and the American courtroom. Whatever problems existed in Sheppard were magnified a hundred times as the Simpson case unfolded. The preliminary hearing was just the start of Simpson's legal—and media—travails, and an ominous warning of what yet was to come.

5

THE RACE CARD

In the days following the Bronco freeway chase, the Simpson case touched off a national dialogue on wife battering. Nicole Simpson's murder had given a face to the issue of spousal violence, and women's groups seized on the chance to bring media attention to the problem. A torrent of horrific, personal biographies suddenly became an integral part of the Simpson coverage. One woman recounted in the *Fresno Bee* a week before the preliminary hearing: "As the terrible story of [Nicole's] murder unfolds, I find myself slammed to the wall by my own memories of years of terror at the hands of my abusive husband."[1]

The prosecution and the police gave the media even more ammunition. With the release of the 911 tapes and other police documents, Simpson's public persona was transformed in a matter of days. No longer exalted in the media as a celebrity role model, Simpson was seen as a wife abuser, and worse. If Simpson could so violently abuse his wife, critics charged that certainly he had the potential to commit her murder. Women's activist Andrea Dworkin, in the *Los Angeles Times,* forcefully made that connection, stating: "You won't ever know the worst that happened to Nicole Brown Simpson in her marriage because she is dead and cannot tell you."[2]

The messages struck deeply but were soon overpowered by an even hotter topic—race. By the time Judge Kathleen Kennedy Powell decided that Simpson would be tried for murder, the "race card" was

already out of the deck. Even though mainstream media at first tried
to downplay or just ignore the significance of Simpson's skin color,
they soon become enmeshed in a case that had been transformed
into racial theater.

The Two-Headed Beast

Two main reasons were responsible for turning the Simpson case
into a story about race. The first was obvious. From the very start,
Simpson's lawyers kept reciting their loosely scripted race story,
again and again, refining it over the months. According to writer
Jeffrey Toobin, this story—or "counternarrative" about a police
conspiracy to frame Simpson—was the defense lawyers' answer to
their dilemma of "what to do about a guilty client."[3] Faced with
overwhelming evidence pointing to Simpson as the killer, said
Toobin, the defense decided to try another case: This one was
against Mark Fuhrman and the LAPD.

The defense's tale began with Fuhrman, whose psychiatric
evaluation in his police records contained angry, racist remarks,
giving Simpson's lawyers their initial "hook." And then the story was
shaped and expanded to encompass the LAPD, a department with a
stormy relationship within the city's minority communities. The
defense's problem was connecting Fuhrman's professed history of
bias, and the LAPD, to Simpson. Since there was no direct evidence
implicating the police with framing Simpson (if anything, there was
clear evidence that the police, for a long time, treated Simpson-the-
celebrity with soft gloves), the defense lawyers came up with an
alternative attack. They chose to take their case out of the courtroom.

To win, Simpson's lawyers needed to go beyond Department
103, where they were limited by the rules of evidence and the rulings
of a judge (who in this case allowed them enormous leeway to explore
their theory). They had to create a public milieu saturated with race
commentary, with the hope of turning the murder case into a
national political trial. If they could succeed in moving the public
debate away from the precise legal question of "Who killed Nicole
and Ron?" to "Was O. J. Simpson the victim of a police conspiracy to
frame him?"; if they could succeed in creating a social climate that
could turn the trial into a civil-rights contest—they believed they had
a chance to win Simpson's freedom. To be effective, their message
had to reach a receptive audience, which they believed they had in
the predominantly black jury. Just as they believed that the media's

race talk would seep back into the courtroom, they also believed that it would easily infiltrate the thinking of the jury.

But the defense lawyers clearly understood that without the means to spread their message, the race-conspiracy strategy would fall apart. And here they counted on the media. The lawyers were adroit dealing with the media, taking every opportunity to spin their case. But they counted on more than just an aggressive public relations campaign: They were keenly attuned to how the media worked and could be used to their advantage.

The mainstream press, in fact, was a two-headed beast. One side was the "reasonable" press trying to temper, if not outrightly avoid coverage that could ignite racial confrontation. The other side was a press, wild and frantic, ready to pounce on and tear into any and all revelations coming out of the case. The clash between these two media "personalities" created a schizoid coverage, in which the press was both severely criticized for failing to be more candid about racial aspects of the case, and then condemned for ratcheting up racial tensions and polarizing the public caught up in the conflict. Both critiques held merit.

In the beginning, most mainstream reporters and editors actually sought to minimize coverage they perceived as having inflammatory racial implications. According to critics like Toobin, reporters and editors were generally squeamish about dealing frankly with aspects of the case that might have racial undertones, especially after the uproar over the infamous *Time* magazine "mug shot."

That propensity was first exemplified in the editing of Simpson's "suicide" note, written shortly before the Bronco chase—a note with numerous grammatical mistakes, with sentences like "My momma tought me to un to other," and, regarding Nicole Simpson, "All her friends will confrim that I'v been tottally loving. . . ." But when the letter was reproduced in the nation's newspapers, virtually all editors had cleaned up the language, making Simpson seem more literate than he was. Toobin suggested that these decisions likely were based on a fear that by exposing Simpson's intellectual short-comings, editors were opening themselves to charges of racism. Toobin contended that this "fear of being called racist" would hang over the case and seriously inhibit the mostly white press corps from vigorously challenging the defense's controversial theories.[4]

Yet, Toobin's critique failed to account for the other side of the beast. In the final analysis, the media could not stop themselves from being pulled into the case's racial conflicts. And then they exploited them. Simpson's lawyers had assumed that once the race card was on the table, the media would be compelled to play it. They were shrewd in that respect. Once unleashed, the media seized upon the debate as an opportunity to create more stories about race with their commentary, spins, and use of "scientific" public opinion surveys. Witness testimony, the lawyers' strategies, the jury make-up, and Ito's rulings were now filtered through the media's prism of race.

The race story, even to the amazement of trial participants, would finally overwhelm the boundaries of the case, turning the murder trial of O. J. Simpson into a political trial of tremendous public consequence. The healthy distance that normally separates the public from most trials disintegrated as black and white Americans discovered that they had been shoved into racial camps, virtually forced to take sides. But, ultimately, it was the Simpson courtroom itself that was most affected. A public furor over race could only help one side achieve its ends. Unwittingly or not, the media played right into the hands of the defense.

Race Polls

In a city already struggling with heated racial divisions, the local, mostly white media were on guard against specious racial analysis. Leo Wolinsky of the *Los Angeles Times* said his newspaper was "very careful not to create race differences where none existed."[5] When a *Times* survey two weeks after the murders gave the first indication that many black and white Americans had different perceptions of Simpson's legal plight, the results were published in a brief story buried in the middle of the newspaper.

The newspaper, though, was determined not to *invent* a race case. The city was slowly recovering from the Rodney King trials involving Los Angeles police officers, the subsequent riots, and the trial of two black men accused of the near-fatal beating of a white truck driver during the street violence. The very last thing Los Angeles needed was another race-related calamity, much less one linked to a popular black sports hero. And the *Times* was by no means the only news outlet minimizing the race angle. Within the daily press, Simpson continued to be characterized by his cultural "transcendence" and "colorlessness.

But some critics were not convinced that the media could maintain their equanimity. *Newsweek*'s Ellis Cose said, "The first inclination of the responsible media is to play it as straight as they can, to bend over backwards to make race not a factor. The irony is that it was coming through the back door." And, stranger yet, it was the media themselves that opened the door.

A week after the *Times* poll in early July, a nationwide *USA Today*-CNN-Gallup survey was published, and the race "secret" was out of the bag. The *USA Today* poll reported that 60 percent of black Americans thought Simpson was innocent; 68 percent of whites called him guilty. In the coming months, media pollsters would continue to survey black and white attitudes toward the case, driving home the perception of a national racial rift.

These public opinion surveys were a favorite weapon of the media early in the case. Polls were an easy way to tell the race story and carried with them the imprimatur of scientific truth. But few media critics dared to question their unreliability and inherent bias, and even fewer understood the dangers they posed to national race relations. Jessica Seigel, a white reporter for the *Chicago Tribune*, said that the polls did much more harm than good in "creating [racial] divisions where there might not be any."[6]

Some black voices also were weary of a trend that Ishmael Reed, a writer, called "zebra journalism," where "everything is seen in black-white." Angela Davis, the black activist, also intoned that the media were at least partly responsible for promoting a racial divide by "putting white people on one side and all the black people on the other side."[7]

Surveys were instruments that could *construct* monolithic perceptions of "us versus them" that typecast Americans along color lines. They encouraged the belief that all whites felt one way and all blacks the other regarding Simpson's guilt or innocence. The polls claimed to be representative of American opinions, yet surveys were superficial, asking for close-ended "yes" or "no" responses that failed to uncover the complexity of beliefs among respondents. Some reporters did not buy into this facile "social science" that painted a quick picture of a racially divided America. Speaking of the black community, Marc Watts, a black CNN reporter, said, "We all don't think with the same brain and speak with the same voice. It's unfortunate, but polls are a part of journalism and a lot of people swear by them. I don't."[8]

Besides the inherent flaws of these survey questions was the problem of who was asking them. Pollsters were limited by a sort of "Heisenberg effect"; that is, the very way responses were elicited could severely influence the "truthfulness" of the results. Since most pollsters were white, and represented the white-owned-and-operated media, it was quite likely that their very presence altered the nature of responses, particularly from black respondents.

Sam Fulwood III, a black *Los Angeles Times* reporter, conducted an informal poll in a Washington, D.C. barbershop, which was patronized largely by blacks, and soon discovered the fallibility of media surveys. "I don't think any blacks want to give up any black man. . . to the white racist criminal justice system," he said. "If pollsters, 99 percent of whom are white, ask blacks if he's guilty, then the 'race gene' kicks in and they all say no. Privately, like in my barbershop, they may say, 'Oh yeah, he did it. But I wouldn't tell a white person that.'"[9]

In fact, it wasn't clear what these polls actually assessed—they certainly didn't measure public opinions based on the merits of the case. The *USA Today* survey was compiled even before Judge Powell had decided whether sufficient evidence existed even to try Simpson. It would take another five months before evidence would be presented at trial. What then did these polls represent?

According to Cose, "The opinions of blacks and whites, in short, rested on something other than deep knowledge—and they were not much subject to change." If these polls had any meaning, they were simply to comment on deep racially held beliefs: Blacks generally had a greater mistrust of the criminal justice system than whites. This was hardly a startling revelation. The Reverend Cecil Murray, an influential Los Angeles religious leader, noted, "I don't know how we can be surprised about a poll that shows African-Americans are suspicious of our system of jurisprudence."[10]

The Mug Shot

The media did not fully comprehend the tremendous psychological effect the Simpson race coverage had on their readers and viewers—until their audiences reacted forcefully. And when they did, the shock was felt throughout the media industry.

Such was the case with the infamous *Time* magazine cover featuring a police mug shot of Simpson. The cover was nearly identical to one featured in *Newsweek* that same week, with one difference: *Time*'s "photo-illustration" altered Simpson's coloration to make his face darker. Critics charged that the magazine had deliberately made Simpson look more sinister and guilty—that the photo was altered to play into the stereotypic image of a black criminal.

The magazine's editors claimed to have a different intent, one cued by the cover line, "An American Tragedy." In an unusual editorial letter addressing the public outcry over the photo, Jim Gaines, the managing editor, explained: "The harshness of the mug shot—the merciless bright light, the stubble on Simpson's face, the cold specificity of the picture—had been subtly smoothed and shaped into an icon of tragedy." More simply put, what *Time's* editors thought represented the face of "tragedy" many of its readers interpreted as "criminal."

As the editors and their critics argued over the symbolic meaning of the *Time* cover, lost in the controversy was the fact that the *Newsweek* mug shot cover may actually have been far more prejudicial in conveying Simpson's culpability in the killings. The untainted mug shot was accompanied by the cover line, "Trail of Blood," explicitly linking Simpson to the murder scene. Yet what would be remembered was not *Newsweek's* cover implicating Simpson, but *Time's* cover implicating Simpson's race.

At least one reporter believed the controversy was widely overblown and ultimately harmful to the general coverage of the case. Jeffrey Toobin argued that the decision by *Time's* editors to run the recomposed photograph was within the boundaries of fair journalism. "Photographs are altered all the time," he said. "Choosing a photograph of someone smiling or frowning is itself an editorial judgment. The distance between that and painting a photograph is not all that significant."[11] Toobin believed that the very "color" debate over the Simpson cover was itself racist. "I think it's outrageous to suggest that *Time* magazine is racist in any way. Are darker skin black people worse than lighter skin people? That's more racist than anything *Time* magazine ever did."

The writer contended that the furor over the photograph had a lasting media effect. By the time the Simpson case came to trial, Toobin said that the press corps was far too intimidated to seriously challenge the defense claims. Fearful of being branded as racist themselves, reporters gingerly balanced the defense theory that Simpson was framed by the police (even if they thought such sinister plotting was highly specious, as many did) with the prosecution's substantial evidence pointing to Simpson as the murderer.

"The reaction to the cover was a shot across the bow of the mainstream press," stated Toobin. "Everybody is watching this trial, and if you don't behave with superhuman balance and treat everything the defense says as credibly as everything the prosecution says, you're going to be called a racist. And reporters, being human beings, don't like being called a racist. So it was simpler for all of us to give the benefit of the doubt to the defense even if in our heart of hearts we didn't believe it."

Simmering under the surface early on, the race issue finally erupted following the preliminary hearing. Virtually any media account or photographic image was open to a racial interpretation. The cover of *People* magazine published the week of the hearing depicted a smiling family shot of a barechested O. J. Simpson with Nicole and their daughter Sydney. Earl Ofaru Hutchinson, a black author, said the picture made him shudder. "Would this be a chilling reminder to many whites that a black man, albeit a wealthy and famous one, not only was suspected of murder but also violated America's last taboo against interracial sex?"

"Many black men cringed when O. J. became a suspect in the murder of his wife," he continued. "Many of us were reminded of Bigger Thomas, the character in Richard Wright's *Native Son* who murdered a white woman, reinforcing the ancient white fears of black men as hypersexual and dangerous. To many black men, O. J. may become the new Bigger Thomas."[12]

Ellis Cose, a black *Newsweek* editor, agreed that media images of Simpson were seen through a different prism by many black Americans. The picture of Simpson in handcuffs prior to his arrest and then his omnipresent mug shot—a visceral shock to most Americans familiar with Simpson's celebrity visage—had opened old psychic wounds about black men and law enforcement. "For many blacks, every black man is on trial," said Eleanor Holmes Norton, a District of Columbia congressional delegate. "O. J. Simpson has become a proxy not because the black man is a criminal but because the black man increasingly is seen as a criminal by virtue of his sex and color."[13]

The racial spins continued. Jacqueline Adams, a black CBS News correspondent, conjectured that the media would never have carried the Simpson story with such "lip-smacking vigor" if he had been white, or if he had been accused of murdering his first wife, who was black. Simpson was guilty of "forgetting the reality of racism, for thinking or acting as if he were white," she stated. As for Nicole Simpson, Adams maintained that she "embodies a little discussed wound in the heart of many African-Americans: the white wife," the siren who lures black men from their community.[14]

Despite such forceful rhetoric, many prominent black leaders refused to help fan the embers of racial division, and they sought to publicly distance the Simpson case from more bona fide civil rights issues. Simpson, they declared, was not Rodney King.

If the videotaped beating of King was emblematic of racist police action, the pictures of the car chase promoted the image of a restrained, professional police force. If some Los Angeles cops acted with brutal, unprovoked force against King, other police officers now possibly erred for acting too deliberately by delaying Simpson's arrest and allowing him to voluntarily surrender. Of course, then, he fled. Simpson was cheered by his fans during the highway chase for his celebrity, a symbol to a hero-worshiping culture. Following his beating, King was embraced for being black and unknown, a symbol of black victimization.

Joe Hicks, the director of the Southern Christian Leadership Conference of Greater Los Angeles, warned that media race chatter could "suck out bigger issues" facing the black community. He feared that "the longer [the case] goes on, it gives people time to develop some sort of racial posture, so that the races, both black and white, can snipe at each other."

Intended or not, the black-white news slant had the effect of creating the very race divide the media first sought to avoid. The black scholar Henry Louis Gates Jr., in the *New Yorker,* bridled at the media's exploitation. The Simpson case was the latest and grandest TV show to trivialize critical issues that are central to the daily existence of black Americans. "So there you have it," he sardonically noted. "Black entertainment television at its finest. Ralph Ellison's hopeful insistence on the Negro's centrality to American culture finds, at last, a certain tawdry confirmation."[15]

For Gates, the elevation of Simpson as a political civil-rights symbol was a crude joke. Simpson had long separated himself from the Los Angeles black community, and to link him with the plight of many ordinary blacks was bound to "suffocate" any serious discussion concerning America's race problems. "The Simpson trial spurs us to question everything except the way that the discourse of crime and punishment has enveloped and suffocated the analysis of race and poverty in this country," he said. "And so an empty vessel like O. J. Simpson becomes filled with meaning, and more meaning, more meaning than we can bear."[16]

"An Incendiary Defense"

Following the preliminary hearing, with the Dream Team now in place, Simpson's lawyers went on the offensive. Their attempt to win public support with publicity schemes was easily transparent and, less than convincing. Following the hearing, the defense released a toll-free telephone number for people with "important leads" to the "real" killer or killers. "Experts in a field relating to the O. J. Simpson case" were also invited to call. The telephone number itself—(800) 322-3632—was devised from Simpson's jersey numbers during his football career, 32 and 36, a ploy playing on Simpson's former fame and status. The defense team also released Simpson's mailing address at the Los Angeles County Jail, for those who wished to send "a letter of support."

Shortly afterward, Simpson would offer a $500,000 reward for leads that might point to a suspect other than him in the double murder. Despite swamping investigations by the police, the media, and private investigators, no person or organization would ever collect.

When Garcetti waged a highly visible media blitz following the Bronco chase, he was severely and rightfully criticized for undermining Simpson's chance at a fair trial. Simpson's lawyers were under no similar obligation to conduct themselves as state officers representing the public interest. They needed only to serve their client's best interests, and they did so with élan. With the district attorney's office now quietly on the sidelines, the media's playing field was left open to the defense, and in the lobby of the criminal courthouse the newly formed law firm of Cochran, Shapiro, and Associates gave its daily spins through ad hoc press conferences and informal interviews.

Those efforts soon paid off as the media lunged after the bait. After the flurry of spouse abuse stories—playing into the prosecutor's dominant story line—the media's focus quickly shifted amid a flurry of news leaks and public pronouncements from the defense. The racist cop–police conspiracy theory emerged front and center.

The first salvos were delivered on July 25 in a *New Yorker* article written by Jeffrey Toobin, called "An Incendiary Defense." Soon after his arrival in Los Angeles the writer managed to wedge himself into Shapiro's law office where he was fed the latest defense strategy from sources he hid under a cloak of anonymity. According to Toobin, "leading members of the defense team" were floating a "provocative theory" concerning the investigation of the murders: that Mark

Fuhrman, one of the first detectives at the murder scene, had likely set-up Simpson as the killer.

Toobin cited Fuhrman's professed racist feelings, documented in his psychiatric records compiled earlier in his career when he unsuccessfully sued the city for permanent disability pay owing to job-related stress. He told psychiatrists of the pent-up rage and depression he experienced from dealing with violent gang members and other "slimes and assholes." He also spoke of "Mexicans and niggers" and the stress that came with working the anti-gang detail in East Los Angeles between 1977 and 1981. As his second marriage was falling apart, Fuhrman had grown increasingly violent and out of control. During this time he was also being sued for brutalizing a suspect, although the case never came to trial.

While Fuhrman's psychiatric record had been the subject of previous media accounts, the *New Yorker* article went further. It disclosed for the first time that Simpson's defense would be grounded on the presumption that Fuhrman had framed Simpson. "If Simpson did not bring [one of two bloody gloves found at] the murder scene to his home, who did?" posed Toobin. "At the preliminary hearing, Robert Shapiro had no answer. He does now—Mark Fuhrman." Citing unidentified defense team members—one later identified as Shapiro himself—the article labeled Fuhrman a "rogue cop, who rather than solving the crime, framed an innocent man."

One defense team source described to Toobin a possible scenario in which "[Fuhrman] transports one [glove] over to the house and then 'finds' it back in that little alleyway where no one can see him." Solving the murder mystery would make Fuhrman "the hero of the case," so spun the defense theory. Toobin's article hinted that the "rogue cop" theory was brokered by the defense team during backroom strategy meetings. One unnamed attorney asserted that the team "will not claim that [Simpson] was framed unless it truly believes it," but another source claimed that "the Fuhrman defense is a done deal."

For some observers, the defense plan was a cynical scheme to float the race balloon to a pool of prospective jurors, most of whom were black. Bill Boyarsky, the *Los Angeles Times* columnist, said: "The maneuver was like tossing a boulder into the unfathomable pool of public opinion. When the rock hits bottom, mud and sand rise, clouding the water."[17] The *New Yorker* piece had greatly helped the defense serve up an unproven and inflammatory story that, Boyarsky charged, was "no better than saloon speculation."

The *New Yorker* article immediately opened the gates to other media talk. The defense theory would later expand to indict the LAPD for conspiring against Simpson and tying the double murder to a Colombian drug hit. With each repetition, such charges won some degree of attention within media circles, especially the tabloids. The *Globe* eagerly took up the defense's cause, running stories declaring "How Cops Framed O. J."

For *Times* reporter Jim Newton, the *New Yorker* piece was an example of journalism at its worst. He accused Toobin of being "careless" for allowing defense lawyers, without going on record and without proof, to publicly indict the detective of felonious conduct. "There's no way I would have let an [unnamed] person on background accuse someone of a felony," said Newton. "I don't think this newspaper would allow it if I wanted to. So I think that's a problem."[18]

Although many found Fuhrman's racial views abhorrent, the fact remained that evidence was weak or nonexistent to show that the detective had planted evidence to implicate Simpson. "There's a link between Fuhrman's [racist attitudes] and planting evidence that has always been very thin, if there at all," said Newton. "It's primarily because of the *New Yorker* piece."

It was, indeed, the height of irony that Toobin found himself excoriated for helping the defense. He was, after all, the very same writer who later condemned the Simpson press corps for caving in to the defense team by failing to sharply challenge the lawyers' outlandish theories. After the trial, Toobin went so far as to report that Cochran and Shapiro were convinced from the start that Simpson was guilty of the murders and contrived the only defense they could—the race defense—to win their client's freedom. Still, while later decrying the defense plan as "monstrous," it was Toobin who first publicized it, winning national notoriety in the process. "Like Johnnie Cochran," said Wendy Kaminer in the *New York Times*, "Mr. Toobin was simply doing his job."[19]

Toobin was unapologetic for his story. "The fact is that they were going to argue this about Fuhrman and they did," he stated. "And I said it first and I was right. I'm enough of an old school journalist that if you're first and you're right and you're accurate and give both sides of the story, that's good journalism to me. What would have been embarrassing was if after the story the defense lawyers never said another word about Mark Fuhrman or never claimed he planted the glove—but that was the heart of their defense, so I don't have any problem being the first one to report that."

Fuhrman sued the *New Yorker* and Toobin for their "bald and untruthful claim"—a move that failed to unnerve Toobin, a former federal prosecutor before turning to full-time journalism. "I know enough about libel law to know that [the lawsuit] had zero chance of success," he asserted. "The notion that the *New Yorker* or I personally would ever have to give this person a dime never crossed my mind."

To induce Fuhrman to drop his $50-million suit, the *New Yorker* offered to publish his response to Toobin's article. The magazine also warned Fuhrman that "such litigation can be destructive and have the paradoxical effect of extending the life of a public controversy long after it otherwise would have faded."

It took a year before Fuhrman dropped his lawsuit. The *New Yorker*'s warning was prescient, although the magazine could not have predicted just how clamorous the "Fuhrman issue" would become. Indeed, the only person to be convicted of any criminal charge stemming from the Simpson trial would be Mark Fuhrman, for perjury.

In yet another bizarre twist, Toobin discovered his most vehement critic was not Fuhrman after all, but Robert Shapiro, one of the article's primary unnamed sources. Toobin recounted in his post-trial memoir that when his controversial story first hit the stands in July 1994, Shapiro had been nothing less than gleeful, reportedly calling F. Lee Bailey in London to tell him, "It's over. I won the case." But as the trial moved into an explosive race case, Shapiro began to backtrack as he found himself dead center in a national fight over Simpson. As the architect of the defense's race-conspiracy scheme, Shapiro was now worried just how fast and furious the race fires he helped to ignite had spread across the nation. His strategy had worked all too well, especially in racially-charged Los Angeles.

Shapiro would soon try to distance himself from his own legal maneuvers. He denied in open court making any derogatory remarks about Fuhrman to Toobin, and then lambasted the *New Yorker* for illustrating Toobin's article with a full-page photograph of him holding a poster-sized facsimile of the *New York Daily News:* Its banner headline read, "Now Let the Jury Decide." Shapiro believed that the photograph implicitly cast him as the unidentified source who had thrashed Fuhrman in the accompanying article.

After the trial, the lawyer publicly went after Toobin. He contended that he had spoken to the writer as a courtesy to Alan Dershowitz, Toobin's teacher at Harvard Law School, and then only in "general terms" as "two professional people" talking about potential strategies. That conversation was clearly off the record, claimed Shapiro, with Toobin forbidden to record the interview or take notes. When the article was published, Shapiro said he felt like he'd been "sucker-punched."[20]

Toobin steamed at the accusation. "There was no doubt in my mind that Shapiro knew I was there as a journalist working on a story taking notes. And if that isn't proof, he said the same thing to Mark Miller at *Newsweek*, the same week, the same subject, much the same comments about the same person, Fuhrman. And he also claimed that Mark Miller made the same mistake I did, thinking that an off-the-record comment was really on the record. To me, that's what I call powerful circumstantial evidence that Mark Miller and I did not make the identical mistake with the identical person, the identical week on the identical subject."

It was one thing to deny in public that he spoke to the media, but Shapiro went further by telling the court that he had never discussed evidence in the case with any reporter. "It's a pretty amazing thing for a lawyer to say in court," said Toobin. "What he said to the judge was not true. And that's a very troubling thing."

The writer said he was actually relieved when Shapiro went public after the trial to accuse him of betraying their private conversation—a charge Toobin considered a lie to begin with. But with Shapiro's disclosure that he was, in fact, the prominent unidentified source of the article, Toobin no longer felt obligated to protect his anonymity. "I wanted to deal with this subject in my book in complete detail, but I also had an obligation to him as a confidential source. But by announcing to the world that he was my source, my obligations to him were over."

Footnote: Garcetti's Trials

The battle to win over the public—and reach a jury yet to be selected—was a calculated and cynical exercise by both sides. Following the preliminary hearing, the defense stopped publicly talking about their posted reward for the "real" killer. They would be more concerned with devising a defense strategy based on a "police conspiracy" and then selling it to the public and the future jury pool.

Meanwhile, Gil Garcetti, grappling with political and legal uncertainties, still remained intensely concerned with public reaction to his case. Looking for any edge, he took the extraordinary step of hiring a consulting firm to help him gauge the effectiveness of the prosecution's case. His consultants traveled to Phoenix to conduct focus groups, selecting residents at random to evaluate how the prosecution case was being perceived. Tactics originally devised by advertisers to judge consumer attitudes now were being used to evaluate just how well the prosecutors were coming across. The results could not have been very gratifying. In a detailed questionnaire, the majority of respondents indicated that they were put off by Marcia Clark's "pushy," "strident," and "aggressive" attitude. The word "bitch" kept cropping up in their analysis. On the other side, Robert Shapiro was described as "smooth" and "sharp," someone who showed "chutzpah."

The prosecution's reaction was largely, and literally, cosmetic. Heading into trial, Clark's long and curly hairstyle was shortened and straightened, a look that created a wave of fashion spins across the media. Media observers also quickly noticed that Clark had softened her characteristically tough demeanor. She was no longer wagging her finger so often in court or being easily provoked by the defense team. The public had spoken and prosecutors listened. On the surface it came across as an absurd dance. But in a case that was increasingly becoming a show, there was nothing more normal than for performers to dress properly and act out for their audience.

6

JUDGE ITO AND THE MEDIA

JULY-AUGUST 1994

O. J. Simpson took sure strides into the courtroom for his arraignment in Superior Court, smiled slightly and flashed a thumbs-up to supporters in the spectator section. He exuded a determination familiar from another time, when he was simply O. J. the football star. During his first court appearance a month earlier, television showed a dazed and depressed Simpson, who could barely be heard uttering his name and was prevented from wearing a tie or belt for fear he might kill himself. Now, with a newfound confidence, he entered his plea in perfect sound-bite fashion: "Absolutely, 100 percent, not guilty." With the preliminary hearing over, reporters commented that Simpson seemed ready for the run of his life.

In the days following the hearing, a flurry of media reports swirled around the judicial candidates for the top spot in the case. What was certain, whoever was assigned as presiding judge in the Simpson trial was assured instant fame. The winner of the Simpson lottery turned out to be Superior Court Judge Lance Ito, an appointment that took the press corps by surprise. At the time, Ito was an administrative judge, in charge of assigning trials rather than presiding over them. And he had seemed eager to eliminate himself from the running when he told a Los Angeles legal paper that a judge "would have to be crazy" to take on the Simpson case and the scrutiny it would receive. "I was amazed that he took the case—he seemed much more savvy than that," said Associated Press reporter

Linda Deutsch. "He must have realized the pitfalls."[1]

But to legal pundits, Ito was an ideal selection. A Japanese-American, he could not be accused of showing allegiance to one side or the other on the basis of race. He was seen as one of the brightest legal minds to come out of the district attorney's office and an example of moderation on the bench. And he wasn't a novice in high-profile cases either. Ito won a measure of public recognition presiding over the televised trial of savings-and-loan financier Charles Keating, convicted of 17 counts of securities fraud (a decision later thrown out on appeal). But that trial wouldn't come close to the global interest in the Simpson case, and the intoxicating power the media would bring to the judge's bench. Looking ahead to the Simpson trial, he sardonically noted: "The sirens of mythology pale in comparison to the allure of seeing yourself on CNN. The results, however, can be about the same."

Ito could not have known how foresighted his remark would be. An amiable and cheerful man when he first took the bench, Ito appeared as an angry and nearly tyrannical figure in the closing weeks of the trial. The picture was of a judge belatedly seeking to exert an iron-fisted rule long after the case had spun out of control. For well over a year he would endure the rigors of overseeing a hotly disputed case before the eyes of the world while contending with a zealous press corps that threatened to overrun the legal workings of his court. Even outside the courthouse, Ito faced a fatuous popular culture that had appropriated his likeness and hawked it on nearby street corners. His face appeared on T-shirts, Halloween costumes, posters, and other Simpson-related souvenirs. With his distinctive hirsute features and owlish eyeglasses, he was also an easy mark for TV talk-show jokes.

Keenly aware of the pressures facing the presiding judge in the Simpson case, even Ito underestimated the physical and mental toll the trial would take on him. From the moment he donned his robe and took his place on the bench in Department 103, the site of the Simpson trial, his life belonged to a pervasive media-pop culture.

The overwhelming presence of the media confronted Ito each day as he peered across from the Criminal Courts Building. Soon after he took the bench, the huge media encampment dubbed "Camp OJ" came to life. The makeshift media shantytown situated in a nearby parking lot had housed reporters, anchors, and television crews during the preliminary hearing. It now rose again to handle the crush of news purveyors. Eighty miles of television cable were strung in and around the Criminal Courts Building to serve the 121 video feeds connected to a score of television production trailers. Nine towering TV platforms, some 40 feet high, were built to give reporters a backdrop of the courthouse during their on-air reports.

Some 2,000 reporters, representing more than 100 accredited news organizations from across the nation and the world converged on the Los Angeles courthouse. The case had even attracted more nontraditional "news" outlets. *Dog World* magazine assigned a reporter to cover the trial based on the heightened interest among dog lovers attuned to the plight of Nicole Simpson's pet Akita, whose agitated cries had first beckoned neighbors to the murder scene.

The courthouse area itself had the air of being under siege, which, in reality, it was. A sea of photographers, television camera crews, and radio and TV announcers joined the gawkers, local agitators, souvenir vendors, and the "crazies" in their best carnival attire. The raucous, festive crowd reminded Robert Shapiro of a "medieval mob about to witness a beheading."[2]

The courthouse area also became a meeting ground for other types of public "communicators"—local and state politicians vying for office in the fall elections. Across the state, California politics had been supplanted by the Simpson case on television screens and news pages. Now, scrambling for new ways to get their faces seen and their messages out, some politicians opted to try the courthouse steps. They even checked the Simpson case calendar to anticipate potential conflicts should controversial matters come from Ito's courtroom. Kam Kuwata, campaign manager for Senator Dianne Feinstein, said, "You have to start with the realization that on certain days, you don't try to schedule media events in L.A."

Ito provided some solace. His court stood in recess on Election Day "to allow the democratic electoral process to go forward without the distraction of news media coverage of the trial."

Department 103, on the ninth floor of the courthouse, seemed a much smaller and intimate place in person than it did on television, a strangely private setting for this very public trial. From the start Ito found himself embroiled in two overlapping struggles. One dealt with the state's murder charges leveled against Simpson; the other pertained to an aggressive media presence that threatened to overwhelm the justice process at every turn in the case.

The proceedings bounced between serious matters of law and

nettlesome problems related to the media. Almost on a daily basis, Ito found himself acting as a constitutional arbiter weighing the scales of justice between Simpson's right to a fair trial and the press's right to report the case. Pretrial publicity had so pervasively infiltrated the case that Ito legitimately feared that impaneling an unbiased jury was becoming an increasingly futile task. Even before the first legal fusillade was fired, the judge was desperately trying to contain a case already hemorrhaging with press ink and TV chatter.

When news organizations asked to view the grisly crime scene photographs of the murder victims, Ito turned them down, concerned that they would be publicly exploited. The press finally did see other photos laid out on a courtroom table, but these were less explicit pictures of items found near the bodies of the victims: a bloodstained envelope; a blue watch cap; Goldman's left shoe; a bank card bearing Goldman's name; shoe prints in blood; and a brown leather glove that matched one later found at Simpson's estate. But Ito refused to go any further, imagining aloud the "graphic, sensationalistic, and lurid" media coverage that would ensue over photographs of the murder victims' corpses—images that would "paint mental images in the minds of potential jurors and prejudice the right to a fair trial of both parties."

Ito, however, also had other things on his mind and used the hearing over the photos to lash out at the media, especially the tabloids, as "glaring examples of rank rumor and speculation, prurient sensationalism and outright fabrication." And Ito wasn't through. He rebuked the news media for illegally eavesdropping on a conversation between Simpson and Robert Shapiro. Their words had been captured by a television microphone and published in news reports, which he said "violated the sanctity of the attorney-client relationship." Ito threatened to "terminate" in-court media coverage if a similar violation occurred again—a threat that echoed throughout the trial.

Running parallel to Ito's tirade against the media was the battle between trial attorneys, with each side accusing the other of leaking information and fueling the explosion of media accounts. Marcia Clark was indignant, denying that prosecutors had been the source of such leaked reports. She then aimed her wrath at the defense attorneys, pronouncing: "Some of the outrageous and unfounded accusations that have been publicized by the defense have only fed the media frenzy."

An angry Shapiro bounded to the court lectern. It was his turn to deny responsibility—no member of the defense, he claimed, had ever discussed evidence connected to the case with any reporter. That assertion, however, squarely contradicted statements by reporters who said that Shapiro had, in fact, spoken to them and lied in court when he denied it. The charges and countercharges seemed to overwhelm the trial's *raison d'être*—deciding whether O. J. Simpson was guilty of murder. The trend would continue throughout the upcoming trial. As the media watched and chatted about the case, the major players watched and blathered about the media.

Gagging Lawyers

On August 29, three weeks before the Simpson trial was scheduled to begin, a *Los Angeles Times* story revealed that Ito was considering a plan to curtail press leaks. The plan called for "gagging" trial participants and sealing all legal motions to the court, effectively cutting the media off from their major sources of information. The *Times* account depicted Ito as furious with recent news reports in which evidence was disclosed to the press before being admitted into the case. One account, which appeared in the *Times* and on KNBC, revealed that lab tests determined that the strands of hairs from a blue knit cap found at the crime scene closely resembled Simpson's hair. Ito was also angry with another reported leak that the "mysterious envelope" first presented during the preliminary hearing was said to contain, in fact, a knife, in pristine condition and with its original price tag. The envelope's contents had been kept under court seal since the hearing, seen only by trial attorneys and the judge. Somehow, someone had leaked the confidential information to the press. The news report said the disclosure was "confirmed by a defense source."

Ito appeared to be fed up. Unable to curb the prejudicial media accounts, he targeted the trial lawyers. If he issued a gag order, anyone connected with the murder investigation would be legally prohibited from publicly discussing any legal aspect related to the case. Declaring that it was his "duty" to protect the trial process from media excesses and the loose lips of opposing parties, Ito bound the lawyers to silence outside the courtroom. "Given the amount of media interest and coverage this case has ignited," he said, "the court must use its inherent authority to control the judicial process."

Media representatives immediately challenged Ito's authority to give such an order. The issue, in fact, was murky, and Ito was well aware that he had entered a legal maelstrom over fair-trial and free-press rights. Few gag orders stood up on appeal, and silencing lawyers was a gray area that even the U.S. Supreme Court had yet to decide definitively. California state bar associations were also among the few nationwide without rules regulating what trial attorneys could say to the press.

Having thrown down the gauntlet, Ito now invited challengers and received them before his bench. Attorneys for the media and the American Civil Liberties Union joined to argue that the judge reconsider his proposed gag order. Ito's plan didn't sit well with the defense team either. Shapiro asked Ito to stay the order, declaring that he might find himself in a position to publicly respond to misleading news reports about the case. Simply, Shapiro did not want to forfeit his right to use the "media card" so freely used by the defense.

ACLU attorney Douglas Mirell argued that no "clear and present danger" existed to suggest that jurors might be tarred by media publicity. That empty declaration gave way to a more cynical rationale. "The horse is out of the barn," said Mirell—media coverage has already saturated the case and whatever damage has incurred could not now be reversed.

But Ito countered that "numerous pieces of evidence [still exist] that are still confidential." "They are very important and have a direct bearing on this case," he asserted. "The horse is not out of the barn."

Kelli Sager, an attorney representing various news outlets, discounted the judge's contention that media publicity could taint the upcoming jury selection process. The answer for Sager was not having jurors exposed to less media coverage, but to more. She told Ito that "if all the evidence is out there, the jury can focus on the evidence and neither side needs to be worried about prejudice."

Given that the courts historically have tried to protect jurors from being unduly influenced by news accounts of their case, Sager's argument was a novel idea. Since there was no hope of curbing media publicity in high-profile cases—be it inadmissible or misreported evidence and testimony, or the slanted spins and commentary by trial attorneys and pundits—the courts should no longer bother to do so. Even with full access to media coverage, Sager maintained that jurors would still be able to reach an undistorted, unbiased verdict.

Some jurists might have been flabbergasted at Sager's reasoning. Ito, however, was not one of them. Apparently, he found such arguments persuasive and decided against implementing the gag order. It would not be the last time Ito brandished a stick at the press before tossing it aside. The judge, too, was learning how to "play" the media by floating controversial proposals before the public—such as the gag order itself—prior to moving on them. These sideshows guaranteed Ito that he would dominate headlines for the day and television's Simpson shoptalk. For all his public anguish over the media "problem," Ito seemingly vied for the media's accreditation.

This early episode was revealing of Ito's *modus operandi* in handling press problems—a pattern in which the judge would issue a stern reprimand, threaten sanctions, derail the trial for a lengthy debate, and then typically back off his original threat. Without any clear-cut rules regarding media coverage, Ito's quixotic temperament and mixed signals confused the working press. And, eventually, it created the impression of a judge who could not make up his mind.

SEPTEMBER-DECEMBER 1994

Lines Are Drawn

Ito's worries about the media only escalated as the formal trial began on September 19. Coverage of the case had in effect become institutionalized, symbolized by "Camp OJ." With major news organizations entrenched and squadrons of reporters, producers, and technical staffs fully deployed, the media were the equivalent of an invading army. Having committed extensive resources to covering the case, this massive media contingent was propelled to feed the growing fires of publicity. Some national news programs refused to enter into the fray, such as CBS's *60 Minutes* and the PBS's *McNeil-Lehrer News Hour*. Virtually all others, however, were swept away in the adrenaline rush to tell the Simpson story.

From the very beginning, the courtroom was often a battleground between a contemptuous judge and a contentious press corps. For their part, the media reacted to Ito's fluctuating moods, first portraying him as being fair and likable but then as being mercurial and impulsive. In the early stages, especially, Ito projected a low-key, professorial equanimity, willing to engage lawyers and media representatives in long-winded arguments more akin to an academic seminar. But he was also easy to anger, at times deliberately confronting the media and creating a public (and televised) debate to voice his own views. To this end, Ito himself was directly responsible for dragging the trial on for so many months, and for perpetuating an image of a dysfunctional courtroom.

Ito was media-sensitive and throughout the trial he kept one eye on the courtroom and the other on news reports and commentary of the case. From the closed-circuit television at his bench, the judge could monitor the behavior of reporters seated in the gallery, and the threat of expulsion faced anyone who violated his stringent rules. Reporters from the *Los Angeles Daily News* were nearly barred from the courtroom after publishing a story about a confidential jury questionnaire. Other times, the issues were less imposing. Like a grade-school teacher, Ito permanently threw out two reporters from *USA Today* and Court TV for talking while court was in session, chastised two others for chewing gum, and embarrassed another reporter by playing a videotape of her caught in the act of chewing gum.

Ironically, what soon became the focus of the media was Ito's attempt to control them. Not even these reports escaped the judge's notice, and during one session he accosted the *Los Angeles Times* for its front-page story critical of his handling of the press. Ito's grumblings soon became emblematic of his own lack of effectiveness in dealing with the media. Television pictures from the courtroom only belied the image of a judge seemingly helpless in coping with the wave of media problems.

Ito had a complicated, even schizophrenic, relationship with the media. He could reprimand a reporter for the slightest infraction. Yet, he went personally to the twelfth-floor pressroom to make certain that the press corps had access to the audio feed coming from his courtroom during the jury selection process. Nothing, however, was more illustrative—and embarrassingly so—of Ito's contradictory mindset than the controversial interview he gave to WCBS midway through voir dire. After weeks of voicing his disdain about media coverage, threatening to bar trial participants from speaking to the press, and warning prospective jurors to avoid publicity about the case, Ito agreed to be interviewed on a local news program, which was aggressively promoted in full-page newspaper ads and TV promos and aired in a five-part series during the week.

Among reporters the interviews earned him the sobriquet "Judge Ego." Other commentators were even less gracious, viewing the judge, as *Times* columnist Bill Boyarsky remarked, as "just like everyone else, a sucker for a favorable story about himself." Howard Rosenberg, the *Times* television critic, sneered at the hypocrisy of Ito's judicial declarations and his actions. "Ito's curious partnership with

Channel 2 has him exchanging judicial garb for the robes of a hypocrite," he said. "You'd think that he was taking lessons from Michael Jackson or Tom and Roseanne by using for self-aggrandizement the very media he complains about."[3]

Throughout the trial, a confused picture of Ito emerged. On one hand, he sought to restrain the media frenzy to ensure some degree of judicial control. To do so, he used his bench to publicly excoriate members of the media who had deviated from his prescribed boundaries—sometimes with good reason, other times with an unflattering petulance. But the other side of Ito was someone captivated by the celebrity and attention, appearing to revel in the spotlight and the fame that went along with presiding over the Simpson trial.

Peter Neufeld, a defense team lawyer, complained about Ito's preoccupation with his celebrity status. Neufeld recalled one instance in which the judge brought the entire prosecution and defense teams into his chambers to tell them Simpson jokes he had heard and to show a clip of the "Dancing Itos," a comedy routine from Jay Leno's *Tonight Show*. "On a professional level it is so unacceptable for a judge who is presiding over a murder trial where two people lost their lives in the most gruesome and horrible fashion, and where a third person has his life on the line, to bring lawyers into chambers to show them comic revues," he said. "As someone who has tried cases for 20 years, I found it deplorable, and I was shocked."[4]

Neufeld wasn't alone. Christopher Darden also lambasted Ito. "This was L.A. and Ito was drunk with media attention. He was becoming one of those people so famous they need only one name: Madonna, Prince, Ito." This was a judge, said Darden, who would invite Hollywood actors into his chambers, and gave celebrity writers and TV personalities the best seats in the courtroom.

Jeffrey Toobin was one among a group of reporters invited into Ito's chambers over the course of the trial, and he recounted a small but telling incident. After a brief personal chat, Toobin commiserated with Ito, remarking that he thought the judge had a very tough job. Ito smiled and asked him if he wanted to see "something great." "Ito reached into his desk and pulled out an envelope that he cradled like a precious heirloom and handed it to me," said Toobin. "I opened it and found a letter that the sender had thoughtfully backed with cardboard, suitable for framing. In the brief message, the author said he had been watching the Simpson case unfold on television, and thought Ito was doing a terrific job under difficult circumstances. It was signed with a flourish: 'Arsenio Hall.' I said it was a very nice letter. Ito beamed."[5]

The relationship between the judge and the media was exacerbated by the physical limitations of Department 103—a room just 35 feet long and as wide, with 63 seats divided among the press, the Brown, Goldman and Simpson families, random spectators, and supporting lawyers for the defense and prosecution. Further crowding the room were an array of laptop computers and a huge high-tech projection system that allowed trial participants to view visual evidence. Ito's bench, cluttered with computer equipment and hourglasses, lent to the overall cramped look of the room.

Before the start of the trial, Ito had declined to move into a larger space, forcing the news media to compete over places in Department 103. Five news organizations and two writers, Joe McGinniss and Dominick Dunne, were given permanent seats. The other 17 seats were shared by 41 news organizations and two other writers, Toobin and Joe Bosco. The remaining 12,000 media representatives coming in and out of Los Angeles were forced to observe the trial in much the same way as everyone else. They watched TV.

Seats were highly coveted and members of the national press corps resented the show of favoritism to local news organizations like the *Los Angeles Times,* and to celebrity authors like McGinniss and Dunne. David Margolick, the *New York Times* correspondent, was annoyed to be sharing a courtroom seat with three other New York dailies, maintaining: "You have to be inside to get the sound and smells of the case." And Margolick would have been happier to have the sounds and smells to himself, not in rotation with the competition.

The seating assignment itself soon became a media story. Dunne had earned the instant enmity of some reporters after being awarded a front-row seat next to the Goldman family. In his "Letters From Los Angeles," Dunne told of being "raked over the coals" by a L.A. *Times* reporter who was indignant that he hadn't been more apologetic about receiving the sought-after seat. Paul Pringle, the bureau chief of the Copley News Service, accused Dunne of being nothing more than "Judith Krantz in pants" and hardly deserving of special treatment. But, as Dunne acknowledged, Ito's decision to award him a valued seat was an act of kindness toward the author who a decade earlier attended another Los Angeles trial—this one involving a man accused of killing his daughter. "What touched me was he had the class not to mention it; it was implicit," said Dunne.[6]

Ito's Dilemma and Resnick's Book

The jury selection process began on September 26, 1994. The court's quest to impanel an impartial jury, untainted by media reports, would be a formidable, if not an impossible, task. And Ito was worried. "This keeps me up at night, I've got to tell you," he told lawyers during a closed-chamber meeting. Ito wasn't the only one feeling anxious about the jury pool. In an unprecedented move, prosecutors asked the judge to sequester jurors from the time they were *selected* until they were discharged (a period that would amount to nearly a year, as it turned out). Ito denied the request.

Most participants agreed on one thing: that excessive media coverage had undermined the normal workings of the court. Although the lawyers were themselves largely responsible for feeding the media frenzy, now, with feigned innocence, they vowed to protect the jury selection process. Such utterances, of course, were little more than public posturing. The defense lawyers, in particular, continued to seek out reporters, leak information, and instigate controversy, even as the selection process was underway.

Out of a pool of roughly 1,000 Los Angeles residents, the lawyers had the delicate task of selecting two jury panels of 12 members each. The second panel would provide alternates. An extensive questionnaire designed by jury consultants was engineered to discover the attitudes and life experiences of potential jurors in such areas as interracial marriage and sports violence.

Soon, the composition of the jury, and the questions arising about ethnicity and gender, became the latest media focal point. Jury consultants made the talk-show rounds to promote their "science," and, specifically, to endorse the prevailing view that Simpson would be better served by black middle-aged male jurors. Prosecutors would benefit from a jury of well-educated men or women, preferably white, with an eye for detail and a capacity for math to cope with the intricacies of DNA evidence. These so-called jury experts were the newest breed of court intruder. Disguised in quasi-social science jargon, their racial and gender stereotyping failed to raise even a ripple of well-deserved criticism.

Each day Ito's courtroom was a spinning wheel, with one or another media problem the central focus of the day. Important legal decisions spun off volatile confrontations about media coverage. On October 19, for instance, Ito decided against setting a deadline for the completion of DNA tests, despite the defense's accusation that the prosecution had delayed testing to gain a tactical advantage. The fight over DNA testing was a critical one. Had Ito acquiesced to defense arguments and set an early deadline for test results, the prosecution would likely have lost as evidence two dozen blood samples taken from Simpson's home and car. The ruling should have been the news headline of the day, but it wasn't.

Ito had barely resolved the DNA issue before starting a fight with the media. A newly released book about Nicole Brown Simpson was inciting the next wave of media attention. It now drew the ire of Judge Ito. The book, *Nicole Brown Simpson: The Private Diary of a Life Interrupted*, was a pastiche of purported experiences in the private life of one of the murder victims, with explicit references to drug and sexual experimentation. It also dealt with O. J. Simpson's violence toward his former wife during the final months of her life. The book was written by Faye Resnick, who called herself Nicole Simpson's "best friend," and Mike Walker, a columnist for the *National Enquirer*. A two-cassette abridged version, read aloud by Resnick, accompanied the release of 750,000 books.

Resnick described O. J. Simpson as a violently obsessive man who stalked his ex-wife and threatened to kill her if she slept with another man. Resnick quotes Nicole as telling her: "O. J. loves me so much he's going to kill me. . . and get away with it." And then she has Simpson as stating: "I can't take this, Faye, I can't take this. I mean it. *I'll kill that bitch.*"[7]

After reviewing the book, Ito addressed some 80 prospective jurors, telling them that the book, which he did not identify, "has caused the court deep concern about Simpson's ability to get a fair trial." In a startling move, Ito then suspended jury deliberations so he could deal with this newest controversy. Before dismissing the panel, he restricted it further because of "the change in the intensity of the coverage." In addition to staying away from newspapers, magazines, and television and radio reports, panelists now were banned from bookstores.

Ito's public challenge of the Resnick book proved to be a serious misstep. The lurid accounts of Nicole Simpson's lifestyle and relationship to her husband were controversial, but Ito's attempt to curb this latest sensation was counterproductive. The book, which might have made a quick sales splash before disappearing, was guaranteed a much longer and more profitable shelf life now that it was embroiled in a court controversy. Resnick and her publishers could not have asked for a more beneficial bolt of publicity. Within days of Ito's public notice, the book climbed to the top of national bestseller lists.

In another move that ensured more publicity for Resnick, Ito issued a written appeal to broadcasters asking them to refrain from interviewing the book's authors until a jury was chosen. In letters to CBS News president Eric Ober, syndicated talk-show host Maury Povitch, and CNN's Larry King, Ito asked them to "find it in [their] conscience, corporate and otherwise," to hold off the interviews. They would only serve to "fan the already raging fires of adverse publicity." After much ballyhoo within the media about "free press rights" only CNN acceded, citing the court's "fair concerns."

Though giving lip service to Ito's attempt to protect the jury selection phase, most news organizations reflexively sided against any proposed limits on the press. Their arguments boiled down to a simple argument: First Amendment press rights. Secure that the Constitution was in their pockets, the media decried the court's attempt to keep the Simpson story in check.

Some media critics, however, were beginning to break ranks, and their dissent sent a forceful message: Perhaps the press should start showing some small degree of civic responsibility. "At some point news organizations have to stop citing the First Amendment as giving them an imprimatur to do whatever they want," said Jeff Greenfield, an ABC media analyst. "I do believe there are times when journalists use the First Amendment the way a diplomat uses his passport when he is stopped for drunk driving. We have to go beyond asking, 'Do we have a legal right to do this?' and ask 'Are there other things at stake?'"

As her salacious book splashed across the media, Resnick evolved as the next instant celebrity to be born from the Simpson case. It was a role she apparently relished as she made her way around the TV talk-show circuit and other promotional venues. (Following the trial, she would take the next step in her newfound career with yet another "expose"—this one as the cover girl for the March 1996 issue of *Playboy*.) Seeking justice in court for her murdered best friend was another matter. By publishing details about her own drug use and sexual liaisons, Resnick had virtually destroyed her worth as a witness. She was removed from the prosecutors' witness list, now seen as "completely useless" to their case. "There are few witnesses worse than someone who has profited because of her testimony," said Darden.[8]

The defense also took advantage of Resnick's admitted addiction to drugs, floating the latest theory that it was Resnick, herself, who was targeted by the Colombian drug cartel, and that the throat-slashing "necktie" murders of Nicole Simpson and Ron Goldman were a tragic case of mistaken identity. The defense's claim was nothing more than vivid speculation, but it floated freely throughout the trial.

Meanwhile, the media pounced on the most inflammatory aspects of the book, creating the very hype that Ito had feared. The book, written in three and a half weeks, was a sordid tale: Resnick was disinclined to spare even her friend's reputation. Nicole Simpson is portrayed as a brainless, sex-obsessed woman with an enthusiasm for fellatio with strangers and open to lesbian encounters with Resnick and a fling with Marcus Allen, the football star and O. J. Simpson's close friend.

The L.A. *Times* reporter Jim Newton said that the media placed "too much importance in this immodest little tell-all book." But he also blamed Ito, who should have been less heavy-handed and more savvy about inciting a national furor over the book. "Ito shut down jury selection for a couple of days to deal with this thin little book," said Newton. "It shows the same qualities that have gotten him into this immediate sense of crisis—the need to react aggressively, and then back off."[9]

But Newton's colleague, Bill Boyarsky, pointed a finger at the media themselves for hyping a book about "a cocaine addict recalling memories of a woman who can't answer from the grave." The columnist asked: "Why should anything in it be believed?" It wasn't long ago that his editors at the *Times* would have ridiculed any reporter for even suggesting a story about the Resnick book. "I bet a reporter would have had the same reaction at NBC *Nightly News* or the KCBS newsroom," he said.[10] But over the last decade the spreading tabloid fever had overwhelmed even more serious journalism: The Resnick book, much to Boyarsky's dismay, was now the stuff of big news.

Other media-on-media critiques were more basic. In her lengthy commentary on National Public Radio, ABC correspondent Judy Muller characterized the press as a pack of insecure youths just looking for a no-nonsense authority figure. "We're like a bunch of adolescents who stay out every night partying because of peer pressure [and] secretly hope Dad will set a curfew and make us stick to it." She then urged Ito to lay down the law, declaring that he was "one guy in America in a position to say, 'Enough, already,' even in a symbolic way." "Which is why, I suspect, so many people are cheering the guy on, even reporters. Especially reporters. 'Stop us,' we seem to be saying, 'before we kill again.'"[11]

Actually, Ito *would* try to set limits on media coverage in the wake of the Resnick debacle. The judge took a hard line, deciding to clear Department 103 of reporters and spectators during portions of jury selection. The press still had access to an audio feed from the courtroom, but the proceedings were blacked out on television. For all intentions, the press corps found itself shut out of the trial.

For once, there was unanimity among the principal lawyers. Marcia Clark gave the judge a vote of confidence—the presence of the media, she said, would only increase the likelihood that prospective jurors would give far from truthful responses to the lawyers' questions. Unless prosecutors were allowed to speak privately with each juror, Clark said she "will not be able to obtain the kind of candor we require." Robert Shapiro said, in his trial memoirs, that he found himself in the "ironic, uncomfortable position of agreeing with the prosecution, and a very conservative judge, that the press and public should be banned."

The decision to close the courtroom doors to the press came after a morning of interviews with potential jurors, two of whom complained about being thrust into the media circus. One told the court that neighbors had recognized her on television when she was shown leaving the courthouse—a violation of a court order prohibiting the photographing of jurors. Another said she asked reporters to refrain from talking about the case on the elevator leading to the ninth-floor courtroom.

In curtailing press coverage, Ito discounted criticism that his order may have violated a U.S. Supreme Court decision that severely limited judges from restricting press access to the courts. News about the case was being shown as far away as Tibet, he said, and his clerk had determined that some 27,000 articles about the trial had appeared to date. Struggling to keep the selection process free of inflammatory media coverage, Ito believed his decision was within the proper legal limits: The door to Department 103 would, for the time being, remain closed. The reaction by the media and civil libertarians was swift and predictable.

A *New York Times* editorial condemned the judge for his "ham-handed efforts at news censorship." Douglas Mirell, an American Civil Liberties Union lawyer, declared: "We have a Star Chamber going on the ninth floor. That is intolerable." Mirell's ostensible concern for Simpson's legal welfare would otherwise be scintillating comedy. Public oversight was meant to protect Simpson's fair trial rights, but the real problem facing the defendant was hardly a suppressed news media. What Simpson *did* have to worry about was not keeping the press inside the courtroom, but keeping the media's damaging coverage out of the jury box.

Bill Boyarsky said that if Ito thought that the secret proceedings would produce a news blackout, then "he doesn't understand the process of news gathering." He warned that unless reporters were allowed into court, they could be forced to rely on overblown guesswork and rumor to move forward their coverage of "the nation's hottest trial." "Leakers will be happy to help them," said Boyarsky. "The wildest of speculation will abound, with nobody except those inside the courtroom having any idea of the truth."[12]

In railing against the court order, Boyarsky unwittingly provided rare insight into a journalistic mindset that sounded all to like professional extortion: Should the courts fail to acquiesce and allow coverage of the jury selection process, the press would have no choice but to be forced into wild speculative coverage. Let us in, or else, Boyarsky forewarned. If this argument was meant to make a case for media inclusion, it could not have assuaged the court's fears, or that of the public, concerning the workings of the press on the Simpson story—and the Simpson trial.

A day after Ito's order, Simpson's lawyers used the Resnick controversy to again rock the murder trial and create the latest headline story. In a stunning change of tactics, they asked Ito to delay the trial for an entire year with the provision that Simpson be released on bail. The move, they argued, would allow the flood of media coverage to abate before a jury heard the evidence. "This is an unprecedented case that requires an unprecedented remedy," declared Shapiro, demanding that Ito "take charge" of the stampeding media. "They're selling [Resnick's] book on the courtroom doorsteps," he said in exasperation.

The lawyers, of course, neglected to mention that they had played the media game themselves and were partly the cause of the court's "media problem." Having helped to muddy the public waters with wild accusations, unsubstantiated crime theories, and cries of racism and conspiracy, the lawyers now were perturbed that the "spin" was not originating from their camp but from a purported friend of one of the victims.

In an attempt to ingratiate himself with the bench, Johnnie Cochran urged Ito to promote his judicial stature by releasing Simpson on bail, this in spite of state law forbidding bail in capital murder cases. "This affords Your Honor a place in history," said Cochran. "This is your opportunity."

But Clark told Ito that by defying judicial precedent "the defense invites this court into the chasm of disaster."

After a brief recess, Ito denied the defense motion, stating that while he "appreciates the call to judicial greatness. . . a trial court has to be guided by statutes and case law."

Following his initial decision to entirely bar press coverage of jury selection, Ito modified his order, allowing a small pool of journalists to attend the proceedings. They would in turn give daily reports to colleagues who had access only to the court's audio feed.

Dan Abrams of Court TV and Linda Deutsch of the Associated Press were two reporters to observe the selection process. They also had the distinction of getting the first pretrial "interview" with the celebrated defendant. The legal challenges to potential jury members were held in a small room consisting of tables crowded with lawyers, Simpson, and a few reporters. Waiting for the proceeding to begin, Abrams and Deutsch turned to Simpson and asked him if he had anything to say to them. He thought for a moment and quipped: "O.J. Simpson number 32, age 47." The banter continued. Simpson told the reporters that a news account had incorrectly identified a song he had been singing the day before. Only in the Simpson story would such musings make news, but Abrams and Deutsch had the exclusive of the day.

In most cases, the media would find little interest in voir dire, but there was no respite from this story. In the overcrowded pressroom, reporters huddled around the audio feed taking notes. Ironically, their accounts about jury selection often were pegged to a "media problem" that confronted Ito. The judge's admonition to the jury panel was severe: Prospective jurors were instructed to resist all television, radio, newspapers, magazines, and bookstores to be eligible to serve on the jury. The attempt by Ito to shield the panel from any coverage of the case was fraught with obvious difficulties. Said one panelist who had inadvertently overheard a report while traveling to the court by bus: "Everywhere you stand or walk, everyone has a TV or radio on. It's in the air."

The panel was also instructed not to discuss the case among themselves. That order was quickly disregarded, according to one member, who said she was shocked to hear several co-panelists in an animated discussion about the Resnick book and the latest rage in Halloween costumes—O. J. and Nicole Simpson masks.

Jury prospects were routinely dismissed for seemingly innocent violations of Ito's strict mandate directing them to steer clear of all media. One man admitted to having listened to an innocuous broadcast after his clock radio woke him up one morning. A 66-year-old retiree said he watched television cartoons with his grandson one day; another saw a program on clairvoyants on PBS. One woman watched a Spanish soap opera; another tuned in to an old Barbara Stanwyck movie. One man said his entire exposure to media was when he overheard a snippet of a news report about a senatorial race in Massachusetts while in a bar where a television was playing. Another read the sports section of a newspaper. A 29-year-old woman, who tried to circumvent the court order, had her husband tape her favorite television shows deleting all commercials. Ito was not impressed. "The order is no TV at this point," said Ito. "Watching tapes of TV programs is a no-no."

In rapid-fire succession, he dismissed them all. While Ito had told panelists that he was not looking for "Rip Van Winkles" to join the jury, he summarily excused anyone who deviated from his court order. Linda Deutsch said: "He doesn't want anything electronic in their lives and that is very difficult."

There were other serious concerns about the selection process. The Simpson case had become the hot ticket in town, and hundreds of eager jurors were lining up to "audition" for a role in the drama. Shapiro told Ito, "We have 300 people begging to be on the case of the century and will give you any answer you want."

Clark was more blunt. During a meeting in Ito's chambers attended by both sides, including Simpson, she accused prospective jurors of lying during voir dire and called upon Ito to disband the entire 300-member jury pool. "Many, if not most, are lying to the detriment of the People because they are sitting there as fans of the defendant, saying, 'We want to get on this jury because we want to turn a blind eye to your evidence and a deaf ear to the testimony so we can acquit this man no matter what.'" Then Clark suggested that panelists be given a polygraph to make certain that they were responding truthfully.

Without the media present, the prosecutor appeared to be lulled into a false sense of privacy, forgetting that transcripts of her remarks would be part of the public record. Clark's anger, however, was directed not only toward the panel, but also to the media. Even for a case so saturated with hyperbole, Clark was extraordinarily high-pitched. At one point, she cited a celebrity's comment that he "wouldn't allow his dog to urinate" on a tabloid scandal sheet.

But the closed-door session also gave the Dream Team a chance to shrewdly choreograph its next public relations move. Requesting to address the judge, Simpson declared his innocence and discussed his state of mind during the now infamous low-speed chase.

> Simpson: Well, I feel I've been attacked here today. I'm an innocent man. I want to get to the jury. I want to get it over with as soon as I can. . . . I've got two young kids out there that don't have a mother. And I didn't do it. . . . I've been told by everybody that I know, everybody that I spoke to, that it is impossible for me to get a fair trial at this point. . . .Mrs. Clark, Miss Clark, said I was trying to run. . . . I was not in a frame of mind. I admit that I was not in the right frame of mind at the time I was trying to get to my wife. . . .
> Shapiro, interrupting Simpson: Your honor, excuse me.
> Simpson, undeterred: I was headed back home.
> Shapiro (sharply): Mr. Simpson, I am telling you that I will not allow you to speak and I will resign as your lawyer if you continue to do so.

Simpson immediately stopped, but not before his declaration of innocence was on record. Legal critics said the scenario, despite the appearance of spontaneity, could have been a deliberate act designed for media and public consumption. Harland Braun, a legal commentator, said: "The defense really won by getting this thing out. You get O. J. declaring his innocence and the prosecutor saying the jurors are liars."

With the release of the transcripts, Clark found herself on the defensive having failed at first to comprehend the full weight of her statements. The prosecutor backtracked, stating that her remarks about issuing a lie detector test to jurors were meant to be facetious—that the context of the remarks were lost through the written transcripts. Outside of the courthouse, Cochran pounced, calling Clark's remarks "one of the most idiotic statements ever made in a courtroom anywhere."

Most significant, by characterizing jury members as liars, the prosecution team had possibly laid the groundwork for a defense appeal if Simpson were convicted. Then, the prosecutors would find themselves in the awkward position of having to defend a guilty verdict reached by the very people whose credibility they had publicly assailed.

With the prosecution lambasting the prospective jury pool, and the defense team requesting that the trial be placed on hold for a year, Ito pondered the future of the case. In his decision to carry forward the jury selection, Ito remarked: "I'm not willing to say this panel is lost at this point. This panel is our best hope."

Cochran agreed, though unintentionally he pointed to the utter futility of assembling an uncompromised jury. "You'll never find a panel that knows less than the panel we have now," he said, "and they know everything."

As jury selection progressed, Simpson's lawyers continued their legal gamesmanship, aggressively using the media to attack their adversaries. During an impromptu press conference in the courthouse lobby, Cochran and Shapiro lashed out at prosecutors, accusing Clark and William Hodgman of treating black jurors differently from nonblacks during voir dire.

"It implies an insidious effort," said Shapiro, "to try to get black jurors removed for cause because they are black, because they have black heroes, and because O. J. Simpson is one of them." To make certain that the message was clearly understood, Cochran ventured to the twelfth-floor pressroom to express his "[real] concern about the tenor of the [prosecutions'] questions and the way they go after certain jurors." Charging the prosecution with racial discrimination was seen as a deplorable ploy. Gil Garcetti had purposely moved the case to downtown Los Angeles to *ensure* a racially mixed jury. Clark also believed she had a strong rapport particularly with black female jurors.

But Cochran and Shapiro's accusations were covered live by television, and once the charges were literally in the air, the story took on a media life, as the lawyers knew they would. Their allegations of racial prejudice had been contradicted by the pool reporters who failed to notice any bias by the prosecutors during their questioning. Neither did Judge Ito. And Clark and Hodgman disdainfully refuted the charges. But, still, the defense had played the race card, and the press had gone along. The "race bias" story became the news peg of the day.

After three months, the tedious selection process finally came to an end. On November 3, 1994, a jury of eight women and four men was impaneled, and a month later an alternate jury was chosen. The controversies surrounding the Simpson jury, however, were far from over. Indeed, they were only beginning.

7

THE GREAT CAMERA
DEBATE

AUGUST-OCTOBER 1994

Court TV's Revolution

By the time Ito took the bench in August, the major broadcast networks had already begun to back off live coverage. Their early pitch—that the public would be "educated" by watching gavel-to-gavel coverage of the hearings—dissolved to a more honest appraisal. The threat of lost advertising revenue quickly superseded any notions about "the public good." Had ABC, NBC, and CBS decided to preempt even half of their nearly 1,300 30-second daytime commercials during the trial, they stood to lose almost $13 million per day. It would have been a risky decision, especially if audiences and advertisers lost interest in a lengthy trial. Network executives assumed they would.

No one could have been happier at the news than Steven Brill, the founder of Court TV. Brill privately wished that the "Big Three," along with CNN, would just leave television court reporting to his three-year-old cable network.

"We want to be the franchise of legal news," said Fred Graham, Court TV's senior anchor. "If there's a war you turn on CNN, and if there's a trial you turn on Court TV."[1] But other cable networks also had Simpson on their minds. CNN would not back off live coverage, and the E! Entertainment Channel, best known for its glossy, gossipy programming, also planned to cover the trial from beginning to end.

Still, the broadcast giants were out of the running, and the Simpson trial became Brill's golden opportunity to showcase his cable station.

Court TV's decision to cover the case in its entirety was made a month prior to the trial. There was little debate about choosing the trial for air-time, but serious concerns arose about the scope of coverage. Some staff members argued for treating the Simpson case like all cases selected for coverage by Court TV—with a single reporter and technical crew on location. Those staffers wanted to undercut the hype and excessive reporting already surrounding the case.

But that thrust was soon overwhelmed by the judgment of most other staff members who saw the trial as a keen opportunity to draw in new viewers and promote the network's identity. Gregg Jarrett, a Court TV co-anchor and also a former California lawyer, lobbied for coverage anchored live from Los Angeles: "I thought there would be such competition from [the major media] that we needed to visually tell people we were there and on top of it." Jarrett also believed Court TV coverage would be improved immeasurably by being on location and tapping into the large pool of Los Angeles lawyers to serve as guest commentators. He contended that "being in L.A. would give us better informed lawyers and better information."[2]

Brill had the final word and left little doubt how he felt about the Simpson case as a commercial property. For the first time in its three-year history, the New York-based network would relocate a staff of nearly 30 associate and senior producers, technical people, on-air anchors and reporters to cover a criminal trial.

The decision could not have been terribly angst-ridden for Brill. With the birth of Court TV in 1991, Brill, with the zeal of an ideologue, envisioned bringing local trials into the nation's spotlight. Since then, that idea had become very much a reality. For better or worse, Brill's television trial was a revolution within the American justice system, and the TV industry at large. Criminal trials were no longer seen as community-based—they were now national events open to anyone with a television set. The birth of the living-room trial gave viewers a central meeting place where cases could be debated and verdicts drawn. The American courtroom, in essence, was now an interactive experience. Television viewers were hardly distant observers but involved *participants*—new-age "jurors" for a new-age courtroom. In the Simpson courtroom, especially, their "presence" was tangible.

But in the days leading to the trial, Brill shrugged off complaints that the legal process could be harmed by infusing the courtroom with this new public jury. He believed that, if anything, public criticism would only make trial participants "act better" and work more efficiently. Even Brill, though, must have come to realize as the Simpson trial entered into a political minefield, just how seriously he had misjudged the medium and its constituency. But, by then, it was far too late.

Steven Brill, at age 43, had become one of the country's most powerful legal media moguls as the Simpson trial was about to begin. Brill was a Yale Law School graduate who never took the bar exam, opting to write about the law rather than practice it. His 1978 book *The Teamsters* earned him a national reputation as a hard-nosed investigator, but he soon turned his eye on the legal profession.

At 27, just two years out of law school, he convinced a British media conglomerate to back his idea for a $2.5-million publication called *The American Lawyer*. Brill was off and running heralding his own pugnacious style of legal journalism.

Until that time, coverage of the legal profession was primarily left to the national and local bar journals, which treated their members with deference, if not slavish devotion. *The American Lawyer* changed the rules of the game and immediately trampled on the clandestine grounds of the country's legal industry. Brill's magazine investigated the ethical practices of major law firms and their treatment of lower-level associates. Stories detailed the phenomenal salaries of law partners and the revenues their firms had amassed, insider secrets once zealously guarded. Major law firms immediately took notice. A senior partner at Shearman & Shearman called the network and warned Brill: "We're the biggest firm in New York, and we're going to run you out of town."[3]

From New York, Brill took his journalism crusade across the country, establishing a network of regional legal newspapers. They further enhanced Brill's reputation as an intimidating presence within the legal community. But nothing would establish his empire more than the Courtroom Television Network.

The idea for Court TV had come to Brill in the back of a taxicab, in 1988, after he overheard a radio news report about a sensational murder case in New York City. That trial—involving a criminal defense lawyer named Joel Steinberg accused of killing his 6-year-old daughter, Lisa—was televised under a recently enacted state law allowing cameras in the court. Predictably, television moved the Steinberg case onto the national scene, and the pictures were vivid. Few viewers would ever forget the haunting testimony of Hedda Nussbaum, Lisa's mother, whose face and body was scarred and deformed from years of torture at the hands of Steinberg.

The Steinberg televised trial intrigued Brill, and he approached Steven Ross, chairman of Warner Communication, with a bold plan to create a 24-hour-a-day, 7-day-a-week cable network devoted entirely to broadcasting trials and other matters of legal interest. Brill envisioned the network as "a mixture of soap operas and C-Span," and Ross soon bought into the plan.[4] The newly constituted Time Warner Inc. was committed to investing $40 million in the new network with Brill at the helm.

On July 1, 1991, Court TV officially went on the air. Brill still retained control of *The American Lawyer,* but with Court TV he held a high-gauge weapon that targeted the American courtroom.[5]

Brill professed lofty goals for his new network, touting it as an electronic law school educating lawyers and laymen to the workings of the court. And, granted, his network delivered, covering trials and legal affairs with sober and intelligent analysis. Still, for all the good intentions, Court TV could never survive on the highly competitive, glutted cable dial by offering only a well-meaning civics seminar.

The network's coverage of such matters as parole hearings and small-town courts dealing with minor crime had public value, but it also attracted infinitesimal ratings. As a commercial entity seeking to expand its reach on the cable dial, Court TV could only work if viewers tuned in. To that end, the pressure on Brill was to choose trials less for their legal significance and more for their inherent social drama and sensational appeal. Those trials that could be translated into strong story lines—bizarre murders, sordid cases of spousal abuse and rape, violent cases of police brutality, and the like—were prime candidates.

Brill shrewdly positioned Court TV as a powerful force within the legal community. A "Court TV trial" brought exposure and fame to judges and lawyers—and the potential to make (and break) careers. Brill also could now anoint favored lawyers as instant "experts" by giving them a chance to be on television in his rotating cast of legal commentators.

Intentionally or not, the network was also the prime mover in fashioning a popular culture that made celebrities of well-known defendants, featuring a gallery of such stars as the Menendez brothers, Lorena Bobbitt, Betty Broderick, Christian Brando, Joey Buttafuoco, Amy Fisher, and William Kennedy Smith.

Court TV's revolution would spill over to the major broadcast networks, now compelled to pay more attention to the justice system. Even before the Simpson case, trial footage had become a routine part of network newscasts, newsmagazines, and tabloid shows. But, unlike Court TV, the Big Three certainly had no qualms about exploiting the most lurid aspects of an ongoing televised trial. Now nestled in the medium's entertainment culture, real trials easily took their place alongside popular courtroom dramas. Hollywood's script-writers found themselves hard-pressed to match true-life stories about parent-murders, sexual mutilation, date rape, and a Lolita-esque love triangle turned violent.

Despite the spate of sensational trials to hit the nation in the early 1990s, Court TV still struggled to capture a wider audience and a more expansive advertising base. Then the Simpson case broke, and, perhaps, no other single media industry profited more than Court TV. Paradoxically, as Brill's network aggressively pursued the Simpson story, old questions arose about the use of television cameras in the courtroom, an issue that had flared periodically over the past 40 years.

In fact, serious questions remained unresolved about placing American trials on the television stage. Did the camera endanger the fair-trial process by turning the courtroom into theater? Were trial participants—judges, trial attorneys, witnesses, and jurors—now actors compelled to "perform" before an involved and opinionated American audience? Was the nation's criminal court system being absorbed—and trivialized—by the entertainment television industry? Simply, was justice being served under the glare of the TV camera?

As the Simpson case inflamed a national debate on "cameras in the court," Brill took on the public role as defender of the faith. He contended that, with the exception of a few critics like Alan Dershowitz, the overwhelming majority of judges, lawyers, and citizens were in favor of televised trials. In at least one respect, Brill was wrong: Dershowitz applauded courtroom television; he just didn't like Brill. Their early feud—the result of an *American Lawyer* article criticizing Dershowitz—heated up after Court TV made its debut. Dershowitz told *New York* magazine at the time: "I'm in favor of bringing TV cameras into the courtroom—but there couldn't be a worse person to do it than Steve Brill."[6]

There were, of course, other critics from legal, academic, and media circles raising red flags about televising the upcoming trial. The zealous coverage given to Simpson's preliminary hearing should have been enough warning. Even a wary federal judicial committee voted, prior to the start of the Simpson trial, to stop a national experiment allowing televised civil trials in federal courts.

But during the pretrial proceedings, the public euphoria over the Simpson "event" was too high to allow such thinking to be taken seriously in state criminal courtrooms—even in Los Angeles, which had recently suffered through several humiliating high-profile cases carried on television. Like a nation going to war, virtually all media organizations—print and electronic—rallied around the courtroom camera. Their main allies included the principals in the Simpson case. Together, they heralded the camera as a revolutionary weapon for democracy.

SEPTEMBER-OCTOBER 1994

The Savage Brushfire

Television's most important and contentious friend was Judge Lance Ito, whose love-hate relationship with the camera grew over the course of the Simpson trial. Unhappy with the media's "inaccurate and irresponsible" reporting during the pretrial hearings, Ito professed ardor toward the in-court camera had noticeably cooled. Even before a jury had been selected, Ito was already thinking about pulling the plug on the camera.

What started the brushfire over the court camera was not anything that had occurred in the courtroom, but an erroneous television news report. Although Ito had complained before about media coverage, his reaction to a KNBC television report was the most serious yet and marked the first time he accused a mainstream news organization of damaging factual error. At issue was the news station's report that blood on socks discovered in Simpson's bedroom had been DNA-tested and found to match his ex-wife's. The account, if true, was highly damning to Simpson. The information, attributed to police sources, was quickly picked up by the wire services, newspapers and newsmagazines, and widely broadcast in TV and radio reports. But the story was wrong.

In open court, Ito told reporter Tracie Savage that her report was erroneous and seriously prejudicial to the defense case. Although bloody socks had been found at Simpson's home, a final determination on the DNA composition of the blood stains had yet to be made. Savage's "scoop" could not possibly have been verified and amounted to little more than idle speculation.

But rather than back off the story, KNBC amplified it that very evening. The next day in court, Ito was furious. "I'm beyond being outraged," said the judge, visibly irate. "For this kind of information to come out and for it to be incorrect and to be so prejudicial is outrageous." (DNA analysis would later confirm that blood on the socks did, in fact, match Nicole Simpson's blood. But at this juncture, the socks had only been tested with conventional techniques that were not as conclusive as DNA analysis.)

Having warned KNBC that the station's access to Department 103 might now be jeopardized, Ito took wider aim at the media at large. Although he had limited power to curtail press coverage, he did have the prerogative to halt the televising of the case. Apparently he blamed the court camera for the fierce media competition outside his courtroom and for the bad journalism it helped to ignite. Ito now planned to cut off the fuel from the fire—the judge said he was prepared to throw the camera in the court out onto the street.

The very threat sent a collective chill through networks and stations electronically primed and heavily invested in televising the case. From the standpoint of most reporters, the camera was a necessary tool. Only a few reporters were allowed inside the cramped courtroom: How else would the rest of the press corps get to tell their stories unless they could watch it on TV? Besides, they argued, Americans had a right as citizens to freely watch the trial.

Most of the press believed that the judge's judicial stance— blaming the court camera for sloppy reporting—was irrational. Brill, whose network provided the live camera feed to the rest of the television industry, said that, if anything, the televised proceedings gave Ito a forum in which he could denounce KNBC or any other media outlet. To ban the camera because of one bad report from one station "is not throwing out the baby with the bath water," he said. "It's [only] throwing out the baby."

If Ito had gone ahead and barred television from his courtroom, the effect on the entire media industry would have been traumatic. Twenty-six television and radio organizations had constructed booths around the Criminal Courts Building that connected to satellite dishes on the courthouse roof that beamed the word—and the image—of the trial to the world. With a relative handful of courtroom seats reserved for the media, most print reporters, as well, would be shut out of the proceedings. For two days, Ito's tirade against KNBC was the lead story, overshadowing news about serious defense motions the judge had to consider, including whether evidence found by investigating detectives had been improperly seized.

Savage watched Ito's blistering denunciation of her report from a TV monitor in the press area on the twelfth-floor. Immediately, she became a sought-after interview. From Bill Boyarsky's vantage point, "the media machine [had] turned on one of its own, treating Savage as if she was just another celebrity in a jam." Savage replied to a few questions from her colleagues before her phone rang. When she answered, her editors told her to stop talking to the press, and she did.

Stage Set

In mid-October, Department 103 became a curious tableau for a public debate on the camera issue. Ito would preside over this "trial" as well. The judge went so far as to convert the courtroom into a veritable TV stage set, surrounding his bench with stacks upon stacks of boxes containing some 12,400 letters. Most were triggered by an article from syndicated columnist Mike Royko, who had urged readers to write to Ito to complain about televised coverage. And they did. Some letters were handwritten on frayed binder paper or on the backs of prescription order forms. Almost all asked the judge to turn off the camera. For Ito's purposes, the letters were ideal props for his contrived theatrical drama.

The Simpson trial stopped dead in its tracks as the judge entertained arguments from media representatives intent on persuading him to continue televising the trial. A line of lawyers took up his invitation to address the court—and a huge television audience—about the democratic virtues of a free press and an open courtroom. These ideals were served, they said, by putting the Simpson trial on television.

Floyd Abrams, representing Court TV, scored the sound bite of the day. "The camera pleads absolutely, 100 percent, not guilty," he said, mimicking Simpson's own court plea during arraignment.

Abrams, a leading First Amendment-rights lawyer, asserted that justice could be best served by having the largest possible audience view the proceedings—an idea that was inherent in a public trial. Of course, the nation's Founding Fathers would never have recognized his argument. The constitutional call for "public trials" was in reaction to the secret, repressive tribunals of Old Europe. It never occurred to Thomas Jefferson or the others that a national arena of millions was needed to guard a defendant against abuses of the State. More recent U.S. Supreme Court decisions also held that broadcasters had no absolute right to use cameras in the courtroom. That decision was left up to individual states, three of which had banned court cameras altogether at the time of the Simpson trial.

Kelli Sager, representing CNN among other major news outlets, derided those letter writers who urged Ito to stop the Simpson television show. At the same time championing individual rights, she pressed Ito to ignore the letters and base his decision on what she perceived as the larger public interest in the case. "A minority [should not] dictate what the court should do simply because they would rather watch *All My Children* than watch gavel-to-gavel coverage of a criminal trial. And my suggestion to those who are sick of watching the television coverage of the case is simple—turn it off."

Sager and Abrams were cheered on by television's hired guns—the legal experts—resulting in a curious collusion to control the public debate. Expectedly, the pundits almost unanimously voted along with their bosses, leaving the impression that, with the exception of a few out-of-touch naysayers, there was near-universal agreement that the cameras should stay. But though pundits spoke with authoritative confidence, they offered muddled explanations.

CNN's Greta Van Susteren declared that the camera had the "enormous effect of making people do their jobs right. It's like having Big Brother watch." Her Orwellian analogy was an unfortunate choice. Surely Van Susteren wasn't endorsing the notion that TV viewers act to intimidate or unduly influence the independent process of law in Ito's courtroom. Yet, unwittingly, she gave credence to that very idea. Trial participants clearly understood that they were being watched and judged—and they were hardly more "professional" as a result. What *was* true: Not one trial member in Department 103 felt free of the stifling public clamor: Television coverage had changed *everything* about the case—their performance, the unfolding of the trial, and, in the end, perhaps the very verdict.

This was not merely a theoretical argument. Throughout the proceedings, the trial attorneys and Ito himself continued to pay obeisance to the notion that the "whole world was watching." As long as the camera was present, the case would be tried before two juries—one in the courtroom and the other in television studios and living rooms across the country. If Ito was serious about protecting the trial against the buffeting media storm—his inherent duty as the presiding judge—then it's hard to fathom how he could have let the camera into his courtroom in the first place. But he had, and the tempest grew only stronger.

For all his public posturing, Ito's decision to continue television coverage of the case was preordained. The camera "debate" had been a contrived legal exercise that only served to delay the proceedings. Ito had made up his mind prior to the daylong seminar, if, truly, he ever seriously considered banning televised coverage. In patronizing language, he offered his thanks to the thousands of Americans for their "so many intelligent, well-thought-out letters to the court." But, he maintained, "the court cannot make its decision based on the perception of the pulse of popular opinion"—a remarkable declaration from a judge who appeared to sway in the winds of public opinion. The camera would continue to bring the world pictures of the Simpson trial.

Ito had been duplicitous, critics charged. For all his bombast directed at the media, the judge seemed enamored at the idea of taking a leading role in his electronic "civics lesson." What lessons *this* trial could provide, however, were debatable. From a judicial viewpoint, the Simpson case was an anomaly. In California, 93 percent of all defendants never even get to trial, their cases ending in a plea bargain. Across the country, eight out of ten defendants are indigent, and of those remaining, very few can afford high-profile lawyers, high-priced scientific experts, and private investigators. If anything, televising the Simpson trial, with its ties to fame and wealth and extravagant litigation, presented a drastically distorted picture of the law and the justice system.

Ironically, by the time the trial ended about a year later, most Americans, and many jurists, thought that allowing trials to be televised was a serious mistake. The Simpson case was seen as a judicial mockery, and judges in other high-profile cases vowed not to make Ito's mistake. Across the country, they said "no" to television.

Even the primary players were blaming Ito for allowing the trial to be televised (though they neither protested during the trial, nor were they shy about accepting post-trial fortunes gained by television's imprimatur of fame). Christopher Darden said he tried to ignore the camera and shut out the cacophony of commentary about the case. But the Simpson trial averaged 60 hours a week on television over the course of the year-long trial, and the day-to-day pressure had an effect. "It was like walking past a fun house mirror, over and over, a mirror that distorts your appearance. It isn't long before your very identity is in doubt [and you say], 'is that really how I am?'"[7]

Ito, himself, came to rue his decision in the midst of the trial, even shutting down the camera briefly on two occasions for violating court rules. In one instance, a camera operator inadvertently panned to two alternate jurors seated in the gallery, capturing their image for a split second. In another, during Marcia Clark's closing statement, the camera caught Simpson scribbling a note to his lawyer, a move which Ito charged had violated Simpson's right to legal confidentiality. But the problem was not really the incompetence of a camera operator—the problem was that the courtroom camera worked all too well. From the moment the camera began to roll, the Simpson case evolved, literally, to another stage—the television stage.

Ito's relationship with the media continued to ride a high wire. An erroneous news report, or an errant television picture coming from the courtroom, could set Ito off. But, despite reprimanding the media, the judge refused to forsake his "partner." His place in history and the full breadth of a case he saw as "historic" could only be realized through televised coverage.

Prior to opening arguments, Ito announced to the courtroom—and a world audience—that "finally, the most anticipated case in history has begun." He told the trial attorneys that he anticipated that they would be "walking on the edge of the legal envelope."

"I want you all to remember that your conduct here [will shape] the image of the profession for years to come," he said. "Those who say that the criminal justice system itself is on trial may be correct in that observation."

But Ito's idyllic vision of the television trial soon disintegrated to a sobering reality. Even before jury selection was finished, Ito was grappling for control over a case turned inside out by the enveloping media frenzy. He well understood that unless the free-wheeling coverage was curtailed, Simpson's legal right to a fair trial was endangered—a matter certain to be part of an appeal should Simpson be convicted. The U.S. Supreme Court was emphatic in its landmark decisions overturning the convictions of Billy Sol Estes in 1965, and Dr. Sam Sheppard in 1966, that high-profile cases must be shielded from pervasive and prejudicial publicity.

Above all else, Ito did not want to be known as the judge who "lost" the Simpson case.

8

MEDIA WARS

SEPTEMBER-DECEMBER 1994

As the Simpson case drew closer to trial, it became impossible to extricate the workings of the courtroom from the workings of the media. These were not two parallel universes: The media and the court often zigzagged in confusion, colliding at various junctures, and then erupting into open dispute. Judge Lance Ito argued over the media's excesses; reporters and pundits in turn criticized the judge for his own failings on the bench.

While Ito could have defused much of the controversy by dealing directly with problems in private chambers, his decision to "take on" the press in open court created yet another sideshow. Ironically, the in-court camera—which Ito had so eagerly embraced early on—conveyed an indelible impression of a presiding judge easily unhinged and overreactive.

In his running battle with the media, Ito had a most unusual ally of sorts—the media. When journalists weren't telling Americans about the trial, they were usually talking about themselves, and their view was not flattering. As the media lambasted the circus surrounding the case, they often neglected to mention that they were the ringmaster whipping the crowd into a frenzy under the big tent. Their harsh critiques about "the media" were an out-of-body experience, as if the problems under discussion belonged to someone else.

Trash Journalism

The favorite whipping boy of the mainstream press was the tabloid press—both the supermarket papers and their television counterparts. They were an easy target with their over-the-top stories and controversial reporting methods. Some critics went so far as to blame the tabs for the very decline of Western journalism, with their penchant for hypersensationalism, gossip news, and cash-for-trash stories.

But what critics were really fearful of was something far deeper and more personal. It wasn't that the Simpson story had helped to boost the tabloids as the newest members of the national press club, as some argued. The real fear was that it wasn't entirely clear which side had joined the other. By the time the Simpson trial was over, few distinctions were being made between the "legitimate" media and the tabloid press.

For millions of readers and viewers, the print and electronic tabloids were the media of choice for their dose of the Simpson story. Diane Dimond of *Hard Copy* stated matter-of-factly that the Simpson story "was our turf." The tabloids swaggered with "inside" stories, "shocking" new evidence, "graphic" reenactments of the murder scenario, and the latest scandal and gossip involving the trial's leading participants.

Simpson was a story that could have only been conceived in Tabloidworld, as *Vanity Fair*'s Dominick Dunne clearly came to see: "The Simpson case is like a great trash novel come to life, a mammoth fireworks display of interracial marriage, love, lust, lies, hate, fame, wealth, beauty, obsession, spousal abuse, stalking, brokenhearted children, the bloodiest of bloody knife-slashing homicides, and all the justice that money can buy."[1]

Not all media observers bought into Dunne's romanticized notion of life imitating pop art. Their critique was more basic and angrier. Gregg Jarrett, Court TV's co-anchor during the case, was openly contemptuous of the TV tabloids for routinely hyping stories to the point where they had lost any tie to the truth. "What *A Current Affair* and *Hard Copy* have done is horrible, reprehensible," he said. "I saw the way they twisted the truth, and it no longer resembled honesty and accuracy. I knew because I was doing the same story and knew what the truth was."[2]

The major networks also did their best to marginalize the tabloids as profiteering hustlers. NBC's *Dateline*, in its report called

"Cashing in on O. J.," began with footage of streetwise entrepreneurs selling shirts emblazoned with "Free O. J." slogans, and trading cards with the pictures of the celebrity defendant and the two victims. In the show's next segment, the huckster image was linked to the tabloids. Graham Smith, a senior reporter from the *National Enquirer* confidently told *Dateline* that his paper "pays the most money for the best stories." Smith made it clear that his major concern had more to do with personal safety than the tabs' controversial practice of buying information. He told of flying to Los Angeles to cover the Simpson story with "cash to the left of me, cash to the right: I was sweating buckets—$50,000 in cash."

The networks' habit of thumbing their noses hardly slowed down the tabloids. Even conflicts with Ito's courtroom failed to deter editors from aggressively pushing the Simpson story forward. When the *Enquirer* paid three witnesses for a story about a knife they had sold to Simpson shortly before the murders, the prosecution was confronted with yet another witness credibility problem. Richard and Allen Wattenberg, owners of Ross Cutlery, and their employee, Jose Camacho, pocketed $12,500 for an *Enquirer* exclusive, "How I Sold a Stiletto to O. J. Simpson." The tabloid's deep pockets had enticed them to ignore the court's admonition about talking to the press. And each time witnesses came to the stand with the tabs' money in their pockets, the case against Simpson suffered.

"Our case was being sold out from under us, a C-note at a time," said Christopher Darden. "I can imagine no case has ever lost so much testimony that way." The prosecution could not "compete" with the tabloids when it came down to what it had to offer. "They were offering thousands of dollars," he said. "We were offering them the chance to be humiliated. . . to be carved up by ruthless defense lawyers."[3]

Surely the Simpson case wasn't the first undercut by the tabs. Anne Mercer, a key witness in the 1991 William Kennedy Smith rape trial, was paid $40,000 by *A Current Affair* for implicating Smith in the sexual assault of her friend. But the Simpson case was different for the tabloids' utter tenacity, and success, in luring sources to talk, especially those most closely associated with the case. Among them were members of the Brown family, who were paid for O. J. and Nicole Simpson's wedding video; Dominique Brown pocketed $25,000 from the *National Enquirer* for a nude photograph of her sister Nicole.

The tabs, though certainly not alone, were instrumental in feeding the sheer avarice that infected the case. Witnesses, jurors, and trial attorneys—and journalists, as well—clearly understood that the Simpson trial was lined with gold, and soon it would be their turn to collect. The pervasive psychology of greed was articulated by Jose Camacho, the cutlery store employee. In explaining his reason for taking the *Enquirer*'s money for his story about Simpson's knife purchase, he said, "I thought [that since] I'm taking all this pressure, I might as well get something for it."

From his Court TV perch, Jarrett was incensed at the tabloids' irreverent disregard for long-standing journalistic practices in a case where the media themselves were under intense public scrutiny. The practice of paying sources had dangerous consequences. Inevitably, it could induce witnesses to lie or to hype a story to earn substantial sums. "You're inviting people, giving them motivation to lie," he said. "It's rarely the truth that I see up there."

The tabs did not back down from the flurry of criticism. To the contrary, they accused their detractors of being sanctimonious while playing the very same money-for-talk game. The *Enquirer*'s executive editor, Steve Coz, acknowledged that paying for information had its risks: "People will embellish for money. Once that's on the table, you understand it and you cross-check." But the legal establishment and major news organizations should be the last to criticize such practices—indeed, they were hypocrites when then did. "Let's face it," stated Coz. "The police pay informants, prosecutors offer reduced jail sentences, defense attorneys pay thousands of dollars for expert witnesses, and newspapers and radio stations are hiring legal consultants at $2,000 a day. We don't go through that elaborate game. We say: 'We pay cash.'" [4]

The *Enquirer* was hardly shy about flaunting its pay-for-talk policy. Soon after the infamous Bronco chase, the paper's gossip columnist, Mike Walker, appeared on *Larry King Live* to announce that the paper was offering Al Cowlings $1 million for his inside information on Simpson. Walker brought along a prop: a cardboard check for that sum in Cowlings' name. Cowlings turned down the offer.

For the mainstream media, the troubling habit of paying sources was only part of the problem—the tabs were simply having too much fun with the Simpson story. Tantalizing stories about romantic entanglements among the leading players; investigative articles "proving" Simpson's guilt (or innocence); stories about mysterious, secret witnesses; recomposited photographs featuring Simpson in a disguise; or actual photographs of a much younger, and topless, Marcia Clark on a beach vacation, were all part of the mix. Just when readers believed that the tabloids had gone as far as they could, new lows of titillating sensationalism were reached. The September 24, 1994, issue of the *Star*, featured an all-Simpson cover, topped by a banner headline announcing "Nicole's Last Confession," with bulleted subheads charging that "Ronald Goldman was one of her lovers," and that "O. J. panicked after sex with AIDS victim Ray Sharkey's mistress." A separate headline had Paula Barbieri visiting Simpson in jail during the day and sleeping in what had been Nicole's bed at night.

Consistency was not necessarily a virtue among competing tabloid papers. On the very day the *Enquirer* reported that a fearful Barbieri was hiding out in France to escape Simpson following the murders, the *Star* had the couple planning to marry and living in Mexico. "About all that the tabloids haven't offered—so far—is a story based on a posthumous interview in which the victims positively identify their killer," said media critic David Shaw.[5]

By far the most disturbing aspects of tabloid coverage were the no-holds-barred depiction of the murder scene. The tabs seemingly reveled in the carnage. The *Globe* went so far as to publish the autopsy pictures of the victims. Then it went after the "real killer."

In the September 27, 1994, edition of the *Globe*, the tabloid reversed course rallying behind the defense team's contention that someone other than Simpson was the killer. It heralded its "world exclusive" with the banner headline: "O. J.'s Defense: Who *Really* Did the Murders?" The paper devoted five pages to a reenactment of the murders, featuring an unidentified stalker, a black man given the pseudonym "Bobby." With actors playing the roles of Goldman and Nicole Simpson, the *Globe*, in a series of 15 photographs, had the hooded assailant attack "Goldman," plunging a knife into his chest and abdomen. As "Nicole" emerges from her townhouse, she is pounced on by the now-unmasked killer. In close-up, he slits her neck. The chronology ends with a photograph of the two bloody corpses, and the editors noting: "Nicole gazed with horror-filled eyes into a face she had never seen before."

The *Globe*'s latest assailant was decidedly different than the one featured earlier in the case. The killer then was white and was depicted in a front-page drawing with the bold headline: "This Man Did O. J. Murders." According to editor Phil Bunton, "[Simpson's] friends were telling us their conspiracy theories, so we decided to explore those. It sold very well, so it has been valuable."[6]

Times vs. Times

For many in the Simpson press corps, the tabs were a grotesque parody of serious journalism and were repulsed to be even remotely associated with them. Linda Deutsch threatened to remove her byline when an editor tried to insert a report taken from the *Enquirer* into one of her stories. Even Joe Bosco, whose work appeared regularly in the nation's major soft-porn magazines, expressed his moral outrage in *Penthouse* over having been offered money by an *Enquirer* reporter for tips.

Still, even the strongest critics of tabloid journalism grudgingly acknowledged that the tabs had gotten the early jump on the Simpson story. While the mainstream press primarily dealt with official sources, tabloid reporters worked at the grass roots level, cultivating sources from bartenders to chambermaids, those who were privy to gossip and "inside" information. "When the tabloids clasped the Simpson story to their heaving journalistic bosoms," said David Shaw, "the mainstream media suddenly found themselves panting alongside—and not always winning the race against competitors far more experienced on this tricky and often treacherous terrain."[7]

Siding with the tabs, however, had its price. When *New York Times* reporter David Margolick dared to suggest in one of his stories that the *National Enquirer* played a significant journalistic role and, in actuality, was often ahead of the Simpson press corps, he evoked a stream of invective from more blue-nose journalists. In his piece, "The *Enquirer*: Required Reading in the Simpson Case," Margolick said: "The *Enquirer* has probably shaped public perceptions of the case more than any other publication. In a story made for the tabloids, it stands head and shoulders above them all for aggressiveness and accuracy."[8] He went on to note that it was not the *Enquirer* that bore responsibility for the deluge of inaccurate and false stories published and broadcast in the days following the murders. Those mistakes had been the fault of many of the so-called "reputable" news organizations.

Unlike his fellow press corps members, Margolick chose not to deride the *Enquirer*'s story alleging that an unidentified jail guard overheard Simpson tell his minister, the former football player Rosie Grier, that he, in fact, "did it." Margolick repeated the *Enquirer*'s allegation that Simpson had, in effect, confessed, a reportorial decision that rankled other reporters. The question of Simpson's alleged confession later seeped into legal motions in the courtroom, and Ito was left to decide on the admissibility of the guard's testimony. (The statement was not admitted into the court record.)

The media fight was far more vitriolic. In praising the enemy, Margolick had left himself open to broadside attacks by competing news organizations. He found himself vilified by reporters and editors for daring to suggest that tabloids elevated the Simpson coverage. Because he wrote for the *New York Times*, Margolick had done more than give credence to the Simpson confession story—he had legitimized the *Enquirer*.

One leading newspaper to question Margolick's article was none other than the *New York Times*. The *Times* chief editors went so far as to publish a follow-up story that clearly was meant to distance the paper from their own reporter. Joseph Lelyveld, the paper's executive editor took seriously the criticism leveled against his paper. Had editors worked more closely with Margolick on his story, Lelyveld said, they would have asked him for "more context" about the *Enquirer*'s journalistic practices.

Jim Newton of the *Los Angeles Times* was more direct. He charged that Margolick was guilty of "laundering information" by repeating Simpson's alleged confession. At the very least, he said, the information was inherently untrustworthy coming from a paper with a reputation for buying stories. "You have no way on knowing whether the *National Enquirer* bought and paid for that information and whether it violates your own standards of trustworthiness," contended Newton. "[Margolick's] defense to that was that the *Enquirer* has generally done good work on the case and has generally been reliable, which is just not borne out in the record. He continued to repeat that because I think he feels defensive about having used those quotes and took a lot of heat for it."[9]

Margolick bristled at such criticism and shot back at his critics. "The fact was that the *Enquirer* had beaten [the L.A. *Times*] on their own stories several times," he stated. "They could pretend the *Enquirer* didn't exist if they wanted to."

But Newton insisted his criticism of Margolick was not jealous backbiting but "a disagreement about how to handle attribution to other news organizations, particularly a news organization whose general record I consider deplorable and whose particular record on this case is average."

The fact is, said Newton, for Margolick to applaud any tabloid for its Simpson coverage was, essentially, absurd. Even if an occasional scoop made it onto a tabloid page, it was virtually impossible to tell whether the story was based in reality or fantasy. Such "blockbusters" included a story about an eyewitness to the Simpson-Goldman murders who police were secretly hiding in a safe house. Another story reported that the prosecution planned to introduce aerial photographs of Simpson's estate showing that the Bronco—and therefore Simpson—was not at the Rockingham estate at the time of the murders. The tabloid claimed that prosecutors had received the photo through a U.S. national security agency. These stories were just a few that never came to light during the trial.

But equally nettling were the tabs' gossip news that often disparaged the murder victims and had little relevance to the case. "A fair number of disputed pieces went to question Nicole's behavior in using drugs, philandering," said Newton. Whether or not such stories were accurate, he said, they were "unquestionably tasteless." The *Enquirer* ran front-page headlines about "Topless Nicole in Lover's Arms," and featured pieces on her "sizzling" affair with the football player Marcus Allen.

Margolick's recognition of the *Enquirer* was a resounding blow leveled against his own newspaper, the staid *New York Times*. The *Enquirer* story only exacerbated an underlying tension that existed between the paper and the reporter. The *Times*' Simpson coverage was far more reticent than other national papers, and Margolick had grown increasingly frustrated by how little space and editorial support he had been given. Some colleagues concluded that the *Times* editors were embarrassed by the sensational media coverage already given to the case and purposely downplayed the story's significance on their news pages. Margolick conceded that his newspaper was "uncomfortable with stories the tabloids are fixated on."[10] Not surprisingly, Margolick's stay at the *Times* would last only as long as the Simpson story. Following the trial, he left to work for the glossy entertainment magazine *Vanity Fair*.

The *National Enquirer*

The *National Enquirer* had come a long way since William Randolph Hearst sold the paper in 1952 with its flagging circulation to Generoso Pope Sr. for $17,000. Pope was then called a marketing genius for reinventing a paper that combined some celebrity gossip with a huge dose of outrageous human-interest yarns. Later, when the paper was sold on checkout lines in supermarkets, the *Enquirer*, and other rising tabloids, turned more heavily to the celebrity world where the papers were described as being somewhere between an entertaining scandal sheet and "an unholy blot on the fourth estate." Whatever the critique, the tabs apparently were immune—they were the most widely read newspapers in the United States, with a combined readership in excess of *20 million* weekly.

The Simpson story changed one important aspect of the *Enquirer*—its status within the general media industry. Once barely tolerated by the mainstream press, the *Enquirer* was being spoken about in the same breath as the *New York Times*—by the *New York Times*. Although Margolick was the most prominent journalist to publicly laud the *Enquirer*, the *Columbia Journalism Review* called the *Enquirer* senior editor David Perel and his boss, executive editor Steve Coz, "the Woodward and Bernstein of tabloid journalism."

Other reporters even began to note that the *Enquirer*'s bold slant spoke directly to their own social and political sensibilities. Said L.A. *Times* freelance writer Kathy Butler: While the Simpson press corps was losing sight of the murder victims by focusing on the day-to-day minutiae, the tabloids never forgot the human elements of the case.

> I have been a newspaper reporter for more than 16 years and, until the trial began, I thought of the *Enquirer* as an impeccable source for news of space-alien abductions and Liz Taylor's latest surgery. My mind changed in August 1994, when I picked up 'Nicole's Secret Life' and read the first perceptive analysis I'd seen of her life of violence and intimidation. It was a time when many journalists were still using the lukewarm phrase domestic discord or avoiding the subject altogether. Not the *Enquirer*. I wanted to know why the *Enquirer* was running stories I wanted to read. I wanted to know how it managed to cover a story of gender conflict and sexual crime for a mostly female readership while beating the pants off the mainstream press.[11]

Still, much of mainstream media remained unconvinced, if not outrightly cynical of the growing media crusade that heralded the tabloids. Jeffrey Toobin remained expressly disgusted that papers like the *Enquirer* were not condemned across the board as charlatans of the trade. "Some of us in so-called respectable journalism get a lascivious charge out of saying how good the *Enquirer* is," he said. "But it's unreliable crap, and it's important to remember that."[12]

The *Enquirer* editors scoffed at Toobin's self-righteous stance. It was Toobin after all, and not the *Enquirer*, who helped to float the defense theory that Mark Fuhrman had planted a bloody glove on Simpson's property, a story that *Enquirer*'s senior editor David Perel said he never would have run. "That story was a blatant plant by the defense," said Perel, "and printing it was the height of irresponsibility."

And so went the battle between the tabs and the so-called legitimate press to take the high ground in the Simpson story.

When news of the Simpson-Goldman murders broke, the mainstream media were already trying to catch up to the tabloids. The *Enquirer* was sufficiently in the know to get to the murder scene at about the same time as the Los Angeles coroner, beating out much of its competition. The result was a series of stories and sensational photos of the crime scene. The paper's rich network of sources also helped the paper score a number of exclusives, including a report of the 1989 New Year's Eve fight between O. J. and Nicole Simpson. With a large team of reporters, the paper soon launched its own investigation to find suspects other than Simpson who may have been involved with the murders. It did not find any. The paper spent $150,000 to keep Simpson sources talking to its reporters, and it was a worthwhile investment—over the life of the Simpson story, as many as a half-million new readers were added to its three-million weekly circulation.

The *Enquirer* was accustomed to being shunned by the established press, relegated to the journalism trash heap at just another scandal sheet. But the Simpson story had leveled the playing field, and the tabloid aggressively ran with the ball. "They simply couldn't dismiss us this time because they were covering the same story that we were," said Perel, who supervised much of the Simpson coverage.[13]

The tabloid, in fact, was impossible to shun having assigned some 20 reporters to the Simpson beat and boasting of a vast network of inside sources within the celebrity world of Los Angeles. "The first thing a lot of journalists did was grab the *Enquirer*," said Perel. "They were reading it down by the courthouse. Johnnie Cochran was reading it. And I know that O. J. read it. Some of them did not want to admit it; they still don't want to admit it."

Perel stated that there was "no question" that his newspaper drove the Simpson story from the earliest moments in the case. "It was in our backyard," he said. With a bureau in Los Angeles, and a large network of sources centered around celebrities, "we had a head start on a lot of our competition."

As a wave of bad information bounced among major news outlets early on, the *Enquirer* was one of the few newspapers to carry only those stories its own reporters had ferreted out. "We were consistently right," claimed Perel. Ironically, it was left to his paper to set the record straight on faulty stories circulating in the mainstream press. When it was first reported that Ron Goldman had come to Nicole Simpson's condominium the night of the murders to return a pair of eyeglasses she had left at the Mezzaluna restaurant that evening, the press had been wrong. The *Enquirer* followed up noting that the glasses belonged to Nicole's mother. At first glance, this may have seemed like a minor point, but the story had significant implications. Goldman had not been induced by Nicole to come to 875 South Bundy that night—he was simply doing a good deed for her mother. The original story fed the rampant speculation that Goldman was romantically linked to Nicole—an impression that if proven could be used to promote the picture of O.J. Simpson as an obsessed and spurned lover driven to murdering his ex-wife and her lover.

The *Enquirer*'s Simpson stories were typically provocative, and, occasionally, they broke news. Within weeks of the murders, the paper said that Simpson was preparing for an upcoming NBC-TV drama called *Frogmen* by learning techniques of commando combat, including how to slit a human throat and muffle screams. It was during the filming of the show that Simpson purchased a stiletto. Before police spoke to Nicole Simpson's housekeeper, *Enquirer* reporters already had paid her $18,000 for an interview. She told the paper that Simpson followed a pattern: He would terrify and hurt his ex-wife, then seek to reconcile by sending her flowers. The house-keeper also disclosed that Nicole had noticed that a set of house keys had mysteriously disappeared, and she suspected that her former husband had taken them. A few days later Nicole was murdered outside her home.

In November 1994, the paper was the first to report that completed DNA tests revealed that the blood types of both victims were found in Simpson's Bronco, two months before any other news organization reported the same story. Later, it printed photographs of Simpson wearing brown Aris leather gloves similar to the pair found at the crime scene and at Simpson's Rockingham estate. In the trial's aftermath, the *Enquirer* published Nicole Simpson's diary, which documented a personal history of abuse suffered at the hands of her husband. The paper reproduced the original handwritten entries, giving the story a powerful, emotional edge.

The paper also broke ground in other ways. Perel said that the *Enquirer* was the first to report on sidebar conferences between the judge and lawyers, often an insightful sidelight to the main proceedings. "Everybody was watching on TV as they broke for sidebar . . . and nobody knew what was going on. We were getting the transcripts every day, and this was newsworthy, interesting stuff. I said, 'Let's do a story.' My editor asked me, 'Why hasn't anybody else done it?' I said, 'I don't know, but we should do it.' After that everybody starting doing it."

Even after the verdict, the *Enquirer* continued to push the story, at one point producing critical evidence linking Simpson to the murder scene. A photographer from the paper uncovered an old photograph in his files of Simpson wearing Bruno Maglis shoes—the type of designer shoe identified as the one worn by the killer. The paper also disclosed that the head of the Nicole Brown Simpson Foundation, which helps victims of spousal abuse, was a convicted swindler accused of beating his wife. Perel said that it took the Los Angeles papers several months before finally picking up on the story.

Perel discounted the suggestion that the Simpson case had put his tabloid on the map: The *Enquirer*, he contended, had always been there. "I just think [Simpson] became a story by which certain elitists could no longer ignore us. There are certain [news organizations] who would like to believe that people who read the *National Enquirer* don't watch their TV shows or don't read their newspapers. That's not true. There are people who read the *National Enquirer*—and read the *New York Times*. What we do is never sell our readers short or take an elitist view."

Following the Leader

For all the self-righteous tabloid bashing, the major media had failed to take stock of their own dubious practices in the Simpson story. For one, they had few qualms about producing stories based on unidentified sources. That such anonymous sources may have their own axes to grind, and their own agendas to sell, did not appear to faze the more reputable media in their single-minded search for the next exclusive. Nor did the secondary effects of their coverage—that the furious blast of pretrial publicity could damage Simpson's ability to get a fair trial and severely erode the workings of the court.

Unabashedly, reporters acknowledged that their pretrial manic coverage could endanger the upcoming trial—a concession that did nothing to restrain them. Their mantra had long since become a worn cliché: Journalists simply were not responsible for problems created by their stories; their job was to get the story, not to worry about its consequences. So, while there was plenty of empirical evidence to demonstrate that pretrial publicity could prejudice a future jury panel, the thought of curbing the Simpson story scarcely crossed reporters' minds.

Ironically, the L.A. *Times*, which had railed against Margolick's story lauding the *Enquirer*, was in large part responsible for fueling the media frenzy. As a nationally renown daily, the L.A. *Times* set the tone for news coverage in Los Angeles, and when the Simpson-Goldman murder story broke, the paper's saturation coverage sent a message that was loud and clear to the rest of the news media.

Once the trial began, the newspaper devoted three to five stories *a day* about the case—more than 1,500 over 16 months. The coverage ranged from the trivial (articles about Ito's hourglasses; the flowers sent to the courtroom; the court stenographer now engaged in the "biggest typing test" of her career; and the Court TV technician responsible for turning off the audio sound during sidebar conferences), to the sensational (stories about Johnnie Cochran's extramarital relationship and Marcia Clark's divorce entanglements), to solid daily court reporting about the day's testimony, individual stories that ran as long as 3,000 words, twice the length of most ordinary news stories. News reports and features were buttressed by columns specifically invented for the Simpson case that focused on the legal and political "spins" enveloping the trial.

Nothing in the L.A. *Times* history equaled the pervasive, unrelenting coverage given to the Simpson story—not Rodney King, not the Los Angeles riots, not the recent San Francisco earthquake, and certainly not weightier issues such as the sweeping conservative "revolution" in Washington, D.C., with its potential to create devastating social changes for California citizens.

Coverage reached an apoplectic height after the jury verdict was announced. The Simpson story took up the paper's entire front page that following day, and dominated 11 of the first 12 pages of the 26-

page main news section. In addition, the verdict story took over the
first two pages of the metro section and was the centerpiece of the
editorial and op-ed pages. The L.A. *Times* credited an astounding 94
staffers and correspondents with contributing to the Simpson's "day
of judgment" story. Following the verdict, the newspaper ran a
special 12-page supplement related to the case each day for a week.

This time it was Jim Newton, an outspoken critic of tabloid
culture, who offered no apologies. "I don't think there's any need to
apologize for covering it because it's interesting," he said. "That's a
good reason to cover it in and of itself." Newton believed that the
implications of the Simpson case reached far beyond that of a
criminal trial, addressing important social issues that warranted the
paper's extensive coverage. In particular, the case highlighted the
dramatic rift between black and white communities, and the tenuous
relationship that continues to exist between the LAPD and blacks in
Los Angeles. "You don't want the newspaper to just pander, you
want it to serve, [and] I do think there are important issues raised
by this case. Just because we happen to piggyback on a very
interesting trial, so much for the better."

But Newton finally conceded that his paper may have crossed a
line that separates genuine in-depth coverage from outright exploitation. "I don't know where the line is, and we may be over it," he
said, "and we may be so far over it that we've lost track of how far
over it we are." Other staff members went further, complaining that
the *Times* had, in fact, gone over the deep end in its coverage, and
that other more relevant stories had suffered as a result. Narda
Zacchino, an associate editor, said that while she was captivated by
the Simpson story, it "affects far fewer people than the radical
transformation of our government. That affects everyone in this
country."[14]

Among the L.A. *Times'* casualties, strangely enough, was coverage normally given to the country's criminal justice system. News
reports about other criminal cases came to a virtual standstill except
for those the paper could connect to the Simpson case.

While the newspaper claimed to hoist the banner of responsible
journalism, its very commitment to Simpson coverage gave its
readers a false message—that *this* story was more important than
every other story of the day (and year). Clearly, though, it was not.
The region was still suffering from a sluggish economy, and the city
itself was facing continued fallout from the 1992 riots and the
genuine racial problems involving the LAPD.

The newspaper justified its excessive coverage by claiming that the Simpson story was a remarkable vehicle for telling larger stories about race, the police, and the courts in Los Angeles. But even that rationale was misleading. The murder case had a scant connection, if any, to the lives of its readers and was atypical of the way law enforcement and the courts dealt with ordinary people of any race.

If such coverage was also meant to help Americans confront and deal effectively with race-related problems, then the paper failed on this front as well. Lifting the case into an epic struggle about race in America, the L.A. *Times,* and the media at large, served to only polarize the country and drown out a genuine dialogue about American race relations.

Simpson himself was an unlikely—and, in truth, an irrelevant—symbol of racial victimization. Throughout his adult life, he had moved within the circles of privilege and status, ensconced in a predominantly white, wealthy, celebrity world. His life—and the heinous crime of which he was implicated—bore no resemblance to that of blacks victimized by ugly racist actions, such as Rodney King; Medgar Evers, the slain civil-rights advocate; or Emmett Till, a 14-year-old Chicago boy lynched in Money, Mississippi, in 1954, after he was accused of flirting with a white woman. Yet the Simpson case was soon elevated to an even greater political dimension than these others, ignited in large part by the media's extraordinary search to tell a story.

Mirror Images

Blaming the tabloids for the breakdown of journalistic culture was a weak cry into the wind. It wasn't the tabloids that had changed: The best of American journalism had. In the 1990s, the national press was in dramatic transformation—a shift that had not gone unnoticed within the news industry. The blurring of hard and soft news, the rise of "infotainment," the trend toward "celebrity" news, were topics of serious discussion well before Simpson was charged with two murders.

There were other changes, however, that were less noticeable. The very *structure* of news stories was changing. Straight hard news, tied to objectivity and facts, had been challenged by a newer type of "storytelling" that was more stylistic and subjective. There were consequences to this shift: Stories that lent themselves to this narrative form, those with dramatic elements and distinct characters, tended to push out stories that were more "fact based."

The tabloids were long experienced as flamboyant storytellers, and in that sense the mainstream media were catching up to them as the Simpson story broke. In any case, the Simpson story itself was a dream story for a new media era.

This transition in the news collided with another trend—television was moving into the courtroom. For the first time, viewers were seeing pictures of ongoing trials, and the stories and images from the courtroom were captivating. Trials with lurid and violent themes played to the inherent "values" of the commercial medium. Stories about familial murder and sexual violence danced across the television screen, feeding the networks' coffers and the public's salacious appetite. The trials of the Menendez brothers, the Bobbitts, and William Kennedy Smith were ideal for their sensational appeal and ratings-readership potential—trials selected for how well they fit into this storytelling structure. But, still, no modern trial compared with what the Simpson trial offered with its multitude of story lines involving murder, sex, celebrity, and race.

Without question, the Simpson saga would have made headlines in any era. But *this* story was something much larger. The Simpson story had entered a realm of such saturating, sensational revelation and gossip—excess of phenomenal dimensions—that it was astonishing even by modern trends in tabloidism.

As much as the mainstream media sought to distance themselves from tabloid philosophy, their editorial choices reflected that very mindset. How else to explain *Newsweek*'s article about Simpson's "double life," a man who was "a hard partyer . . . on the prowl at wild parties in Los Angeles [who] thought his real addiction was white women."[15] It was *Newsweek* that also reported that Simpson's father was homosexual and that Simpson himself indulged in drugs. It was the *Los Angeles Times* that reported about Cochran's extramarital affair. It was the *New Yorker* that published a 16-page photo essay by noted celebrity photographer Annie Leibovitz, with pictures of the family victims at the gravesites of Ron Goldman and Nicole Simpson; a barechested Brian (Kato) Kaelin, preening into a mirror while blow-drying his hair; and a centerfold-type spread of Paula Barbieri, Simpson's girlfriend, draped over a sofa and seductively eyeing the camera, nude, except for a loosely buttoned shirt open from her navel to her neck, exposing her breast.

Such "important" media coverage did not go unnoticed by the trial's principals. When the *Enquirer* published a computer-generated photograph of a bruised and battered Nicole Simpson, Gerald

Uelmen, a defense team member, asked: "Who would have thought that the *National Enquirer* would have stooped to the level of *Time* magazine?"[16] Uelmen's cutting commentary served to remind critics that it was *Time,* after all, that had published the infamous "mug shot" recomposited to make Simpson look more black.

Underneath the self-serving rhetoric, the "legitimate" press continued to be upset because the tabloids simply weren't playing fair under the terms of *their* rules. As the mainstream media loudly criticized the *Enquirer* for paying witnesses for their story about a knife purchase made by Simpson, they zealously pursued the very same story for all its worth. *Newsweek* ran a full-sized photograph of an open-blade, 15-inch stiletto across two-pages to emphasize the weapon's size and killing capacity. TV tabloids also exploited the violent aspects of the case, with reenactments of the murders featuring actors disguised as victims and the assailant. But a Los Angeles KCBS report went further to recreate the murders using a computer-animated figure, depicted as an African-American, slashing the throat of another computer-animated figure, white and blond.

Often there was little to distinguish the more "serious" TV newsmagazines from the TV tabloids in their Simpson coverage. Media critic Neal Gabler remarked: "What is the difference between *A Current Affair*'s Steve Dunleavy and *PrimeTime Live*'s Diane Sawyer, save that one is overtly smarmy, and the other earnestly smarmy and gets invited to better parties?"

What the tabloids could offer their guests in terms of money, the newsmagazines countered with ego gratification—sources could appear on national television next to Diane Sawyer, Stone Phillips, Connie Chung, and Barbara Walters. Regardless of which venue they chose, sources faced the same questions. Walters, famous for her "intimate" interviewing style, had little reservation in bringing up Nicole Simpson's purported lesbian relationship with Faye Resnick. Nor was she reluctant in an interview with Simpson's first wife, Marguerite Thomas, to ask about rumors alleging that the couple's son Jason was gay. Walters asked Simpson's personal assistant if it was true that the former football star had lost his sexual desire for Nicole.

She was at the height of her titillating journalistic style in her interview on ABC's *20/20* with the Goldman family. Walters is among the best in asking, with apparent sincerity, the "did you beat your wife" question. For Walters, it wasn't the Goldmans' predictable answers that were the point, but rather her "tough-minded" questions, loaded with tantalizing insinuations. In her interview, Walters aimed her sights at Ron Goldman's love life and rumored romantic link to Nicole Simpson, a report widely publicized by the tabloids and now validated by *20/20*. Her questions were devised for their maximum effect.[17]

> Walters: You know, we have read about Ron being in the fast lane, you know, driving Nicole's white Ferrari. What does that mean, the "fast lane?" What was his life like, as much as you know?
>
> Fred Goldman (Ron's father): Well, I don't know. I guess that some people could hear the term "fast lane" and I guess it could bring about some negative images. But knowing Ron, I mean, he liked to dance, he liked to be around people. I don't . . . I never got the impression that. . . you know, that Ron saw himself as quote-unquote in some sort of fast lane.
>
> Walters: Or a ladies man?
>
> Fred Goldman: But I don't . . .
>
> Kim Goldman (sister): But my brother . . . my brother wanted to be married and he wanted to have a family.
>
> Walters: Did he have a girlfriend?
>
> Kim Goldman: He was dating a young lady.
>
> Walters: Did Ron ever mention Nicole Simpson?
>
> Patti Goldman (stepmother): Never.
>
> Michael Goldman (brother): Never.
>
> Kim Goldman: Never.
>
> Walters: Did you ever know. . .
>
> Fred Goldman: Never.
>
> Walters: . . . that she existed?
>
> Patti Goldman: No.
>
> Fred Goldman: I had never heard of her.
>
> Walters: You know, so many rumors. First there were rumors that Ron and Nicole were lovers. Then there were rumors that he was gay. Did you hear these, too?
>
> Kim Goldman: Far from it.

The Walters interview added more grist to the media's wild rumor mill, spinning tales about Goldman's involvement with drugs. Although no evidence had been disclosed in court then, or ever, linking Goldman to illegal drug trafficking, Walters pushed on, creating the impression that it was the Goldman family that sought to "set the record straight" about Ron.

> Walters: There were even, at one point, rumors that he wore a beeper. . . and so that it might have meant something about drugs and being targeted . . .
> Kim Goldman: He wore a beeper because he had a. . . he was a tennis instructor and he was running his own lessons. So people beeped him if they needed to get a hold of him that way.

Having fostered a public image of the murder victim as a reckless womanizer and possible drug dealer—and, therefore, a non-innocent victim vulnerable to and perhaps deserving of retribution, a favorite media stereotype—Walters adeptly victimized the Goldman family a second time. Despite the family's protestations, Ron Goldman's lifestyle, as framed in Walters' pernicious probes, had been brought to the mainstream table and was now a "legitimate" topic of public conversation. Walters previous line of questioning failed to deter her from asking Fred Goldman a final, astonishing question: "As we have seen in other cases, often the victim is put on trial, and there is an unrecognizable figure to the family. Are you prepared that might happen?" This from Walters, who had done her share to promote that insidious journalistic subtext which translated meant: The victim asked for it.

Dr. Rivera and Mr. Geraldo

Rather than take a back seat to the Goldman interview, Walters' intention, of course, was to call attention to herself—she was, after all, a *celebrity* news personality—a self-serving trait that she had finely honed into a lucrative career. And she did this very well. Viewers could all but turn their ears away from Walters' shameless and misleading queries.

By comparison, Geraldo Rivera was viewed as a voice of reason by Simpson watchers. Rivera's star had risen no higher in recent years than that of a self-promoting, talk-show provocateur—that is, until the Simpson case broke. Except for CNN's Larry King, no other television personality linked his reputation so tightly to the Simpson story. His cable network show, *Rivera Live*, was a repository for daily Simpson analysis and spins. It was a shrewd move on Rivera's part; he had become a key player in the daily Simpson conversation.

Moreover, Rivera found himself back among the network newsies that once had kicked him out of their club. In truth, however, it was the mainstream news media that had come to him.

Rivera began his career as a poverty lawyer in New York City, and found his way into the media spotlight representing the Young Lords, a Puerto Rican activist gang, which grabbed headlines back in the late 1960s. The young, flamboyant lawyer was noticed by WABC-TV news executives and was hired as a reporter. Rivera emerged as a star following his investigative reports about abuses at the Willowbrook State School, a psychiatric clinic in New York, and soon was on his way to the network news division. His stints on *Good Morning America, World News Tonight* and a seven-year hitch at *20/20* earned him a reputation as a hard-nosed, arrogant reporter with a penchant for self-aggrandizement. The joke at ABC was that if Rivera had been sent to Vietnam, he'd begin his piece by saying, "Behind me, the Vietnam War." His style of "advocacy" journalism meant telling Charles Manson, "You're a mass-murdering dog, Charlie."[18]

Rivera also butted up against network executives. When ABC reporter Sylvia Chase put together a report about Marilyn Monroe's romantic involvement with John Kennedy, network executive Roone Arledge nixed the piece. Rivera blasted Arledge, who was a friend of the Kennedys, and took on Chase's cause as if it were his own. It was a fateful decision, and Rivera soon found himself out of ABC, and out of work. Few major media outlets were willing to risk taking on a reporter who had established himself as the bad-boy of network news. For much of the early 1980s, Rivera was, in his own words, "the most famous unemployed person in America."[19]

Then, in 1986, he returned to the national spotlight in one of the more embarrassing episodes in television history: the Al Capone debacle. In a heavily promoted syndicated special, Rivera promised to take viewers, literally, inside a recently discovered vault said to have belonged to the infamous mobster. On live television, Rivera hyped Capone's violent exploits while workmen busily worked to open the vault. As the two-hour show came to a climax, Rivera's breathless commentary offered the promise that Capone's secrets might soon be at hand. And then the vault was finally opened. Except for a few dusty gin bottles, it was empty.

Rivera found less tenuous work as host of the syndicated *Geraldo,* another in a line of gossip-titillation talk shows. Not surprisingly, he was the daytime personality that critics loved to hate. Although his guests were not unlike those found on other talk shows, he alone held the sobriquet of "Mr. Sleazoid" for his low-ball programming.[20] The closest he had come to regaining national attention was when he had his nose broken in an on-air altercation with a group of skin heads, his guests that day.

The evening cable show on CNBC came on the air as Rivera grappled with his own role in the talk-show sleaze game. "You can't get down there, still survive, and look in the mirror every day," he said. If Rivera was having an identity crisis, so were his critics jumping between the daytime and nighttime Geraldo. The visceral difference prompted one critic to describe him as "Dr. Rivera and Mr. Geraldo."[21]

Rivera sought to abolish "this kind of schizophrenia," as he retooled his syndicated daytime program, moving it away from the tawdry circus that daily talk-show programming had become. But it was *Rivera Live* that, at last, gave him the status and respectability that had escaped him for much of the latter part of his career.

Rivera Live was relatively subdued compared to his frantic, hyperbolic daytime talk show. Donning glasses, a jacket and tie, and a less pugnacious attitude, Rivera deftly positioned his nightly program within a virtually all-Simpson format. His newfound role as a moderator in the great Simpson debate was embraced by a record-breaking audience for the fledgling cable network. With CNBC programming ratings in the low fractions, Rivera's audience numbers were multiplying ten-fold over the length of the trial.

Rivera's entry into the Simpson story had begun with a strange coincidence. On June 13, 1994, a new book claiming that athletes were more likely to beat their wives or girlfriends was the focus of *Rivera Live*. At the center of attention was Mike Tyson, and his history of violence toward women. As the program was being aired, Steve North, the show's coordinating producer, came across a story over the news wire, that a woman, who had been found brutally murdered the previous night, along with an unnamed man, was now identified as the former wife of O. J. Simpson. He took the story to his boss. "Oh, my God," exclaimed Rivera. But North reassured him: "It looks like it had nothing to do with O. J. The story says he was in Chicago."[22]

Rivera Live placed enormous pressure on weekly newsmagazine shows with his nightly analyses and spins, and an occasional

Simpson bombshell. When the Browns spoke on-air to ABC's Diane Sawyer, they were subdued and nonaccusatory. On the Rivera show, Denise Brown told viewers that, without question, "[Simpson] did it—he murdered my sister." It was not the first time she publicly fingered Simpson, but it was the first time her message was transmitted to so many millions in a formal television interview. Her accusation made headlines across the country. Howard Rosenberg, the L.A. *Times* television critic, said the comments "were a deadening cannonball that resonated on newscasts louder than the guns of Bosnia-Herzegovina."

Lou Brown also made an appearance on Rivera's show, infuriating Simpson lawyers, who were trying to keep a lid on negative publicity leveled against their client. They couldn't have been too happy when Brown discussed photographs that his daughter Nicole had shown him after her 1989 New Year's Eve fight with Simpson. In the photos, Nicole had dark bruises on her forehead and arms and an injury to her left eye. The program aired on the eve of a scheduled hearing on the admissibility of Simpson's abuse record.

These scoops instantly boosted the visibility and reputation of the shows that aired them. The established press, which once had turned their noses at Rivera, now embraced him as a long-lost member of the press club. On NBC's *Today* show, Katie Couric asked Rivera, her guest, for the inside "scoop" on the Brown interview. Strange enough was this incestuous back-patting. More telling, though, was that Geraldo Rivera was "back" among his network news colleagues and looking toward the future. He told another reporter that he'd like to cap his career as, of all things, a network anchor. He envisioned holding the "center chair" on network news as "one of the wise men of the century."[23]

Backlash

As careers were being built and the Simpson story forged ahead, the backlash against the media continued to escalate in the month-long recess before the trial—and the loudest voices of criticism came from the media themselves. When Simpson news was slow, the press spoke and wrote about the "messengers," and their tone was frequently acrimonious. Ironically, their public agonizing helped to feed the growing cynicism that the media were shamelessly exploiting the Simpson case.

The inability of the media to place the Simpson story in a less heated and more responsible journalistic context was not lost on the

Simpson press corps. Reporters and commentators were among the most acerbic observers of the media scene. Having committed the sin of excess, they turned to purge themselves and did so by blaming other journalists. But this media-on-media commentary created a certain dissociative quality as journalists stepped outside their skins to report on how their bodies were behaving. "TV reporters increasingly report condescendingly on the media circus outside the courthouse, conveniently forgetting that they are part of it," opined critic Howard Rosenberg.

"Self-loathing among journalists is becoming something chic in the Simpson case," said correspondent Judy Muller on National Public Radio. "But even so, such comments reveal a fear that we can't stop ourselves—that we're on a bottomless binge."

Part of that destructive mindset emanated from a perception that the media were, in effect, being used, compelled to do the combatants' bidding. Jim Moret, the CNN anchor, acknowledged: "We are as much a tool and a conduit for each side as we are an investigating arm of our own individual organizations."[24]

The media catharsis became a strange sideshow to the big event. Some though refused to join in the self-flagellation, instead taking aim at the media's critics. Jon Katz in *New York Magazine* lifted his voice "in praise of O. J. overkill," and then went after *New York Times* columnists A. M. Rosenthal and Walter Goodman: "Like aging ingenues peering into their mirrors every night for too many years, these mandarins can no longer take their eyes off their terrible dilemma, which is this—the more interesting a story, and the more it's covered, the more hands must be wrung about it."[25]

For media types like Katz, the frenetic coverage of the Simpson case was a welcome trend. It represented among other things a trend in the democratization of journalism. The proliferation of alternative news outlets, according to Katz, has "shaken an industry once run entirely by a handful of powerful white men and their narrow editorial agendas. Even as the media slowly became more diverse, the old-time legacy lives on." Under the rules of the old established order, headed by network news anchors like Walter Cronkite and David Brinkley, the Simpson story would have been short-lived, stated Katz. "It wasn't their type of tale. It didn't come out of Washington. It wasn't about the cold war."

But if Katz envisioned a more democratic news industry, it was hard to comprehend his glee over the Simpson story. Rather than produce a more diverse journalism, news outlets tightly narrowed their agenda to target one particular story suffused with popular appeal. The Simpson story was just the latest—albeit the most sensational—tabloid episode in a new-age history of American journalism.

Katz's reasoning, though, was in line with current-day thinking regarding "newsmaking." Americans once looked to the major news organizations for their professional decisions concerning the important news of the day. Now media outlets were increasingly *asking their audiences* what they wanted to see and read—and then they delivered. The ultimate criterion regarding what is "news" was the public's demand. For Katz, and others, a market-driven journalism industry was equivalent to a more "democratic press." And since the sensational always sells better than the nonsensational, the end result has meant more enticing stories—but not necessarily more responsible—for media audiences.

In this new world order, it is not difficult to see why the mainstream media moved onto the Simpson story with such voracious appetites. Indeed, the story was Katz's idyllic world come true, with its promises of ratings, readers, and money for the media; and sensational soap opera for their audiences. Certainly the Simpson story was big news; the press always has gravitated toward stories involving the rich and famous. But the magnitude of coverage was something never seen before. Not every major news organization pursued the Simpson story with the same ferocity, but, fairly or not, the "media" were painted with the same broad strokes of criticism. By the time the Simpson trial ended, the general consensus was that the media *in toto* had failed to take command of the story. The story had overtaken them.

To a certain extent, the public was well prepared for the Simpson onslaught. It had been just a short distance, after all, from the recent Michael Jackson story and the media fury surrounding the singer and allegations of child abuse. Also a product of a Los Angeles celebrity culture, Jackson was helpless in dealing with the overwhelming publicity, particularly on local television news with its less-than-genteel attitudes toward the entertainer. "Their whole point was to put on the air Michael Jackson on stage grabbing his crotch," said Leo Wolinsky of the L.A. *Times.* "I don't know how many thousands of times I saw that on television."[26]

A product of a hyperactive media, the Jackson story also highlighted the troubling changes overtaking even once-respected news organizations. CBS network's morning news program, featured a segment with co-host Paula Zahn interviewing Diane Dimond, a reporter for tabloid TV's *Hard Copy,* about the latest news regarding Jackson. A perplexed Howard Rosenberg remarked: "Here you have this formerly hallowed [news] institution now using a *Hard Copy* reporter as a source."[27]

Whatever the excesses in the Jackson story, they would soon be forgotten as the media charged to the next hot spot: Simpson. For all of the pretrial publicity and tremendous hype, the murder story would only grow larger. Soon it was to become a tale of American life itself, and, most pointedly, of the media, inextricably caught in the rising frenzy, and grappling with a profound sense of lost identity, as they approached the beginning of the great trial.

PART TWO

THE TRIAL OF
O. J. SIMPSON

FIRESTORM

JANUARY 1995

Opening arguments began January 24, 1995, with all the feverish anticipation and hype of a grand sporting event.

"May the trial begin," declared Jennifer Siebens, the Los Angeles bureau chief for CBS network news. "We're ready. We've had six months to get ready."

And Stephen Seplow, a *Philadelphia Inquirer* reporter, said: "Ready does not really do justice to television's level of preparation. The 49ers were ready for the Cowboys. But that was minor compared with the way TV has gotten ready for *The People of the State of California* v. *Orenthal James Simpson,* a.k.a. O. J. Simpson."[1]

Sports metaphors littered telecasts and radio talk shows, while newspapers and magazine ran lineups of the two teams. *People* magazine devoted a special issue to the key "players" replete with mini-biographies and pictures.

If anyone missed the point, *Newsweek* proclaimed in its banner-sized headline, "And Now, Let the Trial Begin." Indeed, the Trial of All Trials had finally arrived.

Few events in the world could galvanize the force of media outlets gathered in and around the Los Angeles courthouse. Although some 1,150 journalists were given press credentials for the trial, many more followed the case much the same way people across America did—by tuning to television coverage. From both a media and cultural perspective, the Simpson case was a mega-TV event. No other medium could compete with television's immediacy and visual dynamism, or its fantastic reach around the globe.

In those first days, it was almost impossible to turn to television and see anything but the Simpson story. In addition to what was offered on the major broadcast networks, cable networks like CNN, Court TV, and the E! Entertainment Channel carried complete coverage of the proceedings. In Los Angeles, viewers could also choose among six local stations, which televised little else but the trial. The promise of ratings, again, was too seductive to ignore. During opening statements, local TV ratings skyrocketed 30 percent.

After that, the major networks left live trial coverage to the cable networks. Going gavel to gavel was risky business with no guarantee that audiences would keep watching over the long run. Besides, their regular soaps were simply too profitable. But the networks did not intend to simply hand the Simpson story over to their cable competitors. Instead, the trial was swallowed into their 24-hour entertainment-news schedules as the featured story on morning talk shows, evening newscasts, prime-time newsmagazines, late-night and overnight news programs.

CNN had much less to lose by committing its daytime hours to complete coverage. Its morning and afternoon audience share barely registered more than a single rating point. The preliminary hearing had given the network an adrenalizing shot with audience numbers quadrupling over the week-long proceedings. Those ratings bolstered confidence that the trial could lift the flagging cable network to the unprecedented heights it had reached during its Persian Gulf War coverage.

Ted Turner's network was battle-ready with 70 reporters, producers, and technical staff situated in and around the courthouse. Camera crews were stationed at the courthouse entrance and also at the jail in which Simpson was being held, ensuring that no one would enter (and no potential story would be lost) without being caught on camera.

Jim Moret, the California-based co-anchor for *Show Biz Today*, received the plum job as CNN anchor for the trial. But complete trial coverage was only part of a larger plan. Once the day's proceedings were over, resident talk shows like *Larry King Live* would continue to keep the case in the spotlight. New interactive programs were introduced with audience members invited to the CNN studio, and others encouraged to call-in from their homes to comment on the latest Simpson "issue of the day." Viewers were expected to do more than just watch: They were positioned as quasi-jurors and required to *act* in a simulated tele-trial.

Over the previous few years, CNN had faced a growing swell of criticism for failing to hold to its original mission as a 24-hour-a-day news service. The network's devotion to Simpson would hardly silence its critics. CNN programming, in fact, had fragmented, and the network's past hard-news edge was undercut by more profitable entertainment programming. Complete coverage of the Simpson trial would largely wipe out the remaining daytime news coverage as the network vied for higher audience shares.

There was little question that the Simpson story was a tremendous moneymaker, and it also placed CNN in the position to challenge the major networks' popular soap operas. Two months into the trial, CNN reported a 600 percent ratings jump. Its advertising rates jumped from $3,000 for a 30-second spot to $24,000. In the first quarter alone, the network pocketed $15 million in Simpson-related ad profits—and the trial had another six months to go.[2]

The network's plan to televise the entire trial was instrumental in keeping the Simpson case alive as a media phenomenon. But CNN's coverage was not universally applauded. Mike Wallace, the veteran correspondent for CBS's *60 Minutes*, said: "With everything happening in the United States and around the world, to have CNN devoting hour after hour to the trial—not because of its news value, but solely because it raises their ratings—is damned cynical."[3]

Much like the preliminary hearing, trial coverage transcended all other news of the world. Opening arguments coincided with President Bill Clinton's State of the Union address, and the press's treatment left little doubt about which event was more important—at least in the judgment of news executives. The "headline news" of the day was Simpson. Never mind that the White House was caught up in an acrimonious political climate, and that the embattled Democratic president confronted a hostile joint session of the first Republican-controlled Congress in 40 years. That night, the networks turned to other matters of national concern. The opening arguments in *California* v. *Simpson* led all three network evening news programs. News "specials" about the case preempted all regular programs. Clinton's national address did not even detract the politically oriented *Nightline* from focusing its attention on the impact of the prosecution's opening remarks on the state of O. J. Simpson.

Clinton himself was not oblivious to the turn in the media's agenda. Typically, Washington politics is at the epicenter of national news, but in the Year of Simpson, the president struggled to get his message across. To be criticized by the media could be grievous; to be ignored was political death. Briefing reporters at the White House on his latest plans for welfare reform, Clinton said ruefully, "The O. J. trial hasn't started yet today, has it? Thank goodness it's in California or you all wouldn't pay *any* attention to what we're doing."[4]

Inside the courtroom, Judge Lance Ito told the trial lawyers: "I expect at the end of this trial that we will all go out and have dinner together, on me, and that we will all be professionals and be able to deal with each other accordingly." If ever a wish was denied, this was it. In the days to come, few would mistake the interaction among the lawyers and the judge for something resembling professional camaraderie. And, following the trial's verdict, there were certainly no reported sightings of Ito and the lawyers breaking bread or toasting one another's good fortune.

Ito's initial optimism was hardly shared by the public. Even before a single witness had taken the stand, an ABC-TV poll revealed that a vast number of Americans already thought Simpson was guilty—most also believed he would not get a fair trial.[5] The poll was a shattering indictment of how far the trial had already disintegrated into a political and media firestorm. Still another warning signal went unheeded. Nearly nine out of ten respondents told ABC that they were "sick of hearing" about the case—a finding that failed to deter the networks from their frenzied pursuit of the Simpson story in their newscasts, newsmagazines, and news analysis programs. The media clearly believed that if they continued to "build" the Simpson story, their audiences would come.

Meanwhile, across television, a new legion of lawyers-turned-pundits offered the latest wave of predictions. Most guessed that the Simpson trial would last as long as four months—at the outside, five. Ito himself told jurors that they would likely be home for Memorial Day. But some analysts found it hard to believe the case could possibly go until May. NBC's homespun pundit Gerry Spence chimed in half-facetiously that he'd never heard of a murder trial lasting longer than five *weeks*. Indeed, the original "Trial of the Century"— the kidnap-murder of the Lindbergh baby—barely lasted seven.

The pundits, of course, sorely missed the mark—the Simpson trial would not end until nine months later, closer to Halloween than Memorial Day. And if there were higher expectations—that, for instance, the case could illuminate the highest standards of American justice—these and other promises were dashed against the hardscrabble reality of a courtroom debacle.

Shapiro, Bailey, and Company

In the days leading to the opening, the trial lawyers jockeyed for position as the television world watched. Prosecutors told Ito they had uncovered a diary written by Nicole Simpson that documented the defendant's abusive and violent behavior. According to her entries, Simpson had thrown her out of a moving car, beat and humiliated her, and threatened to decapitate her boyfriends. Prosecutors painted Simpson as a fiercely jealous man, filled with rage, who after 17 years of an abusive relationship, killed his ex-wife.

On the defense side, the diary was belittled as a document written by woman marshaling her "evidence" against her estranged husband for an impending divorce. Simpson himself asked Ito for permission to address the jury prior to his lawyers' opening statement—a request that Ito denied. But Simpson was allowed to show jurors his old football injuries, presumably to demonstrate how the injury would have prevented him from overpowering and killing the two victims.

And then there was the less-than-amusing sideshow of the Dream Team feud. Even the facade of professional civility wilted under the strain of high-powered egos and childish charges and recriminations. Just days before opening arguments, Robert Shapiro angrily accused co-counsel F. Lee Bailey of denigrating his legal skills in the media to win Simpson's trust and an enhanced position on the defense team. The feud was all the more peculiar since Shapiro and Bailey were close friends. Bailey also was the godfather of one of Shapiro's sons.

But this was not their first public fight—nor their last. Bailey's investigators accused Shapiro of accepting $5,000 from a tabloid newspaper, the *Star*, in exchange for transcripts of Simpson's interview with police the day after the murders. Shapiro vehemently denied the accusation, but admitted he did meet with the tabloid's reporters at a restaurant, in what he described as a "set-up." Shapiro had brought Bailey onto the team, but now told the press he was fed up with Bailey's attempt to discredit him and wanted him off the case. "We can't have snakes in the bed trying to sleep with us," he said.

Shapiro's attack was a far cry from his past remarks lauding Bailey for his behind-the-scenes legal work. But even fellow Dream Teamers said such designs to keep Bailey on low profile were unrealistic for an "old warhorse" who had represented such celebrated defendants as Dr. Sam Sheppard, Patricia Hearst, and Albert DeSalvo (the "Boston Strangler"). "Some wag once quipped that the most dangerous place in a courtroom was to stand between Alan Dershowitz and a television camera," said Gerald Uelmen. "It's probably more dangerous to stand between F. Lee Bailey and the podium. That is precisely where Bob Shapiro was standing."[6]

Uelmen conceded that the public fight was "painful" to observe. And it would only get worse. Bailey was accused of cultivating a close relationship with Simpson in order to undermine Shapiro's position as lead attorney and give him the starring role he sought. The feud painted a picture of small-minded, egocentric lawyers more interested in gaining the media spotlight than in tending to their client's needs.

That mentality also crossed over into Shapiro's relationship with Johnnie Cochran. Though Shapiro insisted that he was still "captain of the ship," Cochran had clearly moved him aside. That point was crystallized the previous December in a power play over a media photo opportunity. Shapiro recounted in his trial memoirs that he had agreed to have the photographer Annie Leibovitz take a group portrait of the defense team for *Vanity Fair*'s annual "Hall of Fame" issue. But Cochran refused to show at the last moment, and the shoot was canceled. He told Shapiro that his *other* famous client, Michael Jackson, "hates" *Vanity Fair* and asked him to pull out of the shoot. But when Shapiro apologetically explained to Leibovitz what Cochran had told him, the photographer was astounded. "That can't be true about Michael Jackson hating *Vanity Fair*," she told Shapiro. "I've just been contacted to do a cover story on him!"[7]

An admittedly bewildered Shapiro said he canceled the shoot because with Cochran and his staff absent "there wouldn't be a single black face in the picture," an image that would not "represent the spirit of the defense team." Shapiro wasn't deterred, though, and found his way into the magazine's "Hall of Fame" issue without Cochran's help. Leibovitz took his picture, alone.

The power plays were bizarre by any standard of professional behavior. But they were revealing nonetheless of the ego-driven mentality that existed among the lawyers, and particularly in their dealings with the media. Cochran's primary interest in "using" the media was to promote Simpson's innocence in terms of his own political and racial agenda. Cochran told an associate, "I'm a hero to my community," a public persona enhanced by his shrewd use of the platform given to him. Cochran had the clearest order of business. The Simpson case was nothing short of a major civil rights battle— which he planned to lead. Shapiro and Bailey's priorities were more obtuse. They were more interested in sculpting media images that promoted their self-perceived high-profile status. Being front-stage was their driving motivation.

The media were a means to the lawyers' own narrow ends, and each sought control. But, finally, Cochran prevailed not only in the courtroom as Simpson's chief attorney but also in the media game. About a month before the verdict, Cochran sent a memo to all members of the defense team, dictating that "effective immediately, per Mr. O. J. Simpson's request, all media appearances must be approved by yours truly. There will be no exceptions to this policy."[8]

As the trial began, any pretense of team camaraderie had already collapsed under the weight of individual egos. Following the Bailey feud, and his own demotion, Shapiro sat mostly in silence at the defense table during the trial. When the camera panned to the defense side, he appeared at times to be sulking. After the verdict and free of legal constraints, Shapiro publicly turned against his former colleagues. In network and newspaper interviews, he blamed Cochran for turning the trial into a racially-charged courtroom fiasco. As for Bailey, he vowed never to speak to him again.

Even before the first witness was called, the Dream Team resembled the royal palace, flush with internal conspiracies and backstabbing enemies, and set to explode into public battle. Ironically, the lawyers' feuding may have unwittingly helped their client. As they publicly bickered and pointed fingers, the lawyers captured, however clumsily, the day's headlines, diverting media attention away from the bodies found at Bundy.

Cochran and Darden

Cochran and Christopher Darden all but guaranteed that the opening statements would be a sellout show following two weeks of ugly, contentious hearings over evidentiary matters. The disputes seethed into open animosity with accusations of racism and race-pandering. The preliminary battle over critical legal issues soon broke down into angry charges and personal attacks regarding the

lawyers' racial identities and their ties to the Los Angeles black
community.

In hearings prior to the opening statements, Darden pleaded
with Ito to prohibit defense lawyers from using the "n-word" before
the jury. The prosecutors were well aware that Simpson's lawyers
planned to vigorously challenge Mark Fuhrman regarding his racial
attitudes. They anticipated that racial invectives, like the word
"nigger," would be included in the type of rhetoric the defense would
use to deliberately inflame the mostly black jury.

"It is the dirtiest, filthiest word in the English language,"
Darden told the court. "It will upset the black jurors. It will issue a
test, and the test will be: 'Whose side are you on, the side of the
white prosecutors and the white policemen? Or are you on the side of
the black defendant and his very prominent black lawyer?' That is
what it is going to do. 'Either you are with the Man or you are with
the Brothers.'"

As Darden spoke, O. J. Simpson was captured in the frame of
the in-court camera, turning in his seat to squarely face the
prosecutor, shaking his head in apparent amazement and searching
out supporters in the gallery with whom to make eye contact. Then
Cochran took the lectern and excoriated Darden. "African-Americans
live with offensive words, offensive looks, offensive treatment every
day of their lives," he said. "To say they can't be fair is outrageous. I
am ashamed that Mr. Darden would allow himself to become an
apologist for [Fuhrman], to justify the fact that he's a police officer."

The angry banter continued. Before a single witness took the
stand, the race issue was out of the bag. Each time Darden
attempted to limit the racial elements of the case, Cochran pounced
at the opportunity to remind the court, and a television audience,
that this case was "all about race." Seeking to show that prosecutors
were not gratuitously attacking Simpson's character, Darden chose
an explosive example. "We're not running around, talking about or
seeking to introduce to the jury the notion that this defendant has a
fetish for blond-haired white women. . . . That would be outrageous."

Then it was Cochran's turn, and he angrily denounced Darden's
argument as "the most incredible remark I've heard in a court of law
in the 32 years I've been practicing. . . . When you talk about the race
card, how outrageous is it to say that 'I'm not going to talk about Mr.
Simpson's fetish for blond women?' Is that what was said in this
court of law? Did I hear that? That is outrageous. If this man loves
somebody who is purple in this country, he has the right to get

married to that person. His first wife was an African-American. That's the beauty of America."

In his signature oratory, Cochran's courtroom appeals invoked God and the spirit of America. But his firebrand rhetoric came off as overheated in his attempt to reach beyond the courtroom to an international audience. Reaction at the defense table made the scene even more stilted. As Cochran spoke of the "beauty" of America, Simpson wiped his teary eyes, bending forward as Robert Shapiro draped an arm across his back to comfort him. When Cochran took his seat, he too reached out to Simpson. The proceedings had come to an emotional pause, with the defense table—a *tableau vivant*—arranged around the aggrieved defendant, a victim himself, unjustly accused by a vengeful prosecution.

Ito, visibly disturbed by the incendiary language, deferred his decision on whether to allow the defense to challenge Fuhrman on the "n-word." The judge, however, would soon discover that he could not avoid the pending race fight: Indeed, he found himself directly in the middle of it, attacked by both sides for his rulings related to Fuhrman and the LAPD.

Ito, also, could not break free of television. Under normal circumstances, he might have clamped down on the trial lawyers and held a tighter grip over collateral or extraneous matters that seeped into the trial. But having told the nation that the televised trial could teach Americans about law and justice, the judge had in one sense given up his authority to the medium.

The judge was reluctant to shackle the trial attorneys, sensitive about his public-media image—and the televised *impression*—that somehow he had not allowed a full airing of the case. The lawyers on both sides quickly understood the open-ended ground rules and immediately took advantage, with the result a judicial travesty of unprecedented scope. Only later, after the trial had dragged on for months past its original timetable, did Ito realize how far he had allowed the case to crumble. By then, however, his outward effort to become "tough-minded" was seen as a pathetic, desperate move to take charge of a process that had long since slipped past his control.

Televising a case steeped in racial overtones had the effect of casting Cochran and Darden as adversaries beyond the walls of the courtroom and into the arena of American racial politics. If Cochran had hoped that the cloud of a race controversy would further obscure the proceedings, he could not have been more pleased.

Cochran's scathing pronouncements against the LAPD seemed designed to reach well beyond the jury and into the homes of millions of Americans. As the trial progressed, he no longer merely represented O. J. Simpson, but was now seen as an outspoken voice for civil rights, and an outright hero among black organizations. When he opened his new law office in Los Angeles two months after the start of the trial, he invited many black community leaders, and the event became a celebration of Cochran himself. The lawyer was compared to a modern-day Joe Louis, a hard-hitting black man challenging a criminal justice system that had been so unfriendly to black Americans. It was an image he carefully cultivated. Among his stops during breaks in the trial were Washington, D.C., to attend the Congressional Black Caucus, and then a Florida college where he received a honorary doctorate.

Cochran had craftily exploited his newfound status beyond the legal parameters of the trial. Jim Newton, of the L.A. *Times*, recalled watching Cochran during a CNN interview in which he compared Police Chief Willie Williams with his controversial predecessor, Daryl Gates. Though Williams was black, Cochran accused the chief of doing little to weed out racist cops. "These are issues well beyond his role as a lawyer in this case," said Newton. "But that's an example of him using the platform he has from the Simpson case to really address issues far beyond the case specifically. The case has invested some authority in him, and I think he's used it."[9]

Darden was quick to anger by Cochran's race-baiting tactics, which the defense lawyer used to gain a tactical advantage. "Cochran knew how to get under Darden's skin; he knew how to bait him at every turn and did," said Court TV co-anchor Gregg Jarrett, "It unnerved and disrupted Darden, [and] he fell right into the hands of Johnnie Cochran each time."[10]

The prosecutor soon found *himself* under assault and thrust into the very center of a vicious race case. And it had begun even before opening statements when Cochran accused Gil Garcetti of only choosing the black prosecutor because of his skin color. "All of a sudden [Darden] shows up here," Cochran told the media. "Now why is that, after we have chosen eight African-Americans [on the jury]? We're concerned about that. Why now?"

Darden said he watched in disbelief as his former colleague— someone he had admired and had once worked alongside in the district attorney's office to ferret out racist police officers—accused him of being a black "token," and a sellout to his race. Cochran had sent a "private message" to the black community, said Darden. "Blacks could hear what he was saying between the lines: 'This brother is being used by the Man. This brother is an Uncle Tom.' It was the most offensive thing a black can be called by another black, and hearing it repeated on television and in the newspapers was the equivalent of publicly being called a nigger by a white lawyer."

The prosecutor said he waited for black leaders to support him against Cochran's charges, but "they were silent."[11] Instead, Darden found himself branded as the resident "house Negro" on radio talk shows catering to black audiences, in the black press, and in the nonstop chatter about the case in the black community.

Darden did not get much more support from the white mainstream media. *Nightline*'s Ted Koppel commiserated: "Poor old Chris Darden, what does he do now? As the only black man on the prosecution team, and as the man expected to examine Mark Fuhrman. . . to put him in the best possible light, what a difficult job."[12]

His guest Leslie Abramson responded: "You have to have some empathy for his position, but you have to wonder why he let himself be there."

Cochran's vilifying "message" seeped into Darden's personal life, and he saw friendships destroyed. Midway through the trial, he threatened to quit the legal profession altogether because of the personal strains he had suffered. As Cochran played to the emotions of his black constituency, Darden said he faced "long nights" contending with the political backlash, and worse—death threats and racist letters. In his cramped office, the telephone rang incessantly, one caller warning him: "If I ever see you on the streets of Los Angeles, you're one dead nigger."[13]

The defense lawyer had largely succeeded in "defining" Darden's role in the case to the black community. Such characterizations were exacerbated by daily television images that resonated on a deeper symbolic level. They implied that Darden was out of touch with many in the black community who were suspicious of the LAPD and its handling of the case. Worse, he was doing the white man's bidding, seeking to put away one of the great black athletes of all time.

Cochran's race-labeling compelled the press corps to investigate the public mood toward Darden, and the prosecutor was helplessly thrust into the maelstrom. The L.A. *Times* sent black reporters to local malls, restaurants, and barber shops in the black community to gauge community sentiment toward Darden. The piece came out in anticipation of Martin Luther King Jr. Day, the prosecutor recalled bitterly—a "perfect day to announce to Southern California that I was reviled in the black community."

The community reaction was a stunning blow to the prosecutor who had spent six of his 15 years as a deputy district attorney prosecuting corrupt police officers. "Am I supposed to surrender my skin color just because I'm doing my job? I'll tell you, when this case is over, the families of black victims will be asking for me."

Cochran's manuevers had clearly placed him on the defensive, and Darden considered responding with his own media campaign. In truth, there were *two* trials of O. J. Simpson: The case being tried in the media was one that Darden also felt strongly compelled to win. But when he approached Garcetti about his desire to speak to the press, the district attorney turned him down. Garcetti feared that Darden would divert more attention to the racial aspects of the case, further distancing the trial from Simpson and the two murders.

Darden abided by Garcetti's order but regretted doing so. He wrote in his trial memoirs: "Maybe [press interviews] would've kept me from being alienated from my community, from being stranded in this inhospitable borderland where I've found myself, smack between black anger and white anger, between retribution and condescension, between two very different kinds of fear."[14]

The Split-Second Mistake

The week of opening arguments crackled with the type of confrontation and histrionics endemic throughout the case. Prosecutors exposed the "private side" of the once-popular celebrity, contending that Simpson was obsessed with his ex-wife and a violently jealous man. "He killed her out of jealousy," Darden told the jury. "He killed her because he couldn't have her. If he couldn't have her, he didn't want anyone to have her."

Then it was Marcia Clark's turn. On an overhead 87-inch television monitor, Clark displayed the gruesome pictures of the butchered corpses. Ito had ruled these pictures off-limits to television viewers, who watched the gallery spectators as they, in turn, watched the photos. Fred Goldman wept at the sight of his murdered son; Nicole Simpson's three sisters also quietly sobbed. Step by step, Clark laid out the prosecution's case, walking the jury through the murder scene, describing the hairs found there: a brown, blood-soaked glove; a telltale, bloody, size-12 shoe print; and blood drops—

all evidence consistent with Simpson's hair, blood type, and shoe size. Another bloody glove matching the one at the murder site was found on Simpson's estate by Detective Mark Fuhrman. That glove would become one of the most controversial pieces of evidence in modern legal history.

The prosecutor continued, tracing a trail of blood from outside Nicole Simpson's condominium to O. J. Simpson's Bronco van, to the pathway leading to his home, into the house leading to an upstairs bedroom, and onto a pair of crumpled socks in the middle of the room. Clark's opening statement was devastatingly vivid—and then Ito abruptly interrupted her.

His complaint was not with the prosecutor's presentation, but with the camera operator. As the camera scanned the courtroom, the technician had inadvertently captured the face of an alternate juror who was sitting in the gallery—a transmission expressly forbidden by Ito. The televised image of the juror could be seen for all of eight-tenths of a second, about the duration of an eye-blink. But when the mistake was brought to Ito's attention, he erupted. The judge immediately dismissed the jury and recessed the court before the defense could deliver its opening statement. "My inclination is to terminate all television coverage at this point," said Ito. And then he did precisely that.

The move sent shock waves through a huge national television audience glued to the opening statements and now thrown into a pit of media darkness. They weren't the only ones discombobulated. The most visible confusion was seen on Court TV, the network responsible for the camera faux pas and likely to suffer most from Ito's edict. Steven Brill quickly went on the air to apologize for his network's mistake, but Ito was not assuaged and refused to immediately reinstate the camera. Had the judge refrained from his dramatic play over the minor mistake, the technical glitch would have passed without notice. But Ito again was bent on asserting his authority, however obtuse or irrational his ruling about the camera may have been. Defensively, he told the court: "My credibility as a judge is at stake."

For the defense team, Ito's move to halt camera coverage was "devastating" and caused Simpson "irreparable harm." Shapiro claimed the defense was "deprived of that very important moment" to answer the prosecution's charges—not to the jury but, specifically, to television viewers. For six months, the lawyers had worn alternate hats as both trial advocates and high-powered media pitchmen, and now they were being cut off from their most valued resource: a vast TV audience. From a legal perspective, Ito's ruling should have made no difference at all, but not in this trial driven by personal ego and ambition.

An enraged Bailey provided the day's memorable sound bite. Speaking to reporters outside the courthouse, he first denigrated the media for their "character assassination" of his client, before railing against the much-beleaguered camera operator. As if he was speaking directly to the technician, Bailey bellowed in perfect sound-bite precision. "If you were flying an airplane instead of a camera," he said, "you would have killed several hundred people."

Inside the courtroom, Shapiro called upon Ito to reinstate the camera, but with a new provision: that witnesses be allowed to decide for themselves whether they wanted their testimony televised. "We have some witnesses who have been intimidated by the media," admitted Shapiro. "We have some witnesses who are now very reluctant to come to court. We have some witnesses who don't want to have their face on television." The prosecution had also a similar experience. Clark said that some of *her* witnesses felt frightened by the camera. But she was not in favor of giving witnesses the discretion of whether or not to be on television; she just wanted to turn the camera back on.

Throughout the daylong suspense over whether Ito would relent and pardon the camera, the stunning revelation that the camera might be making witnesses fearful was shunted aside. CNN commentators presented their own spin, but none took Shapiro and Clark's remarks at face value. Media pundits refused to pursue their accusations for to do so meant charging the camera with "crimes" against the fair workings of the courtroom. And without a camera, television had no pictures, and they had no job. The camera's effect on witness testimony (and, indeed, the behavior of *all* participants) was a story that would remain untold.

It would be wrong to conclude that only the media had a self-serving interest in the debate over the camera. All major participants were heavily invested in this Trial of the Century, a media tag they eagerly embraced for it brought them attention, fame, and the promise of riches. It also gave something more—the grandiose sense that they were central players on the world scene. In a fit of pique, Ito turned off the camera while failing to understand the reality of what had become of the Simpson trial: The case no longer belonged to Los Angeles, much less a lone presiding judge. "This case is larger than one person," argued Garcetti, in reaction to Ito's decision. "I believe, truly, that the criminal justice system is in fact on trial."

Garcetti's unlikely supporter was Shapiro, who went even further in defending television. "It's up to 12 people to decide," said the defense attorney, "but more important, or equally important, the world has to judge O. J. Simpson."

This perception ultimately would lead to the trial's downfall. Once television thrust the Simpson trial into a public arena, it no longer existed as merely a legal entity but a powerfully *political* one that reached a worldwide TV constituency. The lawyers remarks were telling, as if to convey that Ito himself had become superfluous to the trial's overriding political mission. Ito did not preside over the Simpson trial, they seemed to be saying: television did.

Virtually the entire day of January 25 was devoted to Court TV's transgression of Rule 980, which forbids camera coverage of jury members. Brill issued an apology to the court, noting that the network covered 288 legal proceedings in the previous three-and-a-half years, and that this had been its first mistake. Brill hopscotched between Court TV and CNN studios where he went on air to pitch the values of televising trials. The Simpson story once again was more about the media than about the murders.

CNN commentators continued their coverage that day without benefit of video images from the courtroom. They denounced the judge's decision to bar camera coverage while reading computer-generated transcripts from the proceedings. CNN became more radio than television, its audience now listeners instead of viewers. The visual blackout sent another message, too—one that broadcasters did not mean to convey. Had the Simpson trial faded permanently into black, the proceedings, free of daily microscopic coverage, might finally have taken on a more normal legal stance. But such talk, of course, was heretical under television's big tent.

As the trial stalled and jurors remained sequestered, Ito spent the day listening to appeals from media lawyers. After flexing his muscles, Ito now played the role of conciliator. "The court has had the benefit of a night's sleep on the issue," he said in his ruling the following morning. "I find there was no bad faith involved." The television camera was turned back on in Department 103, but this time there were no cheers from the Simpson press corps.

Even the legal community was growing tired of Ito's pattern of outburst and retreat, a habit that reinforced the picture of an erratic, if not an egotistical jurist. "Saying, 'I may pull the plug on all TV coverage and then not doing it is just plain silly," said former Los Angeles County Superior Court Judge Jack Tenner. "Did anybody really believe he was going to pull the plug on the television camera? I don't think even he knows why he did that."

Simpson Economics

If television trials no longer seemed strange in the new world of American justice, neither did the pervasive exploitation of the case as a commodity to be bought and sold over the counter. The Simpson case had evolved from its station as a high-profile story to become a self-sustaining "economy." Even before the trial had ended, Simpson goods and services generated $2 billion, more than the gross domestic product of some *countries*.

Simpson himself quickly realized the value of his newfound infamy and went so far as to hire a law firm to fight bootleg T-shirt makers, trading-card manufacturers, and other entrepreneurs using his name and picture without permission. Soon after the Bronco chase, his lawyers filed applications to federally register the terms "O. J. Simpson," "O. J." and "The Juice" as trademarks. At the same time, 300 limited-edition football cards, signed and dated by Simpson from his jail cell, were being sold to the public for $850 each.

From his cell Simpson expanded his marketing empire, approving the sale of "limited edition" commemorative coins and bronze figures bearing his likeness. The 21-inch, 30-pound statuette depicting Simpson wearing his trademark No. 32 jersey sold for $3,395. A week after being introduced, more than a 1,000 statuettes were reportedly sold, some to investors as far away as Tokyo.

Two days after opening statements—a day the court was not in session—Simpson's book, *I Want to Tell You*, hit the market and was an immediate bestseller. Simpson deftly used about 100 of the 300,000 letters he received in his cell to deny his culpability in the murders. This may have marked the first time in American jurisprudence that a defendant commercially published his defense even before it was presented inside the courtroom. The book was another in a line of public relations ventures by his defense team. With the book, Simpson had the chance to sell his story to the public without the problem of being cross-examined, and earn a hefty $1 million advance at the same time. With 500,000 copies and 250,000 audio versions, Little, Brown and Company, the publishers, forecast more than $13 million in sales.

Simpson's money-making schemes were far-ranging. His prepaid phone cards came with an autographed "certificate of authenticity." For their money, card-users heard Simpson's voice, recorded in jail, extending an upbeat welcome that thanked them for their support by using "The Juice" line. Sports Communication Inc., which produced the phone card, expected Simpson's cards to bring in over $5 million.

Reports surfaced that Simpson was also negotiating a pay-per-view interview to take place after his murder trial, which could net him as much as $10 million. According to Dominick Dunne, in *Vanity Fair*, the pay-per-view ploy "would be similar to the handling of certain major sports events" in the way it would be marketed and sold. Simpson's attempt to sell the rights to his post-trial interview later failed, but it didn't stop him from finally hawking a videotape interview he helped to produce.

Writer John Gregory Dunne and other critics were appalled by the crass profiteering. "Shame seems not to have crossed the ken of anyone involved in this case," he said. Steven Brill refused to advertise Simpson-related products on his network. "The question is," he said, "do you want to be involved in the general coarsening of our society?"

But most media outlets showed little concern for such matters. Too much money was there to be made by all. "Murder mania" drove Simpson to the top of the magazine cover chart, as ranked by *Ad Age* in its monthly survey of 30 leading national publications. Book publishers also got into the act with mega-selling "instant books." Less than three weeks after Simpson was arrested, three Simpson books were released, all selling for $4.99.

Don Davis, the author of *Fallen Hero: The Shocking True Story Behind the O. J. Simpson Tragedy*, began working on his book three days after the double murders. Just a *week* later, he delivered a 50,000-word manuscript to St. Martin's Press. Globe Communications, which publishes the supermarket tabloids, the *Globe* and the *National Examiner,* also came out with *Juice: The O. J. Simpson Tragedy*. The writers, Larry Browne and Paul Francis, began working with the *Globe* editorial staff immediately the case broke. Two days later they finished the book. Among their "surprising new revelations," said a *Globe* press release, was that Simpson's father left his wife for a man, a traumatic event that was said to have scarred Simpson's psychological makeup. Browne contended that this was a "fascinating nugget which may shed light on the how and why of O. J."[15]

Other book publishers zealously joined the book marketing frenzy. Michael Viner and Deborah Raffin, owners of Dove Audio Inc., signed up four books before the trial had barely started. Viner found a blockbuster in Faye Resnick's salacious diary of Nicole Simpson, which sold about a million books and audio versions. Viner's marketing schemes irritated Ito, who was desperately trying to maintain control of media publicity. It was the controversial Resnick book that had earlier caused so much trouble for Ito during voir dire.

The judge also subpoenaed Viner to answer accusations that another of his books about dismissed juror Michael Knox had been far too revealing about the Simpson jury. Viner insisted he was performing a public service by publishing a book that "could end up changing the jury system in terms of sequestration." His rationale was, to say the least, perplexing. Indeed, it was Viner's media exploits, like the publication of Knox's book, that had made sequestration necessary in the first place.

Viner wasn't the only publisher reaping enormous profits in the name of a self-professed higher ethic. According to Clifford Linedecker, who published *Marcia Clark: Her Private Trials and Public Triumph*, "A lot of information you get from the O. J. books helps people understand the legal process, the investigative process and things like DNA testing." Author Marc Eliot, who received a six-figure advance from Harper Paperbacks for his Kato Kaelin book, gave a franker appraisal—the Simpson story was just too tantalizing for publishers to pass up. "There's lesbianism, other men, sex, drugs," he said. "It's got everything everyone wants, and it's real."

Bill Burns, the press agent for a Simpson biography called *Juice*, was the king of the "instant-books," paperbacks about high-profile crimes that are published, almost literally, overnight. Written within days after the murder, Burns said his book was "real lightning." Using information gleaned from the Internet, the book took 72 hours to produce. In an interview with *Dateline*, an exuberant Burns had few qualms about discussing his philosophy: "If you live in the media, you die in the media," he stated. Whether or not Simpson would be found responsible for the crime was beside the point—his purpose was to make "gazillions." "Either way," he said gleefully, "start it rolling."

For other more mainstream writers, the Simpson case also was a lightning rod that flashed across the publishing horizon. Even before the case came to trial, Joe McGinniss and Dominick Dunne had signed with Crown Publishers; Jeffrey Toobin with Random House. The book publishing industry was remarkably inventive in making money even before the first witness had taken the stand. As opening arguments ensued, *Raging Heart*, Sheila Weller's account of the Simpsons' marriage, immediately hit the bestseller list. The book was written with the cooperation of Nicole's sister Denise Brown.

The film industry was also gearing up for the Simpson story. Television trials were fertile feeding grounds for made-for-TV movies, and, in recent years, Hollywood had immortalized the likes of the Menendez brothers and Charles Manson. Amy Fisher, the 16-year-old "Long Island Lolita" who shot the wife of her lover continued to hold the prime-time record with three television movies airing *in a single week*.

As for the Simpson case, Hollywood would not wait: A film was produced for the Fox network even before Simpson was brought to trial. "The O. J. Simpson Story," was set to air on September 13, 1994, six days before the scheduled start of jury selection. Shapiro responded and appealed to the network executive's "common sense and principles of fair play" in urging postponement of the movie.

A caustic Howard Rosenberg chided Shapiro for "using words not in the vocabulary of Fox executives, who probably thought he was speaking a foreign language." Now, said Rosenberg, if Shapiro had appealed to their "principles of cynical opportunities" he might have gotten somewhere. After having its nose tweaked in public, Fox relented and postponed the movie. The network had in mind, anyway, a more opportune moment. The "O. J. Simpson Story" aired January 31, 1995, during the opening week of the trial.

The Simpson economy was a Ronald Reagan dreamworld, with money trickling down to street vendors selling "Don't Squeeze the Juice" T-shirts, and to local radio stations touting 900-numbers where listeners paid for the privilege of voicing their opinions about the case. Los Angeles tour operators were among the first to cash in on the murders, designating new routes that ran past the "homes of the stars"—the Simpson stars. One operator offered customers tours—in a 1971 silver Cadillac hearse—past Simpson's Rockingham estate, Nicole Simpson's condominium on Bundy, and the Brentwood restaurant Mezzaluna, where Nicole had her last meal and where Ron Goldman worked as a waiter. Since the murders, the restaurant had become the latest hot spot, with patrons willing to wait hours in line for a table.

The Simpson imprimatur could turn individuals into celebrities and goods into collectibles. The Simpson "trademark" could be found everywhere. A stretch Town Car that took Simpson to the airport the night of the murders, was offered at auction. And model Paula Barbieri, Simpson's latest girlfriend, used that connection to land a movie deal and a photospread in the October 1994 issue of *Playboy*.

The crass commercial exploitation of a trial involving two murder victims was another ugly statement about American values to have arisen out of the case. "Who isn't cashing in?" asked *Washington Post* writer Henry Allen. "In York, Pa., the Maple Donuts chain has covered a billboard with huge letters saying, 'FREE O.J.'—and underneath, in finer print revealing the 'orange juice' word play— 'when you buy a dozen donuts.'"[16]

For Allen, the Simpson case, and the culture it spawned, had reached the nadir of American greed:

> Meanwhile, sitting in the sky boxes, running the concessions, selling hot dogs to the crowd, are the lawyers, politicians, racism-mongers, white and black, opportunists of every variety. The rest of us watch while the wrestlers sweat and thunder. We watch, thanks to the biggest casher-in of all, the huge, dish-linked, lap-topped, ad-powered, fame-fueled, deadline-tooled media luring us so far into the myths, the dream, the beastliness, the spectacle, that we hardly notice the fact that we've become the spectacle ourselves.

10

EXPOSED

FEBRUARY-APRIL 1995

The Scene

Throngs of spectators pinned behind police lines waited each day for the defense lawyers to make their entrances into the courthouse. Robert Shapiro and Johnnie Cochran had become major stars, and the lawyers seemed to relish their celebrity roles. Both were chauffeured to the front entrance where their arrival set off an astonishing media onslaught. They treaded individually through a gauntlet of sound booms, microphones and hordes of reporters shouting questions. On occasion they deigned to take a fan's outstretched piece of paper and sign an autograph. For those present, there was an unreal feeling about the scene, as if they were taking part in a movie experience. Since very little genuine news was actually passed from lawyers to reporters, the scene itself *was* the news with reporters seemingly acting out their roles as loud, aggressive inquisitors.

The lawyers generally arrived by 8:55 a.m., and camera crews jockeyed for position to get the first pictures of the day. CNN lined up its crews on the bottom and top of the courthouse stairs and near the building's rear parking lot to cover all possible entryways to the courthouse (save the private underground lot reserved for the prosecutors). Following the morning photo shoot, a "runner" delivered the tape to a news producer stationed in a network van at nearby Camp OJ, who selected a quick sound bite to accompany the video pictures, before feeding the media package to CNN headquarters in Atlanta.

Other participants involved in the trial chose to exit from the rear parking lot, and they, too, were immediately mobbed by teams of reporters and camera and sound technician crews nicknamed the "gangbangers." Occasionally, a lawyer or expert witness stopped to answer media questions, but those who refused continued to be bombarded by a barrage of questions and jostled by camera crews, which made passage difficult. There was little pretense about manners. Said one camera operator, "They could make it hard for themselves or easy."

Not every trial member relished the scene as it played out each day. Barry Scheck complained that the defense lawyers were not given the same perks as prosecutors who parked their cars in the building's underground lot, and away from the madding crowd. Scheck was forced to park his car in the outdoor lot, and there he was confronted *en masse* by the gangbangers. "Even in the parking lot we were surrounded," he said. "They'd say, 'What do you have to say to us today?' And I'd say, 'What I want to say today is, I want to get from my car to that courtroom without talking to you.'"[1]

The scene on the courthouse steps was replayed in reverse as the principal defense lawyers left the building after the day's proceedings. Typically, Cochran and Shapiro stepped onto the top stairs at separate times, each taking his own theatrical turn before an eager media contingent. "Fans" also joined the crush around the court building. One woman strewed long-stem roses on a rug she laid at Cochran's feet as he walked by. Others shouted "Johnnie, Johnnie," with the adulation usually given to a rock star. Some onlookers were merely curious; others were "the lunatics." As *Newsday's* Shirley Perlman noted, the latter were those "who didn't take their medication that day." Some carried boom boxes turned to maximum volume; others drove oversized tricycles; some came dressed in bizarre party costumes; still others had messages from God. The "Grim Reaper" carried a sign proclaiming, "Meat eaters are all potential murderers."

Expressiveness turned to performance art, and the streets in downtown Los Angeles took on the sounds and sights of carnival time. Nothing in Perlman's long experience covering trials matched this scene as L.A. law met L.A. counterculture. Perlman encountered one woman, dressed like an angel with wings and bright Kelly green hair, who struck up a conversation with her. The reporter, whose white hair lends dignity to her professional demeanor, said the angel suggested that "the aquamarine would look great on me and she told me where to go get it done."

The show found its way to Judge Lance Ito's courtroom as street people managed to find some of the precious few passes to the gallery. Perlman recounted:

> This one guy showed up dressed like a clown. He had soiled his pants, nobody wanted to sit next to him. But he gets into the courtroom wearing a black boot, a white boot, two sports jackets, red pants—an outrageous get-up. A few days later he shows up again. I recognized him because I saw the same black boot-white boot, but this time he was dressed as a woman in a wig and a pink sweater stuffed with grapefruits or God knows what. We [reporters] can't get into the courtroom, but that person, of course, could. He got in and sat down and then the person next to him sat on his skirt. He got so angry he took his pocketbook and whammed him with it. Ito saw it and ejected him from the courtroom.[2]

Ito: "Child" of the Television Age

Judge Lance Ito continued to be an object of criticism among at least some reporters. Although generally seen as a well-intentioned and "decent" human being, his critics—and they would grow during the trial— believed he had made serious mistakes in running the courtroom. The trial was moving ahead far too slowly, largely because the judge failed to limit the lawyers' arguments, examinations of witnesses, and legal motions argued before the court. Ito was also accused of running a sloppy courtroom that often started late and had extended recesses. By the time a "tougher" Ito emerged, the trial was already crumbling.

Ito's downfall, said critics, was that he sought the press's recognition and, even, affection—desires that proved to be a serious flaw. The judge "very desperately wanted to be liked by the press" and tried to ingratiate himself with the Simpson press corps, said Jeffrey Toobin. "And I think reporters, as much as they like being stroked, also recognized that it was inappropriate, and Ito paid the price for it." The judge lacked "gravitas," contended Toobin—he "lacked the ability to say, 'Look, I'm going to do my job, and I don't care what anybody's going to say.'"

Toobin contended that Ito failed to understand how reporters "think"—journalists are essentially "children" in that "they only understand discipline." The writer referred to his own experience as a federal prosecutor in the 1989 Oliver North trial, and said that the person who routinely received the most positive press was North's lawyer, Brendan Sullivan. "He never gave an interview, he never held a press conference, never appeared to give a damn what was written about him and the case. He only cared about the judge and the jury. The press loved him."[3]

Reporters agreed that Ito worried too much about what they said and wrote. At home the judge reportedly watched three television sets at a time and read as many as five newspapers a day. Critics complained that his demeanor often reflected the media spins of the day. When stories were printed or aired criticizing him for letting the case drag on, the judge immediately responded by discouraging sidebars and long-winded witness examinations, or, at one point, lengthening the court day. After Ito found his picture on the cover of *Newsweek* next to a cover line, "What a Mess," he struck back, throwing two reporters out of the court permanently for talking in their seats.

Ito's mistake was that he believed the media were more important than he should have, maintained Bill Boyarsky, the *Los Angeles Times* columnist. "He was just a child of the television age. He didn't have a broad enough experience to put this in any kind of perspective." Ito was like many TV watchers "transfixed by the media thing," said Boyarsky. "He liked the limelight but I don't think that was it. He just paid too much attention to us. He got himself involved in where people would sit, all the details of press management, the pressroom. He micromanaged the press, and he didn't do that to increase his own publicity. He did that because he believed too much in the power of television."[4]

The Talkers

Throughout the trial, each participant kept one eye on the courtroom and the other on the press. Even those who purposely avoided speaking with reporters could not escape the news reports, commentary, and tabloid gossip that shadowed them. Darden was contemptuous of legal "experts" who were no better than "armchair quarterbacks—book lawyers—who'd spent no more than a few hours in the courtroom themselves, if that much." Still, Darden himself also watched and was sensitive to the daily gossip.

Cochran found it necessary, as well, to knock down media speculation that often seemed to take on a life of its own. When the *National Enquirer* reported that a plea-bargain agreement was being negotiated calling for Simpson to serve a seven-year prison sentence, Cochran immediately took issue in court. "This is a case where there is no plea bargain, will be no plea bargain," he said, "and I thought I should make the record clear in that regard." His statement had no relevance for the court, and, indeed, what Cochran was "making clear" was the public record. While appearing as if he was speaking to Ito, Cochran's intention was in reaching the media and the public at large. And he did so with the camera as his conduit to a national audience.

All trial participants had to live with the reality that television's newest celebrity—the legal pundit—was constantly gabbing about them. These lawyers-turned-pundits now commanded the ultimate platform—television—and they took advantage of the opportunity by offering up their pithy analyses. Gerry Spence, a Wyoming lawyer who defended Imelda Marcos, was better known to TV audiences as a folksy, straight-talker who looked like Davy Crockett in his fringed buckskin jacket, jeans, and long, shaggy gray hair. His legal pronouncements on NBC, CNBC, and CNN were pointed, and he made no pretense about tempering his remarks or judgments, even if it meant publicly prejudging Simpson. On a Geraldo Rivera panel, Spence pondered whether the jury would buy into the defense's conspiracy theory. "If you're O. J. Simpson, and your glove is there, and it's got blood on it, I mean, what are you going to do? You going to say, 'Well the dog dragged it in'? Or are you going to say, 'The tooth fairy dropped it?'"

Other legal analysts tended to be more circumspect. NBC's senior legal correspondent Jack Ford was both a prosecutor and defense lawyer before being hired by Court TV and then NBC. Ford shied away from being the "consummate armchair quarterback" and criticized commentators who anointed daily winners and losers. He was wary that the new trends in legal journalism mimicked the very worst trends of modern-day political reporting—a type of facile journalism that sought to create drama by turning serious public discussion into a type of sports-talk chatter.

Ford's fears were justified. Simpson commentators at various times compared the trial to boxing, dart-throwing, football, bull-fighting, and mud-wrestling. Lawyers scored points, were knocked down, or failed to connect for a knockout. One day they were ahead, and the next they were behind. Viewers listening to CNN's Martha Smilgis's preview of F. Lee Bailey's continuing cross-examination of Mark Fuhrman must surely have been confused about which arena they were actually in. Comparing the defense lawyer's strategy to a "pit bull attack," she concluded: "I don't think he is doing as well as we expected. Bailey's running around, he's throwing out a lot of verbal darts, but Fuhrman's got a little sense of humor there, and he's coming across very well. So I think Bailey is down a few points and Fuhrman is up a few points as we start today."[5]

The sports analogy was a trite device to keep viewers anxious to stay tuned to the next Simpson episode. Defense team lawyer Gerald Uelmen charged that the very choice of analogy reflected the analyst's personal bias. Pundits awarded the defense a "touchdown" or "a 20-yard loss" depending on their sway for or against the defense team, he said. Some news outlets chose variations on the theme, as did *Newsweek,* which published its weekly "Trial Scorecard." Participants were awarded one to four gavels based on how effective the magazine judged their performance.

It was this very type of oversimplification that Simpson's defense lawyers said they worried about. The medium forced commentators to report instantly but without a keen sense of the broader scope of the trial. "Lawyers have to put on witnesses to prove one piece of evidence that will connect to another two or three weeks later," explained Barry Scheck. "So it's very hard to have [this type] of instant analysis. Yet the coverage is at a point where the pundits are asked every day who had a good day, a bad day."[6]

Scheck said such immediate pseudo-commentary skewed viewers' perceptions about Simpson's defense. Most could not see past the overwhelming media coverage already given to the prosecution's case beginning with Simpson's arrest—the coverage fostered a presumption of guilt that carried throughout the trial. By the time the defense team had the chance to respond to the state's charges seven months into the trial, Scheck contended that viewers had already made up their minds regarding Simpson's role in the murders. Few were receptive to the defense arguments or the possibility that "reasonable doubt" existed. Most of the country by then was implacably resistant to Simpson's side, despite the fact, argued Scheck, that Simpson's lawyers "put up a hell of a defense."

The role of the legal pundits was controversial. Their job was not actually to report *what* happened, since viewers could watch the trial's developments for themselves. Their job was to analyze *why* something happened, and what it meant. Though some experts were highly regarded, many others were accused of even failing to keep track of the day's proceedings. Toobin, a regular on the media talk-show circuit, said it was clear that "easily more than half of the [commentators] flat out didn't watch. I was appalled that they did not know what was going on, and they were gassing on."

The trial attorneys also were often flabbergasted by the incompetent level of commentary. "All the lawyers in this case will tell you," said Scheck, "that we would turn on the set every day and were stunned because we knew all these [pundits] commenting about us had not watched the full day of trial, or they hadn't watched the last three weeks that led up to this important point. We couldn't believe it."

Uelmen said he soon became aware that the pundits were relying on a 10-minute "briefing" on the day's proceedings just before going on the air. Occasionally he watched the evening talk shows and "found it hard to believe that these were intelligent adults speaking." The view from the television screen was far different from his table in Department 103.

"I will never forget the day I argued a motion regarding the scope of cross-examination of the coroner," he said. Uelmen explained that the prosecution had filed a motion to prohibit the defense team from cross-examining Dr. Irwin Golden about mistakes he had made in previous autopsies, and also about an incident in which he purportedly brandished a gun and made threats against Simpson's lawyers during the preliminary hearing. Ito ruled that Golden's mistakes could be cross-examined but the threats could not. The point became moot when the prosecution failed to call Dr. Golden at trial.

"That evening, I watched Gerry Spence pontificating on [*Rivera Live*]," recounted Uelmen. "He took the defense to task for making a motion first. [He said the defense] should just get up and ask the questions without seeking the judge's permission first. Obviously he never looked at any of the papers filed in the case, or he would have known that the defense did not even file a motion; we were responding to a motion filed by the prosecution to *prevent* us from asking questions they anticipated. Apparently, he had not watched the argument."[7]

Scheck said that the commentators' emphasis on "spin"—"the inside baseball, the strategy, what must be going on in the councils of the defense and the prosecution"—disguised their lack of preparation. "They weren't prepared," he said. "They couldn't discuss the facts well enough, they couldn't discuss the substance of complex testimony, particularly in scientific areas. You didn't have commentators saying 'I don't know.' If they kept on saying that they wouldn't be on the air."

In the final analysis, though, it was the medium itself that was hostile to the justice process. Trials are slow and often tedious when a complex line of argument is developed by both sides over a long period of time. But the medium is impatient, demanding instant judgments and emphasizing "drama" over complex legal matters that may simply fail to make for "good" TV. The pundits did television's bidding, highlighting those moments that were visually arresting or confrontational. But in the end, Scheck argued, viewers were cheated out of a "true" picture of the Simpson trial. "[The pundits] were more interested in [the lawyers] arguing with each other, the ways lawyers do, you know, or the judge yelling at us," rather than the most significant legal point of that day, he said. "They were more interested in Marcia's hair."

There were ethical problems as well for networks hiring "celebrity lawyers." Although these experts were obligated to provide trial analysis, they indirectly acted out of their own self-interests. ABC's main expert, Leslie Abramson, also represented Erik Menendez, who was about to face a second trial for murdering his parents. Abramson was not an independent "legal eagle," but a lawyer who clearly had a vested interest in portraying the LAPD as, at the least, unprofessional. It was the very same police department that would play an important role in the upcoming Menendez trial. Critics believed that Abramson had an ax to grind with the LAPD, and was grinding it. "She is unrelenting in denouncing the LAPD for inept work," said Stephen Seplow, a reporter for the *Philadelphia Inquirer*. "At least once, she said the prosecution's tactics raised questions about whether they really wanted to win."

Her steady appearance on *Nightline* gave her the added credibility of a highly respected news organization, one that reached into the homes of the next Menendez jury. By portraying the Simpson prosecution as incompetent and in denouncing the LAPD, Abramson was in the enviable position to help her client and increase her own clout in future trials.

But few critics questioned the networks for giving their lawyer-experts the opportunity to sell their platforms, win new clients, and influence future jury panels. Ironically, one critic was Abramson herself, who admitted she was not a fan of the courtroom camera; nor did she like legal pundits. "All of us should get off the tube," she told her *Nightline* audience, adding, "I've always been against television in the courtroom. And I still am."

That sentiment was a likely carryover from her experience at the first Menendez trial a year earlier. She had condemned the media frenzy surrounding the case, postulating that the U.S. criminal justice system would be better off following the British system with its strict rules limiting trial coverage. That sentiment was more dramatically captured in a *Vanity Fair* photograph of Abramson thrusting her middle finger at an NBC cameraman. In a BBC documentary produced after the first Menendez case, she said: "[The press] selects the people to discuss these cases who have a particular point of view. And they are in my opinion corrupting the jury system."[8]

Now Abramson found herself on the other side. She continued to give lip service to the idea that pundits, and the media at large, were contaminating the legal process in high-profile cases like Menendez and Simpson. But she apparently had few qualms about sacrificing her principles for the chance to join the show. Whatever her personal philosophy, the defense lawyer was shrewd enough to understand the benefits of television exposure. The medium that had "discovered" Abramson as a hard-hitting and often mesmerizing courtroom presence during the telecasting of the Menendez trial, now promoted her as a celebrity lawyer. The several thousand dollars a day she earned for her TV commentary was relatively small change compared with other media opportunities that would come her way. Even before the Simpson trial was over, Abramson, as one of the hottest legal personalities on television, was negotiating a TV series and had in hand a lucrative book deal.

Curiously, as her celebrity star rose, her reputation as a legal advocate declined. During the penalty phase of the second Menendez trial, she was accused in open court of convincing an expert witness to alter his notes and eliminate material prejudicial to her client, a criminal violation of court rules. The revelation left open the possibility that Abramson might be disbarred, although the issue remained pending more than a year after the Menendez verdict. According to her foremost critic, Dominick Dunne, Abramson's over-the-top adversarial act and legal tricks had "finally caught up to her."[9]

The Delicate Balance

Through television, the trial reached deeply into the culture and with often strange consequences. According to Court TV senior anchor Fred Graham, some people who sent flowers to the Simpson courtroom did so "because they wanted to see their flowers in the courtroom on TV."

The camera, however, did more than broadcast pictures. It changed the very delicate balance between the media and the courts. Each day as trial images were sent to millions of television screens, scores of TV correspondents and pundits searched for new ways to tell and sell the Simpson story. Print journalists as well were compelled to compete with television. The *Los Angeles Times* originated new columns, called "The Spin" and "The Legal Pad," to buttress its more straight news reports.

Henry Weinstein, the paper's legal analyst, found his job almost entirely recast around the case. In 1995, of the 154 stories he wrote, 126 were about Simpson—82 percent of his entire workload for the year—and more than two-thirds made the front page. No other topic in his 26-year-career had so dominated his work. "There are subjects I have covered rather regularly off and on for years, stories about farm workers, asbestos litigation," he said. "I'll bet I haven't written 126 stories on asbestos litigation in all of the 20 or so years that I've been covering it."

Much of the analysis, the commentary, the investigative reports, and even the gossip filtered back into the courtroom. Court TV appeared stunned at this near-instantaneous connection between media coverage and the courtroom. Gregg Jarrett, the network's co-anchor, recalled a Court TV report about defense witness Rosa Lopez that after being aired was immediately brought before the bench and scrutinized. "Within 45 minutes, that report was being played in front of Judge Lance Ito," he said. "So we know that they are watching these things very closely."

Rita Ciolli, a media critic for *Newsday*, said that she had never before seen a daily package of stories in which witness testimony was first reported and then chewed up in the media grind. "You now have outside people, interested people on both sides, discrediting a witness's testimony, or the press independently saying he's lying, it can't be true," she said.[10]

Graham explained that the media's daily pressure to "move the story forward" had the Simpson courtroom on the defensive, looking over its shoulder waiting for the next revelation. "There is a kind of reciprocal dynamic going on in the O. J. Simpson case," he said, "in which things happen during the day [in court] and then later in the day the very aggressive TV news programs go out and move the story or the trial forward. And then the next day it is reflected in court and on and on. . . . I'm not sure if this is a very healthy thing for the judicial process."

The Arena

As the media drove the Simpson story forward, the case inevitably entered into a minefield of social and political agendas. Celebrity trials of the past resonate because of their links to sympathetic issues of the time. Never, though, had one ongoing trial apparently meant so much to so many people. No longer merely a murder trial, the case entered an electrified social arena, and by its end, few in the country could distance themselves with a "no opinion" on such a hotly disputed national "issue" as Simpson.

The trial soon became a political touchstone with principal witnesses, wittingly or not, assuming a role far greater than that required by the courtroom. For some, their immediate media access gave them a forum for espousing their agenda. For others, the media—most notably television—was an invasive intruder that forcefully cast them in political roles.

Denise Brown, Mark Fuhrman, and Kato Kaelin were among the most high-profile witnesses, whose public personas transcended their roles in the courtroom. With their televised images constantly bombarding the public consciousness, they had become so much larger than their ordinary lives. More than simply momentary celebrities, they became symbols of the larger social and political milieu of Los Angeles, if not the nation.

One of the most outspoken prosecution witnesses was Denise Brown, who took up the cause of battered women after her sister was murdered. She used television to promote her agenda, and also to indict Simpson, telling Geraldo Rivera that "O. J. did it. He murdered my sister." On the witness stand, Brown tearfully told jurors how Simpson publicly humiliated and brutalized Nicole. She told of a drunken Simpson who once grabbed her sister's crotch in a crowded bar, bragging, "This belongs to me." On another occasion he smashed Nicole against a wall and threw her out of his house. During a dance recital for the Simpsons' daughter, Brown said that Simpson had "a very bizarre look in his eye—it was a very faraway look." Later that night her sister was viciously stabbed to death.

Brown's uncanny resemblance to her sister gave her testimony a haunting quality. She was the surrogate voice and face of her dead sister. On the stand Brown wore black, with a large cross hung on her neck, and golden angel earrings and pin. In the gallery, her mother and sisters also wore the pins. When Clark pinned an angel on her own suit lapel in open solidarity with the Brown family, the defense complained, well aware of the poignant symbolism. Ito ordered Clark to remove the pin.

The pundits focused on the "sincerity" issue following Brown's testimony, which had seemingly left her emotionally wrought. Some questioned whether her tearful episodes on the stand were genuine or contrived for the jury. With her testimony interrupted by the weekend, TV pundits were left to relentlessly speculate for two days how the jury would interpret her performance. Despite the fact that the trial still had another eight months to go, with more than 120 witnesses and 1,000 pieces of evidence left to consider, the legal experts were already calling Brown's testimony a defining moment for the prosecution's case.

The Bailey-Fuhrman Showdown

By the time Mark Fuhrman took the stand in March he had been vilified as the second-coming of the Rodney King cops. He was the LAPD cop to give "a face" to racist cops everywhere.

Among the Simpson press corps, few reporters dared to challenge the Fuhrman racist stereotype that the defense tried to paint. *Time* magazine writer James Willwerth, however, was one who presented a more complex picture. "Many people who knew Fuhrman, including African-American friends, a black former reporter, and black crime victims he has helped, insisted he is not, and never was, a racist." Fuhrman was "a foul-mouthed street cop, a nasty anti-gang cop who didn't like the people he was dealing with," but, said Willwerth, "his prejudices were class, not race." The detective was "very, very, very angry" at the black and Hispanic criminal class within Los Angeles gangs. His work on the gang detail had taken its toll and "nearly made him snap." He finally went to a psychiatrist "to straighten out his act."

Willwerth maintained that defending Fuhrman was the one Simpson story the media refused to consider. Even his own editors at *Time* had been reluctant to publish his story. "It was information that ran against the grain of public sentiment," he said. "We're all looking around for a nasty racist to pillory. . . particularly in Los Angeles with the police force that beat up Rodney King."[11]

But standing up for Fuhrman was a risky business and Willwerth paid the price. Only later, after the infamous Fuhrman audiotapes surfaced, did the reporter realize he had made "a terrible mistake" for failing to be more skeptical of the detective. Willwerth's instincts to be "fair" to Fuhrman had betrayed him after hearing the detective's racist meanderings. Admittedly, he had been burned for placing too much trust in sources, who had painted a much more positive picture of the controversial detective. "Even when your sources are absolutely convinced they're right," he said, "they may be wrong."

No other confrontation was more hyped by the media than F. Lee Bailey's cross-examination of Mark Fuhrman. As one of the first detectives at the crime scene, Fuhrman was targeted by the defense as a rogue cop who was out to "get" Simpson. Bailey all but promised the media that he would prove that Fuhrman framed his client.

Charlie Rose on his nightly PBS show declared that this was "the moment many people had been waiting for." Gerald Lefcourt, a CBS legal commentator, chimed in, reporting that Bailey was "champing at the bit" to get a piece of Fuhrman. "He's lying in wait. He knows exactly where he's going. He knows exactly the vulnerabilities this witness has."

Bailey was not shy about self-promotion and repeatedly vowed to dismantle Fuhrman's testimony. He had earlier boasted: "If ever there was a case where an 1,800-pound marlin was hooked, gaffed and in the boat, this is such a case."[12]

The "showdown" was akin to a "a heavyweight fight," promoted by Bailey, said *Newsday*'s Shirley Perlman. "Bailey was lethal and he can be very foreboding. He said he was going to tear Fuhrman apart. And people were looking for a knock-down, drag-out fight."

The media highlight of the three-day cross-examination came when Bailey grilled Fuhrman on his use of the racial slur "nigger," and then, having failed to shake the detective, promised to deliver a witness named Max Cordoba to discredit him. "I have spoken with [Cordoba] on the phone personally, Marine to Marine," Bailey intoned in his best theatrical inflection, "and I don't have the slightest doubt that he will march up to the witness stand and tell the world what Fuhrman called him."

In a plot development audacious enough to make even a veteran Hollywood screenwriter blush, Cordoba could be seen that very evening on NBC's *Dateline,* declaring that he had *never* spoken to Bailey. (Modifying his viewpoint on the next *Dateline*, he said he suddenly recalled such a conversation with Bailey—his memory had been jogged in a dream.) The following day, the prosecution's reaction was swift and furious. With open disdain, Clark accused Bailey of being an outright liar, and when the famed defense lawyer tried to protest, she told him, in essence, to sit down and shut up. The moment for millions of TV viewers was pure *LA Law*.

The Clark-Bailey contretemps evolved into farce as Bailey dramatically displayed a men's leather glove stuffed inside a plastic bag. Without the jury present, Bailey said that "Marines tend to carry things in their socks," suggesting that Fuhrman smuggled the bloody glove by storing it in the plastic bag, hiding the bag in his sock, and then planting the glove in Simpson's yard. The experiment did not go over well. Ito barred Bailey from showing his "evidence" after Clark pointed out that the real glove, a size extra-large, was different from the sealed glove. "Size small," the prosecutor snidely remarked, as she examined the glove in question. "I guess it's Mr. Bailey's."

Such bickering, a constant during the trial, had already begun to wear thin. Court TV, the standard-bearer for this new genre of television programming, found the legal antics hard to believe. An exasperated Gregg Jarrett remarked: "It makes you wonder what's going on here."

The bloody glove episode led to bizarre bursts of talk-show chatter that propelled the sports-drone commentaries to a new level of macho locker-room bluster. Clark's snide retort was thrust into the late night TV banter, spawning dialogue that was vaguely a cross between Sigmund Freud and Lenny Bruce. That night on CNN's combative *Crossfire,* legal expert Barry Tarlow was incensed about Clark's venomous attack. "We heard Marcia Clark making jokes about the size of F. Lee Bailey's penis," he said angrily. "If it was in a bar, Lee Bailey might think that's funny, but in a courtroom, in a murder case? This is disgraceful and it's appalling."

In case Tarlow had become too analytical for a TV audience, Roy Black, on screen from Miami, interrupted to offer his rejoinder: "What? I missed a colloquy on a penis?"

"Come on, Roy, I don't think you have to be too swift to pick up on that," chided Tarlow. "When I was young, condoms were referred to as gloves, and I think it's an obvious sexual reference to the size of his penis."

John Sununu, one of the program's moderators, accused the duo of having "a one-track mind" and changed the subject to racism.

Had Bailey been wiser, he might have told reporters that he planned to use the Fuhrman cross-examination as the legal foundation for questioning other witnesses concerning the detective's veracity. Instead, he bragged about going after Fuhrman on the stand, virtually inviting the pundits to treat his "battle" with the detective as a war game. And they did, but it was not what Bailey had expected. The pundits ridiculed Bailey's *mano a mano* challenge to Fuhrman, belittling the defense lawyer's skills and caustically suggesting that he was, essentially, washed up. The media typically sides with winners and, for this day, Bailey had the look of a loser. That characterization, however, would take a dramatic turn five months later after the disclosure of audiotapes made by Fuhrman and a screenwriter. Then, Bailey's cross-examination would be called "foresighted" and "brilliant."

But at this point, two months into the trial, Bailey's major mistake was his failure to "break" Fuhrman on the stand—to reveal the detective as the racist and bad cop he had characterized from the start. Having pumped the public to expect a Perry Mason-like cross-examination, the media were not in a forgiving mood when Bailey's performance failed to live up to the hype. Neither was his co-counsel, Robert Shapiro. Shapiro shrewdly saw this as a chance to take the moral high ground and get a measure of revenge against Bailey, who earlier had tried to backstab him. Shapiro told reporters that he "regretted" that the race card—so aggressively played by Bailey—had become so central to the case. Shapiro had failed to mention that it was he who was responsible for engineering the race defense from the start.

By the third day of Bailey's cross-examination, the media were openly contemptuous of the lawyer's courtroom tactics. Commentary was more akin to theater "reviews" than analysis, and, clearly, the famed attorney had flopped. *New York Times* reporter David Margolick concluded: "Mr. Bailey's theatricality and bombast seemed silly at times, the kind of shtick that may have worked well when lawyers still wore flowers in their boutonnieres but no longer."[13]

Columnist Frank Rich cut even deeper: "Mr. Bailey all but exulted in bellowing out the word ["nigger"] for a national TV audience, as if he were looking forward to capping what seems to be a waning legal career by playing the role of Bull Connor in a prequel to *Mississippi Burning.*"[14]

For Dominick Dunne, an outspoken critic of the defense, Bailey's performance was a cynical attempt to move the mostly black jury away from the overwhelming evidence against his client. "When F. Lee Bailey said the word 'nigger' nine times, he knew that was like a stab wound in that jury every time he said it. Yet he was saying it as if he was the voice of right and justice. I later saw it from a legal point of view, and it was brilliant."[15]

Kenneth Noble, a black reporter for the *New York Times*, also contended that Bailey's strategy to infuse his questions with the word "nigger" was a calculated ploy to "elicit an intensely emotional and unforgiving response from the predominantly black jury." "The word 'nigger' occupies a place in the soul where logic and reason never go," he said. And then Noble issued a warning, which would echo well after a decision was reached in the trial: "The danger in the Simpson case is that by cynically playing the race card, the defense may unleash emotions not only inside the courtroom, but well beyond." Should Simpson be found innocent, "there will always be a flicker of doubt as to whether the mostly black jury was swayed more by the weight of America's racial history than the voluminous evidence laid before it."[16]

Bailey was hardly unaware of the storm surrounding his performance and sought to control the damage to his reputation, and to the case. From Department 103, he went immediately to the media. He told reporters that he had gotten "very good vibes" from the jury, and that Simpson was "extremely pleased," believing that the jury did not buy Fuhrman's story. There were also positive messages from well-wishers who had called him. "Norman Mailer said it was flawless," he said, "so I feel good."

That evening he took to the airwaves. With ABC-TV's Cynthia McFadden, he charged that amateur legal analysts had misjudged the cross-examination and that his performance had actually gone quite well. Bailey was not the only Dream Team member on television that evening. On CNN's *Larry King Live*, Alan Dershowitz tried to sell the defense line that police corruption was endemic across the country—that cops throughout the country were trained to lie in court. Fuhrman was just the latest example.

The defense team's public relations move to refocus the media's perception of a failed cross-examination was transparent. Still, many reporters suspected that the Fuhrman story was not over. "The first time he took the stand he seemed believable, but every [reporter] knew that lurking in the background was Fuhrman's racism," said Court TV's Dan Abrams. And, in fact, the defense team later got very lucky. Stunning new evidence eventually materialized sealing the fate of Mark Fuhrman, and of O. J. Simpson.

Kato

Some witnesses recoiled in the spotlight and were extremely apprehensive about taking the stand. "We had witnesses who were afraid to testify, who were afraid of what it would do to their reputations," acknowledged Uelmen. Televising the proceedings carried this dangerous potential. Still, at this stage few could predict just how many lives would be seriously changed by the time the trial was over.

Other participants, however, reveled in the trial's notoriety. They saw the case as a chance to sell themselves to a media industry all too willing to embrace them. Brian "Kato" Kaelin, in particular, was an instant "star." When Uelmen said that certain witnesses "treated their testimony like a gig," undoubtedly Kaelin was on his mind as someone who played to television's command as a shaggy-haired, boyish, and irrepressible spirit.

Kaelin's newfound fame was very much a scripted Hollywood cliché. Having spent most of his adult life meandering around the L.A. scene as an unsuccessful actor, and, most recently, as a houseguest of Simpson's, Kaelin found himself "discovered," his life now grist for the media's gossip mill. Kato sightings were now being counted and reported at high-powered political dinners and Beverly Hill parties. As the penultimate "celebrity witness" he had become the latest, peculiar fascination in American pop culture.

Kaelin himself was astonished by the media reaction. But with his telegenic, surfer-boy looks and stumbling, good-humored nature, he fit well into the television world. Ironically, casting Kaelin as a sort of innocent caught up in a gruesome murder scenario, belied the man's media savviness. A would-be actor whose film credit consisted of a soft-core porno film called *Beach Fever,* Kaelin saw the Simpson trial as an extraordinary opportunity to enhance his career. He told a writer: "I'm an actor. Shouldn't I be allowed to pursue my career? I'm going to make a career for myself that's going to last longer than 15 minutes. Wait and see."[17]

Although called to the stand for the prosecution, Marcia Clark branded Kaelin as a hostile witness for his "selective memory" in recalling his relationship with O. J. and Nicole Simpson and the events surrounding the day of the murders. A parallel media world also "tried" Kaelin. When Kaelin told the court that he was not working on a book about his role in the case, a writer, Marc Eliot, went on television to tell the country that Kaelin was a liar.

According to Eliot, Kaelin had collaborated with him on a book during the previous six months, sitting for 16 hours of taped interviews. Unhappy with the final draft, though, Kaelin pulled out of the deal in the final stages. His noncooperation failed to deter Eliot, who wrote his Kato book anyway. In this version, he pointed out the "inconsistencies" between what the "star witness" told him and what he testified to in court. Eliot traveled the media talk-show route, promoting his book and selling Kaelin as a perjurer.

Still, whatever his shortcomings as a witness, Kaelin was ensured salvation as a bona fide media darling. His visage was ubiquitous in magazines like *Entertainment Weekly*, *GQ*, *People*, and the *New Yorker*, and a cable TV program called *Duck Soup*. He was also the hot topic among the newsmagazines. NBC's *Dateline* ran one segment called "The Kato Phenomenon"; Barbara Walters' segment on *20/20* was simply entitled "Kato Kaelin." Walters thought so much of Kaelin that she invited him back for a live interview in October as the Simpson verdict was being handed down. There was little question that America's "most famous houseguest" had found a niche within the popular culture. Indeed, he was afforded an honor given to just a few select stars. Like Madonna and Cher, Brian Kaelin had arrived. He was simply Kato.

Still, by the time Kaelin's five-day testimony ended, the Kato phenomenon was beginning to falter. His stumbling innocence had lost its precocity, replaced by the common perception that he was a mere opportunist. In a Los Angeles culture accustomed to this "type" of hanger-on, said Dominick Dunne, Kaelin was the quintessential example of someone looking for fame, though not too strenuously, latching on to those who are famous. Only through Simpson and the magnified attention to his trial could Kaelin squeeze inside this elite, celebrity world. Kaelin was the very type of unscrupulous celebrity-climber, Dunne said, that inspired Hollywood films, like *All About Eve*. Kaelin was "Eve Harrington in grunge."[18]

Footnote: Blank Screens and Pages

The Simpson trial did not stop the nation's criminal justice system—it only *seemed* as though it was the only case being tried in America. There was little question that other ongoing trials had social and legal significance far greater than Simpson's. The trial of foreign terrorists responsible for murder and mayhem in the bombing of New York City's World Trade Center had enormous implications for the nation. But out of the reach of television, it could not budge Simpson from the media's grip.

Even the bombing of a federal building in Oklahoma City, midway through the trial, was just a temporary distraction. When the story broke, CNN spokesman David Talley announced that the bombing "certainly supersedes" the Simpson case. And when the network turned to continuous coverage of Oklahoma City, for many people it seemed as if the Simpson trial had suddenly disappeared, which without television, in effect, it had. The images from the courtroom were so much a part of the everyday consciousness that viewers felt a palpable disorientation as CNN moved elsewhere. By the following week, though, even the horrific tragedy at Oklahoma City, with 168 dead and hundreds wounded and its ties to domestic terrorism, could not compete with the proceedings in Los Angeles. The Simpson story returned to the airwaves with as much zeal as it had before the bombing in Oklahoma City.

Certainly not all news outlets welcomed back the Simpson story, and in a few instances, an occasional protest was turned into action. The *Times-Georgian* newspaper, with its 11,600 circulation, proclaimed in a front-page editorial headline, "No More O. J.," next to a photograph of Simpson with an X scrawled through his face. The editorial was a declaration of journalistic independence. Publisher Pat Cavanaugh announced that his paper would be free of Simpson stories until the end of the trial. "Never in my career have I witnessed such a farce and such buffoonery in any news media as in the trial coming from California," he said. "We choose to refrain from running the inane absurdities of the O. J. soap opera until the Fat Lady sings. In other words, we are going to tough it out, go cold turkey, and 'Just Say No!' until the trial is over."[19]

11

HOUSE OF MIRRORS

FEBRUARY-MAY 1995

This Trial of the Century had already leaped far beyond the boundaries of a mere media circus. It was an event, one columnist described, that had "hijacked" American culture.[1] Virtually all types of media consumption not related to the trial were victims of the "Simpson effect," as Americans, absorbed in Simpson coverage, pushed aside other sources of news and entertainment. A dramatic drop in newspaper readership and TV news viewing was blamed on the trial. Book sales also shriveled, and non-Simpson-related TV ratings plummeted.

Other high-profile *legal* disputes withered from headline news in the torrent of ink and air-time given to Simpson. Not even the travails of other celebrities could compete. As the Simpson trial geared up, the pandering trial of the so-called Hollywood madam Heidi Fleiss drew to a close down the hallway from Ito's courtroom. At one time, the Fleiss case was the talk of the town—if not the nation—with sex-driven stories about high-priced call girls dallying with some of the film industry's most illustrious stars. During the early days of the Simpson case, Heidi Fleiss hardly had her picture taken.

But the Simpson fascination was not confined to national borders. The trial quickly became a leading American export, and the rest of the world tuned in through international CNN, the London-based Reuters news service, and other worldwide news outlets.

Media organizations from more than a dozen foreign countries sent reporters to the trial, giving the Los Angeles courthouse the appearance of an international conference. Simpson news was broadcast live in Britain, bannered across the front pages of Israeli newspapers, and debated at dinner tables in Iman and Beirut. Eugene Roberts, the managing editor of the *New York Times*, said that during his trip to Asia he found "people who don't even understand the [English] language were watching [the trial] on TV and having it explained to them."[2]

Smaller stories told volumes about the trial's global reach. Linda Deutsch, the Associated Press reporter covering the trial, told of her friend who traveled to the outreaches of Western Samoa. When the friend's car broke down in a remote village, word was passed to a neighboring village that she was in need of a car mechanic. Finding out she was an American, the mechanic excitedly engaged her in conversation, asking, "Oh, did you hear what Judge Ito did today?" Said Deutsch: "It turned out they had one hour of CNN every day. Judge Ito was even a celebrity over there."[3]

Scores of anecdotes were told about the Simpson effect on the world political scene. Dominick Dunne, the *Vanity Fair* chronicler, recounted a story about Pakistan Prime Minister Benazir Bhutto's visit to the United States. When Bhutto was asked with whom she would like to dine at a Beverly Hills restaurant, she named Marcia Clark and Robert Shapiro. The wife of the actor Michael York told Dunne that on her trip to an ashram in India, the resident guru had enjoined her: "Tell me about O. J." And even Russian President Boris Yeltsin on his visit to the country, reportedly asked as he came off his plane, "Do you think O. J. did it?"[4]

There was no way to account for the incredible impact of the Simpson trial, without understanding its deep-rooted relationship to the media, and specifically, television. Airing the Simpson trial turned it into a carnival house of mirrors where law and journalism were refracted into a strange, hybrid image. The trial was immersed in a television environment, inextricably bound to both the commercial entertainment format of the medium and the real world of the courtroom. The case of O. J. Simpson had become a TV maxi-series with as many distortions as a daytime soap opera.

It was more than a little ironic that CBS's venerable *60 Minutes* found itself the only TV newsmagazine among all the network news-related programs, to completely shun the Simpson story. *60 Minutes* had built a reputation for its confrontational and dramatic style of storytelling. Now those associated with the program publicly condemned the media for taking that practice to its extreme in the Simpson story. According to executive producer Don Hewitt, coverage of the trial no longer resembled "the news" but old popular TV soap operas like *Dallas*. "The box office smash in television this year is, 'Who killed Nicole?'" he said. "It wasn't too long ago the box office smash was, 'Who killed J.R.?'" With the same format, title music, commercial interruptions, and credits, "there are those [television viewers] who don't know the difference between Nicole and J.R."

The Bronco chase and preliminary hearing had gotten the Simpson soap off to a smashing start. And television played to the case's most sensational elements, or created its own. The success of the medium to produce an event of such enormous popularity was not lost on others in the media. In that respect, American television was a teacher showing the rest of the world how they too could take advantage of the trial's entertainment potential.

International media outlets mimicked the provocative style of television "news commentary." The results turned out to be a bizarre parody of American journalism. Much of the English-speaking world outside of the United States, for instance, learned of the Simpson trial through the BBC radio, Britain's respected news organization. The network's choice of commentators was, to say the least, unconventional. To cover the trial in Los Angeles, the BBC employed the comedian Jackie Mason and New York divorce attorney Raoul Felder—the clown and the straight man—as its Simpson experts. The duo provided a weekly 15-minute commentary and analysis of the trial that was broadcast around the world.

Mason, a comic provocateur better known for appearing on Broadway or the hotel circuit in the Catskill Mountains of New York, had covered the pretrial hearings for the BBC. Now, joined by Felder, he took his act again to Los Angeles. Though the pair were not quite Laurel and Hardy, the BBC thought they would provide a distinctively American perspective to its coverage. And the network's instincts were correct, although its decision was unwittingly a scathing commentary on the state of American justice and media. Choosing a comedian and a lawyer to tell the world about the Simpson trial began to seem perfectly natural.

Images produced by the house of mirrors were used to poke fun at the American justice system—the carnival house had reshaped a murder trial into something funny, strange looking, and, ultimately, ridiculous. Trial participants took their turn before the television mirrors transformed, in essence, into the medium's offspring— celebrities.

In the early stages of the case when he still held the reins as Simpson's lead attorney, Robert Shapiro easily settled into the world of fame and glitter that came his way. He flitted across the media scene, basking in the role of "celebrity lawyer," and taking on the posture of a star by signing autographs outside the courthouse. This was a role he took seriously. Shapiro was said to give photographs of himself to admiring fans, signing his name with a gold pen.

The lawyer had become one of the nation's recognizable "personalities." In national magazines like *People*, he was seen posing in his pool, pounding a punching bag, and lounging in bed. Shapiro-sightings were recorded in Dunne's "Letters from Los Angeles" in *Vanity Fair*. The writer noted that Shapiro had been one of the most photographed "superstars" at a recent upscale charity bash, right along with Hillary Clinton, Barbra Streisand, Dustin Hoffman, and the Duchess of York. One of the hottest auction items was lunch with Shapiro. It went for $2,000.[5]

Even Shapiro was amazed at his star status within Hollywood culture. "It's one thing to garner respect, congratulations, and praise," he said. "It's another thing entirely to glance up during a Lakers' game and see one's face juxtaposed with Jack Nicholson's on the massive video screen in the Great Western Forum."[6]

Shapiro apparently adjusted quite nicely to his newly discovered fame. In his trial memoirs, he recounted having dinner at the chic restaurant Spago, joined by actors Martin Landau and Warren Beatty, where they struggled with such great metaphysical dilemmas as how to cope with "all this celebrity stuff." Later, however, during closing arguments, Shapiro had greater difficulty with his high-profile status among more ordinary folks. At his synagogue, observing the sacred holy days of Rosh Hashanah, Shapiro recognized that he was less a celebrity in the eyes of the congregation than "a symbol of lawyers using the system to gain an acquittal."[7]

Two Died for the Show

Inside the courtroom, the house of mirrors provided more distortion. If life imitates art, the Simpson trial mimicked the stuff of Hollywood's "Dream Factory." It evolved as a Los Angeles cliché with "character actors" playing roles as the judge, lawyers, witnesses, and even reporters. The trial eerily resembled Tom Wolfe's dark novel *Bonfire of the Vanities*. Although Simpson was not much like the fictional Sherman McCoy (except that they were both wealthy and had reputations as philanderers), he shared a similar trial experience: a highly publicized case turned racial and caught in the tabloidesque throes of the media. What seemed outrageous in Wolfe's imaginary flight of fiction, had inexplicably taken form in this real life tele-event.

In the hallway outside the courtroom, "experts" lined up for their chance to help fill airwaves already swollen by opinion and comment. Among them was attorney Gloria Allred, a regular at the Criminal Courts Building, who prepared to meet the press each day in full pancake makeup and a telegenic wardrobe. Using her association as the attorney for Denise Brown, she sought out the media, which in turn helped to position her as an "insider" and expert to discuss spousal abuse and other social issues tied to the case. Building a celebrity status meant persistently seeking the media's attention, and Allred was persistent.

For some observers, the proceedings were surreally disconnected from the normal trial experience. If a public space could manifest a split personality, then Ito's courtroom was clinically psychotic. It was both a serious place to uncover the grave matters of Simpson's role in a double murder, but also a frivolous place to be recognized and "discovered."

Reporters themselves were not always quite sure just what "event" they were attending. On one hand, the courtroom was overly restrictive, with Ito taking a hard hand against any reporter or spectator who dared to speak or squirm in his seat. Should a reporter be forced to leave the courtroom for any reason, he could not reclaim his seat that session. Yet, at the same time, walking into Department 103 could be like attending a Hollywood bash, where "being seen" or simply basking in the glow of the glitterati was a primary indulgence.

Robin Clark, who covered the case for the *Philadelphia Inquirer*, counted himself among the media "outsiders," unlike other press members who were natural "insiders" and very much at home in this Hollywood-like milieu. Clark found himself watching, incredulously, the often absurd encounters in the strange, insular celebrity world that had become the Simpson trial. Unlike most reporters, he had not vied for the spotlight and was anxious for the trial to end so that he could move on to other assignments. But, tragically, the Simpson story would be his last. Six weeks before the trial ended, Clark and his two passengers were killed in a car accident. His "Simpson Show" was published posthumously.[8]

Marcia Clark doesn't lean over the rail to bat her famous eyes at me, as she does author Joe McGinniss.

Robert Shapiro doesn't dial my home number to dish dirt on rival F. Lee Bailey. He calls the *New York Times*.

And heaven knows Nancy Reagan has never button-holed me in the lobby of the Biltmore Hotel to pick my brain about Faye Resnick and Heidi Fleiss. That kind of access is reserved for *Vanity Fair* columnist Dominick Dunne, a gossip with such awesome connections that he's known simply as The Dominator.

I hate to tell you, folks, but here in Tinseltown, scene of the O. J. Simpson trial, the *Philadelphia Inquirer* is chopped liver.

When I'm not in court, my "office" is a stuffy trailer on the ragged fringe of Camp OJ, the sprawling media ghetto across the street from the Los Angeles Criminal Courts Building.

The Port-o-lets are nearby, which is convenient—except when the wind blows hard out of the west. There is a gourmet catering truck next door, which recently posted a luscious menu of grilled ahi tuna, fresh asparagus spears and chocolate cheesecake. Also posted was a sign reading: "CNN Employees Only! No Exceptions!"

I even had to battle the *National Enquirer* for a seat in the courtroom. And lost!—until I reminded one of Judge Lance Ito's minions that we still held a slight lead in the Pulitzer count. *Inquirer* 17, *Enquirer* 0.

These days, I occupy seat C-16 in the Simpson court pretty much full time. It's not exactly ringside. In fact, it's just one row ahead of the winos and cross-dressers who fill the public seats. But occasionally I catch a glimpse of O. J. when he turns to smile benignly at Annie Leibovitz or some other celebrity photographer whose motor-drives whir constantly in my ear.

One day, Barbara Walters sat just to my left and made sympathetic goo-goo eyes at Kato Kaelin through an entire morning of incomprehensible testimony. Three days later, he was a guest on her show, which explained everything.

Famed Wyoming defense lawyer Gerry Spence, who commentates on the trial for just about everybody, sits to my right. His costume never varies: black turtleneck, fringed leather jacket and elephant-skin boots.

After cornering him for a quote one day in the hall, I innocently asked how he'd like to be identified.

"The legendary," he said.

Spence hasn't been in court much since Ito overheard him cracking wise one day and told him to shut up. (I bet that won't be in Gerry's book.)

Talk-show host Larry King created the biggest stir so far during a courtroom appearance early in the trial. After receiving a private audience with the judge in chambers, King bounded into court like an overheated Labrador retriever, drooling over the famous lawyers and waving to the audience as if he were the grand marshal at a parade.

Flanking King were two jewel-encrusted blondes half his age, both of whom looked embarrassed to be holding up the Trial of the Century.

Not King. After yukking it up with the lawyers, he eagerly shook hands with the judge's staff, the court reporters and everyone else in sight. Only when he approached Simpson did King learn that, in Superior Court, even celebrity has limits.

As King extended his hand with a hearty "Hey, O. J.!" two surly sheriff's deputies stepped between them and firmly reminded the TV host that double-murder defendants aren't allowed to press the flesh.

King smiled and shrugged sheepishly. Simpson smiled and shrugged back. Then, seeing no one left to shake hands with, the famous man turned to leave. Unfortunately, he picked the wrong door, walking toward the holding cell where Simpson is detained before court.

Deputies turned him around, pointing to the exit, where King paused to wave again before departing. "So long, everybody," he said.

So long, Larry.

With so many stars in orbit, the Simpson trial often takes on the excited air of a Hollywood cocktail party, especially in the morning when everyone gathers in the ninth-floor hallway to wait for court to open.

O. J.'s sister Shirley greets Ron Goldman's stepmother, Patti.

The Dominator—who describes himself not as a gossip but as a "social historian"—tells us about his dinner with Maggie Thatcher, who was dying to hear about the trial.

When Johnnie Cochran pauses to make a pit stop on his way into court, half the male members of the press corps follow him into the men's room, hoping for some crumb of new information to spice up their stories.

It's quite odd, really. And a little pathetic.

I mean, it's swell to be on a first-name basis with Johnnie and Marcia and Lance and the rest—even if they don't know me from Adam's house cat.

But it seems a shame that two people had to die to make this show possible.

Toobin's Fame

Most print journalists worked in relative anonymity prior to the Simpson case, their identity confirmed by a simple byline. The trial now gave many of them "a face." Linda Deutsch said that for the first time in her career—one that spanned more than a quarter century—she was recognized by strangers who had seen her on television. Even Dunne, who first earned fame as a Hollywood producer in the 1970s and then as an author of bestsellers and magazine articles, thought of the Simpson case as a defining moment in his professional life.

Jeffrey Toobin was another who parlayed his *New Yorker* assignment into a broad-based media career. Like a number of reporters on the Simpson beat, Toobin was first a lawyer before delving full-time into journalism. His first forays into journalism started when he was a Harvard law student, freelancing for the *New Republic*. It was during his freshman year that he had taken a course in criminal law, taught by a nationally recognized legal figure: Alan Dershowitz. Following graduation, Toobin stayed in touch with his mentor, but neither the student nor the professor could imagine how their lives would entwine 13 years later in Los Angeles. They had become adversaries: Dershowitz, defending Simpson's innocence;

Toobin, convicting Simpson of murder in his *New Yorker* columns, and subsequently, in his book about the trial.

Toobin was bright and ambitious and, after graduating magna cum laude from Harvard Law School, continued to feel the "tug of two worlds" as a lawyer and writer. He first pursued the law and after a judicial clerkship, he landed a job as an associate counsel for Lawrence Walsh, who was running the Iran-Contra investigation in Washington, D.C. Toobin wrote a book about his experiences at the Oliver North trial but still was not prepared to leave law to take on a full-time journalism career. He had another job in mind: to try his own cases as a prosecutor. For the next three years Toobin worked in Brooklyn as an assistant federal prosecutor, but when the job started becoming less challenging, he was ready to take the plunge into journalism. He heard that Tina Brown, recently hired as editor of the *New Yorker*, was looking to revamp the venerable but flagging magazine, and applied for a writing assignment. He was hired to write "Talk of the Town" stories, but that assignment soon changed.

Toobin realized that his comparative advantage as a writer lay in his ability to take dense matters of law and make it interesting to nonlawyers. His early *New Yorker* pieces dealt with Supreme Court Justice Clarence Thomas and Polly Klaas, the 12-year-old Petaluma, California, girl abducted from her home and murdered. When the Simpson-Goldman murders broke, Toobin was just finishing a piece titled "Cash for Trash," about the widespread tabloid practice of paying for interviews. He quickly "rejiggered" it to include some aspects of the breaking murder case. From that moment, he was officially on the Simpson story. When Tina Brown sent him to California to find something interesting to write about, he came back with a story about Mark Fuhrman called "An Incendiary Defense." The article squarely placed Toobin at the controversial center of the Simpson story.

Up until that time, no single article had created as much fury. Toobin's piece detailed for the first time the defense team's strategy to "try" Mark Fuhrman, whom they described as a racist cop out to frame Simpson. Such rumblings had simmered under the surface of the case early on, but it was unclear then what impact, if any, it would have on the trial. "This [defense theory] had everything, and it seemed as if race was going to be there, but no one knew how it was going to manifest itself," said Toobin. "My piece comes out and everyone's going, 'Ah-ha. Race is not only going to be a part of the trial, but it's going to be at the center, and the defense is going to use it for everything it's worth.'"[9]

But his article was also read with disdain by other reporters who believed that Toobin had all too eagerly gone along with the defense's unsubstantiated story. Dominick Dunne said he thought he was going to "hate" Toobin for failing to scrupulously challenge the defense claims. But as Dunne watched Toobin's work over the course of the trial and came to understand its full context, his respect and friendship grew for the young reporter.

The trial was a heady experience for the relatively unknown writer. There were personal sacrifices and the long length of the trial was frustrating as Toobin found himself commuting between coasts to be with his wife and two children in New York. But the Simpson case was an extraordinary gift for the driven writer just beginning his career. Toobin soon realized that he was one of the most recognized writers in the country. "What was so great about it as a journalist was that people cared so much [about the case]. People would ask you a million questions, read your stories, see you on television. I am a journalist who writes for other people, I don't write to amuse myself, and to have so many people engaged in what you're writing was a tremendous thrill."

Ironically, it was television more than the *New Yorker* that brought him intense national exposure. Toobin was among the roving band of "insiders" commenting about the trial on the talk-show circuit, and his high profile paid off professionally. "I found that my sources took me more seriously for having seen me on television," he said. Toobin also found access to information to which he ordinarily would have been excluded. "I actually was the first reporter to be inside the house on Bundy [after the murders], and I knew that I never would have been allowed to do that if the person who let me in did not see me on television. In our society, being on television is an important form of validation for better or worse." Being "known" was also important in other ways. Conscious that other, more famous writers like Dunne were also writing books on the trial, Toobin believed that he had to get his name better known to have a competitive advantage when it came time to sell his book.

Toobin's hard-hitting TV analysis frequently undercut any claim of Simpson's innocence, and throughout the trial he proved to be a thorn in the Dream Team's side. Despite his original piece seen as favoring Simpson, Toobin would persist as an outspoken critic of the defense. He made no pretense about what he felt was O. J. Simpson's role in the slayings of Nicole Simpson and Ron Goldman. Simpson was their murderer.

But in the trial's aftermath, Toobin left himself open to criticism after his book. *The Run Of His Life* painted a different picture than the one he gave to *New Yorker* readers during the trial. His generally favorable, if not glowing reviews of Clark and Darden, were wildly contradicted in the portrayals he offered later in his book. The *New Yorker* portrait of Clark during the trial, was, as one critic described, a "press agent's dream." Here Clark was an exceptionally talented and ethical lawyer, who was not only the equal of her high-priced adversaries, but better. Darden, as well, was lauded as a smart, savvy prosecutor who carried himself with "quiet dignity." Following the verdict Toobin publicly commiserated with the prosecutors, stating that "there was nothing that could have been done—or undone—that would have changed the result."[10]

But this was hardly the same Clark or Darden seen in Toobin's best-selling book. Clark was now depicted as a lawyer "drunk on virtue," whose "arrogance" had blinded her to the realities of the case. She had ignored jury consultants, alienated key witnesses during the preliminary hearing, kept jurors waiting by being chronically late, and bungled Mark Fuhrman's testimony. In his revisionist history, Toobin now sided with those who viewed Clark as "a narrow-minded civil servant who preferred courthouse bromides to solid information." Darden, also, was portrayed as intellectually weaker than his nemesis, Johnnie Cochran, and a hot-tempered prosecutor, whose legal judgments were highly suspect. His decision to let Simpson try on a bloody glove retrieved from the crime scene provided "a classic example of [his] shortcomings as a trial lawyer—his impetuousness, his immaturity, his failure to prepare either himself or his witnesses adequately."[11]

As a high-profile critic both in the *New Yorker* and on NBC's *Today* show, Toobin had told his audience one story during the trial, and a different one afterward. "He is entitled to change his mind," said Wendy Kaminer, in her *New York Times* book review. "But without any explanation his divergent reports raise questions about his credibility."[12]

Regardless of the criticism, Toobin could hardly complain. The Simpson case had given him a level of national prominence he could only have imagined when he first came to the *New Yorker*. With the success of his book, he would also walk away from the experience with a huge royalty check and, later, a new job as legal analyst for ABC's network news and *Good Morning America*. As Toobin acknowledged: "Simpson has been very good to me."

Neufeld's Problem

Few lawyers could resist being sucked into the centripetal forces of fame swirling around the case, whether they were lawyers who curtailed their practice to be on television as pundits, or the principal attorneys who moved aside all other business to work full time on the trial. Peter Neufeld was beginning a controversial murder case in New York involving a man, Pedro Gill, accused of throwing a 30-pound bucket of spackling compound from the roof of a building that struck and killed a policeman. About the same time, Simpson retained Neufeld and his partner Barry Scheck as expert litigators on the subject of DNA.

Neufeld, who had taken the Gill case *pro bono*, prepared for the trial on September 28, 1994, while at the same time accepting membership to the Dream Team. Anticipating that a pretrial DNA hearing would be held in the fall for the Simpson case, Neufeld asked Harold Rothwax, the presiding judge in the Gill case, for a two-month postponement. Rothwax, a judge with a forceful reputation, wrote in his book, *Guilty,* that he was reluctant to grant Neufeld a delay, sensing that the Simpson case was unfolding like "a slow-motion train wreck." But Neufeld persisted, imploring that "as a man of honor" he would return to New York for Gill's trial date even if the DNA hearings were not completed.

As Rothwax predicted, lurches in the Simpson case pushed back the DNA hearing, and Neufeld found himself stuck between two trials and two coasts. When he asked Rothwax for a second postponement, the judge reminded him in open court about his claim of "honor" and commitment to the Gill case. Rothwax then revealed that Neufeld had privately pleaded with him: "Judge, you've got to let me go. My fame and fortune rely on Simpson."[13]

Neufeld erupted after being confronted with the judge's accusation. "That's a lie, your honor," responded a furious Neufeld. "That's a lie and you're doing it to distort the record. . . and you should be ashamed." Rothwax told the lawyer to sit in his seat, outraged that Neufeld had failed "to see the injustice of his position." But the lawyer persisted, again charging that the judge had lied. Rothwax had heard enough, halted the proceedings, and threw Neufeld in jail until he simmered down.

For Rothwax, Neufeld's actions spoke to a much graver problem—lawyers who believed that *they* were what mattered rather than considerations of law and justice. "Neufeld had made himself [and, consequently, Simpson] the center of the system," he said. "The family of a dead police officer in New York City didn't matter to him. Nor did the court's calendar. Nor did the rights of Pedro Gill and the state of New York."

Price of Fame

What Neufeld did foresee, however, and what every other lawyer connected to the Simpson case also well understood, was that the Simpson trial would eventually pay off grandly. Indeed, the main players in the trial walked away with million-dollar book contracts, TV series, lecture tours, or other lucrative deals. For the trial lawyers in particular, the case would define their careers, enhance their law practices, and earn them a coveted niche in celebrity culture. On a broader scale, each lawyer relished the idea of having a place in one of the most celebrated trials in American history.

But the price of fame was costly. All trial participants found their lives open to media meddling. The daily television attention made certain that they could no longer lead normal lives, and private lives collapsed under the constant media surveillance. Johnnie Cochran recalled that he had been in a media trailer in Camp OJ one day making a phone call when he noticed his mother's death certificate tacked to the wall. When he angrily confronted a reporter, she told him, without a hint of embarrassment, not to be concerned. "We got a tip that your mother had died penniless in a welfare hotel in Las Vegas," she explained, "and we had to check it out."[14]

Other journalists, though, said they were reluctant to pursue personal stories about police officers and prosecutors who were just "doing their jobs," or witnesses and jurors involuntarily caught up in the trial. They also tried to stay away from the "who's sleeping with whom" stories, despite being well aware of the personal relationships that existed among some participants,

Still, the frantic competition to tell the Simpson story generally overwhelmed the rules of professional conscience. Local television news stations and tabloids gravitated toward the more personal and gossipy side of the Simpson story. And once such stories were out on the airwaves and in newsprint, few reporters on the Simpson beat could just ignore them. Eventually, these stories, too, became an integral part of the media mix.

Tabloids reveled in the rumor-mongering and prattle and virtually no key participant was shielded. Cochran was caught in the middle of a very public and ugly palimony suit brought by Patricia Cochran, his mistress and the mother of his son. Christopher Darden's brother was identified as a crack addict, alienated from his family; a tabloid ran a picture of him, painfully gaunt and dying of AIDS. Nicole Simpson's sister Denise was reported to be the former lover of an ex-mobster turned FBI informant. A college roommate of Ito's recalled to the tabloids a story about the judge, then a student at UCLA, running naked through the dormitory hallway on the anniversary of the Pearl Harbor attack, yelling, "Banzai! Banzai!"

In this hyperintense setting, even members of the Simpson press corps found themselves on the receiving end, victimized by their own titillating and mindless reports. Traci Savage, the controversial KNBC reporter, discovered that she was the focus of salacious media reports, her high profile apparently making her open game for fellow reporters. Reports surfaced that identified her as a former actress who performed barebreasted in an early Hollywood horror film. She was also romantically linked to David Gascon, the LAPD commander and official spokesman for the department during Simpson's flight from justice.

In New York, the daily newspaper war turned personal. *New York Daily News* reporter Michelle Caruso became the subject of a leering *New York Post* article in which she was described as attending a barbecue thrown by writer Joe McGinniss, plunging naked into a pool, and "declaring her admiration for E! [Entertainment] Channel anchorwoman Kathleen Sullivan," before jumping into a hot tub with *New York Times* reporter David Margolick.

Mainstream news organizations were less reticent reporting about Clark's and Darden's latest romances. The most publicized speculation early on was whether Darden was dating Anita Hill. But by the end of the trial, the lead story seemingly everywhere was whether the prosecutors themselves were lovers and even had marriage plans following Clark's divorce.

Such incongruous matters sometimes had relatively short media lives. But other stories lived longer and proved an additional strain for trial participants. Clark had filed for divorce against her estranged husband, Gordon Clark, shortly before the Simpson-Goldman murders. But once she became the case's lead prosecutor, the media floodgates opened to her contentious divorce and child custody battle. Reporters sought out Gordon Clark, who willingly made the media rounds, at one point grabbing $50,000 for an exclusive on *A Current Affair.*

Although Marcia Clark asked the media to "respect" her privacy, both she and her estranged husband exploited their relative positions to gain leverage in their legal battle. The Simpson trial again seeped beyond the confines of Ito's courtroom. Gordon Clark filed court papers asking for primary custody of their children since his wife, with whom the boys lived, was rarely home and worked 16-hour days on the Simpson case. For her part, Marcia Clark asked the divorce court for more financial support to cover additional child-care costs, as well as Simpson-related expenses. The financial drain of having to dress stylishly and groom for a national television audience was an undue hardship, she said, since those expenses were not reimbursed by the county for which she worked.

What ordinarily would have been a private divorce contest soon became a quarrelsome public dispute between the Clarks, and the media were in the middle of it. The prosecutor became the central figure in the media's new round of "social awareness" stories. No longer did Clark stand as a mere attorney. She now embodied the Modern Working Woman, caught between the obligations of motherhood and her job. Clark was either a sympathetic, if not heroic, role model for working mothers, or a neglectful mother, who sacrificed her two children for her job. Tabloids were particularly gleeful with scandalous stories of Clark's "dirty divorce" or her "suicide ordeal" or the "men she left behind."

The attention to Clark's private custody battle did not escape the defense team, which also found it a convenient issue to distract from the proceedings. Cochran did not hesitate to expose Clark's personal problems in open court. When Clark told the court that she could not stay late for a proposed evening session because she had to attend to her children, Cochran suggested that Clark may have used child care as a ruse to delay the testimony of defense witness Rosa Lopez. Clark angrily retorted that she was "offended as a woman, as a single parent, as a prosecutor and as an officer of the court."

Heat and fire from the Clarks' family dispute made good copy, but few within the media questioned whether such stories were within the bounds of fair reporting. Mainstream journalists ridiculed the tabloids for featuring photographs of a younger, topless Marcia Clark vacationing on a nude beach in Saint-Tropez, but then exposed sensitive reports dealing with her divorce and child custody fight.

The effects of the unwarranted publicity took its toll on Clark. In court she broke down in tears, overwrought after learning of the published semi-nude photo of her. As it pertained to her contentious divorce, she was, simply, furious at the media's meddling. Jim Newton, of the *Los Angeles Times*, conceded that his newspaper had received complaints that the coverage had strayed too far into "the personal side." "Marcia Clark was upset when we reported about her divorce," he acknowledged. "I can see why she had a hard time in seeing that in the paper."[15]

Newton drew distinctions between covering the private life of a state employee, like Clark—a person who was thrust into the limelight as part of her official duties—and other participants, who aggressively sought out media attention. "We had a magazine piece where Cochran was accused of spousal abuse years ago," he recounted. And then Cochran's former wife published a book detailing how her husband routinely abused her while carrying on a 10-year affair with a woman with whom he had fathered a child. "He was not thrilled to death about that," said Newton. "I'm sympathetic. But Cochran is a big public figure here, he's a big player, he needs to take his lumps. But I understand that there is this zone of privacy that everyone relishes and some of it has been violated and probably by us."

Reporters could suddenly find themselves facing the wrath of lawyers and witnesses angry that they had stepped too forcefully into their private lives. Fuhrman, embroiled in the case's ongoing and heated racial controversy, made headlines for hitting a news photographer in the chest with a steel briefcase after his picture was taken at a Spokane, Washington, airport.

Clark also lashed out at a Court TV reporter she believed had gone too far. Dan Abrams had been instructed by his network to investigate why Clark was arriving late to court each day during a time in which important DNA information was being explored. Clark, who was not the lead attorney on the DNA evidence, told Abrams that she was using the opportunity to spend more time with her children.

"I was out on the air shortly thereafter reporting why Marcia Clark is late for court every day," said Abrams. "And I thought she would actually like this kind of report [that says] 'Look, Marcia Clark is not just messing around, Marcia Clark is not just late, she's been working six months, incredibly long hours, and not getting to spend enough time with her children. This is a woman who cares about her children.'"[16]

But when an associate told Clark what Abrams had reported over the air, the prosecutor was livid. Fearful that the report had somehow endangered her family, an angry Clark confronted the reporter. "She just railed at me [shouting], 'It was off the record, off the record,'" recalled Abrams. "It was a very touchy situation. Her press person told me she wasn't going to talk to me anymore."

Abrams' job for Court TV was to cover the prosecutors' case. He had learned to be very careful in dealing with a prosecution team that was reluctant to put any statement officially on the record. The four words Abrams said he never spoke on the air were "Marcia Clark told me" when identifying the source of any of his reports. Many news accounts were attributed to unidentified sources, and Abrams well understood the "tacit agreement" between reporters and lawyers as to which statements were meant for the public record and which were private. Clark's accusation that he violated that agreement made him angry. He contended that Clark's interview was "for the record," and he had gone so far to inform her of his intentions to file the report. "Clark was under a great deal of stress during the trial," said Abrams. "There were times she may have lost her temper at the press when really it wasn't the press to blame."

Paradoxically, as some participants desperately tried to keep their private lives away from the media's business, others seemed just as desperate to attract the media's attention. The 1980s had seen the rise of the "Oprahization" phenomenon—named after the television personality—that was characterized by ordinary people going on TV talk shows to discuss every imaginable, and unimaginable, sexual, psychological, physiological, and emotional aspect of their lives.

During the Simpson case, the trend reached full bloom, with individuals directly or indirectly connected to the case purging their darkest secrets to an eager TV audience. One *Rivera Live* show was a strange sideshow featuring a discussion between Barbara Berry and Patricia Cochran—the former wife, and the long-term mistress of Johnnie Cochran. The women commiserated. Barbara told of being beaten during her marriage after she had confronted her husband over having an affair. Patricia had changed her legal name to Cochran, though not officially married, and had a child with the lawyer. In effect, Cochran had managed to have two ongoing "marriages" with both women over the span of ten years. Even TV soap operas would be hard-pressed to script a family life to match the Cochran household.

On *Larry King Live*, Ron Goldman's biological mother, who had long been separated from Fred Goldman and her children, used her television appearance to complain of being shut out of family matters surrounding the death of her son. A phone call to the show stopped her short. It was her daughter, Kim Goldman. The young woman bitterly denounced her mother, telling King, and a national audience, that her mother had abandoned her children and had "come back" to exploit Ron's death.

The Simpson saga continued on, far surpassing anything that ordinary TV could offer.

Two Worlds

Television created a vivid picture of the O. J. Simpson trial for its audiences, but the view inside the courtroom was far different. From the jury box, in particular, the case was much more restrained than what the rest of the world saw on television. For half of their nine-month service, jurors were removed from the jury box, purposely sheltered from the squabbling and personality disputes among the lawyers. They were also kept apart from a wealth of evidence that never made it into court. And they were not privy to the judge's rulings on motions or sidebar transcripts.

The media, however, had access to all such information and were free to broadcast and publish it. Evidence and testimony found inadmissible in court, and spins from the opposing camps, were part of the daily media parcel. When, for example, Ito barred lawyers from telling jurors that carpet fibers found at the crime scene matched the carpet in only a few custom-made Ford Broncos—one of which was owned by Simpson—the media duly noted the fact for their audiences.

Later, Ito allowed jurors to hear just snippets of the audiotapes in which Mark Fuhrman was heard to use vitriolic, racist language to describe blacks. But television viewers listened to the tapes in their entirety. When Rosa Lopez testified she became the latest subject of the media's unrelenting Simpson-talk. Her testimony was given in the absence of jurors and videotaped. Lopez, who worked as a housekeeper for Simpson's neighbor, claimed she saw a white Bronco outside of Simpson's estate at the same time the Simpson-Goldman killer was at South Bundy. But her testimony, so riddled with contradictions, dissuaded the defense from ever showing the videotaped testimony to the jury. Unlike jury members, television viewers had a clear view of the near-farcical nature of one of the defense team's key witnesses.

Throughout the case, the media at large continued to give the public a far wider frame of reference than the jurors were privy to. "It was as though we were all in a large coliseum watching a three-ring circus," said Uelmen. "But the jury was wearing blinders that permitted them to watch only the center ring."[17] Even admissible evidence, seen by both jurors and media audiences, was often processed through different filters. Reporters and pundits "framed" the trial for public consumption and were assisted by such inventions as crime scene "reenactments," and other graphics, that supplied pictures to the words. This was the *journalism* rendition of the Simpson story. The story that jurors came to understand—the *court* story—followed from a more severe set of facts. "It is well to remember that what we read in the newspapers or see on television is not necessarily the same story the jury is hearing," cautioned critic John Gregory Dunne.[18]

As much as Americans were exposed to information banned from the jury box, they, too, were limited by the restricted view of the camera. Ito refused to allow TV pictures of certain exhibits, including photos of the brutally slashed bodies of Nicole Simpson and Ron Goldman. To that degree, the public was distanced from the reality of the crime, murders so horrific that jurors and court spectators were visibly repulsed.

There were other pictures absent from the television screen that were more tangential. For instance, viewers could not watch jury members, since the panel was off-limits to the camera. For reporters in the courtroom, like Dominick Dunne, jury watching was "endlessly fascinating." He took note of which panelists had a sense of humor and which ones never laughed. He observed the most diligent jurors and those who fell asleep. As the trial wore on, reporters also looked for other physical traits that might give away what jurors were thinking.

The prevailing myth that O. J. Simpson was being tried before a jury of his peers was given obeisance across the media. But, of course, there were two legal venues—one in Ito's courtroom and the other on television, and Simpson's peers were far more than then 12 men and women in Department 103's jury box. Television had created the illusion that both jurors and the public were watching and experiencing the same event, but clearly they were not. Sequestered from the "public evidence" and the avalanche of commentary attached to that evidence, jurors saw one case. TV viewers saw another. And so, when a controversial verdict was finally reached, many accused the jurors of reaching a racial decision. Few, if any, took into account that the picture from their television set was decidedly different from the one in the jury box.

To that end, television worked against the legal system. The net effect was that viewers believed they *knew* the Simpson case as well as, if not better than, the jury panel. The very idea that these jurors represented *them*, the "people"—so distinctively an American compact—was anathema to their television experience. After all, they also had served—on yet another public jury—and had seen for themselves the evidence and testimony.

"Where people would normally say I wasn't there for every minute, the jury saw more than I did, and I trust what they did— that's not happening anymore," said AP reporter Linda Deutsch. "Television undermines the public confidence in the jury verdict because everybody feels they are the jury and that they were there."[19]

In this collision of two worldviews, it was inevitable in the aftermath of the trial that the Simpson jurors faced the anger and contempt of many "public jurors" who contended that the "wrong" verdict had been reached.

Mutiny on the Jury, and Other Madness

No part of the Simpson story was more bizarre than the coverage of the jury. The lengthy selection of 12 sitting jurors and 12 alternates was merely the first act in an extended serial drama. As the trial proceeded, juror after juror was dismissed by the court, and the media avidly kept count and wondered whether enough jurors would remain at the end of the trial to come to a verdict. Should a nonverdict be rendered—and a mistrial declared—this would, indeed, be the bitterest of ironies. In such an event, Department 103 would likely be the only place in America where a judgment about O. J. Simpson had not been reached.

Ito's decision to sequester the jurors was meant to allow them to work in anonymity unencumbered by the chaos surrounding the case. While out of the public eye view, jurors nevertheless became objects of suspicion and even ridicule, vulnerable to stereotypes suggesting that they were either mentally incapable or racially bent from reaching a proper verdict.

The media consistently packaged the panel by its racial composition. When a juror was replaced, the media treated each dismissal with monumental concern as they probed the new balance of white, black, and "other" panelists. The implicit message was evident, though skewed: With each new black juror, Simpson's chances of freedom were enhanced; with each new white member, they were diminished. The jurors were seen as a microcosm of American society, racially polarized over the case. These assumptions fed into the general coverage. Of all the elements in the case, the most significant, at least from the press's perch, was skin color.

For jurors, by the time the trial was a month old, any glamour from being selected had worn off, being replaced by the sobering reality of living at a hotel in almost virtual isolation while being constantly supervised by the sheriff's deputies. Throughout the trial, jurors found themselves under investigation by the very court that had chosen them. Deputies monitored their phone calls, censored their reading material, and searched their rooms for contraband. Any juror found writing a book, for instance, was subject to immediate dismissal. The only unsupervised activities were sleeping, weekly conjugal visits, bathing, and bathroom visits. Jury members essentially had fewer liberties than *actual inmates*. Compared with the jurors, Simpson had a relatively free existence, with access to reading materials, television, the telephone, and visitors.

Ito himself aggressively sifted through the background of jurors he found, for whatever reason, "suspicious." No longer citizens performing their civic duty, jurors were thrust into the role of political arbiters in a trial being watched daily by millions across the country. Perhaps no other jury in American history had faced such overriding public scrutiny.

One by one they were dismissed: a juror who knew a doctor scheduled to testify against Simpson; a juror for betting a co-worker before the trial that Simpson would be acquitted; a juror suspected of writing a book; a juror who failed to disclose a past personal experience with domestic violence; a juror whom others on the panel felt was intimidating and domineering.

The jury barely held together until the trial's end. Of the original 24 members, only 14 remained.

Ito's inability to run a tight courtroom stretched the case well beyond the four to five months originally anticipated. On occasion he apologized to jury members for keeping them from their families.

Eight months into the trial, Ito wryly offered his congratulations to them for surpassing Charles Manson's jury in time spent separated from daily life. Prior to the Simpson case, the Manson jury had been sequestered longer than any other in the state.

This hardship, however, failed to deter the judge. Ito continued to indulge a process that had disintegrated into a morass of courtroom speeches, histrionics, extended motions, and endless side-bars (in the first three months alone an estimated 460 sidebar conferences had been called). By the end, jurors had spent as much time sequestered from court proceedings as they had listening to testimony.

Ironically, the one critical jury story that the media failed to seriously probe involved a charge of jury tampering. The matter came fully to light in an investigation by *60 Minutes* only after the verdict was reached. During the trial, Francine Florio-Bunten found herself in Ito's chambers answering questions related to an anonymous letter the judge had received. She soon was removed from the jury. The letter writer claimed to be a 20-year-old literary agency recep-tionist suffering from a "moral dilemma" of whether to turn in a juror she knew had signed a contract to write a book called *Standing Alone for Nicole*. She then went on to describe the juror as someone who was "about 40 years old, [and] a white woman." There was no mystery who that was on the Simpson jury: Florio-Bunten, a 38-year-old white telephone company employee.

The problem was that the letter writer apparently was a liar. *60 Minutes* had conducted a survey of all book agents in Los Angeles and found no one to match the description offered in the letter. Florio-Bunten, and her husband, who was also implicated as being part of the book deal, continued to deny that they ever entered into negotiations about the book. And no book, in fact, ever was authored by the Buntens.

But at the time, Ito took the letter seriously, despite the juror's vehement denials and pleas that she was being set up. For the record, Ito dismissed her for lying about a note she had been handed by another juror. But, according to the *60 Minutes* investigation, the larger injustice had been committed against Florio-Bunten. The report concluded that someone close to the defense team likely planted the anonymous letter, fearing the juror's purported pro-prosecution bent. That fear was, in fact, well placed. Following the trial, Florio-Bunten said that, without question, she would have voted to convict O. J. Simpson. The mystery of the anonymous letter writer was never resolved.

Ex-jurors found that they were welcomed as instant celebrities under the media's big tent. Ex-juror Michael Knox, in a publicity tour for his book, *The Private Diary of an Ex-Juror,* told reporters about deep racial schisms on the panel. He said he was skeptical about the defense theory that police conspired against Simpson, whom he believed was guilty of the murders.

A 25-year-old flight attendant, Tracy Hampton, was also excused after she told the court she "couldn't take it anymore." Shortly afterward, Hampton was hospitalized for stress she said she suffered as a result of the case. The former juror would sufficiently recover, however, to pose for *Playboy* magazine.

The Simpson trial had given rise to a new and dangerous phenomenon, the *pre-verdict* juror interview. Never in the history of American jurisprudence had there been circumstances in which ex-jurors took on the role as ex-officio spokespersons for a sitting jury. They traveled the media sideshow, each proclaiming to be the measure by which to judge how the actual jury was thinking. Ostensibly, this was a presumptuous notion—jurors were prohibited from speaking with fellow panelists until the deliberations began. But, apparently, these limitations did not inhibit ex-jurors from making their views known to an avid media.

Only in a theater of such absurdity could such interviews seem commonplace. At one time in pre-Simpson history, many in the legal community strenuously argued against jurors speaking to the media *after* a verdict had been reached. Such "post-trial interviews" were criticized because they disclosed private discussions that were never intended for public consumption. Indeed, the very premise of keeping deliberations private was to ensure that each juror could speak candidly and without fear of being publicly exposed. Post-trial interviews also sent a message to *future* jurors: Their private deliberations could also be thrust into the public arena. The underlying danger was that jurors would be far less confident in challenging a panel's prevailing point of view. Others might be fearful about coming to an unpopular, but correct, decision in cases of high emotional public interest.

The pre-verdict interview that evolved during the Simpson case was a far more insidious trend. Former jury members were now in the position to critique their ex-colleagues and offer "verdicts" even as the case was still being decided. Jeanette Harris, one of the most controversial ex-jurors, rose from anonymity to TV celebrity after being dropped from the panel for failing to tell the court that she had been a victim of domestic abuse. In one TV interview, Harris called the prosecution's case "a whole lot of nothing." Hinting that other jurors shared her view, she said, "to be perfectly honest with you I see a hung jury."

Harris went further. She told reporters she believed that jury members were under intense public pressure to deliver a verdict that would be favored by their respective communities. "The [public] pressure is too great" on the jury, she said. "Black jurors might feel that 'I can't say he's guilty because I want to walk out of here.'" That assessment fed into the media's preconceived notion that the case would be decided along racial lines. To that extent, her statement came as no surprise to the media primed for *that* verdict.

Harris then delivered an even bigger bombshell. In the middle of a case already falling under the weight of racial bombast, she accused several sheriff's deputies of agitating discord by favoring white jurors over blacks. She also told of two incidents in which she was assaulted by white female jury members who kicked her leg and elbowed her in the ribs. She alleged that the only female Hispanic juror told her while sitting in the sheriff's van: "I don't want to breathe the same air as this woman," referring to another black juror.

The allegations came soon after the Bailey-Fuhrman showdown, and if the media were looking to move the race story forward, they now had their next sensational news peg. Harris' story was hyped across TV newscasts and newsmagazines. "One thing is clear," Diane Sawyer concluded after an ABC-TV *Day One* segment on Harris' charges. "This legal battle is veering dangerously close to guerrilla warfare inside and outside the courtroom, and millions of American TV viewers are taking it in. The question is, with all this courtroom chaos, will either party, the state or Simpson, ever see justice?"[20]

Ito, exasperated by the media frenzy surrounding the ousted jurors, complained: "I've got jurors out there writing books. We have jurors running around in limousines to talk shows." The judge, though, still felt compelled to launch an investigation into Harris' allegations that sheriff's deputies were fomenting racial divisions.

A perplexed Cochran asked: "When have you ever seen a case where jurors are continually investigated after a trial has begun?"

But the lawyer took advantage of the chaos surrounding the jury box to accuse prosecutors of "Big Brother" tactics, alleging a "concerted effort" by government attorneys to unseat Harris and other jurors sympathetic to the defense. Cochran failed to mention his own efforts in urging Ito to remove jurors whom he believed were pro-prosecution.

For all the posturing by the defense and the prosecution that race would have no place in choosing a jury panel, their actions revealed a more sobering truth. Of the ten jurors let go, prosecutors endorsed the removal of five blacks; the defense sought the dismissal of five nonblacks.

Three months into the trial, the jurors were first in a state of despair and then rebellion. In the wake of Harris' departure, three jurors suddenly took ill, forcing Ito to suspend testimony. Then, in a dramatic act of protest, 13 of the remaining 18 jurors and alternates marched into court dressed in black, angry that Ito had gone ahead and removed three deputies from their assignments because of Harris' accusations. "In 32 years of practice," said Cochran, "I have never seen anything like this."

The strife over the jury would persist throughout the trial. As Ito continued to investigate the jury, legal groups challenged his right to do so. Midway through the trial, the American Civil Liberties Union petitioned the release of undisclosed court transcripts pertaining to juror dismissals. The ACLU argued that the public was entitled to know whether Ito was being induced by trial attorneys to dismiss jurors. Soon the Simpson trial found itself the middle of yet another civil-rights fight—this one involving the rights of the jurors. In his commentary in the *Philadelphia Inquirer*, attorney Donald Russo likened the harsh day-to-day existence of jury members to those living in a totalitarian state.

> It appears that each juror is being monitored, and is under constant surveillance by agents of the state, on a 24-hour basis. Their phone calls are listened to, their rooms are searched, their personal belongings are inspected, they are placed under surveillance cameras, they are interrogated, and their personal lives are investigated. . . . In a time when all of us have been educated to be vigilant about the denial of basic civil liberties, it is difficult to understand why Ito would sanction a wholesale Gestapo-type investigation of his jurors.[21]

The Siege

Each dismissal brought a new surge of media competition, with news outlets vying to interview the latest Simpson celebrity—the ex-juror. On one occasion, a notice that a juror was about to be dismissed sent the media into a frantic investigative mode more reminiscent of the Keystone Kops than Watergate. When word got out that juror No. 462, a 38-year-old black woman from Inglewood, was being let go, reporters with access to her address converged on her home. By the afternoon, the juror's condominium was surrounded by reporters and producers from every media outlet covering the case.

ABC-TV producer Dan Morris wrote in the *New Republic* that by the time he arrived "nearly a dozen microwave transmission trucks were sending their antennae skyward as fifty or so media types milled about, cell phones to ears." For passersby, it was hard to believe that the media mob was simply there to interview a lone person. But, of course, this was no ordinary person.

As the day wore on, the scene around Juror 462's home became more bizarre. Morris recounted that a young well-dressed woman loudly announced herself as a representative from Sony/TriStar Pictures and demanded to know what was going on. Soon it became apparent, said Morris, she was emotionally disturbed. The woman began flagging down cars, writing gibberish in her notepad, and poking her head inside cars to ask drivers, "Are you an O. J. juror?" Traffic was soon backed up as compliant drivers, believing she was "the media," obeyed her commands. "My colleagues and I cringed, but no one intervened," said Morris. "Her mad playacting was so close to what we were doing that it was hard to come up with valid grounds to stop her."[22]

By 6:30 p.m., with local newscasts over, most of the media mob left, said Morris. Rumors also had spread that Ito was furious at the media siege and ordered the mystery juror to stay away from her home. But then, out of nowhere, the woman appeared from her condo balcony; she somehow had slipped by the media encampment. As the remaining reporters fired questions, she insisted she was not, in fact, a Simpson juror. When reporters persisted, she produced a driver's license and held it up for the cameras. The woman, in fact, bore the same name as that of the real juror—Jeanette Harris—but, undeniably, this was not *the* Jeanette Harris.

The Sony/TriStar crazy woman declared: "We all look like fools."

12

THE JOURNALISTS

FEBRUARY 1995

The Pregame Huddle

Each day before court convened, the hallway outside Department 103 bustled with frenetic energy. For nearly an hour, a crowd of reporters, spectators, and the families of the victims and defendant congregated in the corridor, waiting for the start of the day's proceedings. This unusual gathering ground was called the pregame huddle.

The huddle was a place to shoptalk, exchange the morning's confidences, or discuss what was coming up that day. Sometimes the chatter focused on the gossip-of-the-day, maybe Robert Kardashian's latest romance or other shenanigans supposedly taking place in the lawyers' offices. Some reporters spoke to Goldman, Brown, and Simpson family members. Others avoided them altogether, concerned that such discussions would intrude on the families' privacy or even interfere with their own objective stance in the case. Formal interviews weren't allowed in the corridor, and reporters faced having their courtroom seats taken away if they violated the rule. "You tried to talk to people in a low-key way to get some sense of what was going on," said *Newsday*'s Shirley Perlman, "but we were always walking on egg shells on that floor."[1]

The courthouse was a beehive of rumors for reporters always on the lookout for tips. Even small pieces of news were ardently vied for. Occasionally, Dominick Dunne befriended a reporter he liked by passing along information that he knew would be old news by the time his monthly magazine, *Vanity Fair*, hit the newsstands.

Dunne was a favorite among certain members of the press corps. His stories chronicled the Simpson trial against the backdrop of the rich and famous of L.A., and his "letters" at times were stinging social commentary. Dunne himself was a captivating personality with tales to spill about his forays in Los Angeles high society. "He came in one day and told us he had dinner with a socialite totally hooked on the Simpson trial," recounted Linda Deutsch, the Associated Press reporter. "She informed him that she had made a very serious decision—she was going in for a facelift during DNA testimony. That's the kind of thing only Dominick would get."[2]

The hallway social hour often became so crowded that the deputies were forced to clear the courtroom entryway. On occasion, a famous face would join the crowd. Actors Richard Dreyfuss and James Woods, ex-baseball star Steve Garvey, and network show-biz news personalities Diane Sawyer, Larry King, Barbara Walters, Geraldo Rivera, and Katie Couric all made an appearance, and each one created a buzz among reporters and the spectators lucky to get one of the few courtroom seats that day.

Reporters anxiously waited each day for the trial attorneys finally to appear to toss a few on-the-run questions. Mostly, though, the lawyers joked with reporters; the huddle was not intended to be too serious. One of the biggest flurries was over Marcia Clark's new haircut, a makeover that became the media talk of the day. In the hallway, Clark received an ovation. Deutsch was astonished: "I thought it was the most astounding thing I'd ever seen with the crowd applauding her hairdo."

When the doors opened, the first shift of reporters took their designated seats in Department 103. The relatively few press seats were assigned to groups of reporters, and each group worked out a rotating schedule. A reporter on the morning shift had the primary obligation of picking up a courtroom pass at 8:15 a.m., some 45 minutes before the start of the day's session. Failure to pick up the pass on time meant the entire group would forfeit the seat for the day. In Ito's courtroom, the pass was more valuable than money.

Department 103 was very small, too small to accommodate a trial of such enormous public interest. With Ito's decision to keep the trial within its tiny confines, the courtroom became an insular world for the "regulars." "[While] it was the national attention of focus, it really was our workplace—I include the lawyers, the judge, the spectators," said Jeffrey Toobin. "All of us met there every day and got to know each other very well as colleagues."[3] The angry and petulant behavior displayed by the trial attorneys did not necessarily extend to the families of the victims and the defendant. Juditha Brown and Eunice Simpson conversed and commiserated in the corridors during breaks. Likewise, the esprit de corps among reporters had grown over the months, and despite the daily fight for stories, they shared in the biggest story of their respective careers.

The Pit

Three floors above Department 103 was the pressroom, home to the Simpson press corps. The room was given the name "the pit" for good reason. Two long tables stretched along the walls of the narrow, windowless office space no longer than a bus; two other tables trailed down the middle of the room. Here is where a crush of reporters followed the live TV feed from the courtroom and wrote their daily stories. The pit was constantly crammed, with as many as 30 reporters elbowing for more space. The noise made it a seemingly impossible place to concentrate and write, but reporters managed to shut out the din as their deadlines approached.

"[The court press supervisor] wanted fewer people in there," said Perlman. "We said we didn't care if we had to sit on top of each other, we had to stay there because it was the only way to have access to what was going on." Reporters watched the trial on closed-circuit monitors on either side of the room. Another set of monitors stood ready to carry press conferences that might break on the ground floor or in the district attorney's office on the eighteenth floor.

Nonstop chatter and wisecracks filled the pressroom, and the Simpson case was rich in material. "Somebody would get up there and rip apart some of those dippy West L.A. witnesses, the touchy-feely people, some of the psychiatrists," said Perlman, a member of the club. "Bailey always provoked a lot of comment [and] very sarcastic and mordant, graveyard humor. [Reporters] all hated Scheck as well because he went on and on and wouldn't stop. Then he destroyed [Dennis] Fung and the scene changed. All of a sudden they were transfixed, and Scheck became the star of the show for that day."

Above all, there was the ever-present deadline. "We all had to write our stories," said Perlman. "If you were in that room once court ended, you just heard an awful lot of [keyboard] clicking with people really under the gun to get their stories filed."

"There was incredible intensity because everyone was on deadline every day," said Bill Boyarsky. "As the day went on the intensity in the room was palpable. You could feel it. It was hot, the air conditioner didn't work. And people ate in the room, so it smelled like a boarding house. At the end of the day, everybody felt just wrung out. And then knowing that this was the big story—you had to be right."[4]

The pit contained the concentrated power of dozens of major media organizations, a fact that did not go unnoticed. Boyarsky believed that Gil Garcetti was always worried about what the media were saying about the case, but shrewd about how he approached the press. On occasion, Garcetti exchanged small talk with the pit's reporters, explaining that he was passing by on his way to his eighteenth-floor office. "He always told us that because of the elevator system he had to stop by the twelfth floor and switch to another elevator," said Boyarsky. "I found out there's a direct elevator; he could have gone right to his office."

Boyarsky wrote four or five "spin" columns a week from the chaotic confines of the pressroom. He had the choice to return to his newspaper office located near the courthouse, but he could see that the pit was "the place to be during the trial." Boyarsky had been primarily a political writer for most of his career. He had come to the L.A. *Times* in 1970 after ten years at the Associated Press where he covered the political campaigns of Ronald Reagan, Richard Nixon, and Jimmy Carter. Simpson's was the first criminal trial he had reported on since his early years as a reporter.

His "spin" column was devised by the paper during the preliminary hearings to comment on what the trial's main players were saying. As the column evolved, Boyarsky turned his focus on to the media themselves—how they worked or failed to work in their coverage of the case. And the pit was a central stomping ground for his reports. "When something happened I was there," he said.

The pressroom was, in fact, a perfect perch to watch the trial's strange and inexplicable machinations that seemed more appropriate for a legal thriller than a real-life murder case. Boyarsky's story about the "reporter without a paper" was illustrative. The columnist had befriended a reporter by the name of George Reedy when he noticed that Reedy was taking a strong interest in the jury members, particularly the ones that Cochran didn't like. Then he noticed that Reedy "was really thick" with Cochran and his assistant, Carl Douglas. "Finally I asked him where his paper was published, and he told me it hadn't actually started yet," said Boyarsky. "Then I asked Darden about the possibility of jury tampering, but Darden stopped short [of accusing Reedy]. I did a piece about the mystery man—'the reporter without a paper.' It wound up they pulled his sheriff's pass [to the pressroom]. George was so happy about the notice I gave him that he forgave me."

High Anxiety

The trial was an exhausting, seven-day-a-week job for reporters. Normal reporting routines were dashed by the overwhelming demands by editors and TV executives for more and more of the Simpson story. Local television and radio reporters filed stories throughout the day. The pressure to get something "new" was always paramount. The courthouse hallways reflected the chaotic nature of the Simpson beat, with TV reporters filing their reports, then running back to television monitors to avoid missing any part of the day's testimony.

Print reporters also faced severe deadline pressures. At each early morning break in the proceedings, Deutsch shot out of Department 103 and headed to her upstairs office to write the first Simpson story of the day for more than 1,700 news outlets that subscribed to the Associated Press. Like other reporters responsible for East Coast coverage, Deutsch was handicapped by the three-hour time difference. She sometimes found herself sending a story before a single witness had testified and then updating her account throughout the day in order to keep news organizations with varied deadlines as current as possible.

Some reporters doubled up on their duties, reporting for their newspaper or network while also providing freelance commentary for the panoply of news and talk shows devoting hour upon hour to the trial. Dunne was under contract to CBS for his commentary, and Toobin was a regular on NBC's *Today* show. Twice a week, Court TV's Dan Abrams awakened at 2:45 a.m. to get ready for a 3:20 limousine pickup to the *Today* show studio where he would join Toobin. After his appearance, Abrams returned home for some rest before going to the courthouse. Then he would try to corral a member of the prosecution to discuss the upcoming session before his first live shot for Court TV at 8:30. By 9:00, he was in the courtroom for the day's proceedings.

Despite the general camaraderie within the press corps, competition reigned, and reporters were under extreme pressure to get information about the case, and preferably information no one else had. "At the Simpson trial any piece of information you had that someone else didn't was gold," said Abrams. "It reached a point that if you knew that the defense was going to file a motion, you had a scoop." Abrams counted himself among the small group of "insiders"—those reporters who had developed an informal relationship with the leading trial participants. Along with a few male colleagues, he wasn't above trailing lawyers into the ninth-floor men's restroom for a relatively private interview. Firing questions to Cochran and Shapiro at the wash basin or urinal could possibly elicit some key news. "Some of the best information came in the bathroom," said Abrams.[5]

For many reporters, the Simpson story meant a grueling 18-hour workday. Once their stories were filed, reporters joined colleagues or their contacts over dinner to discuss the day's events. Afterward, they returned to their offices, rented homes, or hotel rooms to "work the phones," calling sources they had cultivated over the months in search of a different spin or a single piece of information that somehow had eluded their competition.

Life on the Simpson beat was the press's equivalent of hazardous military duty. After a less than stellar reporting record in the early stages of the case, reporters had learned to be wary of their sources, while still aggressively seeking them out. Some sources had bad information, or were trying to push their own agenda, or simply were "out of the loop." "You had to be careful—you had to watch out for what information you were getting," said Abrams.

The pressure to be first with the latest Simpson news left reporters in a state of high anxiety. But even more stress-provoking was the possibility of being wrong on a story that was being closely followed by most of the nation. Abrams recalled being told by an "ironclad" source from Simpson's team that the defense was going to attack Detective Philip Vannatter as part of its strategy to implicate the LAPD. Abrams reported the information to Court TV's audience, only to be told later by another lawyer on the team that his account had been wrong. Two other sources had confirmed his story, Abrams said, but "after getting a defense lawyer insisting it wasn't going to happen, I got worried." Abrams pulled back from his report fearing he had been misled. But two days later the defense team went after

Vannatter. "It turned out my sources were right," he said. "This one person was out of the loop."

Reporters were not only worried that their facts were correct but were wary about being conned into accepting heavily biased or misleading legal spins. "You had to make sure that what you were getting was not just an effort by the lawyers to float a theory," explained Abrams. "And I have to say that the defense attorneys did that more than the prosecution. They regularly talked about how absurd something was that the prosecution was arguing." Typically, the reporter found after checking with his independent sources that the prosecutors had not committed the grievous sins of which they had been accused.

Abrams, a Columbia Law School School graduate, was perhaps more adroit in detecting an inflated legal observation than some in the press corps not schooled in the law. Trial lawyers routinely tried to take advantage of an unknowing reporter willing to accept their heavily slanted legal spin. On occasion, they had their way. "The regular reporters who were there every day were generally a savvy group," said Abrams, "even if they hadn't been in the beginning."

Shirley Perlman—A Reporter's Life

I began writing stories almost every single day beginning June 17 [the day of the chase] until the end. I worked on Saturday, Sunday, because I needed to have an advance [story] on Monday. Otherwise we were behind. If I didn't know on Sunday what was going to happen on Monday, I was dead in the water.

What I would do is come back from the courthouse on Thursday night and start reporting out. If I was doing a Sunday story talking about what we expected to unfold that following week, I would go back to the hotel at 7 p.m. and report until 10 p.m. until I couldn't call people anymore. Friday morning I was back in the courthouse. Friday afternoon I'd file my story. That Friday night I'd often write until 3 in the morning because at 10 a.m. [Saturday] I had to push that send button—it was already 1 p.m. in New York— and then start reporting Saturday afternoon for the story I had to write that night and send Sunday morning.

We had to be at the courthouse at 8:15 a.m. If you didn't pick up your [courtroom] pass, you would lose the pass for the entire day, not just for yourself but for everyone else in your group. I shared a seat with the *Daily News* and *New York Post*. Our arrangement was that we would switch at a break, so if I was first up, I would pick up my pass, grab a cup of coffee and go downstairs to the ninth floor where Ito's courtroom was, see Dominick [Dunne] who always wanted a sip of my coffee because I drank it like he did. It was very, very structured, there was not much regard for the press. We had to be ready when court opened. Once the door was locked you couldn't get in. In most other cases, you could walk in and out of the courtroom; that wasn't the case here. Once you were in you were in; if you walked out that was it.

Being in the courtroom was very difficult. Ito had this overhead camera [controlled by a] joystick underneath his desk, and he would scrutinize all the reporters. We weren't allowed to chew, suck or contort our bodies or we would possibly be thrown out. A few were thrown out. Kristin Jeannette-Meyers and Gail Holland were. The lawyers were displaying the RFL-DNA readings during the testimony of Robin Cotton, and these reporters were trying to make sure that the numbers were right. It was absolutely outrageous that they were barred from the courtroom after that. Outrageous.

We had to sit very still, we weren't allowed to pass notes, we weren't allowed to do any of the things that generally are not a problem in the courtroom. Reporters know how to behave in the courtroom, we're all seasoned reporters. Ito seemed to be very contemptuous of the press. Unless you were Barbara Walters, Diane Sawyer, they got an audience with Ito. So did [actor] James Woods, who appeared one day with his mother and his mother's friend. Larry King was able to walk all around the courtroom. But any of us, forget it.

You had to sneak around the courthouse since you couldn't break any news from the pressroom, because you have 60 ears, 30 people, everybody wanting to know who you're talking to. I would find a pay phone at the courthouse where I could check out information and break news rather than just report the day's events. Some reporters were there for analysis and perspective. I was there for analysis, perspective, but I was there to break news. That's why my editor sent me there.

I am married with three grown children, a husband, two grandchildren, one of whom was born while I was in Los Angeles. I got a call at 10 at night that my daughter was hemorrhaging and to come home immediately. I was able to get a red-eye through Dallas, got to the hospital at 11 the following morning, and Geanne had given birth and everything was fine.

While it was very difficult to be away from home, you have to understand, when you have a story like this, it's much easier to be out of town than to be home, because when you're home you have other responsibilities. When you're out of town you have the luxury of focusing all of your energy on what you are doing. For me, I stayed in a hotel the whole time. I know a lot of reporters who rented houses, rented apartments. I didn't want to do that. I didn't want to think about any of those things. I was there to work. In the hotel I had complete support services. I didn't think about food. I didn't think about a cleaning person. I didn't think about anything at all except for doing my job.

My husband didn't join me. I was never really off. This was a story that was happening seven days a week. So I can't have him come out, travel 3,000 miles and not have my time my own. When Orson Welles in *Citizen Kane* said being married to a newspaper person is worse than being married to a drunken sailor—that's true.

Death in the Field

As the trial wore on much of the competitive tension and occasional hostility among reporters was replaced by a sort of battlefield kinship. Many noted that the defining moment came following the deaths of Chris Harris, a TV correspondent for the Fox network, and Robin Clark, a reporter for the *Philadelphia Inquirer*. During the Rodney King case, Harris was stricken with a heart attack on the air. A hard-driving workaholic, Harris recovered but continued his frenetic pace on the Simpson story. Late one evening, near the beginning of the trial, he filed a story before going home. He died that evening. Reporters came together in what Deutsch described as a "family memorial."

Robin Clark's tragic death was even more profound. For the better part of a year, the 40-year-old reporter had been a popular member of the press corps, and, for many, his loss was a bitter blow.

"The most telling thing about Robin was the laugh lines around his eyes," said Perlman. "He liked to be amused, but in addition to that he had a lot of wisdom."

Clark spent his last day at a Friday court session joined by his cousin and her friend. He told Perlman that he planned to sneak his cousin's friend into the courtroom with his press pass. "He was real excited [knowing] that she'd get a big kick out of it," she said. When Perlman came by the pressroom during a break, there was Clark sitting on a chair, slapping his legs, delighted that the courtroom camera had panned over to the family friend who was visible on the screen.

At noon Clark and his two visitors left to go to Santa Monica for lunch. Traveling north on the Pacific Coast Highway, his Volkswagen bus was sideswiped by a Mercedes Benz and turned over on the driver's side. The bus skidded into the southbound lane and was struck by a Volvo station wagon which sent it airborne. Clark and his passengers were killed instantly.

"I got a call at 10 that night," recounted Perlman. "Andrea Ford [of the *Los Angeles Times*] called. Somebody called her from the *Philadelphia Inquirer* and wanted to know if was true. So I called the morgue and she called the sheriff's department. And then we knew it was true."

More than a year after Clark's death, Perlman still carried a memorial card. On one side was a picture of Clark leaning against the *Philadelphia Inquirer* building and a Carl Sandburg poem. On the back were the words to the hymn "Amazing Grace" over a picture of Clark on an open stretch of highway in the Southwest, standing in the middle of the road in Bermuda shorts and hat, strumming his guitar.

At the Monday session after Clark's death, Ito ordered that his seat remain vacant for the day in tribute to the reporter. Clark's press card was hung over the seat. Later, the Simpson press corps gathered at Joe McGinniss' residence in Beverly Hills for a memorial. For some it was a revelatory moment.

"I think that, in a way, this finally made us realize how close we all had become," said Deutsch. "At the base of all of this, we shared a common interest in journalism and in the reporting of stories. And how much we had come to like each other."

Deutsch as Grand Doyenne

Dunne appropriately called her the "grand doyenne" of court reporters. Linda Deutsch's reputation preceded her as she took her customary front-row seat in Department 103. The prized location enabled her to leave the courtroom quickly to meet her early deadline. It also gave her a view of the entire courtroom. The Simpson family was to her left; the Brown family sat behind her; and the Goldmans were to her right. Her job was to report for the AP's morning news cycle; her colleague, Michael Fleeman, had the afternoon cycle.

Her position in the courtroom also had a strong personal meaning for her. Sitting in the front-row seat, she made a conscious effort to maintain a strict impartial appearance. She was disheartened that members of the press corps had lost their objective stance, a trap she sought to avoid. Knowing that a television camera could at any time pan in her direction, she went so far as to consciously suppress any facial gestures that might reveal her private feelings. "That was my aim throughout the trial," she said. "It's an awesome responsibility to have that front-row seat and to bring the word to the public of what happened. I am the messenger, the eyes and ears of the public. They are smart enough to make their own decisions without me telling them how to make it."

She abhorred journalists who "took sides" at the trial and, at one point, refused to visit the courthouse pressroom because of the biased banter among her colleagues. Her professional stature did not go unnoticed. When Ito closed the courtroom for jury selection back in September, Deutsch was chosen to serve as the "pool" reporter. For much of that week, her daily reports were central to all media coverage.

Deutsch was a near-legendary figure among crime reporters. For a quarter of a century she had covered many of the most celebrated trials in modern American history involving such defendants as Sirhan Sirhan, Charles Manson, Patricia Hearst, Angela Davis, Daniel Ellsberg, and John DeLorean. The Manson and Simpson trials represented the "bookends" of her career, two cases she saw as containing lasting social meaning.

"Manson spoke to the drug-induced horrors of the 1960s, the end of flower power and love-ins, the birth of murderous cults," she wrote in her Simpson "chronicles." "If the Manson trial had been on television, the country would have stopped. It was so bizarre that had it been on TV every day there would be no way to do business in this country. It was as if every witness was Kato Kaelin. You really had a situation as explosive, as interesting [as Simpson], maybe more so in that it involved movie stars and hippies and represented an entire era coming to an end."

The Simpson trial was also unique, she explained, largely because of the defendant's status in a celebrity-worshiping culture. "Simpson was the most famous American ever charged with murder, simple as that. He is a beloved figure for many people, a very positive image, whether they knew him for football, movies, commercials. He now was in a role that no one ever expected him to be in. And that's always number one for any drama. In Hollywood, they call it the fish out of water. It's always interesting to us as human beings when someone gets into a scrape you don't expect him to [be in]. And this is more than a scrape."

But from Deutsch's view, the Simpson trial legacy may go beyond the defendant's stature, or even the controversies surrounding the case. The Simpson trial may well enter into history as a story of the media. "Oddly enough," she said, "my guess is that the O. J. Simpson trial will be remembered for the way we covered it and for the way it changed the world of journalism."

Dunne's World

The killing of Fred Goldman's son and Juditha and Lou Brown's daughter struck Dominick Dunne more profoundly than any other journalist covering the case. The murder of his only daughter was a bitterly painful memory that had deeply reshaped his life and, admittedly, altered his perception of O. J. Simpson, who Dunne was convinced was a murderer. Dunne's daughter, Dominique, was just beginning a career as an actress, having appeared in the popular movie, *Poltergeist*. She was stalked by an obsessed ex-boyfriend who finally lashed out and strangled her to death. John Sweeney, a promising Los Angeles chef, was convicted of manslaughter and sentenced to serve a prison term of just two and a half years. Dunne never forgave Judge Burton Katz for handing down such a lenient sentence.

The Simpson case, in smaller ways, brought him back to his daughter's murder trial. During one of his guest appearances on *Larry King Live*, he arrived at the CNN studio only to find that Katz was also a guest. Dunne refused to go on and wanted to leave the studio. The producers sent Katz home, telling the former judge that they would rather have Dunne.

Writers continued to search for "deeper meanings" to the Simpson case. For journalists like Jeffrey Toobin and Bill Boyarsky, Simpson was a story about the intractable racial divisions in America. But for Dunne, the Simpson case embodied Hollywood culture with a cast of beautiful women, powerful men, and a flamboyant lifestyle mix of celebrity, sex, and money.

Before his career as a novelist, Dunne was very much a part of the same Los Angeles milieu as a movie producer and Hollywood "player." After breaking into television as stage manager for the popular 1950s children's show, *Howdy Doody*, Dunne moved to Hollywood where he was hired by 20th Century Fox. Following a stint as a television executive, Dunne's career took off as a major producer when he hired a relatively unknown actor named Al Pacino to star in *Panic in Needle Park*. Other movies soon followed for Dunne, including *Play It as It Lays*, based on a book written by his sister-in-law, Joan Didion.

At the same time, Dunne fed off the excesses that plagued the rich and the famous of Hollywood. "At that time I was a drunk, and took whatever else was handed around," he said. His career failing and a marriage ending, Dunne at the age of 51 was convinced he was through. He was also suicidal. "I had fucked up my whole life," he said. Dunne told a BBC interviewer, "Hollywood is a very cruel place for failures, and I had become known as a failure. [Hollywood society] will forgive your lies, your cheating, your forgeries, and occasionally your murders, but never your failures."[6]

On a drive to Oregon's Cascade Mountains, a blowout turned out to be one of the fortuitous events in his life. Forced to spend a night at a nearby cabin to wait for repairs, Dunne wound up staying six months during which he discovered the writing life. He also regained his sense of sanity. After a few articles, and a first novel that he acknowledged had "flopped," Dunne continued writing about the people he knew best—America's rich and famous, and especially those in trouble. His first editor, Michael Korda, told him that Americans love nothing more than to read about powerful, wealthy people in criminal situations. "It was like a bell went off," said Dunne. "And that has become my whole second career."[7]

Dunne was only beginning his newfound career when he met Tina Brown. In the early 1980s *Vanity Fair* was a failing magazine about to be taken under the wings of Brown, then a relatively unknown editor of a British glossy magazine called the *Tatler*. Dunne met Brown at a dinner party the night before he was to attend the trial of his daughter's killer, and Brown gave him the assignment of covering the case for *Vanity Fair*. The result was a powerful and personal article about the terrifying plight, and death, of Dominique Dunne. "I had never given a thought about justice, except that I enjoyed reading about criminal stories," he said. "When I attended that first trial I wrote about it in a rage—it was all done on emotion but it established me as a writer. It made me a known quantity."

He followed with a cover article on Claus von Bulow, a Rhode Island socialite who was facing a second trial for attempting to murder his wife, Sunny, by insulin injection. His conviction at the first trial was overturned on appeal, won by Alan Dershowitz. In a full-page photo in *Vanity Fair*, von Bulow smirked into the camera, dressed in tight blue jeans and a black leather jacket—a bizarre portrait of a man exuding public contempt. Dunne's piece was equally revealing of the man and the society he inhabited. "After von Bulow had been found guilty and sentenced to 30 years, he was the toast of New York society," recounted Dunne. "After the second trial, when he was acquitted, everyone dropped him like a hot potato. That's the greatest comment on the whole sensibilities of the 1980s I can think of."[8]

But it was through his novels that Dunne was able to expand his reach. His books were a device by which he, cast as a fictional narrator, chronicled celebrated cases involving powerful American families in felonious trouble. His work was a piercing commentary on justice, social mores, and the special world inhabited by people of wealth. "I have had a front-row seat my whole life at a privileged world, and I get the details right, I get the dialogue right, I get the whole feel, I get the ambiance right," he said.[9] Taking two cases involving the Kennedy family—William Kennedy Smith's rape trial and another involving the death of a member of Ethel Kennedy's family—he wrote the best-selling novel, *A Season in Purgatory*.

Dunne was a third of the way through a novel based on the Menendez trial when he heard that Nicole Simpson and Ron Goldman had been murdered. "I just knew when the case broke that I was going to be involved with it," he said. Dunne was about to attend an awards dinner in Las Vegas when Simpson took flight. "I was in my room during the freeway chase and I was supposed to be down for these awards," he recounted. "My face was inches from the TV screen. I was that involved, I was obsessed." Dunne finally broke from the Bronco coverage to go to the dinner, and then he called his editor at *Vanity Fair*. His next assignment was the Simpson trial.

The Simpson case was a pivotal moment for Dunne. After 15 years, it marked his return to the Hollywood of which he once was a part. He had left in 1979 with his career and marriage in shambles and now returned with a successful career and a well-known name. His access to the Simpson case further enhanced the author's popularity within the enclaves of Hollywood's inner circle. "I became the toast of the town," he said. "I was the 'right-of-the-hostess' kind of guest because I had the hot skinny from the courtroom. This was how obsessed L.A. was. Whether I was with the media people, the TV people, or the movie moguls, there was this obsession."

This was, admittedly, Dunne's obsession as well. The Simpson case was a treasure trove for a writer with social antennae as acute as Dunne's. He was one of the few writers to praise Faye Resnick's book about Nicole Simpson. However unwittingly, Resnick's Los Angeles story features men and women whose only purpose in life is in satisfying their own indulgences. "It shows a part of L.A. life that we haven't seen before, of rich people in Ferraris going out, doing nothing with absolutely any intellectual curiosity," said Dunne. "They're going to Starbucks for coffee, then to the gym, then out dancing all night."

But Dunne's own Simpson commentary was even darker, his landscape a wash of Los Angeles culture where celebrities, beautiful women, rich men, and sex mingle with the dangerous realities of murder and racial conflict. As he writes in his "Letters":

> At Fiona Lewis' lunch party for her new book, *Between Men*, at the West Beach Cafe in Venice, Sean Penn, Dennis Hopper and Val Kilmer were all talking about O. J. Everyone has a different perspective. A Beverly Hills butler said that he was disappointed with O. J.'s body in the stripped-to-his-jockey shorts photographs at the trial to prove that he hadn't been hit by Ron Goldman. . . . People at smart dinner parties talk about their fear that the racial issue will be fanned into flames, while being waited on by black waiters and maids. The local joke is about the Beverly Hills woman who asks her maid if she'd kill her if the riots came. The maid replies, 'No, ma'am, but the maid next door might.'[10]

Inside the courtroom, Dunne was a visible figure seated next to the Goldmans for whom he held a deep affinity. He saw them as "good people" caught up in tragic circumstances, much like his own experience a decade earlier at the Sweeney trial. From the beginning, he believed Simpson was guilty and was openly sympathetic to the victims' families. His seat next to the Goldmans symbolically positioned him in the eyes of TV viewers as anti-Simpson each time the camera panned to the gallery.

His "Letters" did not overtly condemn Simpson, but his vivid character portrayals clearly showed his bias. In Dunne's world, prosecution witness Ron Shipp had a "sense of honor" and a "heroic" stance in the courtroom. His inquisitor, the defense team's Carl Douglas held a different stature. "I think that I have never seen a meaner face than Carl Douglas when he went after Shipp in his cross-examination," he wrote. "His eyes bulged almost out of their sockets as he directed a Bela Lugosi gaze on his prey."

According to Linda Deutsch, Dunne was a charismatic personality whom "you had to love whether you agree with him or not." But Dunne's public stance against Simpson still bothered Deutsch who objected to his "spouting of opinion on the case and representing himself as a reporter." "I think he was much more of an advocate," she said, "[and] a trial is not a place to take sides."

Leslie Abramson, Dunne's outspoken nemesis, was more blunt. She concluded that Dunne had taken his anger over his daughter's death and the subsequent trial of her killer to lash out against such defendents as the Menendez brothers and Simpson. His writing had become "therapy," charged Abramson. "He did what I suppose many writers would do under the circumstances: He turned his daughter into material. . . . [But] I happen to believe that there is a necessary distinction between journalism and therapy."[11]

But Dunne was not so easily typecast. Among the people he spoke affectionately about were Simpson's sisters, Carmelita Simpson Duro and Shirley Baker. The sisters themselves seemed to admire the writer who was so outspokenly convinced of their brother's guilt. They even purchased all of Dunne's books and had the author autograph them. Over the course of the year-long trial an unusual bond developed between the writer and the sisters, a relationship that Dunne felt was not entirely surprising. "People talk to me because they think I remind them of a defrocked priest," he said. "It's always been that way."

The relationship between Simpson's supporters and detractors was complicated and not easily broken down into two adversarial camps. The courtroom was an enclosed, intense environment where, interestingly, individual humanity flourished against the foreground of a double murder trial. Dunne understood this peculiar dynamic from his own experience at the Sweeny trial. He recalled speaking on behalf of the mother of the man accused of killing his daughter. She was a "sad figure" that "no one in the courtroom wanted anything to do with," recounted Dunne. "I remember saying on the witness stand that I admired the mother of the murderer because I knew she was a poor, hard-working women, and I knew she was good."[12]

Dunne said that Simpson's sister were also inherently "good"—a trait he admired. But as the trial wound down, he acknowledged that the personal strains overtook their friendship. The "thing" between them—Dunne's belief that Simpson was a murderer—had grown more prominent as the case came closer to the verdict. "We didn't look at each other anymore," he said.

It was near the end of the trial when Dunne himself became enmeshed in a frightening episode. His son Alex was reported missing in the Santa Rita Mountains of Arizona, and Dunne left the courthouse to be with his former wife and family for four agonizing days. He told his other son, the actor Griffin Dunne, that he believed Alex was dead. "From hanging out at murder trials, as I do, I had grown despondent about the goodness of people," he said.

The disappearance of Alex Dunne became a major national news story. Dominick Dunne joined the vast search efforts in a plane sent over from *Entertainment Tonight*, the glossy celebrity television program. In the plane, a camera operator photographed Dunne as he scanned the Arizona landscape looking for his son. Looking back at the scene, Dunne wryly recalled how absurd the photo-op must have looked. "There I was in their plane, with a cameraman focused on me, looking out the window—it was a cheap movie." Only in a scene from Dunne's life-as-a-movie would the *Entertainment Tonight* plane actually be the first to find Alex Dunne's abandoned car. Yet that's what happened. The cameraman took footage of the car for the program's evening telecast. "They felt they got their money's worth," he said.

In this latest chapter of his tumultuous life, Dunne found good fortune on his side. His son was discovered and rescued after surviving a fall down a ravine. Following Dunne's return to the courtroom, Ito began the day's session by welcoming him back. "When I got back to court every single person came up to me and hugged me," he said, "and I realized then I was part of this trial."

13

THE FUHRMAN TRIAL

JUNE 12, 1995

The Bitter Anniversary

Across the country, the one-year anniversary of the Simpson-Goldman murders was a collectively agonizing and mournful moment. Media photographs captured the Goldman and Brown families at the victims' gravesites—a snapshot reminder that two lives had been snuffed out in the rampage at South Bundy on June 12, 1994.

In court the bitter anniversary was acknowledged in vivid reenactment. Earlier in the week, jurors got their first glimpse at the grisly autopsy photos, and two were so shaken that Ito was forced to recess to allow them to regain their composure. Prosecutor Brian Kelberg then summoned Lakshmanan Sathyavagiswaran, the county coroner, to the stand to demonstrate how Nicole Simpson was killed. The coroner grabbed Kelberg around the chest, leaned the prosecutor's head backward to expose his neck, and then held a ruler to Kelberg's throat and made slashing motions.

Ito also allowed a contingent of 48 reporters to privately view the autopsy pictures during a closed-door session. Some 58 photos were mounted on easels, as reporters circled the macabre exhibition. One photograph, in particular, haunted some reporters: It showed the face of Nicole Simpson, her half-closed eyes, frozen in a death mask. Robin Clark wrote in his report that day that Nicole's pale lips "were parted as if to pose a terrible question, the answer to which only one person may know."[1]

For once during the long, fractious proceedings, the brutal reality of the crime seemed chillingly clear. Some reporters were so taken by the horrific nature of the photographs that during the display they sat silently in the gallery as if paying respect to the dead. In a funeral-like procession, reporters passed by each photo, as Ito and Kelberg watched without speaking from the jury box. Except for the sound of reporters' pens scratching against their notepads, the courtroom was silent.

"I'm just undone by it," said Dominick Dunne. "I had prepared myself, but even so it was devastating." In one photo, Nicole Simpson's throat had been so deeply slashed that the insides of her neck were exposed. "It was absolutely faint-making," he said.[2]

As an experienced crime reporter, Shirley Perlman had seen many autopsy photographs. Few compared with Goldman's. "Ron Goldman was absolutely butchered," she said. He had suffered so many stab wounds that it appeared as if his body "was shot full of bullets."[3]

Robin Clark said it was not the pictures of death that he found most disturbing. It was the photographs that "carried small reminders of life interrupted." One was of Goldman's bloody jeans and T-shirt. Another was of the watch worn by Nicole the night of her murder. The watch had been broken from the violent assault, its hand frozen at two minutes before ten.

After six months, many veteran reporters despaired that the trial had crumbled into a senseless legal exercise winding its way to a no-decision. "To many lawyers and lay people alike," said David Margolick in his *New York Times* story that day, "the proceedings in Judge Lance A. Ito's courtroom seem endless, exasperating and ultimately meaningless."[4]

The trial had become a source of national shame, and the autopsy photos were a sad reminder of just how far the case had veered from its primary question: Did O. J. Simpson murder Nicole Simpson and Ron Goldman? It was a question overshadowed by the theatrical sideshows inside and outside the courtroom. The gnawing reality continued to grow that the case had degenerated into a depressing event disconnected from real justice.

Some columnists recognized the anniversary with blistering attacks on what had become of American culture in the year of the trial. Frank Rich was openly disdainful in his *New York Times* column that day, asking rhetorically, "Who is to blame for this circus in which the murder victims have increasingly become forgotten players? Cynical observers might point the finger at a public so ravenous for celebrities that even Faye Resnick will do—and so infatuated with violence that witnesses' descriptions of off-camera autopsy photos take on their own pornographic allure."

The anniversary also marked an emotional turning point for certain key players in the trial. A visibly depressed Christopher Darden admitted to the *Los Angeles Times* that his faith in the courts had been severed. He questioned his own place in a system that had worked so poorly. Each participant had been "tarnished," he lamented. "I don't know if I ever want to practice law again. Everything about this case and these proceedings is imperfect. Frankly, I'm ashamed to be a part of this case."

It was an audacious statement, but Darden had had enough, distraught by the personal attacks he had endured over the year. He was proud of his work within the black community, fighting against corruption and gang violence. But now he found himself a pariah within segments of that same community, branded by the defense, however absurdly, as "anti-black" by his place on the prosecution team.

But it wasn't just the tiresome race baiting that bothered Darden. He believed that his private life had also been torn apart by the media: The public surveillance that the Simpson prosecutors had endured was beyond the limits of fair play. "The intense scrutiny of our personal lives is unfair," he said. "We're just civil servants trying to do the right thing to prosecute a case. Our privacy ought to be respected."[5]

A 15-year veteran of the Los Angeles district attorney's office, Darden said that thoughts of the victims and their families, steeled him against the debilitating effects of the trial. "Sometimes I turn around and I look at the Goldmans, and you could see the hurt and the suffering in their faces," he said. "Sometimes I see them and they're smiling, but. . . sometimes they are dying inside."

This trial was not the civics lesson Ito had in mind. An American Bar Association survey revealed that as a result of the Simpson trial, a growing number of Americans had "lost respect for the justice system," a trend that came as no surprise to Darden who counted himself among those who had lost faith. The court's "search for the truth" seemed more like a battle between undisciplined, long-winded lawyers seeking to manipulate evidence and devise far-fetched schemes. For all the moral rhetoric, the trial had become a high stakes, win-at-any-cost game.

Television pictures from the courtroom continued to reinforce the perception that the trial was out of control. "Some of the interminable testimony seemed to have no other purpose than to showcase the talent of a lawyer for the camera," admitted Gerald Uelmen. He said that when he took a leave from the case for a long-planned family trip to Europe, Lakshmanan Sathyavagiswaran was being sworn in. Uelmen returned to the courtroom *two weeks later* to find the coroner still on the stand. "Brian Kelberg is a brilliant lawyer," he said, "but apparently 15 minutes of fame was not enough for him. He needed sixty hours."[6]

Public contempt was expressed in media commentary across the country: The Simpson trial had become an object of scorn. Those who carried the hope that extended television coverage could have a salutary effect on public understanding of the law were bitterly disappointed. What we have ended up with "is a three-ring circus which would have made P. T. Barnum green with envy," said Donald Russo, a criminal attorney in the *Philadelphia Inquirer*. "Having watched many movies in which prisoners of war were being tortured to reveal military secrets, any pity I may have had for those prisoners has been far surpassed by the horror I have experienced at the sight of attorney Barry Scheck cross-examining Los Angeles County criminalist Dennis Fung for ten days."[7]

The Simpson trial had not only exposed the cracks of the justice system, but had created its own deep fissures. Lawyers and legal representatives across the country tried to cauterize the wounds to their profession. At Vanderbilt Law School, law professor Nancy King cautioned students that the Simpson case furnished "a warped vision of normal attorney conduct—that attorneys get through most trials without whining or calling each other names."[8]

Steven Brill also tried to control the damage inflicted on his most valued partner: the camera. Forced to adjust his public pitch, Brill no longer was selling "cameras in the courtroom" on the worn basis that the medium could "educate" the public about the workings of the court. He now espoused the belief that television was necessary to show Americans what was *wrong* with the courts so that they could then fix it. Brill was scrambling to find *some* rationale to counteract what many critics saw as a spectacular televised failure in criminal justice.

Even the Simpson defense team—heavily pro-camera at the start—accused Brill of being disingenuous. Uelmen said that it was television that had "corrupted" the court as a "bastion of thoughtful reflection and dispassionate analysis." Television changed the way lawyers behaved, with the level of "sniping and snarling" achieving "a new low for the American bar." Witnesses "bore the greatest brunt" being part of a televised trial, asserted Uelmen. "Some may profit, while others will bear lifelong scars. But we have lost our sense of proportion when we strip away any claims to privacy for anyone who approaches the witness box."

Live TV trial coverage had in fact created an event with tremendous popular appeal but dubious legal benefit—a conflict that left Simpson watchers captivated but unsettled. It was one of the great paradoxes of the Simpson trial that while Americans railed against television's exploitation of the case they continued to promote the Simpson "show" by tuning in daily to the proceedings. However intellectually repelled by what had become of the trial, they were emotionally drawn to the media-made soap opera.

This curious personality split was evident as well in California politics. As state leaders expressed disgust at this new genre of "entertainment," local politicians sought to exploit the trial's commercial "values." In an effort to recoup an estimated $9 million that the trial would cost the public, the Los Angeles County Board of Supervisors seriously considered proposals that would allow the city to cash in. Should a retrial be required, one proposal called for booking the Shubert Theater as the legal venue, with tickets selling for $50 apiece (a highly questionable constitutional venture, at the least). Yet another proposal gave the county authority to sell television rights to the highest bidder, much like the way the Olympics or professional sports programs are sold to networks.

Uelmen mused that it might not take too long before prosecutors "went looking for cases that would have greater earning potential as entertainment events. We could end up with a trial of the century every month, instead of the current rate of one every three years."[9]

The public ridicule of schemes to market the Simpson trial belied an underlying sentiment shared by both the trial participants and the rest of world tuning in. The Year of Simpson had become something of a twisted joke.

JUNE-JULY 1995

Simpson and the Glove

O. J. Simpson carried a "star" presence with him each day he walked into the courtroom, his self-confidence disarming given the dire circumstances. It was also an attitude conveyed at the defense table, where he took a highly active role. At times his instructions or comments to his lawyers were audible to gallery spectators.

But on television, Simpson mostly was a spectral presence. During opening arguments, he was allowed to show the jury his arthritic knees, suggesting he was incapable of overpowering and killing two healthy young people. But beyond a brief quiet word to his lawyers, or an occasional animated expression of emotion, in the TV frame Simpson was a fairly stoic figure. In a pivotal moment of the case, however, a glove demonstration gave him the chance to take center stage.

At Darden's request, Simpson stood in the middle of the courtroom well and attempted to try on a single extra-large brown glove stained with blood from the killing scene at South Bundy. As the jury watched intently, Simpson struggled to pull the glove over his outstretched fingers. He had been required to wear a latex glove as protection against possible biochemical effects from the blood-soaked glove. Simpson grimaced and contorted his face, commenting to the jury, "They're too small."

Darden accused Simpson of faking his struggle and tried to recoup by handing the defendant a marking pen to show he could bend his hand and thereby grip a knife. But the experiment was already over: Darden's ploy had flopped, both in Department 103 and on national television.

The picture was dramatic but not sensational television. In this particular instance, the medium failed to convey the emotional impact the demonstration had within the confines of the courtroom. Reporters seated in the gallery were able to more fully observe Simpson's body language, and they also fed off the intense emotion that permeated the courtroom. "This was theater at its highest—Simpson had seized the moment," said Linda Deutsch. "He had the jury mesmerized when he put the glove on. It was when you had a true picture of how self-confident he was, how powerful a persona he was in the courtroom, and how much his charisma affected the outcome. It was one of those Perry Mason moments you rarely see in the courtroom."[10]

Deutsch said she returned to her upstairs office and called Darden to ask him why he allowed Simpson to try on the glove. He told her, "I looked at his hand, and I looked at the glove, and I thought it would fit."

The glove demonstration was like a scene out of *Rashoman*, the classic Akira Kurosawa film, leaving observers with diametrically different impressions.

Deutsch believed it "clearly did not fit."

But Bill Boyarsky contended, "It was clear to me he was acting."

Dan Abrams agreed: "An objective person watching would have to report that it did not look like Simpson was trying very hard to put on the glove."[11]

Media personalities had a field day with the glove experiment. On his late-night CNBC program, Charles Grodin went so far as to perform his own glove demonstration. Wearing a latex liner, Grodin struggled to squeeze into a leather glove to no avail. He mimicked Simpson, grimacing theatrically in his effort. Then, without the liner, he smoothly slipped into the glove, now looking perfectly fitted on his hand. Grodin duly noted that the glove mystery had been solved.

Immediately after the glove demonstration in Department 103, Jim Newton phoned his legal sources from the *Los Angeles Times* newsroom. "Without exception," he said, "they considered it somewhere between a really bad moment and the worst example of trial lawyering they had ever seen."[12]

Darden, however, wasn't the only legal strategist who had miscalculated. Roy Black, best known for his successful defense in the William Kennedy Smith case, said on the *Today* show that the very same ploy occurred to him while he had been watching Darden introduce the glove into evidence. Black admitted he kept thinking, "Have Simpson try on the glove, have him try on the glove!" When, in fact, Simpson was instructed to try on the glove and the experiment seemed to backfire, Black wryly played the omnipotent second-guesser. Watching the televised image of a shaken Darden, he shouted at the screen, with a strong hint of self-mockery, *"You idiot. You idiot."*

Prosecution Rests, Defense Attacks

July 6. After five months the prosecution completed its case against Simpson by wearily announcing, "The People rest."

The Dream Team wasted no time and immediately went on the attack. On the eve of the defense's case, Simpson lawyer's chose the television airwaves as their initial staging ground. When Johnnie Cochran appeared for a *Nightline* interview, he may have expected an opportunity to beat up on the prosecution before a national audience. Instead, Cochran's presence gave Ted Koppel the chance to vigorously challenge the promises the lawyer had made during opening arguments—promises that had gone largely unfulfilled.

Cochran then had told the court that a key witness, Mary Anne Gerchas, would testify that she saw five men wearing knit caps, and carrying what seemed to be weapons, within ten feet of Nicole Simpson's condominium shortly before the murders. Rosa Lopez, a housekeeper who lived next door to Simpson's estate, would testify that she saw Simpson's Bronco van outside his home at the time of the murders. But these witnesses never were called before the jury. Gerchas faced criminal actions herself and was seen as highly unreliable. Lopez testified on videotape in the jury's absence, but her five-day stint on the stand was so riddled with contradictions and memory shortfalls that the tape was never shown.

Cochran could not slip away from Koppel's probes: What was Simpson doing with a large sum of cash during his flight from the law? What proof did Cochran have that there was a conspiracy afoot to frame Simpson? By the end of the evening, Cochran had maintained his composure but had lost the public relations battle.

On CNN that evening Alan Dershowitz was given a much wider berth by Larry King. In this strange television universe, it was difficult to discern the *real* Dershowitz as he switched between his role as a Simpson advocate and a generic celebrity legal pundit. That night on King's show, the subject ostensibly had nothing to do with Simpson but with another famous personality in trouble with the law—actor Hugh Grant accused of soliciting a prostitute. Dershowitz came to Grant's support too, decrying laws that involve such "victimless crimes." But Dershowitz was also delivering another subtle message. The LAPD had gone after yet another Hollywood celebrity who had done little to warrant arrest and the public humiliation that had been heaped upon him. From that stance, Dershowitz let viewers make up their own minds about Simpson.

AUGUST-SEPTEMBER 1995

Downfall

After 92 days of testimony and evidentiary presentations, the defense sought to rehabilitate Simpson's image from the wife beater-turned killer that the prosecution had portrayed. Simpson family members took the stand one by one: his daughter, Arnelle, his sisters, Shirley Baker and Carmelita Simpson-Durio, and his mother, Eunice, all wearing shades of gold in a show of solidarity. Deutsch described the opening as "family day." "With their warm recollections, the courtroom seemed transformed, as if everyone was sitting around the fireplace trading family memories," she said.[13] Indeed the picture of familial love was evident as Arnelle told jurors proudly that she was born the same day her father won the Heisman Trophy given to the best college football player in the country.

The cozy picture of the Simpson family would linger for only a short time. The defense's police conspiracy theory, long thought to be moribund, was suddenly revived in a stunning discovery that would implode the prosecution's case and catapult the race issue to another level.

Six months earlier Mark Fuhrman had told the court how he had scaled the fence at Simpson's estate and found a bloody glove in an overgrown stretch of property near the defendant's house. He had adeptly parried defense accusations that he framed Simpson by planting the glove. When pressed by the defense, he also had denied uttering the word "nigger" during the previous ten years. Now with the discovery of a series of audiotaped interviews, Fuhrman's reputation, and the prosecution's case, would crumble with new revelations of the detective's racist attitudes.

The story behind the Fuhrman audiotapes was as fantastic as any Hollywood courtroom thriller. An investigator from Simpson's team had tracked down the tapes to a North Carolina screenwriter, Laura Hart McKinny. Nine years earlier, Hart had been in a Westwood coffee shop, when a Los Angeles police officer named Mark Fuhrman approached her and struck up a conversation. She was a fledgling writer interested in researching a film script about women police officers. When Fuhrman learned that she was working on a screenplay about the LAPD, he offered his help as a technical advisor, agreeing to a fee if the script was bought. Over the next decade, Fuhrman spun a violent tale of the city's police force in a series of extended interviews that would end shortly after the Simpson-Goldman murders. Neither Fuhrman nor McKinny could possibly foresee the explosive ramifications of those interviews.

On August 11, following the defense team's legal tug-of-war with the North Carolina courts over rights to the tapes, the 17 cassette tapes arrived at the district attorney's office. It was clear that

Fuhrman had lied to the court in March—more than 40 times he could be heard using the word "nigger." But the detective's rhetoric went much further, bragging about vicious acts of police brutality that he had personally been involved in. Fuhrman described one incident in which he and three other officers severely beat four suspects in a 1978 police shooting incident.

> We basically tortured them. . . . We broke 'em. Numerous bones in each one of them. Their faces were just mush. They had pictures of the walls, there was blood all the way to the ceiling and finger marks of them trying to crawl out of the room. They showed us pictures of the room. It was unbeliev-able, there was blood everywhere. These guys, they had to shave off so much hair, one guy shaved it all off. Like 70 stitches in his head. You know, knees cracked, oh, it was just—we had 'em begging that they'd never be gang members again, begging us.

A secondary conflict shadowed the Fuhrman tapes. The detective also had discussed in derogatory language his confrontations with Captain Margaret York, the head of the LAPD's internal-affairs department and the highest-ranking female on the force. She was also Ito's wife. That disclosure prompted the prosecution, already unhappy with Ito's actions, to demand that the judge remove himself from the bench for the remainder of the trial. It was a shocking request coming at the trial's eleventh hour. But prosecutors argued that Ito's ruling on the admissibility of the tapes was now tainted by his wife's indirect involvement in the case.

From the defense team's viewpoint, the prosecution's move was a ruse to throw the trial into turmoil. If Ito was forced off the case, his replacement would need weeks to read 20,000 pages of transcripts and become familiar with all prior evidentiary rulings. The jury, now down to two alternates and already chafing under the strain of the lengthy trial, would also have to remain sequestered for as long as another month. Should Ito leave the case, the general feeling was that a mistrial was all but certain.

In a tearful response from the bench, Ito declared his love for his wife and admitted he could not remain impartial to Fuhrman's insults. "I love my wife dearly," Ito said, his voice cracking with emotion, "and I am wounded by criticism of her, as any spouse would be. I think it is reasonable to assume that this could have some impact." The media typically overplayed the judge's emotional affirmation of love, going so far as to compare the judge with the love-stricken King Edward VIII who abdicated the British throne for matters of the heart. The trial, so long compared to a soap opera, had further evolved as one.

The next day Marcia Clark reversed direction and withdrew her request that Ito disqualify himself. Judge John Reid independently determined that York would not be required to testify, ensuring that Ito would continue to preside over the trial. But the episode lingered, and was indicative of the deep-seated rift between the prosecution and the judge. Said Darden: "Many of the prosecutors were angry with Ito for the way he handled the case, allowing it to spin out of control."

On August 29, Ito allowed the defense to play the Fuhrman tapes for the court, but, in truth, this was a demonstration meant for television. Since the jury was not present, there was no legal benefit in having the tapes played in open court. Ito's concern, in fact, was not based on legalities but on public relations—he admittedly worried that he might be accused of participating in a cover-up if he kept the tapes under wraps. Ito ruled that almost all taped excerpts of Fuhrman were inadmissible in his courtroom—but that they were entirely admissible in the court of public opinion. Department 103 would be the site of this shadow trial.

It was a telling decision. Ito had continually reprimanded the lawyers for presenting arguments deliberately designed to reach and exploit a live TV audience. However, any pretense to keep the case within the boundaries of the courtroom was obliterated as wholesale segments of the audiotapes played in the courtroom and across the United States. Ito had made his own play to the camera. The courtroom gates were thrown open with the McKinny tapes offered up as the latest trial sensation.

The tapes were the equivalent of dropping a bomb into a case already weighted with racial tensions. Fuhrman's invectives pierced through the small confines of the courtroom. Linda Deutsch said that it was as if Department 103 "was under a bombardment by this outpouring of racist venom." "I wrote on my notepad to Dominick [Dunne], 'The case is over,'" she recalled. "And he wrote back, 'The party's at Rockingham.'" [14]

McKinny's scratchy tape recordings played in conjunction with a transcript that scrolled on an overhead screen. "Anything out of a nigger's mouth. . . is a fucking lie," Fuhrman was heard to say. Speaking about police tactics: "The department says we shoot to stop, not kill, which is horseshit. The only way we can stop somebody is to kill the son of a bitch. And what's the big deal? If you've got reason to shoot somebody, you've got reason to kill him."

The tapes played well beyond the courtroom into the streets and communities of Los Angeles, as well as the nation. As the media played over and over the most inflammatory parts, the audiotapes became an incarnation of the Rodney King videotape, confirming to many blacks what they already "knew" or suspected—the LAPD was racist and had few qualms about violating civil rights or tampering with evidence to put away anyone it was convinced deserved it, that the system was rigged against people of color.

For Fred Goldman, Ito's decision to turn the tapes over to the public was yet another misguided step away from judging Simpson's role in the two murders. "There is no reason to have two hours of this hate to be spewed out over the public airwaves," he stated. "My son, and Nicole, and her family, have a right to a fair trial and this is not fair."

Goldman's fears were justified. The media immediately began to focus on Fuhrman rather than Simpson. Reporters now turned to investigate the detective's statements that he had beaten suspects and engaged in other police misconduct. The role of the LAPD was also closely scrutinized.

Reporters contended that the "Fuhrman issue" had now overwhelmed the narrow question of whether or not O. J. Simpson was responsible for the Simpson-Goldman murders. "That issue and the handling of it goes to the question of police management, which I think is ultimately more important than the question of who did the murders in some ways," said Jim Newton. "In this city, at this time, post-Rodney King, these are the social issues that reach decades beyond this case."

Newton's observation pointed to just how far the media had veered from the murder trial. Nothing on the tapes directly contradicted Fuhrman's role in the Simpson investigation. Rather, on tape, the detective denied allegations he planted evidence or set up Simpson. His racial attitudes and purported violent actions were repellent and his perjury possibly criminal, but would such "testimony" override the wealth of evidence linking Simpson to the murders? Apparently, it would. Following the tapes' disclosure in court, the public trial of O. J. Simpson would begin in earnest: At the center of attention was the detective and the LAPD. The tide had shifted for good as the media turned from Simpson to Fuhrman.

Newton was among those who investigated Fuhrman's boastful stories about widespread brutality within the police department. The reporter, in fact, had uncovered internal police reports of a 1978 incident in East Los Angeles that cited many of the facts Fuhrman described, though his role was never clarified. Whether or not the detective was actually involved in brutalizing suspects, his taped remarks carried serious implications. "If he's making all this up, it raises the question whether he's a liar and that's no good for the trial," said Newton. "If he's telling the truth—that he beat people's faces to mush—then it raises real questions about the conduct of the police department and its relationship within the communities, and its willingness to cover up. Those fundamentally are issues much bigger than Simpson."

While the tapes played heavily on the nation's social conscience, the actual recordings, ironically, carried less weight inside the courtroom. Ito had severely limited their admissibility, ruling that the jury would be allowed to hear just two of the 42 tape-recorded instances in which Fuhrman referred to blacks as "niggers"—remarks that were tame compared with other more explosive statements on the tape.

Ito also barred the defense from using any of Fuhrman's damning statements about police violence on the grounds that they were too inflammatory and that the defense had failed to prove the incidents ever happened. Ito, who had previously allowed the defense to capriciously explore its police conspiracy theory, now sought to clamp down. "The asserting of glove-planting is not supported by the record," he said in his ruling. "It is a theory without factual support."

Ito's ruling enraged the defense, and Cochran's first move was to take his case to the media. At an impromptu press conference, the lawyer condemned Ito for holding the tapes back from the jurors—if not the world. Ito's ruling, Cochran charged, was "one of the cruelest, unfair decisions rendered in a criminal case in this country." The emotional outburst was surprising even for reporters accustomed to the lawyer's histrionics. The subtext to his remarks was also disturbing. Cochran was well aware that his remarks could incite Los Angeles' inner city already emotionally charged by the trial. After attacking the judge's decision, Cochran then appealed to the black community for "calm." The lawyer was undaunted, shamelessly

manipulating racial tensions in his win-at-any-cost battle to save
Simpson.

Shirley Perlman said Cochran was "walking a fine line" between
a strong adversarial role in the case and that of a self-professed
spokesman for the black community. But for other observers,
Cochran's posturing was meant to intimidate, and his inferences
were clear—the Simpson case was a hair trigger within the black
community, and Ito's controversial ruling could set off a race war.
Whether Cochran's rhetoric had accurately gauged black sentiment
was beside the point. He cynically used his platform to inflame public
reaction, and then held out the threat that violence might ensue from
perceptions of racial injustice against his client.

Despite limitations placed on the tapes, Fuhrman's record was
hardly concealed from the jury. The defense questioned witnesses
who had heard Fuhrman make racist statements. Kathleen Bell, a
real estate broker claimed that Fuhrman told her years earlier: "If I
had my way, all the niggers would be gathered together and burned."
Another witness, Natalie Singer, who met Fuhrman in 1987, quoted
Fuhrman as telling her, "The only good nigger is a dead nigger."

McKinny also testified fully about her interviews with the
detective. At her references to Fuhrman's racist depictions, some
jurors bit their lips, others recoiled. Reporters in the gallery noticed
that jurors who had been moribund in the waning days of the trial
suddenly became more focused, with some taking notes.

The defense team had also persuaded Ito to permit the jury to
hear one additional taped passage in which Fuhrman spoke of
women police officers. "They don't do anything," he said. "They don't
go out there and initiate contact with some 6-foot-5 nigger that's been
in prison for seven years pumping weights."

On the following day, September 6, the defense brought Mark
Fuhrman back to the stand, this time with the jury absent. When he
first appeared in court in March the detective gave off a visceral sense
of confidence. Reporters then described the detective's self-assured
swagger, which had carried over to his composed testimony. Now,
said Dunne, Fuhrman's eyes were "black holes" belonging to someone
who didn't have a friend in the room. Darden ordered his young black
associates to stay away from court that day to avoid "[taking] with
them the memory of Fuhrman's face, his betrayal to us all." On the
stand, Fuhrman, by then the target of a U.S. Justice Department
probe and no longer with the LAPD, invoked the Fifth Amendment

against self-incrimination when defense lawyers asked him if he had lied under oath, if he'd fabricated police reports, or if he'd planted evidence against Simpson.

Fuhrman's legal culpability became the latest turn in the case, with the defense team arguing that he had repeatedly perjured himself in earlier testimony. From a national perspective, Fuhrman would likely never to be able to overcome being branded "the racist." As the *Amsterdam News* reported, "Finally, Mark Fuhrman was brought back into the mix with those who had seen, heard and watched him. He was erect as an arrow, and as cold as a storm trooper in Nazi Germany as he refused to testify, as was his right, of course."

But for Fred Goldman, it was yet another depressing slide away from resolving O. J. Simpson's part in the savage double murder. Following the detective's revisit to the stand, Goldman implored the Simpson press corps to keep its eye on who he believed was his child's killer. "This is not the Fuhrman trial," he pleaded. But, by that time, trial watchers, including those in the media, were thinking otherwise.

<h1 style="text-align:center">14</h1>

THE BLACK AND
WHITE PRESS

SEPTEMBER 1995

The trial of O. J. Simpson lurched into the final stages of a glum exercise in criminal law, hopelessly slipping from a legal question about murder to a national contest about race. No longer was it possible to speak about the Simpson-Goldman murders without addressing matters having to do with Simpson's skin color. And no longer was it possible to consider race without looking at the press corps and its coverage of the case.

Cochran had told a group of black journalists in Philadelphia that the white-controlled news media were taking sides against Simpson by sympathetically portraying the families of the murdered victims, while ignoring the suffering that his client's family had endured. Simpson himself had been victimized by the media's sound bites, which were calculated "to sell the guilt of Mr. Simpson" and the "insincerity" of the defense team. Cochran then issued a clarion call to black journalists to be "advocates" for the black cause.[1]

There were only a handful of black reporters among major newspapers and networks who played a consistent role in the daily reporting of the Simpson case. Andrea Ford of the *Los Angeles Times,* shared a byline on many news accounts of the trial, and Kenneth Noble of the *New York Times* substituted on occasion for the paper's chief Simpson writer, David Margolick. Covering the trial for the networks were Marc Watts of CNN, Bill Whitaker of CBS, and Ron Allen of ABC. Black reporters were more visible on local news stations and the smaller news outlets, but, for the most part, relatively few blacks were among the 1,159 reporters accredited for the Simpson trial.

The white predominance was even more apparent at the higher levels. Few major news organizations had a single black editor or news director working on the Simpson story. Since it was widely assumed that many reporters, editors, TV correspondents and news directors believed Simpson was guilty, this institutional bias toward Simpson's guilt troubled individual black reporters.

Speaking about the L.A. *Times* coverage, Ford stated: "Most of our coverage is done and directed by white people. No black editor making decisions. No black person actually writing the main story. I think that is truly, truly disturbing."[2] Ford herself was assigned to a nearly all-white team of reporters, columnists, and editors to cover the trial. As the lone black reporter, she was moved off the main trial story partway through the trial and onto secondary trial coverage. Her transfer evoked suspicions that she was being shunted aside because of her outspoken attitudes regarding the case.

Ford admittedly was angry over press coverage of the Simpson case, whether it was coming from her own paper or other major media outlets. She contended that she had been placed in an untenable position working day to day with mostly white reporters and editors who had already made up their mind about Simpson's guilt. Ford was most disturbed by the "disdainful, dismissive attitude taken toward the defense" made evident by comments heard in the pressroom. "The defense is automatically seen as sleazy and dishonest," she said. "The prosecution is automatically seen as virtuous."[3]

The reporter found support from Linda Deutsch, who also maintained that reporters had "taken sides" in the case, and that as a result, the pressroom—the center of Simpson coverage—had become an increasingly inhospitable place to work.

The pressroom, in fact, was often raucous with reporters directing comments to one another or yelling at the television monitors, or poking fun and mimicking the mannerisms of trial participants such as Johnnie Cochran, a favorite target. "I can see where Andrea would feel [offended]," said Shirley Perlman. "These weren't biased people but it hurts when you hear it. It's insensitive, so I can understand why she felt that way."[4]

For Perlman, the reporters were mostly acting out "their cynical selves" in a situation loaded with tremendous day-to-day pressures. "Some people were taken more seriously then they should," she said. "You had to take a look at what they wrote, not what someone was saying when they were horsing around in the pressroom."

Perlman acknowledged that the mostly white press corps likely viewed the case differently than black reporters covering the case. White reporters tended to believe the government's case, that if police say things happened, they happened. Black reporters generally were more leery about evidence and police claims. Perlman believed that at least some black reporters thought Simpson was probably guilty, but were more inclined to keep their opinions to themselves.

Some reporters conceded that they struggled to keep their opinions about Simpson out of their work. David Margolick admitted that he held a "profound skepticism of the defense," a mindset he had to guard against to avoid influencing his stories. But others believed that it was not possible to filter out a reporter's prejudgment. Intentionally or not, that message crept into the coverage. David Bloom, a white reporter who covered the case for NBC's *Nightly News*, said that "to argue against that proposition would be a logical absurdity."[5]

Not all black reporters shared Ford's experience and belief that a white-dominated press had stacked up against Simpson. Marc Watts, a black reporter for CNN, remarked, "Andrea was working in a whole different environment" than he was. Watts said his two main supervisors were highly aware what role race may have played in the trial: "They were never blinded to what may have been a fair story just because they were white."[6]

Watts refused to pillory the "white media," but contended that individual members of the press corps were out of touch with the racial realities of the Simpson case—an attitude reflective of their overall ignorance about race in America. "Some reporters covering the trial were culturally illiterate, so they don't understand, perhaps to this day, the dynamics that race played in the trial," he stated. "And they don't understand Johnnie Cochran when he says, 'I didn't make race an issue, Mark Fuhrman made race an issue.' Unless you've walked in a black man's shoes, you can't understand what he's saying by that. I don't think that as African-Americans we like to go out and make race an issue, but it exists as an issue."

"Because of who I am, I was able to understand the racial elements of the trial," he added. When Christopher Darden argued against allowing the defense to use the "n-word," Watts said he strongly identified with the deep psychological import the word "nigger" had for the mostly black jury, a sensitivity that went beyond the ken of most whites. When Cochran mentioned Simi Valley, the site of the first Rodney King case, he said that an internal "alarm" went off. The reporter believed that his "life experiences" made him better equipped to cover the racial aspects of the trial, most notably Fuhrman's role, which stood at the core of the defense. The question confronting the court, and the press corps, was whether Fuhrman's professed racist views were enough evidence to conclude that he may have framed Simpson. "All the white reporters I talked to said he may have been a racist, but he could have never planted the glove," said Watts. "I will tell you that I would answer that question quite differently."

Black reporters in mainstream news organizations faced public pressures of a different kind from white reporters. Watts found himself no longer being seen as a reporter covering the Simpson story but as a *black* reporter. Black viewers wrote letters and called the network to complain that he was anti-Simpson; others called him an "Uncle Tom" and a "sellout." Then he got responses from white viewers accusing him of automatically siding with the defense because he was black. Watts said that he was neither "pro-prosecution" nor "pro-defense," but that some viewers labeled him as such and could not get past his skin color. "It bothered me," he said. "In a case where race was of such magnitude, people even looked at me through that prism of race. At times I was being judged by the color of my skin, not the content of my report."

The public reaction was so strong that Watts found himself constantly looking over his shoulder, never sure which story would incite a public outcry. A routine profile of Brian Kelberg provoked an angry response from black viewers who believed Watts had been unfair to Simpson. Kelberg was the prosecutor who graphically demonstrated in court how the killer could have attacked the victims. "Obviously that report wasn't viewed very well in the community who felt that O. J . Simpson was not guilty," he said.

Ironically, as the "Fuhrman issue" became the centerpiece of national news coverage, the press corps found itself caught in a trap of its own making. For so many months, the media had portrayed an America racially split over the Simpson case. Now, individually and collectively, reporters faced defending their own racial attitudes and fighting against the presumption that there were two entrenched camps divided by race and lined up for or against Simpson. They now found themselves in the uncomfortable position of justifying their own work on the Simpson story.

Court TV's Dan Abrams maintained that reporters were too caught up in the minutiae of the day to sit around chatting about whether Simpson was guilty or not. But, he acknowledged that by the end of the trial, the majority of the white reporters had reached the conclusion that Simpson had committed the murders. That decision, however, was not a result of any racial motive, he insisted, but from observing the case as it unfolded. "It's insulting when some people criticize the [white] press and say they didn't get it. I can tell you—we got it."[7]

Abrams also warned about drawing conclusions about the mindset of black reporters. "One has to be very careful talking about what black reporters thought," he stated. Only a handful of black reporters regularly covered the trial, and clearly they did not hold a singular view toward the defendant or the issues in the case. Some black reporters publicly positioned themselves with the defense, while others avoided taking sides altogether.

"Andrea Ford on occasion berated the prosecutors and witnesses in ways that other people were surprised she was doing," said Abrams. "Dennis Schatzman would come forward and explain why he thought the prosecution's evidence didn't hold up. He would be writing almost opinion pieces for the *Sentinel*. On the other hand, I have no idea what Janet Gilmore [a black reporter for the *Los Angeles Daily News*] thought. There were a number of black television reporters. . . I have no idea what they thought about [the case]."

Still, for whatever stance they took, all reporters still had to confront a trial burdened with racial antipathy, and many self-consciously struggled to convey those aspects in their stories. That angst played out in newsrooms across the country during the bitter Darden-Cochran exchanges, and then the Fuhrman tapes, as editors wrestled with how to handle the word "nigger"—whether they should print and broadcast the racial epithet, and, if so, how often. The euphemistic treatment of the racial invective was trite, yet the word "nigger" was offensive. In the end, some news organizations solely used the "n-word," others used the full word, while still others concocted formulas in which the word was used on first citation and in euphemistic form in repeated references. This stylistic confusion mirrored the racial confusion that had plagued the trial and the reporters who covered it.

Toobin's Stand

Jeffrey Toobin was among the most outspoken journalists to confront and refute the defense team's theory that Simpson himself was a victim of a racist police frame-up. He also lambasted his colleagues in the press corps for not doing the same. According to Toobin, reporters had become far too sensitive, allowing a form of political correctness to interfere with their reportorial judgments and duties. Instead of exposing the falsity of the defense case, reporters bowed to pressures to remain so completely neutral and "fair" as to play down the barefaced facts surrounding the trial—evidence pointing squarely to Simpson as the Brentwood killer.

Toobin was the very same journalist who had been rebuked by fellow reporters for his *New Yorker* piece that first floated the defense team's "rogue cop" theory. It was no small irony that following the trial he would write another controversial article—this one blaming the Simpson press corps for failing to vigorously challenge spurious defense theories out of fear of being branded as anti-black. "The fear of being called racist transcended everything connected with the coverage," said Toobin. "The case against Simpson was simply overwhelming. When we said otherwise, we lied to the audience that trusted us."

Jim Newton acknowledged that "race was in every moment in this case, and I suspect that racism and the fear of being labeled a racist affected us more deeply than we know. So I can't tell you with any certainty that none of my actions were influenced by the fear of being called a racist." However, the reporter asserted that his paper, the L.A. *Times*, had looked critically at the defense theory linking the police to a massive frame-up, and another that Nicole Simpson and Ron Goldman had been mistakenly killed by a Colombian hit team out to murder Faye Resnick. "Did we hammer it, did we conduct our own inquiry?" he asked. "Probably not and probably we could have done more."[8]

With the press reluctant to directly contest the defense claims, Toobin maintained that Cochran continued to fervently pursue his race gambit in Ito's courtroom. Even in small ways, the defense lawyer pandered to the "experience" of the mostly black jury. In his cross-examination of Detective Tom Lange, Cochran repeatedly reminded the jury that the detective lived in Simi Valley, a locale stigmatized as racist following the acquittals of police officers who beat Rodney King. And, in the middle of the Fuhrman controversy, Cochran arranged for the defense team to wear African kente-cloth ties in front of the jury.

While these antics brought derisive "hoots" from reporters watching the proceedings in the pressroom, Toobin charged that "when it came to actually reporting on the trial we all turned into a remarkably timorous crew. No one was ever worried that their treatment of the defense was unduly favorable."[9]

Toobin accused Cochran of conjuring up the specter of racism at each turn of the case—even when it pertained to his own witness. Robert Heidstra had been walking his dog near Nicole Simpson's condo around the time of the murders and testified that he had not come across the bodies of the victims—a critical point for the defense. But when Darden asked the defense witness to comment on his police statement that he'd heard an angry, loud voice coming from Nicole's home that night that sounded like that of a black man, Cochran went on a tirade. He claimed that Heidstra's statement, and Darden's question, were racist; the witness could not possibly identify a voice as coming from a black person. Cochran argued: "It is totally improper that in America, at this time in 1995, we have to hear and endure this."

The commotion stopped the trial dead in its tracks as Ito dismissed both the witness and the jury to deal with the defense's latest accusation. Cochran's outburst was met with a resigned response from Darden. "That is what created a lot of problems for myself and my family, statements that you make about me and race, Mr. Cochran."

Cochran's ploy was seen as yet another wild attempt to cry "Racism!" in a trial already overwrought with such charges. "Who in America would deny that black people have distinctive speech patterns and language?" said Darden. "Who would equate saying that people are different with denigrating them?. . . . Cochran's principles depended on how it affected an accused murderer. When it benefited [Simpson], he wanted to live in the 'real world,' where black people hear the word 'nigger' every day and steel themselves against it. Yet, at other times, he feigned disgust at someone who asked simply if a voice sounded like that of a black man."[10]

Toobin also saw Cochran's argument as a cheap courtroom trick. "Whether one sometimes can tell if a speaker is African-American on the basis of his or her speech is inarguable," he stated. Cochran's accusation was clearly designed with a singular purpose in mind— "How better to stop an effective cross-examination," charged Toobin, "than by throwing a stink bomb of racial grievance into the middle of the courtroom?"

An accusation that the LAPD engaged in a conspiracy to frame a celebrity for murder would ordinarily provoke the media to investigate. But instead of critically examining the validity of Simpson's defense, Toobin said the press corps followed the defense team's lead to nit-pick over evidence that would incriminate and convict any other defendant. Consequently, Toobin explained, DNA tests showing conclusively that it was Simpson's blood at the crime scene, were given equal weight with defense claims that the blood might have been contaminated [though it was never explained how even contaminated blood would have matched Simpson's type]. Simpson's blood found on a sock and inside his locked Bronco was planted. Hair strands found in a knit cap at the murder scene and on Goldman's shirt were suspect, since matching hair types is not a 100 percent certainty.

If the broad police conspiracy theory was not embraced by the press corps, few reporters seriously scrutinized Cochran's unsubstantiated claims. In the absence of such criticism, the defense theory gained a measure of credibility as it freely floated in the media. Fuhrman, of course, was Cochran's toehold into the alleged criminal machinations of the Los Angeles Police Department. The detective's language of racial hate and retribution muffled whatever meager challenges were leveled at the defense. Only after the trial did Toobin himself finally strike back in the *New Yorker* against the defense's allegations against Fuhrman and the LAPD.

The core of the defense case was, of course, that Fuhrman surreptitiously took that glove from the murder scene to the defendant's home. Not only would he have had to transport the glove with its residue from the crime scene, but he would have had to find some of Simpson's blood [from unknown sources] to deposit upon it and then wipe the glove on the inside of Simpson's locked car [by means unknown]—all the while not knowing whether Simpson had an ironclad alibi for the time of the murders. The other conspirators [conspicuously unnamed] would have had to be equally adept and even more determined.

In his contemporaneous notes from the crime scene, Fuhrman wrote that there was blood on the gate at Bundy; someone would have had to wipe that off and apply Simpson's. The autopsies, where blood samples from the victims were taken, were not performed until June 14th, two days after the murders. Someone would have had to take some of Goldman's blood and put it in the Bronco, which was then in police custody. And someone [the same person? another?] would have had to take some of Nicole's blood and dab it on the sock [found in Simpson's bedroom] which was then in a police evidence lab.

All of these illegal actions by the police would have had to take place at a time when everyone involved in the case was under the most relentless media scrutiny in American legal history—and for the benefit of an unknown killer who, like only 9 percent of the population, happened to share Simpson's shoe size, 12.[11]

The Black Press

Shadowing the mainstream press was another media force: the "black press." This loose conglomeration of 205 papers in 38 states with 13 million readers was a bona fide alternative voice. Since the *Freedom's Journal* was published in New York City in 1827, the rise of black-run newspapers has been a voice of advocacy.

The Los Angeles-based *Sentinel* was at the forefront of Simpson trial coverage for the black press. The paper's lead reporter was Dennis Schatzman. Although the *Sentinel* had a modest circulation of 20,000, it was one of just a few media voices reaching out to the million black residents of Los Angeles. Schatzman's stories were syndicated to black papers across the country, giving him the influence among black communities similar to the Associated Press' Simpson stories in the larger mainstream. Unlike the AP's straight news reports, Schatzman took a clearly "black perspective" that left little doubt as to how he felt about the issues and people associated with the trial.

The reporter was openly derisive of the prosecution's case, calling it nothing more than a "six-million-dollar boondoggle." His work reflected a very different view from that of his mostly white colleagues. When Ron Shipp, a former police officer and a self-described friend of Simpson, took the stand, Schatzman was not impressed. Most reporters believed that the defense was badly hurt after Shipp testified that Simpson, prior to the murders, told him of having had "some dreams" about killing his former wife. But Schatzman called Shipp "a drunk" because of his past problems with alcohol, and a "hanger-on." "Face it," he said, "the man just lied up there."[12]

Schatzman was also unimpressed by the next prosecution witness, Denise Brown, whose tearful testimony painted a horrific portrait of Nicole's life, one in which she was beaten and often humiliated by O. J. Simpson. Schatzman derided Brown's credibility, labeling her as yet another drunk to have taken the stand. He wrote about Shipp and Brown in a story headlined, "Two 'Drunks' Join O. J. Cast of 'Addicts, Liars.'"

From very early on in the case, Schatzman held the conviction that the Simpson story—and the criminal case—had a deep racial subtext. This was not just a murder case, he maintained, but a story of a black man's search for justice in a white criminal justice system. When Simpson was handcuffed by Los Angeles detectives after returning from Chicago, Schatzman's front-page sidebar the following day questioned police motives. "Think hard. How many times did you see convicted cannibal Jeffrey Dahmer handcuffed during his well-publicized arrest and subsequent trial? If you say 'none' you get the prize."

Schatzman also went after the LAPD, as well as the media, for failing to more vigorously pursue leads that might find other suspects. Using his own "highly informed sources who walk Los Angeles' glamorous wild side," the reporter floated the theory that two Cuban hit men, in a black Mercedes 500SL, were seen at the Mezzaluna restaurant on the night of the murders. "Cuban hit men are famous for using their knives, not guns," he said. "Knives—they're very skilled."[13]

While such uncorroborated claims were not taken seriously by the mainstream media, they did take on a life among black papers. And when the defense team announced that it was preparing to accuse the LAPD of conspiring against Simpson, the theory resonated more deeply within the black press. Dorothy Leavell, who publishes the weekly *Chicago Crusader*, said: "Many of us think that there is a conspiracy as far as the police department is concerned, and that has a lot to do with the mistreatment and brutality that blacks have suffered at the hands of police."[14]

There were other underlying themes in the black press's commentary on the case. One held that Simpson was victimized for violating white societal sexual taboos. According to the *Amsterdam News*, the case "was not about O. J. at all, rather about the black American male and the willingness of the criminal justice system to destroy him symbolically, by making an example of a black man who dared to be arrogant as well as rich and famous, who, heaven forbid, tasted the fruit of white womanhood."[15]

Black editors complained that there was an insidious double standard within the mainstream media that targeted black defendants more than whites. George Curry, editor of *Emerge* magazine, a national news monthly based in Arlington, Virginia, said he was bothered that black men were "being used as the poster children for every domestic issue around"—sexual harassment (Clarence Thomas); date rape (Mike Tyson); child abuse (Michael Jackson); domestic violence (O. J. Simpson). "I'm not a conspiracy buff," said Curry, "but I do find it extremely curious that Simpson was accorded far more media coverage than a cannibal like Jeffrey Dahmer. I suspect celebrity has something to do with it, but I think race has something to do with it, too. The white media routinely demonizes the black male."[16]

"That white men—from Senator Robert Packwood to Woody Allen—have also been accused of sexual misconduct is irrelevant," added E. R. Shipp, a black *New York Times* reporter. "With a white man, it is an individual matter, but when a black man is implicated, the entire race may feel impugned."

While black journalists condemned the white media for their wildly overblown coverage, few criticized their own ideological bent toward the race issue. Discussion of the trial often had more to do with Simpson's racial status within the black community—depicted as everything from "a cultural icon" to a "high-class Uncle Tom"—than with his culpability in the murders.

The black press was not a monolithic entity, but clearly its race-conscious mission permeated its editorial choices. Even decisions to *ban* Simpson coverage were based on race considerations. Curry's newsmagazine, for instance, declined to publish a single Simpson cover. It ran just one major story during the year-long trial, and that focused on the media coverage of the case. "We have given little coverage to the O. J. Simpson story because O. J. Simpson is not a person who had cast his lot with African-Americans," he said. "In fact, you could say just the opposite. He's gone out of his way to not align himself with blacks."[17]

Other telling differences separated the black and white press. For one, the white media's overzealous efforts to report the Simpson story were responsible for the waves of pretrial publicity that vilified Simpson and posed dangers to his fair-trial rights. In that regard, the black press was much more conservative, especially in its coverage of the early stages of the case. With far greater resources than the black press, the white press was able to send reporters to Los Angeles to independently pursue the story. White-run newspapers also carved out much more space on their news pages for Simpson stories than did black papers, which kept the Simpson story consistent with other news of the day.

The Simpson case brought out the best and worst of reporting across the media's color spectrum. Although the mistakes in the white press were more well-documented, the black press also suffered from a careless disregard for facts and attribution and, occasionally, it delivered a monumental blunder. (In one case of racial confusion, the *Amsterdam News* identified Jill Shively, a controversial white witness who was barred from testifying, as being black.)

Still, the major difference was ideological. Once the Simpson case jumped from being an ordinary murder story (albeit one involving a celebrated black athlete) to a perceived civil rights fight, the black newspapers became more involved. Their questions were pointedly different from the ones being asked by the white press: Was Simpson being singled out by the prosecution because of his color, or because of his preference for white women, or because the murder victims were white? On a broader scale, was Simpson just the latest victim of a racist society's conspiracy to destroy black men?

"Noticeably absent from much of the debate," said E. R. Shipp, "was the consideration that Simpson might be guilty."[18]

Endgame

With the prosecution's case still reeling from the Fuhrman debacle, the defense quickly moved to its endgame. Among the final witnesses were two mob informants, Larry Fiato and his brother Craig "Tony the Animal" Fiato. They testified that Philip Vannatter, the lead detective investigating the murders, told them that Simpson was immediately suspected as the killer in the case because "the husband always is a suspect." Vannatter had been targeted by the defense, as part of its overall attack on the LAPD, for his "rush to judgment" in presuming Simpson was the murderer. (Brought back to the stand, Vannatter denied he had gone after Simpson until enough evidence was gathered to convincingly point to his guilt.)

With the ugly echoes of Fuhrman's racist rantings still hanging in the courtroom, the Fiato brothers were comic relief. Craig Fiato, with his white hair, black goatee, gold hoop earring, and sandpaper voice was a prime-time gangster out of Central Casting. Ito deferred to the brothers' claim that they would be in danger if seen on television. For the first and only time in the trial, the judge barred camera coverage of a witness's testimony. Apparently, though, the Fiatos weren't all *that* concerned—that evening they turned up in a prerecorded CNN interview for the world to see.

SEPTEMBER 22, 1995

With their case coming to rest, and the jury absent, the defense hoped to bring one final "witness" before the court—he was O. J. Simpson. Cochran told Ito that his client wanted to address the court—and Americans watching—about his decision not to testify. Clark shot out of her chair, excoriating the defense for its latest scheme to manipulate public opinion and to surreptitiously send a message to jurors through their families on the eve of jury deliberations. More than mere trial rhetoric, it was widely assumed that jurors and their families discussed the case during conjugal visits. Then Clark tweaked Simpson, inviting him to take a seat "in the blue chair" to have "a discussion" about his role in the murders.

Ito, weary of the legal muscle-flexing, replied, "Thank you."

Simpson was then allowed to make a statement in the absence of the jury. He delivered the rehearsed sound bite of the day, declaring to the nation's "jurors" tuned to the televised proceedings: "I did not, could not and would not have committed these crimes."

As Simpson continued, remarking how much he missed his children in the year he was imprisoned, Ito finally cut him off. He reminded the defendant of his right to testify on his own behalf. Simpson nodded, but said no more.

In the gallery, a furious Fred Goldman clenched his hands into fists. Dominick Dunne, sitting next to Goldman, overheard him hissing, *"Murderer! Murderer!"*

15

CLOSING CURTAIN

SEPTEMBER 26-29, 1995

The World Watching

A global community of reporters, TV producers and technicians zeroed in on the Criminal Courts Building in downtown L.A., making it futile to even attempt counting their numbers. Most pundits instead merely wondered just who had failed to show up. "There's hardly a country in the hemisphere or in the world that has not paid attention to this trial—only Russia is not here today in serious numbers," said ABC anchor Peter Jennings.

A few hundred spectators merged with the media, many holding signs reading: "Guilty or Not, We Love O.J.," "Support the Jury," "If They Acquit, They're Full of Shit." One sign-carrier held a placard that read "Hitler Is Dead," a reference to Johnnie Cochran's closing argument that compared Mark Fuhrman with Adolf Hitler.

There were other symbols of racial hatred. When Cochran arrived at the court building, he surrounded himself with eight Nation of Islam bodyguards, ostensibly as protection from death threats he had received. For spectators around the courthouse, and viewers across the nation, Cochran seemed to be publicly aligning himself with a political organization that espoused black separatism and anti-Semitism.

As he walked through a gauntlet of microphones, cameras, and sound booms, Cochran popped off an occasional sound bite to anxious reporters. TV crews from dozens of stations were all desperate for

Cochran's attention. Should they be successful in getting any response from the lawyer, they were assured of being featured on their local newscast that day. There also was no better advertisement for the news station itself than to have its reporters on-air, a microphone in hand bearing the station's logo. "TV reporters were under pressure to get some reaction," said Bill Boyarsky. "It was strictly a promotional deal."[1]

Besides the media's presence, roughly 250 locals jammed into the area about a city block long around the courtroom. "There was every loony person in Los Angeles," recalled Boyarsky, and they gathered in the morning and stood in front of the courthouse screaming at each other. "There was this guy named Melrose Larry Green"—a resident "nut" who once ran for mayor—"who shows up wearing a [prayer shawl] and yarmulke during the high holiday [of Rosh Hashanah]." Green got into a screaming match with black Simpson supporters who "had their individual nuttiness." Their demonstrative exchange whipped up the crowd, said Boyarsky, "and then we passed a certain point where the craziness started to look a little dangerous. It started to be not fun."

Television producers played a hand, deliberately distorting the picture, and creating in the minds of viewers a scene of public turmoil, contended Boyarsky. "The [crowd interaction] was totally magnified by television which was desperate for a crowd scene. It looked much worse than it was."

The scene in front of the courthouse was more reminiscent of the political theater unique to Los Angeles, but with television shooting the tightly compacted crowd, Boyarsky charged that TV producers sought to heighten drama, stir public passions, and, intentionally or not, fan the racial flames. The impressions was that Los Angeles was on the verge of yet another riot. Boyarsky believed that "nobody who knew anything about L.A. believed that would happen."

But, perhaps, even Boyarsky was underestimating the medium's influential reach. With TV imagery depicting a racial battleground both in and around the courthouse, no one, with certainty, could predict what final outcome would come to pass on the streets of Los Angeles.

Fade to Black

An exhausted Marcia Clark stood before the jury for the last time. The decline in her physical appearance was dramatic. Dark pockets hung under her eyes; she had lost weight and was suffering from an abscessed tooth. The strain of the trial and lack of sleep was evident in the long lines of her face. Clark's fiery manner was noticeably subdued as she quietly walked the jury, again, through the prosecution's scenario of how O. J. Simpson brutally murdered Ron Goldman and Nicole Simpson.

Clark was drawing to the end of her closing remarks when the in-court camera panned over to the defendant. For a few seconds a tight shot of Simpson scribbling notes stayed on the screen—a decision by the camera operator that sparked the next blast from the bench. Ito could see from his own monitor the video pictures of Simpson, and he was not pleased. After halting Clark's closing argument, Ito asked to see the videotape, and then lashed out at the camera operator for the "flagrant violation and intrusion of the attorney-client privilege." And then, astonishingly, he ordered camera coverage terminated. After more than 250 days of proceedings, and with the end of the Simpson trial finally in sight, Ito played the camera card one last time. As the camera panned to the judicial seal on the courtroom wall, the Simpson trial was blacked out.

Ito had grown increasingly testy in the final few months of the trial. Media critiques that he was too "soft" by allowing lawyers to control the courtroom had given rise to a much less tolerant, even tyrannical, judge. The change was not flattering. Ito's knee-jerk reactions to the lawyers, as well as to reporters seated in the gallery, came off as unduly harsh and vindictive. Lawyers were reprimanded for delays, and reporters were thrown out of the courtroom for talking. And then the camera faux pas.

This time commentators were less deferential, with the rift between the media and the court permanently cemented in mutual animosity. An angry Roger Cossack on CNN called Ito's decision a "rip-off" for the viewing audience (and, presumably, for the commentators) who had spent an entire year tuned to the trial. CNN replayed the errant tape, with Cossack emphasizing that it was impossible to distinguish what Simpson was writing to his lawyer.

Ito's response was a familiar replay and provided a strange symmetry that linked the opening and the closing of the trial. During opening arguments, he had shut down the court camera after a technician accidentally panned for a split second to two alternate jurors. Instead of dealing with the camera mistakes privately, Ito again postured before a national audience before shutting television down. The court camera was a controversial idea from the beginning, but Ito's capricious behavior confused the issue and mired the legal process in yet another tedious sideshow about the media.

The Simpson murder case had literally become once again a media trial. Attorneys from news organizations raced into the courtroom to persuade Ito to lift his ban. The year-long quarrel between the judge and the media would not take a respite even in these waning moments of the trial. The exercise would have been tiresome had Ito's decision not come at such a climactic moment. On the air, CNN anchor Jim Moret was left to reading court transcripts of the ongoing proceedings which now dealt with this latest media problem. The camera shutdown lasted long enough to create additional anxiety among the networks. About an hour later, Ito reversed field and lifted the blackout, levied a $1,500 fine against Court TV, and then apologized to Clark for the interruption. The prosecutor resumed her closing argument to the relief of the networks and their viewers.

Clark concluded with a visual trick devised as much for the jury as for a television audience. Recapping her case, she unveiled a computer-generated image of a 14-piece jigsaw puzzle. As she cited evidence against the defendant, one puzzle piece after the next was revealed. The effect was reminiscent of a TV quiz show, in which the name of the game was to guess the mystery face. There was little mystery to Clark's puzzle. By the end, Simpson's image had emerged from the blocks of pieces, as did the prosecutor's answer to who murdered Nicole Simpson and Ron Goldman. "There he is," she said, as the sullen-looking picture of O. J. Simpson filled the large overhead screen.

Christopher Darden's task was to sell the prosecution's theory that Simpson was a man possessed by jealousy, a "slow fuse" that finally erupted into a murderous rage. He recounted the litany of abuses that Nicole Simpson suffered at the hands of her husband. For the last time, the victim's frightened voice on the 911 tapes filled the courtroom. Darden painted a mental image of the victim's battered face, describing an imprint left on her face after Simpson had struck her. "We submit to you that the hand that left this imprint five years ago is the same hand that cut her neck on June 12, 1994. It was the defendant then. It was the defendant now."

Darden's low-key narrative belied the chilling psychological portrait he called forth of Simpson on the night of the murders. "This is a rage killing. He's using a knife because he's there to settle a personal score, a personal vendetta. He stabs this woman in the neck and he's right there, it's one on one and the rage that he has, the anger, the hate he has for her that night, at that time, it flows out of him into the knife and into her. And he kills Goldman in this rage because he wanted to teach her a lesson. He wanted her to be there, face to face to know just who was doing this to her. With each thrust of that knife into her body, into Ron's body, there is a gradual release of that anger and that rage. And he stabs, and he cuts, and he slices until that rage is gone and these people are dead. And after that rage is gone. . . he just walked away."

Johnnie Cochran was television's dream lawyer. Throughout the trial his practiced preacher's oratory flared, but in these final moments the courtroom was an irresistible pulpit to spread the message that Simpson was an innocent man. On television, Cochran's thundering biblical evocations and emotional appeals appeared to belong on a grand stage rather than in the tiny cramped courtroom. He was, of course, fully aware that his performance was being seen by the largest audience in the history of American jurisprudence, as satellites brought his remarks to most countries of the world.

His impassioned argument was not complete without an occasional prop or rhetorical ploy intended to tap into the jury's racial sensitivities. During his closing a life-sized photograph of a glowing Simpson with his young daughter Sydney was placed before the jury box. Cochran had angled the photograph so it would also be captured on television as the camera panned. Then he showed a video of a smiling O. J. Simpson at Sydney's dance recital taken just hours before the double murder. Cochran argued that the tape was evidence that Simpson was hardly in a murderous mood the day of the murders. And then, in an inexplicable reference to the Rodney King incident, he added: "We know in this city how important videotape can be."

At another moment the lawyer put a knit cap haphazardly on his head, looking intentionally clownish. He asked jurors whether this cap would in fact be a suitable disguise for such a famous face as Simpson's. But the point was more subtle: Could anyone imagine this impeccably dressed, charismatic celebrity looking so ridiculous? This is not the way O. J. Simpson would have dared to be seen, Cochran seemed to argue. Then he tried his own glove demonstration, squeezing his hand into a prop glove. The performance was buttressed with his bumper-sticker, singsong refrain, "If it doesn't fit, you must acquit."

As Cochran spoke, measuring his cadence and inflection, the closing argument had a sweeping pitch more akin to an evangelical sermon minus the hallelujahs than a legal summation. In the background of television's frame of Cochran were the other trial lawyers. Images of a weary Clark and Darden were juxtaposed against the image of an animated Barry Scheck whose head bobbed up and down in rhythm to Cochran's exhortations. The message on the television screen was one of victory and defeat.

The defense team had engineered a public campaign against the Los Angeles police that culminated in Cochran's summation. This case was not about murder but the LAPD's perversion of justice, he intoned. Cochran asked the jury to follow him on a crusade against racism. A vote to acquit, he said, would be no less than a vote to defend the Constitution, and a vote to stop the racist forces that existed in the city's police department. Acquitting Simpson would send a "message" to the LAPD.

Cochran's plea depicted an apocalyptic world inhabited by police detectives like Fuhrman and Vannatter whom he branded as the "twin devils of deception," and the very type of men who beat Rodney King. Fuhrman was "the man who found the glove," and Vannatter was "the man who carried the blood." The defense attorney then unveiled a giant chart, titled "Vannatter's Big Lies." Cochran charged Vannatter with lying when the detective explained his reason for obtaining a search warrant for Simpson's home. Cochran also contended that Vannatter also had lied when he said that Simpson was not an immediate suspect in the case (a preconception that led to a "rush to judgment" and the arrest of Simpson).

Having built the defense around Fuhrman, Cochran's rhetoric soared. He ripped into the detective, branding him as a "lying, perjuring, genocidal racist," and then the lawyer made a startling comparison: "There was another man, not too long ago, who had the same views, who wanted to burn people. This man, this scourge, became one of the worst people in the history of the world, Adolf Hitler. If you don't speak out, if you don't stand up, if you don't do what's right, this kind of conduct will continue on forever."

In a case involving a Jewish victim and his family, not to mention a contingent of Jewish lawyers, Cochran's summoning of Hitler struck raw nerves and spilled over during the court recess. Fred Goldman erupted outside of Department 103, pushing aside the efforts of his wife to restrain him as he excoriated Cochran as "a horror walking amongst us." For Cochran to compare Fuhrman's racist comments with a man who murdered millions—while walking shoulder to shoulder with disciples of Louis Farrakhan—was the behavior of a "sick" man and "the worst kind of racist."

Goldman was joined by critics who charged that Cochran's advocacy had descended into outright demagoguery and racial pandering. "As hateful as the Fuhrman tapes were, they were matched in ugliness by Johnnie Cochran's exploitation of them in his final summation," an angry Frank Rich stated in his *New York Times* column. Rich said it was impossible to keep [his] "Manhattanite's ironic distance," identifying with the rage that filled Fred Goldman. "If anything, I wished Mr. Goldman had gone further and attacked Alan Dershowitz, Robert Shapiro and Barry Scheck for standing idly by as Hitler's crimes were trivialized before a mass international audience."[2]

Across the media, commentators seemed to visibly blanch at Cochran's tactics. The subject of race and ethnicity was a delicate one for pundits, with their discussions usually polite and center-of-the-road. But Cochran's summation came crashing down on the mostly white media. "Cochran's summation, as masterful as it was disgraceful, simply codified what the trial was all about: Whatever the evidence, this trial was about political message sending," said columnist Charles Krauthammer in the *Philadelphia Inquirer*. "In totalitarian countries, trials are just another opportunity for political statement. Even as he portrayed the other side as Hitlerian, it was Cochran who sought to turn this case from a murder trial into that totalitarian specialty, the show trial."[3]

Cochran's Nazi analogy continued to be replayed. As someone who clearly understood the power of symbolic suggestion, the lawyer's manipulation of such historical references to win freedom for his client was seen as an unconscionable ploy. Even the defense-minded Leslie Abramson had heard enough, although her response was more weary than fiery. She said on *Nightline* that night: "To use a Hitler analogy with a Jewish murder victim, in my Jewish opinion, is bad taste and why Fred Goldman went nuclear."

For *Newsweek*'s Ellis Cose, Goldman's outburst was rooted in an all-too-credible fear that Cochran's blatant manipulation of the race card might just be successful in setting his son's murderer free. Said Cose: "Cochran is unfazed by such criticism, maintaining that America, not he, made race an issue. And he has an obvious point.

Cochran did not, after all, manufacture Mark Fuhrman or create the police culture that rewarded him. He did not invent Rodney King— nor blacks' suspicion of police. And he certainly did not write the history of slavery and segregation that divided blacks and whites into separate, unequal camps. Cochran merely exploited those divisions in the service of his client. And if the quest for some idealized notion of justice suffers in the process, that may be an unintended consequence."[4]

In Washington, D.C., Bill Clinton worried about the trial's divisive messages, hoping that Americans "will not let this become some symbol of the larger racial issue in our country." Jesse Jackson, the prominent civil-rights activist, also sought to downplay the race rhetoric and bring the nation's attention back to the victims. "At the end of the day, two people were brutally murdered and two children are motherless. We should never take our focus from the depth of pain of that crisis." But Jackson, like Clinton, must have known that they were already too late. Reasonable talk could not compete with the ugly bluster coming from Los Angeles.

Cochran was followed by Barry Scheck, who told the jury that "something was terribly wrong" with the physical evidence against Simpson. He questioned DNA findings taken from blood-soaked socks found in Simpson's bedroom, and charged that the socks had been drenched in blood after the killings and not during the bloody struggle at Bundy. He also went after Vannatter for carrying a sample of Simpson's blood back to the Rockingham estate during the police search of the grounds. To Scheck, the inconsistent blood evidence carried the sinister implication that Vannatter, and the LAPD itself, had tried to rig the case against Simpson.

Scheck then took aim at criminalist Dennis Fung and his assistant, Andrea Mazzola, criticizing their blood-collection methods, and the Los Angeles police lab, for tampering with blood samples. "Somebody played with this evidence," said Scheck. "We've proved reasonable doubt. Period. End of sentence. End of this case."

Clark had the last word, concluding with an emotional reminder of the heinous nature of the murders—one that was blocked from the sight of television viewers. The prosecutor looked at the overhead courtroom screen, which filled with the photographic image of Nicole Simpson's body lying at the foot of the steps outside her home, followed by a picture of Ron Goldman's crumpled, butchered body.

"I don't have to say anything else," she said.

16

JUDGMENT DAY

OCTOBER 2-3, 1995

Verdict in the Court

Reporters hunkered down anticipating a long wait for the verdict. Some had returned to their newspapers and television stations, others hung around the courthouse pressroom. The first flurry of interest came some two hours into deliberations when the jury requested a read-back of testimony given by Allan Park, the limousine chauffeur who had waited to drive Simpson to the airport on the night of the murders. Linda Deutsch was among the reporters who were in the courtroom that Monday trying to comprehend the significance of this piece of Park's testimony. Following the 70-minute read-back, she left the courtroom, but a deputy told her not to stray too far. The reporter, astonished, asked whether the jury had come to a verdict. The deputy's body language gave her an answer. "He kind of looked at the ceiling," she said, "and I knew there was."[1]

Forty minutes later, Ito summoned the opposing sides a second time to make a stunning announcement. Some reporters never made it back to the courtroom, figuring the session to be procedural. Most of those remaining still had no idea what was to come. Nor did their news headquarters. Newspaper editors and television producers continued to make preparations for their extended end-of-the-trial analyses. A verdict wasn't expected for at least a week, and likely for much longer, and they believed they had abundant time to prepare their articles, pictures, graphics, and videotape presentations. And then, suddenly, at 2:52 p.m., this first day of deliberations, a somber Ito told the court, and the rest of the nation: The jury had come to a verdict.

A gasp from the gallery was audible on television, a sound that may very well have been emitted in the collective shock felt by the nation. The murder case of O. J. Simpson would end in much the same way it had begun—with a sense of disbelief. "We listened in uncomprehending silence as the meaning of the judge's words became clear," said Bill Boyarsky. "The trial was over. It was as sudden as a Round 1 knockout in a heavyweight championship fight."[2]

The twelfth-floor pressroom was emptier than usual. No one had seen this nearly instantaneous verdict coming; nor were reporters prepared to work on the "verdict story" that day. Some reporters placed bets in a press corps pool that a verdict wouldn't be decided until December, two months away. No one bet on *this* outcome. When Ito made the announcement, the pressroom froze. "The room just became silent—there was absolute silence," said Boyarsky. "People looked at each other and didn't have a thing to say. The room was so small you could feel the emotion."

A trial that had lasted an entire year and had generated more than 45,000 pages of transcripts and 1,000 pieces of evidence had come to an end in the relative blink of an eye. Nearly every juror had come to a decision before ever entering the jury room. Minus the time taken for the Park read-back and a lunch break, deliberations had lasted about two hours.

The initial fear of the court was that deliberations would end in a hung jury, a no-decision, forcing yet a second trial. For most trial observers *this* decision held much darker implications—this was a verdict disdainful of the judicial process. Regardless of which way the jury voted, Boyarsky believed the verdict was essentially meaningless: "If they only gave [a few] hours to this thing it didn't matter what they said. If that's all they thought about it, then who cares."

David Bohrman, the special-events producer at NBC, thought that a verdict was at least three weeks away, but he was taking no chances. The network's plan was to keep a "hot" control room, fully manned and operational throughout the deliberations. Correspondents, camera crews, and remotes also were in position ready to move into action at a moment's notice. The setup gave NBC an edge over its main rivals at CBS and ABC. Within seconds—when word that the jury had come to a decision—Bohrman could switch on a powerful machine to connect the Los Angeles courtroom to the rest of the world.

The network was battle-ready with camera crews positioned in Los Angeles and New York. Fiber-optic lines linked Los Angeles to New York headquarters. Commentators Gerry Spence, Kim Worthy, Ira Reiner, Jack Ford, and Roy Black were situated in various locales around the country. All were hooked into Bohrman's control room in Rockefeller Center. From there the NBC signal would carry to a huge outdoor screen in Times Square (called the Jumbotron), to millions of TV sets in America, and, through its international channel, to most of Europe. The Simpson verdict was to be a worldwide communal gathering of stupendous dimensions.

Seated before a bank of monitors in the front row of the control room, Bohrman watched the camera feed from Department 103. The executive producer never anticipated that on the first day of jury deliberations he would actually be switching on this powerful engine. But as Ito called the court to session, Bohrman pulled the trigger. NBC was instantaneously on-air with the startling announcement that the verdict was in. The trial of O. J. Simpson, finally, was coming to an end.

Even Ito seemed stunned as he told the court, and the world wired into the proceedings, that a decision had been reached. He had expected the process to take about two weeks. On television, Department 103, usually bustling with spectators and lawyers, seemed unusually empty and somehow darker as if the courtroom lights had lost their full intensity. Not even the legal teams were in place as the two sides convened. Johnnie Cochran was in San Francisco, and Simpson, looking unnerved, seemed strangely alone sitting at the defense table with Carl Douglas, a second-stringer on the team. Christopher Darden minus Marcia Clark sat thinking, "Nothing shocks me anymore."

Ito had instructed the jury to avoid coming to a decision before reviewing all the evidence and testimony. His instructions were, simply, ignored. Jurors had barely addressed the voluminous court record. The inevitable questions arose: Was this a matter of jury nullification—had jurors simply voted with their emotions in a case so racially bent? Were they just fed up with being sequestered for 265 days? Likely both factors were at work. Cochran's accusation that the police investigation had been a "rush to judgment" took on a paradoxical twist. The jurors had acted impulsively, taking a cursory look at a complex case in their own rush to judgment.

Ito decided that the verdict would be disclosed the following morning, giving time for the principal attorneys to return to the Los Angeles courthouse. Some pundits, knowing the judge's penchant for media attention, questioned whether Ito was deliberately trying to provoke greater drama by holding up the announcement. But more observant court watchers believed there were practical reasons for the delay: Ito was well aware of the circumstances following the first trial of the Los Angeles cops acquitted in the beating of Rodney King. The verdict in the Simi Valley case had been announced during the late afternoon as the city headed into rush hour. When the riots erupted, the police found it difficult to organize and get through the jammed streets and roadways to the hot spots in the city. This time, Ito gave the LAPD time to arm and prepare for any outbreak of public violence.

Whatever Ito's intent, the decision to stall the verdict also allowed the media to gather their forces and, in effect, ratchet up the public frenzy. "[Ito's decision] allowed the hysteria to build," said Deutsch. "Had he taken the verdict right then, even with the handful of us in the courtroom, it would have lowered the temperature. It would have still been a shock. But the delay allowed a big buildup for the television shows, the televising in Times Square."

The upstairs pressroom snapped from its collective shock. "I knew right away what I had to do, which was to write about [the media's] total confusion," said Boyarsky. The pundits had been wrong. This trial was not going to end in a hung jury, but in a spontaneous, unanimous decision. Boyarsky dashed back to his *Los Angeles Times* office, bumping into the paper's editor in chief, Shelby Coffey. Turning to his boss, he remarked: "I guess I oughta write something about this."

A Moment in Time

Media critic Howard Kurtz proclaimed the Simpson decision to be "the most dramatic courtroom verdict in the history of Western civilization."[3] Kurtz wasn't the only media observer to believe that the Simpson trial had transcended the great trials of world history. Making no apologies to the trials of Socrates, Joan of Arc, Alfred Dreyfus, the Nazis at Nuremberg, or the Rosenbergs, Kurtz was awed by the trial-turned-media creation.

Left with hours of air-time before the verdict was read, television commentators plunged into the depths of rampant speculation, indulging in what essentially was the most inane type of prognosis. This was a game show of their making called "Guess that Verdict." Boyarsky was no fan of the pundits, and his column that day, deriding their so-called expertise—not one had forecasted *this* verdict— was written with "a great deal of satisfaction." "I hated all the people who were predicting the verdict," he said.

Across television the only talk was about Simpson. NBC host Bryant Gumbel asked four legal experts for their predictions. The panel was split. Peter Jennings, on ABC *World News Tonight*, stated he would refuse to speculate as to "what the jury should do." Other network anchors were less restrained, encouraging their legal experts to take a shot.

Laurie Levenson told Dan Rather: "Most people thought a quick verdict meant a defense verdict, but I'm not so sure. . . . I think the prosecutors are probably saying, 'Hey, maybe we got it.'"

Roy Black told Tom Brokaw that he was "willing to go out on a limb"—not guilty.

Paul Lisnek, another legal expert, said: "I think we may see a conviction."[4]

But, said Gerald Uelmen, the pundits were "all grasping at straws to bolster a conclusion that was consistent with their own bias." Uelmen had his own guess. It was relatively simple, he said, to figure out that the jury had come to an acquittal in the case. Only seven minutes had passed from the time jurors requested a verdict form until they signaled to the court that they were prepared to return the verdict. The forms were more complex than simply asking jurors to check off whether Simpson was guilty or innocent. If Simpson had been found guilty of murder, jurors would have had to decide on first or second degree, and whether "special circumstances" had been proved—decisions that would require more than seven minutes.

Uelmen found it "most amusing" to listen to the guessing game that filled all of television that morning. With little else to report, instant replays were shown of Ito's announcement that a verdict had been reached; Allan Park's testimony (the only read-back that jurors had requested); and Simpson being taken back to jail. The rest of TV programming consisted of sheer speculation. Through all the chatter, it was clear that the hot air was simply meant to fill air-time.

That night CNN's *Crossfire* had intended to debate Medicare reform. The program quickly adjusted. Ironically, a television show that typically confuses shouting matches for genuine public discourse had a moment of sardonic genuflection. When the show's host Michael Kinsley asked defense attorney Barry Tarlow his opinion of the upcoming verdict, Tarlow replied: "How in the world would I know what the verdict is?"

To which Kinsley responded, knowingly: "Then what in the world are you doing here?"

After serving as a studio co-anchor for much of the trial, Marc Watts of CNN returned to the courthouse beat in the early-morning hours of judgment day. Outside the building he reunited with reporters he had gotten to know 16 months earlier during the dawn-to-night stakeout of Simpson's house in the days following the murders. Watts was back to his old routine, giving three live reports an hour about the courthouse "scene." When jurors arrived at Department 103, he joined his CNN team at Camp OJ across the street. The moment before the verdict was to be read, he said, "you could have heard a pin drop outside on Temple Street." Television monitors in and around the courthouse brought the crowd live pictures from the courtroom.

The police moved thousands of onlookers behind barriers marked with yellow crime-scene tape. Police were dressed in riot gear, some on horses, as helicopters hovered above the scene. Cars had been banned from the area for fear of a car bombing. Some reporters believed this verdict—regardless of the outcome—would not provoke the same community ferocity that followed the Simi Valley decision. But not all reporters subscribed to that belief. For Watts, the Simpson case had tapped the same racial undercurrents, and he felt a palpable sense of anger within the inner city of Los Angeles. He was fearful that the impending verdict might in fact trigger yet another riot.

"Those of us who covered the riots in L.A. in 1992 after the Rodney King verdict were all in anticipation of another riot breaking out if the [Simpson] verdict wasn't accepted by the community. There was this tense feeling in the air that if it wasn't 'not guilty,' we're going to be covering the riots 24 hours later."[5]

The reporter had grown up in Southern California and was living there in 1965 and 1992 when massive street violence erupted. He said the riots were explosive reactions to the "social evils" that surround the black community. "People are still economically depressed, there's a lot of rage among African-Americans in Los Angeles, that things haven't improved since 1965," he said. "Rioting is the way they carry out their frustrations. It is the only way they feel that society will listen to them. Those of us who are in touch know there's a lot of animosity and anger and rage. So a guilty verdict, regardless of what the facts were in the case, would have been a further extension of that animosity."

Television producers also helped to raise the level of social tension in their choice of images to air. Besides the constant pans of the tumultuous crowd around the Criminal Courts Building, television brought other pictures—Los Angeles police being armed with shotguns. Police Chief Willie Williams told reporters that the city had been through a "traumatic experience" and, though he did not expect widespread problems, he was prepared for the worst.

Cochran arrived at the Criminal Courts Building, again flanked by his bodyguards from the Nation of Islam. Darden and Clark were taken to the court building in separate cars protected by escort vehicles. As they approached the building, they could hear the helicopters swarming above them. The city block in front of the courthouse had been cordoned off by police barriers, and the area was filled with people screaming. "Packs of people ran through the streets and seemed to scream for no reason," said Darden. "I had never seen anything like it—except perhaps in old pictures of V-J Day, after World War II." Some in the crowd shouted to the prosecutor, "Give us Fuhrman! Send out Fuhrman!"

Hundreds of media people and "the locals" converged on the courthouse for word of the verdict. Most of the rest of the nation, and much of the world, watched television coverage. If there ever was a question about the impact of the trial—and of the powerful, tentacular reach of television—viewers were constantly reminded that they were witnesses to a happening of global dimensions. "Around the world, the impending verdict in the O. J. Simpson trial has just captured people beyond anything we would have believed in the beginning," Jennings pronounced on ABC's live coverage.

Yet there were other signs indicative of a new media age. Across America, people not only turned to television to share the Simpson experience but also to their computers to join an interconnected cyberspace community. Throughout the year, the Internet was a primary source of Simpson news, analysis, gossip, trial transcripts, sound files, photographic images, and video clips. Simpson had been the "hot" topic of the year for on-line services, which catered to a vast consumer appetite for trial coverage and Simpson-talk among a worldwide computer community. With the verdict coming down, more than 2,400 people jammed into a special O. J. Simpson "chatroom" on America Online. Even in cyberspace, the talk was all about Simpson.

The force of the impending verdict virtually shut down the nation's capital. A flurry of announcements informed the Washington, D.C. press corps that the daily White House and State Department briefings would be delayed. Senator Sam Nunn postponed his formal announcement that he would be leaving the Senate after a distinguished career. President Bill Clinton reportedly left the Oval Office to watch the proceedings from his secretary's office.

The Simpson decision seemed to obliterate all other on-going news. The very day the Simpson jurors reached their decision, another verdict was announced in a New York federal courtroom. Sheik Omar Abdel-Rahman and nine other militant Muslims were convicted of "seditious conspiracy" in the bombing of the World Trade Center. They were also found guilty of instigating a widespread campaign of terror and violence that included the 1990 assassination of Israeli activist Meir Kahane, as well as a series of aborted assassinations, bombings, and kidnappings. The verdict was a powerful indictment against international terrorism, but the story died on the wires, at TV news stations, and in newsrooms, overwhelmed by the power of the Simpson story.

The impending verdict was like a monster wave crashing across the country. Airline flights were delayed. College classes began late. Medical procedures in hospitals were held up. Phone companies reported a usage drop of nearly 60 percent. And with investors glued to the TV screen, stock trading plummeted. Although the verdict took place during the workday of many Americans, some 150 million stopped everything to catch it "live."

The Simpson trial spilled over national boundaries, exported by the long arm of television to remote parts of the globe. To understand American culture in 1995 meant understanding the Simpson case. Or as Karen Heller of the *Philadelphia Inquirer*, stated, "To not know the latest about the Simpson matter was to be less than fluent in the second language of the day."

The world watched as the verdict was announced. British pubs and sports bars in Moscow turned their attention to Los Angeles. South African television interrupted regular programming to broadcast the verdict live. Israelis were avid Simpson trial viewers. Many trial participants were of Jewish background, including Marcia Clark, Hank Goldberg, Alan Dershowitz, Robert Shapiro, Peter Neufeld, and Barry Scheck. So was one of the murder victims, Ron Goldman. The verdict coincided with the beginning of Yom Kippur, the holiest time of the year in the Jewish calendar. The television broadcast of the verdict presented a dilemma for many observant Israelis. Once the high holy day began, they could not turn on television sets. Some circumvented the problem by turning on their set early in the day and keeping it on.

The hallways outside of Department 103 were packed with media types: Talk-show bookers were ready to snare guests for their respective shows; several movie stars joined the crush, along with a squad of ABC producers eager to get hold of jurors following the verdict.

NBC-TV was prepared, and then some, with 40 camera crews poised for public reaction to the verdict. The network had already been on the air for six hours with pre-verdict programming when the incessant media chatter finally ceased. The network hooked into the courtroom video feed as Ito handed the verdict sheet over to the court clerk to be read. Control rooms are usually a hotbed of noise, with directors and producers giving directions and coordinating coverage. But in the NBC control room, there was an eerie silence that seemed to reach well beyond the confines of the room. Bohrman had the palpable sense that, everywhere, everyone was waiting in the same state of silent anticipation. "You could feel the silence outside," he said. "You could hear the silence in the bar in Fort Lauderdale and the pub in London. Everything became quiet."[6]

In Department 103 the courtroom camera's gaze did not budge from the defense table tightly crammed with lawyers and the defendant. All were ordered to stand for the final judgment.

The court officer stumbled when she came to Simpson's name, but pushed forward with the verdict. *"We the jury in the above entitled action find the defendant Orenthal James Simpson not guilty of the crime of murder upon Nicole Brown Simpson, a human being. . . ."*

The verdict was repeated, exonerating Simpson from Ron Goldman's murder as well. Screams resounded from the hallway outside Department 103; the sound of cheers from the street crowd also penetrated the courtroom.

The trial without end was over with Simpson mouthing a thank-you to the jury. Looking squarely in the direction of the camera, Simpson gave the impression that he was thanking TV viewers. Cochran placed one arm around Simpson's shoulder and nestled his face against Simpson's body. In another context, this might very well have been a glorious picture of a proud father with his son.

The camera panned to other parts of the courtroom, and the images were vivid. Kim Goldman burst into tears; Fred Goldman's face pinched, a muscle jumping in his jaw. Simpson's eldest son, Jason, bent forward, sobbing into his arms in apparent relief as he was comforted by his family. Simpson's mother, Eunice, wheelchair bound, lifted her arms to the ceiling to praise God.

A bitterly dejected Darden believed that Simpson had gotten away with murder. "[Simpson] had told Nicole that he could kill her anytime, anyplace, and that he could get away with it," he said. "And now it was over." The prosecutor was resigned to the verdict even before it was announced, but the quick decision was a powerful blow. Darden maintained he could have accepted a not-guilty verdict had the jurors reviewed the evidence more thoroughly. "Instead, they did what Johnnie Cochran asked them to do," he said. "They sent a message."[7]

In the front row, the verdict came as no surprise to Linda Deutsch. She knew from the moment the jury walked in that Simpson was going to be set free. Her colleague had seen a juror raise his fist in solidarity with the defendant. "She wrote 'NG' on her pad to me," said Deutsch, "and I looked around and the whole mood seemed to be not guilty."

At the defense team's table the lawyers and Simpson gathered in a tight circle, clasped hands, and Uelmen recited a prayer—a quasi-religious ceremony reminiscent of a football team uniting in prayerful thanksgiving after winning the Super Bowl. It was the last time that these lawyers would be caught in such harmonious public unity. Before the day was out, Shapiro would distance himself from the pack in interviews on CNN and ABC. There he singled out Cochran as someone who not only played the race card but had "dealt it from the bottom of the deck."

Sitting behind the Goldmans was Jeffrey Toobin. He believed that the previous day's read-back of Park's testimony was a sign that Simpson would be convicted. Toobin himself had no doubt that

Simpson had committed the murders. When the verdict was given, he listened, in shock. "I felt as if I had been hit with something physical," he said. "I sat there thinking that he killed these two people with a big knife, and he's never going to jail for it."[8]

The announcement that Simpson was about to go free delivered another stinging message to Toobin, a former federal prosecutor, about the state of American justice. "I think the criminal justice system makes all kinds of mistakes," he said, "but murderers who are tried for murders they committed who walk out the door—that's pretty rare. I felt very sad for the Goldmans who I thought were very decent people caught up in something not of their making. It was nothing but a tragedy for them."

Dominick Dunne, seated next to the Goldman family, was also utterly convinced of Simpson's guilt. As the verdict was read the camera caught the writer in what seemed to be a freeze-frame. Disbelieving, his jaw dropped as he stared ahead. "It was like getting punched in the stomach," he said. Shoreen Maghame of the *City News Service* had been with Dunne for two years in both the Menendez and Simpson courtrooms. As the court clerk read the verdict exonerating Simpson of the murders, she turned to Dunne, whispering in hushed disbelief, *"Both! Both of them!"*

Of all the journalists in the courtroom, Dunne was one of those most emotionally involved with the victims' families. Having lost his child to the murderous impulses of a killer, the moment was deeply felt. "I had grown to love the Goldmans, they're fine people," he said. "I just wanted to go hug them."[9]

In the upstairs pressroom, Bill Boyarsky snapped from his initial shock. The announcement—Simpson not guilty—was stunning, but quickly he went on "automatic pilot," focusing entirely on his work. At first the columnist planned to write an impressionistic article about the courtroom scene, but when he went to his newsroom his editor had a different idea—just write what the Simpson verdict means for the city. Boyarsky threw away his original notes and wrote.

His column did not paint an optimistic picture: Los Angeles, he predicted, will pay dearly for this trial in terms of race relations. If the city was moving slowly forward from the ugliness stemming from the King case and the riots, the Simpson case was a huge step backward. When he finished his column, Boyarsky went to a nearby bar with fellow reporters Andrea Ford and John Mitchell. The white reporter and his two black colleagues pulled back a few drinks and reflected on the trial. Boyarsky then went home and, as he remembered, "that was the end of it."

From television's eye, the rest of the verdict story was a wash of moments. There was a network reporter giving a live report outside the courtroom, shifting slightly to allow a line of men from the Nation of Islam to pass into the building. Cochran's bodyguards were another reminder of the charged political climate that had enveloped the trial.

Then the camera moved to Department 103, which had been instantly transformed into a press conference room. Now in Ito's courtroom, the defense lawyers and Simpson family members sat at a long table with their backs to the judge's empty bench and faced reporters sitting in the gallery. The mood was festive as lawyers jokingly introduced themselves to the press. When it came to F. Lee Bailey's turn, he told reporters that he was Johnnie Cochran, drawing a laugh. The scene was Hollywoodesque with Cochran thanking the behind-the-scenes crew of the Dream Team for their efforts. In other circumstances, this could have easily been a movie director's congratulatory speech after receiving an Oscar for Best Picture of the Year. Then, in a statement read by his son Jason, Simpson repeated the sound bite he had made in court near the close of the trial—that he "would not and could not kill anyone." He vowed to find the "real" killer of Nicole and Ron.

In retrospect, the Simpson trial never really belonged to Los Angeles. Ito on occasion had admonished lawyers from addressing their remarks to a public audience, a half-hearted gesture to keep the Simpson trial inside the courtroom. But Department 103 was merely the setting of a television experience for the world to see—the trial belonged to anyone with a TV set. So it was not surprising when the main players, in the wake of the verdict, spoke directly to a satellite audience.

In the district attorney's office, the denouement flickered in a wave of parting statements. "We have come here in search of justice," said Darden. "You'll have to be the judges, I expect, if any of us found it." Then, with perfect dramatic closure, Darden broke down, hunched over in emotional distress, and was comforted by his colleagues before being escorted, literally and figuratively, off stage. But it was a nonlawyer, Fred Goldman, who looked directly at the TV audience and stated: "I'm going to ask everyone who's watching to pause for a moment and remember why we're here. We're here for

Ron, we're here for Nicole, and we're here for every other victim of violent crime."

The political messages about victims' rights could not compete with the resounding racial messages that the trial had evoked. Throughout the country, the Los Angeles verdict played out along color lines, and the media helped reinforce the image of an America divided. Reporters and photographers were strategically stationed at malls, colleges, and businesses at the moment of decision; their stories and pictures were almost all "framed" by the perspective of race. Across the media spectrum was the collective image of an America cleaved into racial tribes. Photos in the newsweeklies caught the very moment of the verdict: blacks outside the Los Angeles Criminal Courthouse, with their fists raised and clenched, reminiscent of the black power salute of the 1960s; white employees of an Orange County shopping mall, their mouths agape, their hands covering their eyes and mouth in shock.

The country, which seemed to come to a virtual standstill as it awaited the verdict, was jolted back to life as if it had been struck by an electric charge. The announcement of Simpson's fate had in one swift blow punctured the collective myth of a unified America, sending a powerful energy release felt everywhere at once. Although students joined in common rooms at universities across the country to watch the trial, any illusion of "community" was immediately shattered by the announcement from the Los Angeles courtroom. Race superseded their social identities as students, citizens, or, simply, TV viewers. Black students exploded out of their seats in jubilation; whites remained seated, disbelieving.

Boyarsky said his daughter, a hospital nurse, watched with her unit, staffed almost entirely with black nurses, which cheered the Simpson verdict. As a victim herself of a violent crime, she identified with the pain suffered by the Goldmans and Browns during the trial. "She felt so hurt and angry at her colleagues, that they would do that," said Boyarsky. "She felt it was an attack on her; it showed that they didn't respect her. And those scenes were all over the city."

Nothing could equal television's intensity in capturing the moment. The print media were effective, though, in creating an almost hallucinatory wash of dreamlike images that bombarded the American consciousness in the days to come. In *Time* magazine's "special report" that week, the lead Simpson story was accompanied by a collage of disjointed photos—Shapiro, in shirt and tie, striking a punching bag; a grinning Fuhrman; an exhausted Clark, with her head resting on a table; a buoyant Cochran waving to the camera; a grieving Kim Goldman at her brother's gravesite; Justin and Sydney Simpson, holding white roses at their mother's grave; Simpson, himself, now back at his home, watching his former adversary, Gil Garcetti, on television.

The verdict unleashed a flood of media judgments. Geraldo Rivera, who throughout the trial had devoted his CNBC program to all-Simpson coverage, pronounced his own verdict minutes after the jury's was read: "O. J. Simpson has gotten away with murder." The talk-show personality was among the most outspoken critics, lashing out at Cochran for "[driving] a freight train through the racial divide in the country." Contending that the evidence against Simpson was "overwhelming," Rivera said the jury decision was nothing more than racial payback. "The trial was a triumph of race over reason," he asserted. "We've now seen 400 years of racism come home to roost."

At least one viewer watching Rivera's post-trial commentary took exception. He was O. J. Simpson. Basking in his newfound freedom, Simpson had turned on the Rivera show during his post-acquittal party at Rockingham. And after hearing Rivera's pronouncement—that a murderer had been set free—Simpson was said to have replied: "Yeah, but look where I am now Ger-al-do."

Reporters were caught in an emotional riptide which carried over to the post-trial coverage. In an interview with Tom Brokaw, Jeffrey Toobin was visibly enraged at the quick verdict and recounted: "I was almost shaking because I was so angry."

But unlike others in the press corps, Bill Boyarsky said he did not feel personally involved in the trial's outcome. "I didn't feel angry that O. J. was found not guilty. It didn't offend me. I know that guilty people get off all the time. I was different than some of my colleagues who took this personally. After a professional lifetime reporting [such stories as] the assassination of Robert Kennedy, the Vietnam War protests, the Los Angeles riots—these were events that were truly traumatic."

Boyarsky's equanimity was unusual. Many reporters continued to express their rage, charging that Simpson was the beneficiary of a jury that had followed the racial call of the defense team. Some on-air commentators, though, tried to hold onto the calm, clearly uncomfortable about placing a racial spin on the verdict. CNN's Greta Van Susteren disagreed with the prevailing commentary that jurors had acted too precipitously. Soon she was involved in a brawl with Dominick Dunne on the air.

In a post-verdict interview outside the courthouse, Van Susteren told Dunne that the jury's decision must be respected—jurors had sent a message to the Los Angeles police. A livid Dunne argued that "it wasn't the jury's function here to give a message to the LAPD." At that very moment a cadre of police walked by and was met by derisive comments from mostly black onlookers.

Pointing to the crowd's reaction to the police, Dunne shouted: "*That's* what happened with your message!" Van Susteren responded, accusing Dunne of being an "anarchist." Dunne, now further enraged, turned to CNN reporter Art Harris and told him: "I don't have to take this." Furiously, he pulled out his earphone and microphone and threw it at the camera operator. He acknowledged later: "That's how nuts I was from that verdict."

Television coverage was spinning.

ABC-TV continued to jump back and forth between live coverage and a Barbara Walters interview with Kato Kaelin, who said he wasn't quite yet ready to pronounce his own verdict. This was not the right time for such personal disclosures, said Kaelin, apparently oblivious that it was, in fact, the perfect time. But he wasn't prepared to just hand over the scoop to ABC. Later, in a widely promoted interview with Geraldo Rivera, Kaelin announced his verdict—Simpson was guilty—leaving Simpson trial addicts to rest easier.

Old feuds refused to die as Shapiro continued his running fight with his defense team cohorts. He told Walters that night on ABC that he was "deeply offended" by Cochran's analogy that compared Mark Fuhrman with Adolf Hitler. He vowed never to work with Cochran again; nor would he ever speak to Bailey. Cochran, reached later by reporters, stated that Shapiro was "the one with the problem." Bailey described Shapiro as "a sick puppy."

The jockeying for "high ground" among the Dream Teamers was a strange pathetic farce. Recently hired by a respected Los Angeles law firm, Shapiro now sought to separate himself from the very race case he had helped to construct. Critics believed that it wasn't a sudden bolt of human concern that drove Shapiro to decry the defense's tactics, but his more pragmatic concerns for the monied corporate milieu he wanted to join. "Shapiro felt personally threatened in his West Los Angeles world by being a part of this racial event, and he wanted to play both sides of the fence," said Toobin. "He wanted to be seen as an effective lawyer for his client, but he also didn't want to be seen as someone who would use race in such a transparent way. You can't have it both ways."

As part of the media's iconic world, O. J. Simpson also evolved. He was no longer the desperate, former football star, taking flight down the freeway, cheered by his fans for his celebrity. He had been relegated to another status: that of the black man, conspired against by a racist police system, now cheered for his blackness. The case, which began as a TV mega-event, would end in a surreal coda.

An ABC helicopter camera caught Simpson entering a large white van that would take him home. The aerial view was eerily reminiscent of other shots taken 16 months earlier along parts of the same California highway. At that time, of course, Simpson had put a gun to his head and was a fugitive at large. This time Simpson was returning as a free man to his Rockingham estate, where he was embraced by A.C. Cowlings, his driver in the infamous chase.

TV cameras peered over Simpson's fence to watch the family's celebratory picnic. The all-day party went into the night as Simpson joined with his lawyers, family and friends—and a photographer taking pictures for the *Star*. In one photo, partygoers mockingly pointed to the floor in Simpson's bedroom where police had recovered a pair of bloody socks. The picture was a final tweak at the prosecution's case—as well as the mainstream media. This was the tabloid's biggest cash-for-trash Simpson story. Wasting no time cashing in on his notoriety, Simpson had sold the *Star* the "exclusive" of his post-trial party for $500,000. As part of the deal, the photo shoot was credited to his company, Orenthal Productions.

The Camera Debate Redux

In the history of American jurisprudence, no single trial, or group of trial participants, had been so publicly and intensely exposed. Indeed, few television personalities of any kind had achieved such intensive national exposure *over the course of their entire careers*. It was estimated that CBS News anchor Dan Rather would need *24 years* to match the air-time given to the lead lawyers involved in the 16-month case.

But there was a cost to being a TV star. By the time the Simpson trial ended, even defense and prosecuting attorneys—strong supporters of the courtroom camera early on—had finally grasped the full consequences of having the case televised. The attorneys blamed much of their excessive lawyering, the feuds, the scores of motions before the bench, the hundreds of sidebars, and the incessant bickering about collateral issues, on the tremendous pressure brought to bear on them through television. The camera's presence not only changed the way trial attorneys and the presiding judge behaved, it also added another risky element—the case became a political battleground with participants *personally* invested in the trial's outcome.

Darden blamed Ito. The judge's "worst decision" in the case was allowing cameras in the court, he charged.[10] In the blame game following the trial, Ito or the "other side" bore the brunt of responsibility for the trial's collapse. But for all of Darden's post-trial hand-wringing, his complaints sounded hollow, if not hypocritical. At no time during the trial did he or any other lawyer in the case seriously consider having the camera blacked-out for their grandstand performances. Only afterward, with their celebrity status firmly intact, their book contracts in hand, their lecture tours, TV shows, and movie deals in place, did they loudly protest and, typically, they pointed an accusing finger away from themselves.

In a *Nightline* interview after the trial, Fred Goldman summed up the televised trial experience, stating: "The camera turned the court into a pulpit for agendas, and what was lost was Ron and Nicole." With lawyers making the proceedings "a circus," and a judge failing to control their antics, Goldman said the trial was turned "into a nightmare."

After witnessing the chaos of the Simpson trial, judges in high-profile cases refused to risk having their trials televised. A week after the verdict, a Texas judge in the trial of a woman accused of killing the popular singer Selena banned television from the proceedings. The California trial of Richard Allen, accused of murdering a 12 year old named Polly Klaas, was blacked out by the presiding judge, Lawrence Antolini, who stated emphatically: "Nothing like the O. J. Simpson case is going to happen in my courtroom."

Superior Court Judge Stanley Weisberg said he had learned from his own mistake in the first Menendez trial by allowing gavel-to-gavel coverage. Much like Simpson, the trial was then embraced by the media as a spectacular story about wealth, sexual abuse, and murder, with the brothers emerging as the latest inductees in the culture's hall of fame. And, likewise, the case bogged down for months and ended with questionable verdicts—two hung juries—despite the brothers' confession that they took shotguns and blasted their parents to death in their Beverly Hills home. For the second trial, Weisberg denied Court TV's request to air the proceedings. After a five-month retrial, the brothers were found guilty of first-degree murder—a verdict that was a one-day story in the national media.

The Simpson "lesson" rippled overseas. In Palermo, Italy, prosecutors asked the judge to prohibit live television coverage of the trial of Giulio Andreotti, the former Italian premier accused of corruption and murder. They cited the excesses of the Simpson trial as an example of the dangerous consequences of having trials televised.

On June 12, 1997, three years to the day after the Brentwood murders, a jury in Denver was reaching its final phase of deliberations in a federal murder trial. By the following afternoon, the jurors had unanimously arrived at a decision: Timothy McVeigh, a 29-year-old Gulf War veteran, was to be put to death by lethal injection for killing eight federal agents. The victims were among the 168 people killed when McVeigh set off a huge truck bomb on April 19, 1995 outside the Alfred P. Murrah federal building in Oklahoma City.

The case involving the worst case of domestic terrorism in the country's history—a traumatic event involving the horrific deaths of children among the bombing victims—cut across the nation. The bombing case spurred comparisons to the prosecution of O. J. Simpson, and most observers agreed that Simpson was the antithesis—the "anti-trial"—to McVeigh. Indeed, the two cases appeared as polar opposites. At Simpson, participants were accused of playing to the camera and the nation watching; the principals in McVeigh appeared to keep their eyes strictly focused on the courtroom. Simpson slogged along for 13 months, a perplexing legal process that broke down into salacious sideshows and bouts of racial pandering. McVeigh was seen as an example of the justice system at its most efficient—a swift, five-week proceeding that sought clarity regarding the defendant's role in the bombing in Oklahoma City. A visceral feeling of outrage lingered among Americans in the aftermath of Simpson; a sense of unity and closure was expressed among the victims' families and the country at large following McVeigh.

Various reasons were given to account for these differences, but one was most apparent: the McVeigh trial was not televised. Judge Richard Matsch was mandated by Congress to allow a closed-circuit feed to Oklahoma City for the benefit of the victims' families who could not attend the Denver trial. But he refused to go further: commercial television was banned. And once television was gone, even a case so emotionally tied to the country's psyche for the past two years could calmly be adjudicated.

The McVeigh trial was, of course, still closely scrutinized by the media, but few cries were heard that Americans were shortchanged or the court process diminished by the absence of television. To the contrary, most trial observers asserted that democracy was enhanced in the unfettered unfolding of the bombing case. Court participants were not the only parties relieved of the daily pressures of working under television's microscope. Reporters were free as well from the daily hysteria that had trailed each step of the Simpson case—a situation created by gavel to gavel TV coverage. Certainly there was strong media interest in McVeigh. But without the camera, reporters found that they could be diligent but respectful to their audiences as well as the court. Curiously, it was not necessarily the Simpson trial that finally awakened Americans to the dangers of the courtroom camera. It was McVeigh.

Ito's Lesson

The pundits, of course, hardly cast stones at the nation's media for the Simpson verdict. Instead they directed their collective anger against another "system" they said had failed to work—the courts. The case evoked the outrage of reformists calling for a revamping of the justice system, and their wish list was seemingly endless: Trials should be shortened; attorneys should be muzzled from trying their cases in the media; the buying and prepping of expert witnesses should be replaced by court-appointed experts; the racial makeup of a jury should be diversified; peremptory challenges that allow lawyers to strike potential jurors from consideration without cause should be severely restricted; repetitious cross-examinations should be curbed, and so on.

Other critics, however, argued that a more fundamental problem has corrupted the justice process. Simply, the courts have lost their direction in their "search for truth." That mission has been subverted by a legal machine more interested in obfuscation and legal trickery than in answering the overriding, essential question that is at the heart of every criminal case: "The [court's] central issue, *'Did he do it?'* is the last question we ask," stated Judge Harold Rothwax of the New York State Supreme Court. The Simpson case was just the latest example, he said, of a process that had severely decayed over the years—the search for truth had become unrecognizable. The day Simpson was freed, the judge recalled the sense of betrayal felt by the "hardworking men and women whose task is justice." Rothwax noted that it wasn't the acquittal per se that caused such deep dismay, "but there was something dreadfully wrong with the process that led to this verdict."

"I am not afraid to say what is unquestionably true: that justice was not done in this case," he stated. "O. J. Simpson is free. He will never be criminally prosecuted for these murders again. And society is left with the bitter taste of perverse justice. By law, Simpson is not guilty. Our system, however, *is* guilty, and it is the people who are punished."[11]

The verdict shattered Ito's promised golden civics lesson. In the end, perhaps Ito himself felt the same bitterness experienced by Americans who believed that the trial had exacerbated deep-seated racial tensions. The search for justice had less to do with truth than with wealth, status, and, in the end, a play to racial fears.

Although the jury had come to a verdict, the nagging question remained whether they had reached the *right* verdict. Certainly, that judgment will continue to confound trial observers who believed that a murderer was set free. However, what will persist as an even greater source of distress is *how* the verdict was decided. Ito had warned jurors about reaching a decision before all evidence and testimony were fully evaluated. Nevertheless, the panel essentially nullified a highly complex case involving more than 120 witnesses and 1,000 pieces of evidence to reach a snap judgment.

Many critics tied the verdict to a racial agenda. One was Marcia Clark, who told CNN that Simpson was acquitted because he was black. "Liberals don't want to admit it, but a majority black jury won't convict in a case like this. They won't bring justice."[12] The D.A.'s office quickly claimed that Clark was misquoted, but, regardless, the sentiment hung in the media airwaves and persisted in newsprint.

Explanations other than race were offered to explain the near-instantaneous verdict. And here a finger was pointed at television and its influence on the court. Ito's wish "not merely to *be* fair-minded but to be *perceived* as fair-minded caused the trial to last twice as long as it should have," said the writer Diana Trilling.[13] The case, in fact, was distended beyond recognition, earning it the dubious distinction as one of the nation's longest trials. It finally concluded with a frustrated jury anxious to end nine months of being separated from their families and normal routines of life.

Still, the media, and most of America, almost exclusively saw the verdict in racial terms, and it was a bleak picture they painted. "The Simpson verdict is some of the worst racial news in years," asserted Jacob Weisberg of *New York Magazine*. "It demonstrated, to those who still had any doubt, that the era of racial progress has now given way to a fracturing of black and white America into alternate universes. . . . We simply can't ratify the notion that there is a white reality and a black reality. A nation that lives with separate realities is Bosnia, not America. There is not white reality or black reality about Simpson's guilt. There is only the reality of his guilt, and the tragedy of his exculpation."[14]

In the wake of the verdict stood other serious questions that were largely ignored. These had to do with how the media work and their powerful influence within the culture. Did the media merely reflect existing racial tensions and public attitudes about the case? Or, were they instrumental in creating and then dramatizing them? Ultimately, were the media at least partly responsible for fueling racial anger and severing the country in their 16-month obsession with the Simpson story?

The jury story, the Darden-Cochran story, the Fuhrman story, the police conspiracy story—all were about race conflict, endlessly hyped and hoisted as a metaphor for American race relations. While the media insisted they were simply following a dramatic story for a huge, involved audience, there was a collective sense of denial that somehow they had helped to fan the embers of racial division into a national conflagration. In the final analysis, their excessive, overblown coverage was critical in turning a murder trial into political theater, exploiting American racial tensions, so very real in the country, to sell their Simpson stories. The media claims that they were just aggressively "doing their jobs" echoed precisely the same rationale voiced by the defense team in devising its race-based strategies. And they both could confidently claim victory: the defense, a highly suspect acquittal; the media, soaring ratings, more readers, and huge profits.

In the days following the verdict, the media commentary continued to spin, painting a picture of a bitterly divided America. By this time, Simpson had become the political symbol that few could ever have envisioned when the case first broke in June 1994. The television trial that was supposed to join Americans in a shared lesson about justice had forcefully shoved them to opposite sides. And, in a strange, ironic denouement, the media now served as the messengers delivering a damning message about American life.

A *Time* magazine piece, "A Nation of Pained Hearts," featured a double-page photograph of a crowd in Los Angeles, people standing together—black, white, and Hispanic—looking skyward, hands shielding their eyes from the glare of the sun. Together they watched a huge outdoor television screen of the Simpson verdict. The street scene was reminiscent of those in sci-fi flicks with anxious citizens staring upward as if to anticipate, moments before the cataclysm, the collision of Earth against a celestial force.

The Hollywood allusion was reinforced by the page design. Accompanying the picture of the crowd was the article's lead paragraph, which scrolled down the page in large type like the introduction to the movie *Star Wars*. The message was depressing.

For writer Roger Rosenblatt, the photograph was a final moment of the nation's people "coming together" before the Simpson verdict irrevocably severed their bond.[15]

At least there was one moment of visible black-and-white unity last week. It occurred on Tuesday, shortly after 10 a.m. Pacific time, when crowds of citizens gathered together in the streets like extras in a *War of the Worlds* movie of the 1950s, stood staring up at outdoor television screens, waiting for the word.

They were united, briefly, in an anxious silence of the heart. As soon as the verdict was read, however, they split apart; they could watch themselves do it on the split screens. On one side jubilation, on the other dismay. Afterward it was said that America should have seen this coming, that the division of the races cut so deep, it ought to have been obvious that two nations had always been hiding as one.

17

AFTERMATH

OCTOBER 1995-FEBRUARY 1997

Soon afterward, Camp OJ pulled up stakes as the networks removed their fiber-optic cables, satellite dishes, and trailers and went home. They took their log of hundreds of hours of Simpson footage spanning 16 months, a story of historic proportions judging by the thousands of miles of videotape. CNN alone had delivered some 625 hours of live trial coverage, not including the hours given to its obsessive talk-show chatter. The network's risk in going gavel to gavel had paid off. Its ratings had skyrocketed 100 percent over the year, and with more viewers came huge ad profits.

ABC, CBS, and NBC also packed up their machines, tapes, and personnel, finally leaving the story behind. Moving on to their next assignments were their armies of anchors, reporters, producers, camera crews, and technicians. The size of the force directly reflected the importance that executives had placed on the Simpson story—network newscasts, in fact, had devoted more air-time to Simpson coverage in the year than to Bosnia and Oklahoma City combined.

If the monster story was going to die, the tabloids would not be the ones to drive a stake through its heart. Shortly after the verdict, the *National Enquirer*'s special 14-page "collector's issue" hit the stands with a blaring front-page headline: "Cops Fear Goldman's Dad Will Kill O. J." Other such scoops would follow, some more real than others. After months of negotiating a deal, the paper purchased Nicole Simpson's diaries with her handwritten entries telling of a sad, tortured life. It made its way to the racks of 250,000 checkout counters and into three-million homes.

Well after the verdict the Simpson book writers would continue to tell the story about the famous trial. Jeffrey Toobin continued to be Simpson's main nemesis. His book, released in September 1996, became an immediate bestseller with startling revelations about the trial's main players. His claim: Johnnie Cochran and Robert Shapiro had told friends and colleagues that they believed Simpson had, in fact, killed Nicole and Ron. Then Toobin disclosed that Simpson knew of his acquittal the day before the verdict was formally announced in court. The writer claimed that a sheriff's deputy assigned to the jurors learned of the decision and passed it along to his friend who was guarding Simpson at the county jail. Simpson's emotional reaction the following day to the not-guilty announcement, Toobin contended, was nothing more than an act. "One of the biggest moments in TV history," he said, "is fundamentally a fraud."[1]

Giving in to the Beast

After 126 witnesses, 1,105 pieces of evidence, 99 days of prosecution testimony, 34 days of defense testimony, 857 exhibits, 433 motions, 372 days of jury sequestration, 474 days Simpson spent in jail, and a price tag of $9 million to Los Angeles taxpayers, the O. J. Simpson trial was, at last, over. It did not, however, end the Simpson story. The "television trial," especially this one, possesses a peculiar afterlife. Now unbridled from their legal duties, trial participants cashed in. Most of the key players soon discovered, if they hadn't already known, that they had become the latest hot property.

In the post-trial marketplace, Marcia Clark, Christopher Darden, Robert Shapiro, Johnnie Cochran, and O. J. Simpson, as well, were prepared to take their cut from the pie. Clark and Cochran, the very hottest celebrities of the moment, took the biggest pieces. Publishers opened up their vaults to the tune of $4 million for each of their stories. This was not normally the type of money given to lawyers, regardless of their status—this was money more appropriate for "stars."

Darden and Clark also were handsomely paid for taking their case to the public on lecture tours and at forums. As exorbitantly paid speakers, they spun the Simpson case over and over as a blow against American justice. Clark was a top draw in the months following the verdict, commanding speaking fees of $25,000 as she traveled the circuit. Soon she left the Los Angeles district attorney's office, signed up with the William Morris talent agency, and prepared for her new career as a media personality.

If Clark had been upset during the trial with the media's intrusion into her private life, she had no qualms going public to sell her "intimate" autobiography. The book, entitled *Without a Doubt*, carried a second meaning, intended or not. Though the title was meant to convey Clark's unequivocal belief in Simpson's guilt, it spoke more about Clark herself—without a doubt, she was now a star. That "persona" was completed with a photograph on the book jacket showing the former prosecutor in full makeover, dressed in designer jeans, blouse and boots. Sitting atop a legal container marked with Simpson evidence, an insouciant Clark smiled into the camera lens, no longer the aggrieved lawyer but a successful Hollywood creation.

As befitting a celebrity of her status, she took her life story, with all its sordid details, to television's confessional and its High Priest, Barbara Walters. Clark disclosed to Walters that she had been raped when she was 17 and since then had been involved in a series of abusive relationships. Walters played to her guest's "tough-guy" image as a hard-drinking, chain-smoking prosecutor, even offering her up as a role model for the women of America. As for Clark, she had come of celebrity age, peddling her "secrets" and basking in her newfound status. Only a final question offered by Walters gave her a moment's pause. How did she feel about exploiting the Simpson case to win such fame and fortune? Clark could only reply weakly: "I'd give it all up to get a conviction and a normal life."

In the next months, Darden also took to the stage, quite literally, though with mixed reviews. At New York's Town Hall, he spoke to a less than half-filled house. Theatergoers paid $100 a ticket to hear him speak and join him for lunch. The low turnout compelled Darden to cancel the rest of his engagement, but critics were more disappointed that he had given in and joined the post-Simpson celebrity bandwagon. The Broadway "flop," said Frank Rich, was "a poignant illustration of what can happen to good people when America's Faustian culture of celebrity comes to call. Wasn't this young prosecutor, an impassioned and conscience-stricken foe of domestic violence and the n-word, one of the very few good things to come out of the entire circus in L.A.?. . . On Sunday, he gave in to the beast."

Darden would finally find stardom with the publication of his book, *In Contempt*. The book, an immediate bestseller, was an auto-biographical narrative of a young black man's struggle, culminating with his experience at the Simpson trial. The former prosecutor (having quit the D.A.'s office) was propelled around the TV talk circuit, moving between network newsmagazines and cable shows with the likes of Howard Stern, Geraldo Rivera and Dennis Miller. Like an old beaten prizefighter, Darden replayed his lost championship fight. Ironically, he now found himself in the same ring as the Simpson "experts" he so decried during the trial.

Prominent jurists lashed out at the prosecutors' crass prof-iteering, which they said fed the growing public scorn toward the legal profession. U.S. Appeals Judge Stephen Reinhardt specifically condemned Clark and Darden for seeking to reap the benefits of, essentially, a failed case. "Perhaps the most mind-boggling aspect," Reinhardt asserted, "was how two lawyers who lost a case that most people had thought could not possibly be lost, and who did so through the use of some of the most bizarre trial tactics employed in the history of American jurisprudence, not only obtained book and motion picture deals that will bring them more money than most lawyers make over their entire careers, but that they now also command huge fees as lecturers. That, on the basis of this trial, they are held out as expert practitioners, role models, and examples of dedicated public servants simply defies the imagination."[2]

The Dream Team also would not be shut out of the post-trial bonanza. Alan Dershowitz was first off the blocks with a legal treatise on "reasonable doubt," while the two primary trial lawyers pompously wrote of their "quest for justice." Shapiro's loosely drawn "legal brief" called *The Search for Justice* rivaled Cochran's *Journey to Justice*, but neither book would dent the American consciousness—nor publishers' bestseller lists—with principled insight about larger moral truths. Cochran, though, seemed to impress Steven Brill who handed the defense lawyer his own talk show on Court TV.

F. Lee Bailey was apparently satisfied reaping the royalties from the reissue of his earlier memoir, *The Defense Never Rests*. The paperback included a new promotional blurb that splashed across the cover in the very best of tabloid tradition: "O. J. Simpson's Acclaimed Defense Lawyer Re-Creates His Most Famous Wife-Murder Cases." But Bailey had other things than the publishing business on his mind in the months after the trial. In February 1996, Bailey was found in contempt for failing to turn over to the

U.S. government a $20-million stock portfolio given to him by a client, a major drug kingpin. The lawyer finally had a starring role, but not quite the one he had chased so fervently in the Simpson case. The media carried pictures of Bailey being led away in handcuffs to a Tallahassee federal detention center where he served 44 days before agreeing to give up his claim to the contested stock. The key witness for the government's case had flown from California to Florida to testify against Bailey. He was Robert Shapiro.

Almost every major participant eagerly sought to tell their Simpson story for posterity and, of course, a large book advance. The Simpson library grew with new literary figures such as Mark Fuhrman, Fred Goldman, Denise Brown, Tom Lange, Philip Vannatter, Hank Goldberg, Gerald Uelmen, and Larry Schiller (working closely Robert Kardashian).

O. J. Simpson also took his story into the market, but dreams of a multimillion dollar pay-per-view interview crashed against mainstream reality. Simpson was stigmatized, acquittal or not, as a wife beater and perhaps someone who was far more dangerous. The prevailing wisdom was that Simpson would quietly catch up to the life he had left. Instead, he became a wraithlike presence flitting between one or another media appearance.

Soon after the trial he promised to tell NBC his story in a nonpaid interview but backed down hours before the scheduled time. He stated his concern that the network interview would not be friendly enough. Then he began a strange hit-and-run promotional campaign, calling, without notice, Bill Carter of the *New York Times*, and then Larry King, who was live on-air at the time with Johnnie Cochran. The show soon became a lovefest between Simpson and his stalwart defender.

Simpson apparently was a devoted TV viewer, watching the ongoing spins of his case. During a CNN program with pundits Greta Van Susteren and Roger Cossack, Simpson again made a surprise call to the studio, this time to take offense at some remark. When the hosts tried to engage him in a broader dialogue, Simpson abruptly hung up the phone.

His interview with the Black Entertainment network was interspersed with commercials for his new video. With no takers willing to engage Simpson is his pay-per-interview enterprise, Simpson produced his own "no-holds barred" videotape interview, selling for $29.95. Only in present-day American culture could an exdefendant "testify" to allegations that he murdered two people and then sell his alibi through an aggressive marketing scheme. Simpson, in fact, unabashedly hawked his video at every media opportunity. The image of Simpson the defendant was soon replaced by Simpson the huckster. Later his promotional tour would go worldwide to Oxford University in England and then to Budapest. Simpson had hoped to score a big payday, but sales of an estimated 35,000 copies were considered a commercial bust.

Simpson's post-trial analysis failed to win new supporters. Reciting a well-worn defense theory, he reposited the theory that Colombian hitmen murdered his former wife and Ron Goldman. They had mistaken his wife for Resnick, an admitted drug user living in Nicole Simpson's condominium at the time of the murder. That no evidence was produced supporting his story did not dissuade Simpson from repeating it. It wasn't only the pundits who ridiculed his latest efforts. Ross Becker, the journalist who was paid a fee to interview Simpson on videotape, told NBC *Nightly News* that he believed that Simpson was lying to him when confronted with the facts of the case.

The media were now less enthralled by Simpson's self-styled promotional tour or his forays to Europe. After all the clamor, the case had a remarkable deflating effect, the fatigue finally setting in after a wearisome trial. In the months following, the remnants of the Simpson story continued to play out, prompting the pundits to finally lash out at the insidious relationship between the trial participants and the media. "As long as Larry King lives and as long as the public hungers for more, more. . . . television's panderers, in cahoots with courtroom performers, deal makers and hangers-on, will keep at it," charged critic Walter Goodman. "So don't be surprised if O. J. finds a host willing to let him proclaim his affection for his children, his charitable contributions and his golf swing to an enormous audience. After all, as his lawyer Johnnie L. Cochran Jr. said on *Meet the Press* the other day, 'in black America, we need role models.'"

Goodman's caustic analysis could not have been more prescient. In the days to come, Simpson's post-trial conversion as a "role model" and "social reformer" was a shameless and bizarre exercise in self-promotion. The trial's revelations of his abusive treatment of his wife apparently moved him to organize a seminar in Los Angeles on spousal abuse. His newly found stature within the black community earned him an invitation to speak before a college audience and a church in Washington, D.C., and other friendly forums.

Lance Ito was one of the very few prominent trial personalities to shun the media spotlight in the days and months following the verdict. One news report said he had been so distraught moments after the acquittal that he broke down, sobbing with his wife in his chambers. In the trial's aftermath, he returned to the bench, keeping a low media profile. Following the unpopular verdict, he played his final media role—as the fall guy. To be sure, the televised civics lesson he had promised was a bitter one. For many Americans, the Simpson trial symbolized the collapse of the justice system; a trial that had so dismally failed to dispense justice, owing to the powers of money and the emotions of race. They saw in Ito's courtroom, a legal process made unintelligible by the personal feuds, endless motions, sidebars, and histrionics. The camera, which Ito declared would spread the message of American justice, had instead helped to instigate one of the great, and grotesque, legal debacles of our time.

Well after the verdict, jurists continued to snipe at Ito. One Superior Court judge told the *Los Angeles Times* that Ito had been "a disaster" who had turned what should have been a "a six-week trial into a year-long nightmare." The response from the legal community was so intense that Ito confided in Superior Court Judge John Reid that he was worried about the trial's lasting effect on his career. Ito acknowledged receiving advice from several colleagues that he should simply quit the bench and take the millions of dollars he could earn by writing a book about the case. According to the L.A. *Times* story, Reid compared Ito to a "trauma victim" adjusting to post-Simpson life. Ito's mental state could not have improved when, in April 1996, a federal court in Los Angeles overturned the much publicized conviction of financier Charles Keating on the grounds that Ito had given improper instructions to the jury.

Across the country, Ito was branded as a judge whose authority had collapsed in a runaway case that had turned riotous. Judge Harold Rothwax blamed Ito for allowing lawyers to run roughshod over the court, stating that "judges get the lawyers they deserve." "If they tolerate misconduct they have it in abundance," he said. "If they don't run their courtrooms, then the lawyers will—with all the chaos that implies."

Rothwax had his own experience with a Dream Team lawyer, Peter Neufeld, in a New York City murder case that followed the Simpson trial. Lance Ito had repeatedly warned Neufeld against asking questions that he ruled were out of order—reprimands that the lawyer routinely disregarded. When Neufeld later appeared in

Rothwax's courtroom, the judge warned him not to dare ask an improper question the *first* time. Neufeld responded: "Don't blame me, Judge. Ito let me do it."[3]

Steven Brill had carved out Court TV's place in the history of the Simpson saga, but Brill himself would not survive a corporate takeover of his network and publishing empire. The move was announced on February 19, 1997; however, few notes of sympathy were being delivered that day to his office overlooking Third Avenue in New York. Time Warner had eased Brill's pain with a buyout estimated as high as $40 million.

The Simpson press corps also moved on—some to the next story, many to new jobs. The trial was a defining moment in many of their careers, and they took advantage of their newfound fame. Tom Elias of the Scripps Howard news service and Dennis Schatzman of the *Sentinel*, both left to write books. Jessica Siegal of the *Chicago Tribune* also quit to write a book. David Margolick left the *New York Times* and joined Dominick Dunne at *Vanity Fair*. Sally Ann Stewart quit *USA Today* to become the media director for the Public Counsel, associated with the Beverly Hills Bar Association. Roger Cossack and Greta Van Susteren, the CNN trial commentators, packed in their law careers and moved to Washington, D.C., to host the network's new legal affairs program.

Other reporters adjusted in other ways. *Newsday*'s Shirley Perlman had spent 16 months away from her family, absorbed in a story she admitted "devoured" her life. Like a foreign correspondent returning home from a long tour, Perlman came home to a very different *Newsday*. The New York edition had folded, and the Long Island newspaper had been downsized. Perlman no longer was assigned to the courtroom beat. There were other emotional adjustments. "I became accustomed to a very, very fast pace. That was one of the big changes for me. It was just as if I had gotten off a very fast beltway. I felt like I was at a standstill."[4]

For virtually all reporters, the Simpson story was epic in their professional lives. The story had become all-encompassing, a feeling compounded by working with other reporters sharing the same driving energy. After working 14-hour days under the toughest of deadline pressures, the verdict at first spelled a relief for Jim Newton who was physically and emotionally exhausted. He returned to the police beat to cover the travails of a besieged LAPD Chief Willie Williams, himself picking up the pieces in the wake of the trial.

Admittedly, however, the aftermath of the Simpson case "left a big hole." "To have it end. . . it took me months to get out of the habit of writing about this," he said.[5] What remained were 300 tapes and notebooks filled with reams of notes. Newton was thankful to have avoided the pitfalls that had trapped other reporters: He had kept his Simpson story straight and accurate. The police reporter would, however, find himself in court again soon after the Simpson case—he had been called for jury duty but would fail to be picked for a panel.

Following the verdict, many in the press corps fell into a deep sense of vacancy, a sort of post-Simpson trauma. Reporters pondered how they were ever going to duplicate the experience of the Simpson story. CNN reporter Marc Watts commiserated with Perlman in an on-air discussion, asking her how they would replace the daily journalistic "rush." "We were the lead story every day," he said. "She was almost a daily interview for CNN, and I was on the air a guaranteed five or six times a day with the lead story."[6]

Watts was at first relieved that he could move on to the next assignment for both professional and personal reasons. "Not only was I a journalist, but I'm part of L.A. That's my community, and I wanted the community to heal. I want one day for L.A. to heal." But Watts' mood fluctuated, and the reporter admitted he struggled over the next two months. He was no longer CNN's most visible reporter, forced to decompress after being immersed for a year in the most sensational story of his time. "I felt like I was a forgotten reporter," he said.

After joining CNN's political news team, assigned to cover the national election campaign, Watts was able to divorce himself from the Simpson trial. His fiancée had finally helped him realize that "it's over," that he would never duplicate the exposure as an on-air reporter, or the fame he received as a sought-after media personality. Finally, the correspondent said he was able to "come to grips with this."

Still, months later, Watts admitted that the Simpson case hovered in his professional life, a shadowy presence that followed him from one assignment to the next. "No matter where I go, no matter what city I report in, no matter what politician I seem to walk up to, they always say, 'weren't you the O.J. guy?' And I'd say, 'yes, I was the O. J. guy.' And that's how they remembered me. It's never going to end. I think for the rest of my life, at least, I'm going to be known as the O. J. guy."

OCTOBER 1996 - FEBRUARY 1997

The Civil Trial

Some reporters did in fact go on to cover the *next* Simpson story. Michelle Caruso of the *New York Daily News* and Dan Abrams of Court TV were among the old guard to remain on the Simpson beat. A civil lawsuit against Simpson had been brought by the Brown and Goldman families for the wrongful deaths of their children. But the civil case was remarkable for the way in which it was not covered. On occasion, the trial broke into mainstream news, most notably when Simpson took the stand to deny he ever beat his wife or that he owned the type of Bruno Maglis shoes imprinted at the bloody crime scene. His testimony sharply contradicted the vivid evidence presented to the court—photographs of a beaten Nicole Simpson and 30 other photos showing Simpson wearing the designer shoes.

But the day-to-day intensity of the Simpson story had been extinguished. Judge Hiroshi Fujisaki's decision to gag trial participants from talking to the press eliminated the daily courthouse spins. Even more significantly, his decision to ban television from the trial robbed the medium of its most precious commodity: pictures. Television had been the moving force behind the creation of the gargantuan Simpson story for the previous two years, driving all media to follow its lead. Without courtroom visuals, the case dried up on the networks: Gone were the gavel-to-gavel shows and the army of droning legal "experts." And once television lost interest, the print media as well backed off the story. The competition to tell the Simpson story, finally, seemed to settle back down to earth.

Though Simpson's civil trial was blacked out, the perjury case in Los Angeles Superior Court against Mark Fuhrman was not. With the camera once again in the courtroom, the "Fuhrman story" took another turn around the media circuit. On October 2, 1996, a year to the day after 12 jurors acquitted Simpson of murder, the former LAPD detective pleaded no contest to a single charge of perjury for lying on the stand about using the "n-word." Under the plea bargain agreement with the State Attorney General's office, he received three years probation and a $200 fine. Official investigations completed six months later found no evidence to support Fuhrman's taped statements that he abused suspects or rigged cases. And no evidence was presented at any time to show that Fuhrman had ever planted evidence against Simpson.

Across the television dial the Simpson story was largely left to CNBC's tag-team talk-show hosts, Geraldo Rivera and Charles Grodin, and a somewhat bizarre creation by the E! Channel, which reenacted the civil proceedings using look-alike actors who read from daily trial transcripts. Rivera was the most tenacious and continued to ride the story that had rejuvenated his career. His program, though, was now less than compelling. Without the benefit of trial video Rivera was left to reading deposition transcripts and moderating worn discussions about the personalities, legal theories, evidence, and testimony, that Simpson followers could now recite by rote. However, Rivera would persevere, his nightly Simpson-talk evolving like a picture of Dorian Gray into an eerie reflection of the great trial itself. Soon joining him were two new "expert" commentators: Alan Dershowitz and Christopher Darden. And they had no trouble at all adapting to the combative and loud style of argumentation that passed across TV as serious legal discourse.

In the days leading to the civil verdict, the Dershowitz-Darden dysfunctional relationship sputtered angrily when Dershowitz called for a judicial investigation of Darden himself. Playing the role of the outraged defense attorney, Dershowitz demanded to know what Darden's relationship was with a dismissed juror who had failed to inform the court that her daughter worked for the district attorney's office. The split screen depicted both lawyers simultaneously arguing and name-calling into the camera, each unwilling to give up the screen to the other. An exasperated Dershowitz remarked, "You're not worth talking to anymore," as the camera cut to Rivera, who sighed as if apparently helpless to stop the verbal brawl.

As the primary holdout to carry daily the Simpson story forward into its third year, Rivera saw no need to apologize. Instead, he justified his coverage insisting that the Simpson case rivaled the great political trials of history "This is our Dreyfus case," he stated. "The Simpson case revealed in agonizing dimensions our racial divide, rich man-poor man justice, how people will go to extraordinary lengths" to get a result, no matter how glaring the injustice.

But Rivera was no longer merely covering the Simpson story—he had become a player in it after his post-criminal trial remarks condemning the verdict. Simpson himself declared Rivera his enemy, a man who had "feasted on people's misery and death." Speaking to parishioners at the Scripture Cathedral in Washington, D.C., following his acquittal, Simpson said that "there are people, bottom-feeding, barracudas, jackals, Geraldo. . . . We heard from Geraldo night after night with his foolishness and badness. Well, Geraldo, we got a message from the black nation tonight. We are backing O. J. Simpson up."

Apparently, Simpson's remarks were taken seriously among some supporters. When Rivera countered by taking his show to the same Scripture church for a live, on-air debate, the panel broke down into a racial fight. If Rivera had intended to reach out to the black community, he had seriously misjudged how far the trial—and his nightly show—had inflamed race relations. One of his guests, Dr. Alvin Pouissant, a black Harvard professor, angrily stormed off the stage and out of the church as the cameras rolled, refusing to share the TV platform with a Nation of Islam co-panelist known for his virulent anti-Semitic stance. The program plummeted to new depths of outrageous behavior when one audience member suggested that the black community "get their guns," and "take to the streets," ostensibly over the white reaction to the Simpson verdict.

Final Justice

The country also lurched forward, the sharp racial edges of the trial still embedded in the national psyche. As for the question—who killed Nicole Simpson and Ron Goldman?—that had become largely irrelevant. Their lives snuffed out by dark human forces, their justice lies in the dust. Into history they will likely be remembered in footnote, overshadowed in memory by the very pandemonium and sideshows of the trial. Even a civil judgment against O. J. Simpson, 17 months after the criminal trial, would prove to be a perverse sort of closure. With his checkbook, Simpson would finally pay—literally—for his role in the brutal crimes. For most trial observers, Simpson had gotten away with murder. The language of the judgment—finding Simpson "liable" for the "wrongful deaths" of his victims—was legalese too far removed from the horrific hacking attack of the Brentwood murders.

The timing of the civil verdict broke into prime-time television in dramatic fashion. In a fateful confluence of events, the Simpson case and the Clinton presidency again would compete for the nation's attention. Two years earlier, television had largely ignored Clinton's State of the Union Address to cover the opening statements at Simpson's criminal trial. Clinton found himself competing with the Simpson spectacular a second time as he prepared to deliver the first State of Union since his re-election. Ironically, White House staffers had sought to bypass other competing TV interests and had gone so far as to move the president's speech up a day to avoid bumping into the Miss USA pageant. But Clinton could not sidestep Simpson. He found himself going on the air at the very moment when the civil verdict was being turned over to Judge Fujisaki. As if a gigantic light bulb had been flicked on, the scene outside the Santa Monica courthouse was flashed across the nation via television just as Clinton prepared for his address.

Viewers surfing the channels moved between video images of the president's motorcade waiting to go to the Capitol and that of a car said to contain Simpson on his way to the courthouse. Meanwhile, Clinton aides feared that the president's speech would be visually juxtaposed with the visage of O. J. Simpson, a symbolic linkage they dearly wanted to avoid. As Fujisaki waited for the main participants to return to court before announcing the verdict, worried network execs found themselves in a historical nexus. Their instinct to bolt to the Santa Monica courthouse was tempered by the possible consequences of cutting off the President of the United States in midstream. Instead, the major networks frantically split the screen; accompanying Clinton were ticker-tape crawls with the latest Simpson updates.

The president reached his next-to-the-last paragraph as Fujisaki made the announcement—Simpson had been found "responsible" for the deaths of Ron Goldman and Nicole Simpson; the jury awarded the Goldman family $8.5 million in compensatory damages. (The Brown family joined the Goldmans in the second phase of the suit. The following week, both families were given $25 million in punitive damages.) Like fidgety children, the networks waited for the president to finish before shifting to the Simpson verdict, much to the relief of Clinton's staff members. "A brief glimmer of hope for American journalism," said a rueful Michael McCurry, a White House spokesman.

TV's split-screen imagery unwittingly sent a dark message about American life, contended *New York Times* columnist Maureen Dowd. The medium's juxtaposition of the president and the accused murderer posed dueling symbols of "political power and social reality, of happy talk about race and unhappy talk about race, of what America is supposed to care about and what it really cares about." Television coverage that night, however unintended, "captured" the mood of our celebrity-obsessed, morally riven culture."[7]

Dowd noted that the civil verdict was "an eerie photo negative" of the criminal verdict. This time the jury was white instead of black;

Simpson's van was black instead of white; the public acclamation now came from white voices, instead of black. This time, it was mostly black pundits calling the decision racially motivated and accusing the predominantly white jury of bending to political and racial pressures.

Even in small, peculiar ways, the civil trial's denouement presented a ghostly link from the present to the past. On his way home after the verdict, helicopter cameras captured Simpson stopping to buy chocolate-chip, cookie-dough ice cream at a Brentwood ice cream store. On a cool, clear evening two and half years earlier, Nicole Simpson had ventured into Brentwood to buy the same flavored ice cream for her son Justin. Later that night, it was found mostly melted in Nicole's condominium by detectives in their sweep of the bloody grounds at 875 South Bundy Drive.

Across the media, the Simpson story inexorably slowed but not before a final round of tired arguments and racial spins. The theme was constant as commentators painted the Santa Monica decision as a "white verdict" as opposed to the "black verdict" in the criminal case.

And then, in one inexplicable moment, their message changed.

As if the collective of TV pundits had awakened simultaneously from a long, severe bout of wringing guilt, the conversation across the screen became something else. In a symbolic linking of arms, Johnnie Cochran, now a Court TV talk-show personality, Geraldo Rivera, and other lesser-known commentators pleaded with their TV constituencies for racial harmony, for mutual acceptance of both the criminal and civil verdicts, for respect of the court system. It was time to move on from the Simpson case, they chimed.

Only in such a twisted media universe could self-denial be so prevalent and memory so short-lived. Having unleashed the floods of racial animus, these media voices now begged for reasonableness and civility. Having carved out every bit of flesh and bone from the Simpson story, they called for restraint. Having reaped gargantuan profits from the Simpson industry they helped to create and sell, they pleaded for moderation and mutual respect. Having cleaved the fragile bonds that connect our national community, they now asked Americans to join hands.

As it had begun, the Simpson story ended with a fury, one final blast of incomprehensible, deadening noise, before it was silent.

EPILOGUE

LEGACY

Lasting well beyond the public anguish and painful echoes of the criminal trial will surely be the memory of the media maelstrom. And in that sense the Simpson trial will resound like many of the other historic trials of the century—Scopes, Hauptmann, Sacco and Vanzetti, the Rosenbergs, Sheppard, the "Chicago Seven," Manson, Hearst—all shaped by the frenzy and excess of the prevailing media. Like the others, the Simpson trial transcended the legalities of the courtroom, entering into the popular culture, finally arriving as a neo-mythic American event.

But Simpson *was* different from the rest, and not simply because of the celebrity of the defendant. The Simpson story came at a time when the American media were caught in the throes of a severe identity crisis, confused about their role as news-reporting entities, seduced by the values of entertainment and tabloidism, and faced with increased competition, fragmented audiences, and frantic pressures to keep both eyes on the bottom line.

But, most significant, the media failed to understand the nature of what they are and how they work. They failed to see the powerful influence of their technology, not only on the Simpson story but on the Simpson trial. And so they followed their machines into the courtroom believing in technology's inherent goodness. But as the case slips into the folds of history, the question hauntingly remains: Would the criminal trial of O. J. Simpson have come to a different, more complete closure had a rather inconspicuous machine—a television camera—been absent from Department 103? What is certain is that something was terribly amiss in Ito's courtroom, and perhaps wiser minds within the media will see the pressing need to ask why.

The social legacy of the trial may also be imponderable, and not even a civil judgment will right the sinking sense of despair over where this country has arrived as the century clock is about to turn. Just how damaging the trial was to perceptions of American justice and the national ethic may in fact be incalculable. But assuredly vivid in history's collective memory, the Year of Simpson was a moment when the media, and the nation, surrendered to the lure of a story that they helped to create, market, and transform into one of the most titanic and traumatic events of our time.

The Simpson story was certainly grand entertainment. But after the show remained the sickly feeling that something primal to the American experience was gone for good. And, perhaps, it is *this* that will linger as the trial's saddest legacy. Rather than renew trust in the nation's system of justice—and in the American media—in the end, the Simpson story shattered the credibility of both, leaving us only to ponder what was irretrievably lost in the smoke and thunder of the spectacle.

APPENDIX: JOURNALISTS INTERVIEWED

The following journalists were interviewed by the author between March 1995 and July 1996.

Dan Abrams, reporter, Court TV
David Bohrman, executive producer of special events, NBC-TV
Bill Boyarsky, columnist, *Los Angeles Times*
Rita Colelli, media critic, *Newsday*
Linda Deutsch, reporter, Associated Press
Dominick Dunne, columnist, *Vanity Fair*
Jack Ford, senior legal correspondent, NBC-TV
Neal Gabler, media critic
John Gilmore, executive producer, CNN
Fred Graham, senior anchor, Court TV
Gregg Jarrett, anchor, Court TV
David Margolick, reporter, *New York Times*
Jim Moret, anchor, CNN
Jim Newton, reporter, *Los Angeles Times*
Steve North, coordinating producer, *Rivera Live*
David Perel, senior editor, *National Enquirer*
Shirley Perlman, reporter, *Newsday*
Geraldo Rivera, host, CNBC *Rivera Live*
Jay Rosen, media critic
Howard Rosenberg, TV critic, *Los Angeles Times*
Jeffrey Toobin, critic, *New Yorker*
Marc Watts, reporter, CNN
Henry Weinstein, reporter, *Los Angeles Times*
Leo Wolinsky, metropolitan editor, *Los Angeles Times*

NOTES

PRELUDE—BUNDY AND ROCKINGHAM

1. Interview with Marc Watts, July 1996.

CHAPTER 1—THE CHASE

1. Interview with Jim Moret, March 1995.

2. Ann Sjoerdsma, "Worshipping False Idols," *Virginian-Pilot*, June 26, 1994, p. J1.

3. Interview with Neal Gabler, March 1995.

4. Interviews with David Bohrman, July 1995, June 1996. Throughout this chapter, all quotes from Bohrman are from July 1995, June 1996 interviews with the author.

5. NBC-TV news special on the Simpson chase, June 17, 1994.

6. Walter Goodman, "Television Meets Life, Life Meets TV," Week in Review, *New York Times*, June 19, 1994, p. 1

7. Interview with Leo Wolinsky, August 1995. Throughout this chapter all quotes from Wolinsky are from August 1995 interview with the author.

8. Interview with Howard Rosenberg, August 1995. Throughout this chapter all quotes from Rosenberg are from August 1995 interview with the author.

9. "Primal Curiosity," *New York Times* editorial, July 18, 1994, sec. 4, p. 18.

10. Richard Corliss, "Justice—It's Already the Movie," *Time*, July 18, 1994, p. 36.

11. Interview with Marc Watts, July 1996.

12. Interviews with Jim Newton, August 1995, June 1996. Throughout this chapter all quotes from Newton are from August 1995, June 1996 interviews with the author.

13. Goodman, p. 6.

CHAPTER 2—FRENZY IN L.A.

1. Susan Sward, "OJ's Dramatic Surrender," *San Francisco Chronicle*, June 18, 1994, p. A1.

2. Interview with Leo Wolinsky, August 24, 1995. Throughout this chapter all quotes from Wolinsky are from the August 24, 1995 interview with the author.

3. *Los Angeles Times*, June 24, 1994, p. F1.

4. Interviews with Jim Newton, August 1995, June 1996. Throughout this chapter all quotes from Newton are from the August 1995, June 1996 interviews with the author.

5. Interview with Marc Watts, July 1996.

6. Howard Rosenberg, "'Action News' Lays Another Stink Bomb," *Los Angeles Times*, July 18, 1994, p. F1.

7. Bailey cited by ABC-TV's *20/20*, "The State vs. O. J.," June 24, 1994.

8. David Shaw, "Obsession: Did the Media Overfeed a Starving Public?" *Los Angeles Times*, October 9, 1995, p. S7.

9. Ibid., p. S6.

CHAPTER 3—THE GREATEST STORY EVER

1. From Cambridge Human Resources Group, and cited by David Shaw, "Obsession: Did the Media Overfeed a Starving Public?" *Los Angeles Times,* October 9, 1995, p. S3.

2. For an in-depth examination of the camera-in-the-courtroom issue, see Paul Thaler, *The Watchful Eye: American Justice in the Age of the Television Trial,* Westport, CT: Praeger, 1994.

3. Anna Quindlen, "Order in the Court," *New York Times*, July 13, 1994, p. A19.

4. Interview with Jay Rosen, March 1995.

5. Bill Turque, "He's Going Nuts," *Newsweek,* July, 4, 1994, p. 22.

6. Interview with Steven Brill, on ABC-TV's "This Week with David Brinkley," June 26, 1994.

7. Interview with Gregg Jarrett, August 1995. Throughout this chapter all quotes from Jarrett are from August 1995 interview with the author.

8. Bill Carter, "Television Networks' Simpson Vigil: A Low Cost Reply to CNN," *New York Times*, July 11, 1994, p. D1.

9. Interview with Fred Graham, March 1995.

10. David Shaw, "Obsession: Did the Media Overfeed a Starving Public?" *Los Angeles Times*, October 9, 1995, p. S10.

11. Shaw, p. S4.
12. Interview with Howard Rosenberg, August 1995.
13. "Primal Curiosity," *New York Times* editorial, July 18, 1994, sec. 4, p. 18.
14. ABC-TV's *20/20*, "A View from the Streets," July 8, 1994.
15. Max Robbins, "News Banking on Simpson's Staying Power," *Variety*, August, 15, 1994, p. 25.
16. Interview with Leo Wolinsky, August 1995.
17. "The Complete Guide to the Trial of O. J. Simpson," cover title of *People*, October 10, 1994.
18. Judy Brennan and Greg Baxton, "Big Screen, Small Screen View the Case from Different Angles," *Los Angeles Times,* July 9, 1994, p. A22.

CHAPTER 4—METAMORPHOSIS

1. Henry Louis Gates Jr., "Thirteen Ways of Looking at a Black Man," *New Yorker,* October 13, 1995, p. 56.
2. Mike Royko, "Planted Glove Gives Media a Fertile Field," *Chicago Tribune*, July 19, 1994, p. 3.
3. Interview with Neal Gabler, March 1995.
4. Jeffrey Toobin, *The Run Of His Life*, New York: Random House, 1996, p. 11.
5. Bill Boyarsky, "TV Conveys Drama and Opens the Court," *Los Angeles Times*, July 2, 1994, p. A4.
6. Richard Corliss, "Justice—It's Already the Movie," *Time,* July 18, 1994, p. 34.
7. ABC-TV's *20/20*, "The State vs. O. J Simpson," June 20, 1994.
8. From address by Barry Scheck at the "National Conference on the Media and the Court," National Judicial College, Nevada, August 1995.
9. Gerald Uelmen, *Lessons from the Trial,* Kansas City, KS: Andrews and McMeel, 1996, pp. 98-99.
10. Everette Dennis, "Simpson Coverage Makes for Bad Television," *Communique,* published by The Freedom Forum Media Studies Center, Columbia University, New York, November 1994, p. 2.
11. John Gregory Dunne, "The Simpsons," *New York Review of Books,* September 22, 1994, pp. 36-37.
12. Alan Dershowitz, *Reasonable Doubts,* New York: Simon and Schuster p. 147.
13. "Inside O. J. Inc.," *Newsweek*, October 13, 1994, p. 39.
14. *The Trials of Dominick Dunne*, BBC documentary.
15. Ibid.

CHAPTER 5—THE RACE CARD

1. "Behind the Smiling Portrait: A Model Family's Secret Life of Pain," (anonymous writer), *Fresno Bee,* June 22, 1994, p. B7.

2. Andrea Dworkin, "Understanding the Abuse," *Los Angeles Times*, June 26, 1994, p. M1.

3. Jeffrey Toobin, *The Run Of His Life,* New York: Random House, 1996. p. 11.

4. Jeffrey Toobin, "A Horrible Human Event," *New Yorker,* October 23, 1995, p. 46.

5. Interview with Leo Wolinsky, August 1995.

6. David Shaw, "Obsession: Did the Media Overfeed a Starving Public?" *Los Angeles Times*, October 9, 1995, p. S7.

7. Henry Louis Gates Jr., "Thirteen Ways of Looking at a Black Man," *New Yorker*, October 23, 1995, p. 59.

8. Interview with Marc Watts, July 1996.

9. Shaw, S7.

10. Jill Smolowe, "Race and the O. J. Case," *Time*, August 1, 1994, p. 25.

11. Interview with Jeffrey Toobin, June 1996. Throughout the remainder of this chapter all quotes from Toobin are from June 1996 interview with the author.

12. Earl Ofaru Hutchinson, "Race and Sex, The Last Taboo Lives," *Los Angeles Times*, June 29, 1994, p. B1.

13. Smolowe, p. 25.

14. Jacqueline Adams, "The White Wife," Hers Column, *New York Times Magazine,* September 18, 1994, p. 36.

15. Gates, p. 59.

16. Ibid., p. 61.

17. Bill Boyarsky, "Defense Muddying is Media-Savvy Plot," *Los Angeles Times*, July 17, 1994, p. A15.

18. Interview with Jim Newton, August 1995, June 1996.

19. Wendy Kaminer, "The Client," *New York Times Book Review*, September 29, 1996, p. 12.

20. Robert Shapiro, *The Search for Justice*, New York: Warner Books, 1996, p. 99.

CHAPTER 6—JUDGE ITO AND THE MEDIA

1. Interview with Linda Deutsch, June 1995. Throughout this chapter, all quotes with Deutsch are from June 1995 interview with the author.

2. Robert Shapiro, *The Search for Justice*, New York: Warner Books, 1996, p. 173.

3. Howard Rosenberg, "Judge Ito Feeds the Hand He's Bitten," *Los Angeles Times*, November 16, 1994, p. F1.

4. Howard Chua-Eoan and Elizabeth Gleick, "Making the Case," *Time*, October 16, 1995, pp. 55-56.

5. Jeffrey Toobin, *The Run Of His Life,* New York: Random House, 1996, p. 232.

6. Interview with Dominick Dunne, June 1996.

7. Also cited in "Candor or Pander," *People*, November 7, 1994, p. 59.

8. Christopher Darden, *In Contempt,* New York: ReganBooks, 1996. p. 235.

9. Interviews with Jim Newton, August 1995, June 1996.

10. Bill Boyarsky, "'Diary' Opens a New, Lurid Chapter," *Los Angeles Times,* October 20, 1994.

11. Judy Muller interview on National Public Radio, October 24, 1994.

12. Bill Boyarsky, "Why Not Ban Leno Jokes," *Los Angeles Times,* October 21, 1994, p. A33.

CHAPTER 7—THE GREAT CAMERA DEBATE

1. Interview with Fred Graham, March 1995.

2. Interview with Gregg Jarrett, August 1995.

3. Cited in Laura Mansnerus, "As Brash Publisher's Empire Ends, Quest Begins for Another," *New York Times*, March 3, 1997, p. D10.

4. Ibid., p. D1.

5. For a complete history of Court TV and a media case study of the Joel Steinberg murder trial, see Paul Thaler, *The Watchful Eye: American Justice in the Age of the Television Trial*, Westport, CT: Praeger, 1994.

6. Dershowitz cited in Thaler, p. 63.

7. Christopher Darden, *In Contempt*, New York: ReganBooks, 1996, p. 261.

CHAPTER 8—MEDIA WARS

1. Dominick Dunne, "Letters From Los Angeles," *Vanity Fair*, February 1995, p. 48.

2. Interview with Gregg Jarrett, August 1995. Throughout this chapter all quotes from Jarrett are from August 1995 interview.

3. Christopher Darden, *In Contempt*, New York: ReganBooks, 1996, p. 237.

4. Kathy Butler, "The Accidental Feminist," *Los Angeles Times*, magazine section, December 10, 1995, p. 34.

5. David Shaw, "Obsession: Did the Media Overfeed a Starving Public?, *Los Angeles Times*, October 9, 1995, p. S4.

6. Bill Boyarsky, "A Columnist Comes Clean: Yes, He Likes the Tabloids," *Los Angeles Times*, August 21, 1994, p. B1.

7. Shaw, "Obsession: Did the Media Overfeed a Starving Public?, p. S4.

8. David Margolick, "The *Enquirer:* Required Reading in the Simpson Case," *New York Times*, October 21, 1994, p. A12.

9. Interview with Jim Newton, August 1995, June 1996. Throughout this chapter all quotes from Newton are from August 1995, June 1996 interviews.

10. Shaw, S10.

11. Butler, p. 34.

12. Ibid.

13. Interview with David Perel, July 1996. Throughout this chapter all quotes from Perel are from July 1996 interview.

14. Cited in Shaw, p. S10.

15. Evan Thomas, "The Double Life of O. J. Simpson," *Newsweek,* August 29, 1994, pp. 43-49.

16. Gerald Uelmen, *Lessons From The Trial,* Kansas City, KS: Andrews and McMeel, 1996, p. 79.

17. ABC-TV's *20/20 ,* "Who Was Ron Goldman?" September 16, 1994.

18. Marc Gunther, "Tabloid TV and Beyond," *TV Guide,* December 20, 1995, p. 33.

19. Interview with Steve North, October 15, 1996.

20. This reference is attributed to Eric Mink, critic for the *New York Daily News,* in Gunther, p. 33.

21. Gunther, p. 32.

22. Interview with North, October 15, 1996

23. Gunther, p. 32

24. Shaw, p. S2.

25. Jon Katz, "In Praise of O. J. Overkill," *New York,* July 25, 1994, pp. 12-13.

26. Interview with Leo Wolinsky, August 1995.

27. Interview with Howard Rosenberg, August 1995.

CHAPTER 9—FIRESTORM

1. Stephen Seplow, "For Simpson Trial, Six TV Networks on the Case. . . . Today the Avalanche Begins," *Philadelphia Inquirer,* January 23, 1995, p. D1.

2. "OJ Trial Juices Up Its Own Economy," *Pittsburgh Post-Gazette,* March 25, 1995, p. D1.

3. Gail Shister, "Mike Wallace Says the OJ Simpson Trial is Vaudeville, Not News," *Philadelphia Inquirer,* April 19, 1995, p. E6.

4. "OJ Hasn't Started Yet," Reuters, January 27, 1995.

5. ABC News Day One Poll, released January 12, 1995.

6. Gerald Uelmen, *Lessons From The Trial: The People v. O. J. Simpson,* Kansas City, KS :Andrews and McMeel, 1996, p. 56.

7. Robert Shapiro, *The Search For Justice,* New York: Warner Books, 1996, p. 161.

8. Jeffrey Toobin, *The Run Of His Life,* New York: Random House, 1996. p. 412.

9. Interviews with Jim Newton, August 1995, June 1996. Throughout this chapter all quotes from Newton are from August 1995, June 1996 interviews.

10. Interview with Gregg Jarrett, August 1995. Throughout this chapter all quotes from Jarrett are from August 1995 interview.

11. Christopher Darden, *In Contempt,* New York: ReganBooks, 1996, p. 172.

12. ABC-TV's *Nightline,* February 23, 1995.

13. Darden, p. 206.

14. Ibid., p. 173.

15. Michael Colton, "Pulp Publishers Squeeze Out Instant OJ," *Boston Globe*, July 1, 1994, p. 53.

16. Henry Allen, "One Nation Under OJ's Spell," *Washington Post,* September 26, 1994, p. D1.

CHAPTER 10—EXPOSED

1. From address by Barry Scheck at the "National Conference on the Media and the Court," National Judicial College, Nevada, August 1995.

2. Interview with Shirley Perlman, July 1996. Throughout this chapter all quotes from Perlman are from July 1996 interview.

3. Interview with Jeffrey Toobin, June 1996. Throughout the chapter, all quotes from Toobin are from June 1996 interview with author.

4. Interview with Bill Boyarsky, June 1996. Throughout this chapter all quotes from Boyarsky are from June 1996 interview with author.

5. CNN Simpson Coverage, March 14, 1995.

6. Scheck, National Judicial College, August 1995.

7. Gerald Uelmen, *Lessons from the Trial,* Kansas City, KS: Andrews and McMeel, 1996, p. 94.

8. *The Trials of Dominick Dunne,* BBC documentary.

9. Interview with Dominick Dunne, June 1996.

10. Interview with Rita Ciolli, March 1995.

11. David Shaw, "Obsession: Did the Media Overfeed a Starving Public?" *Los Angeles Times*, October 9, 1995, p. S11.

12. Robin Clark, "For Now, Simpson's Lawyer Seems the Loser," *Philadelphia Inquirer*, March 19, 1995, p. A2.

13. David Margolick, "An Examination Ends and Judging Begins, for Simpson Lawyer," *New York Times*, March 19, 1995, p. A30.

14. Frank Rich, "Dropping the N-Bomb," *New York Times,* March 16, 1995, p. A25.

15. Dunne interview, July 1996.

16. Kenneth Noble, "One Hateful Word," *New York Times*, March 19, 1995, Sec. IV, pp. 1, 3.

17. Marc Eliot, *Kato Kaelin: The Whole Truth*, New York: HarperPaperbacks, 1995.

18. Dominick Dunne, "Letters from Los Angeles," *Vanity Fair*, June 1995, p. 92.

19. "GA. Town's Newspaper Vows 'No More O. J.'," *Philadelphia Inquirer*, April 15, 1995, p. A10.

CHAPTER 11—HOUSE OF MIRRORS

1. Frank Rich, "The Longest Year," *New York Times*, June 15, 1995, p. A31.

2. Cited in David Shaw, "Obsession: Did the Media Overfeed a Starving Public?" *Los Angeles Times*, October 9, 1995, S3.

3. Interview with Linda Deutsch, June 1996. Throughout this chapter all quotes from Deutsch are from June 1996 interview with the author.

4. Shaw, p. S3.

5. Dominick Dunne, "Letters from Los Angeles," *Vanity Fair*, February 1995, p. 52.

6. Robert Shapiro, *The Search for Justice,* Warner Books: New York, 1996, p. xvii.

7. Shapiro, p. 349.

8. Robin Clark, "Much Ado About O. J.—and Lance and Johnnie and Marcia," *Philadelphia Inquirer*, December 31, 1995. Reprinted with permission from the *Philadelphia Inquirer.*

9. Interview with Jeffrey Toobin, June 1996. Throughout this chapter all quotes from Toobin are from June 1996 interview with the author.

10. Cited in Wendy Kaminer, "The Client," *New York Times Book Review*, September 29, 1996, p. 12.

11. Jeffrey Toobin, *The Run Of His Life*, Random House: New York, 1996, p. 369.

12. Kaminer, p. 12.

13. Anecdote related in Harold Rothwax, *Guilty: The Collapse of Criminal Justice, New York:* Random House, 1996, pp. 121-129.

14. Johnnie Cochran, Jr., *Journey to Justice,* Ballantine Books: New York, 1996, p. 376.

15. Interviews with Jim Newton, August 1995, June 1996. Throughout this chapter all quotes from Newton are from August 1995, June 1996 interviews with the author.

16. Interview with Dan Abrams, July 1996. Throughout this chapter all quotes from Abrams are from the July 1996 interview with the author.

17. Gerald Uelmen, *Lesson from the Trial,* Kansas City, KS: Andrews and McMeel, 1996, p. 192.

18. John Gregory Dunne, "The Simpsons," *New York Review of Books,* September 22, 1994, p. 39.

19. Interview with Linda Deutsch, June 1996.

20. ABC-TV's *Day One,* April, 13, 1995.

21. Donald Russo, "Simpson Case Is a Sorry Example of Our Nation's Judicial System," *Philadelphia Inquirer*, July 15, 1995, p. A15.

22. Anecdote by Dan Morris, "Stakeout," *New Republic,* May 1, 1995, p. 11.

CHAPTER 12—THE JOURNALISTS

1. Interview with Shirley Perlman, June 1996. Throughout this chapter all quotes from Perlman are from June 1996 interview.

2. Interview with Linda Deutsch, June 1996. Throughout this chapter all quotes from Deutsch are from June 1996 interview with the author.

3. Interview with Jeffrey Toobin, June 1996. Throughout this chapter all quotes from Toobin are from June 1996 interview with the author.

4. Interview with Bill Boyarsky, June 1996. Throughout this chapter all quotes from Boyarsky are from June 1996 interview with the author.

5. Interview with Dan Abrams, July 1996. Throughout this chapter all quotes from Abrams are from July 1996 interview with the author.

6. *The Trials of Dominick Dunne*, BBC documentary.

7. Interview with Dominick Dunne, June 1996.

8. *The Trials of Dominick Dunne*, BBC documentary.

9. Dunne interview, June 1996.

10. Dominick Dunne, "Letter from Los Angeles," *Vanity Fair*, April 1995, p. 90.

11. Leslie Abramson, *The Defense Is Ready*, New York: Simon and Schuster; 1997, p. 288.

12. Dunne interview, June 1996.

CHAPTER 13—THE FUHRMAN TRIAL

1. Robin Clark, "Autopsy Photos Shake Journalists," *Philadelpia Inquirer,* June 13, 1995, p. P1.

2. Ibid.

3. Interview with Shirley Perlman, June 1996. Throughout this chapter all quotes from Perlman are from June 1996 interview with the author.

4. David Margolick, "A Year Later: The Simpson Case Has Permeated the Nation's Psyche," *New York Times,* June 12, 1995, B8.

5. Christopher Darden, *In Contempt*, New York: ReganBooks, 1996.

6. Gerald Uelmen, *Lessons from the Trial: The People v. O. J. Simpson,* Kansas City, KS: Andrews and McMeel., 1996. p. 98.

7. Donald Russo, "Simpson Case Is a Sorry Example of Our Nation's Judicial System," *Philadelphia Inquirer*, July 15, 1995, p. A15.

8. Margolick, p. B8.

9. Uelmen, p. 101.

10. Interview with Dominick Dunne, June 1996. Throughout this chapter all quotes from Dunne are from June 1996 interview with the author.

11. Opinions about the glove are from respective interviews with Linda Deutsch, June 1996; Bill Boyarsky, June 1996; and Dan Abrams, July 1996.

12 Interviews with Jim Newton, August 1995, June 1996. Throughout this chapter all quotes from Newton are from August 1995, June 1995 interviews with the author.

13. Linda Deutsch, Michael Fleeman, *Verdict: The Chronicle of the O. J. Simpson Trial,* Kansas City, KS: Andrews and McMeel, 1995, p. 75.

14. Interview with Linda Deutsch, June 1996.

CHAPTER 14—THE BLACK AND WHITE PRESS

1. Peter Nichols, "O. J. Simpson a Victim, Cochran Tells NABJ," *Philadelphia Inquirer*, August 20, 1995, p. B1.

2. David Shaw, "Obsession: Did the Media Overfeed a Starving Public?" *Los Angeles Times*, October 9, 1995, p. S8.

3. Shaw, p. S8.

4. Interview with Shirley Perlman, June 1996. Throughout this chapter all quotes from Perlman are from June 1996 interview with the author.

5. Shaw, S2.

6. Interview with Marc Watts, July 1996. Throughout this chapter all quotes from Watts are from July 1996 interview with the author.

7. Interview with Dan Abrams, July 1996.

8. Interviews with Jim Newton, August 1995, June 1996. Throughout this chapter all quotes from Newton are from August 1995, June 1996 interviews with the author.

9. Jeffrey Toobin, "A Horrible Human Event," *New Yorker,* October 23, 1995, p. 46.

10. Christopher Darden, *In Contempt,* New York: ReganBooks, 1996, p. 339.

11. Toobin, "A Horrible Human Event," *New Yorker,* October 23, 1995, p. 46.

12. Jeffrey Toobin, "Putting It In Black and White," *New Yorker,* July 17, 1995, p. 31.

13. Toobin, p. 34.

14. Ibid.

15. "OJ Simpson: Beyond a Reasonable Doubt," *Amsterdam News,* September 23, 1995, p. 12.

16. E.R. Shipp, "OJ and the Black Media," *Columbia Journalism Review*, November 1994, p. 41.

17. Shaw, p. S9.

18. Shipp, pp. 39-41.

CHAPTER 15—CLOSING CURTAIN

1. Interview with Bill Boyarsky, June 1996. Throughout this chapter all quotes from Boyarsky are from June 1996 interview with the author.

2. Frank Rich, "The Circus Folds," *New York Times,* September 30, 1995, p. A19.

3. Charles Krauthammer, "Trial of O. J. Simpson Was Not About Justice But About Sending a Political Message," *Philadelphia Inquirer*, October 9, 1995, A8.

4. Ellis Cose, "Shuffling the Race Card," *Newsweek*, October 9, 1995, p. 34.

CHAPTER 16—JUDGMENT DAY

1. Interview with Linda Deutsch, June 1996. Throughout this chapter all quotes from Deutsch are from June 1996 interview with the author.

2. Interview with Bill Boyarsky, June 1996. Throughout this chapter all quotes from Boyarsky are from June 1996 interview with the author.

3. Howard Kurtz, "Media Bursting With Speculation," syndicated to *Philadelphia Inquirer,* October 3, 1995, p. A7.

4. Ibid.

5. Interview with Marc Watts, July 1996. Throughout this chapter all quotes from Watts are from July 1996 interview with the author.

6. Interviews with David Bohrman, July 1995, June 1996. Throughout this chapter, all quotes with Bohrman are from July 1995, June 1996 interviews with the author.

7. Christopher Darden, *In Contempt*, ReganBooks: New York, p. 381.

8. Interview with Jeffrey Toobin, June 1996. Throughout this chapter all quotes from Toobin are from June 1996 interview with the author.

9. Interview with Dominick Dunne, June 1996. Throughout this chapter all quotes from Dunne are from June 1996 interview with the author.

10. Darden, p. 260.

11. Harold Rothwax, *Guilty: The Collapse of Criminal Justice,* New York: Random House, 1996, p. 232.

12. CNN interview cited by Ann Bollinger, "Marcia Blasts Jurors," *New York Post*, October 6, 1995, p. 19.

13. Diana Trilling, "Notes on the Trial of the Century," *New Republic,* October 30, 1995.

14. Jacob Weisberg, "The Truth Card," *New York*, October 16, 1995, p. 33.

15. Roger Rosenblatt, "A Nation of Pained Hearts," *Time*, October 16, 1995, pp. 41-42.

AFTERMATH

1. NBC-TV's *Dateline*. September 8, 1996. Katie Couric interview with Jeffrey Toobin.

2. Judge Stephen Reinhardt, in address to Beverly Hills Bar Association, June 4, 1996.

3. Harold Rothwax, *Guilty: The Collapse of Criminal Justice,* New York: Random House, 1996, p. 227.

4. Interview with Shirley Perlman, June 1996. Throughout this chapter all quotes from Perlman are from June 1996 interview with the author.

5. Interviews with Jim Newton, August 1995, June 1996. Throughout this chapter all quotes from Newton are from August 1995, June 1996 interviews with the author.

6. Interview with Marc Watts, July 1996. Throughout this chapter all quotes from Watts are from July 1996 interview with the author.

7. Maureen Dowd, "Schism of the Union," *New York Times*, February 6, 1997, p. A25.

INDEX

About the Author

PAUL THALER is Director of Journalism and Media at Mercy College. A former newspaper reporter and freelance writer for *The New York Times* and *Forbes MediaCritic*, Thaler has been a noted media expert for many national publications and network programs. He is the author of *The Watchful Eye: American Justice in the Age of the Television Trial* (Praeger, 1994).